The English Lyric
from Wyatt to Donne

The
English Lyric from
Wyatt to Donne

A HISTORY OF THE PLAIN AND

ELOQUENT STYLES

BY DOUGLAS L. PETERSON

PRINCETON, NEW JERSEY

PRINCETON UNIVERSITY PRESS

1967

Publication of this book has been aided by the Whitney Darrow
Publication Reserve Fund of Princeton University Press

Printed in the United States of America by
Princeton University Press

Preface

NEARLY THIRTY YEARS AGO in an essay published in *Poetry: A Magazine of Verse*, Yvor Winters demonstrated the presence of a plain and an ornate, decorative style in the English lyric of the Renaissance.[1] The reader who is familiar with the essay—it remains, incidentally, among the best available critical accounts of the English lyric of the sixteenth century and should be reprinted—will recognize the extent of my indebtedness to it. It has provided a starting point for the present study. I have gone on to reconstruct something of the intellectual, social, and rhetorical contexts in which the development of the sixteenth-century lyric occurs and to consider events in that development which are beyond Winters' original concerns: the medieval origins of the plain and eloquent styles; the reasons for the eloquent style's domination of the lyric throughout the greater part of the sixteenth century; the confluence of the two styles in the verse of Wyatt, Gascoigne, Googe, Shakespeare, Greville, and Donne; the processes by which the eloquent poet's experimentation with tropes, schemes, and modes of *dispositio* contributed to the refinement of the general verse tradition; the impact on the lyric in the last decades of Elizabeth's reign of the growing anticourtly opposition to love as a subject suitable to poetry; the decline at end-century of the Court's cultural and intellectual influence in English society.

I should also like to express my appreciation of the professional help and encouragement I have received from Virgil K. Whitaker, who read several earlier drafts of the present study and offered a number of helpful criticisms; to Jack Conner, a good friend and colleague, who read and criticized an earlier version of the chapter on Thomas Wyatt; to Richard Matthews for bibliographical and proofreading help; to Margaret Peterson, whose patience as a wife, proofreader, and critic made completion of the work possible; to the Research Foundation of

[1] "The Sixteenth-Century Lyric in England," Vols. 53-54 (February, March, April 1939), pp. 258-72, 320-35, 35-51.

the California State College at Hayward, for financial assistance; to the staff of the Huntington Library, for the services they so willingly provided during the summer of 1963.

DOUGLAS L. PETERSON

Hayward, California
March 1966

Contents

*The English Lyric
from Wyatt to Donne*

Introduction

DISCUSSIONS OF THE DEVELOPMENT of the English lyric in the sixteenth century are still confined mainly to textbook clichés about the "birth" of a new poetry of the imagination and the domestication of the Italian sonnet. Modern poetry, we are told, began prematurely with the appearance of Tottel's *Miscellany* in 1557—specifically, with the appearance of Wyatt's and Surrey's translations and adaptations of Petrarch—endured a quarter-century of uninspired imitation, and finally "burst forth" in the last two decades of the century. This was Sidney Lee's view: "The promise of a poetic revival in England, which the effort of Wyatt and Surrey gave, was not fulfilled. Surrey's death in 1547 was followed by a barren quarter of a century, and only at the close of that period did a great literary era dawn on England."[1] C. S. Lewis, writing some fifty years later, reaches conclusions not much different from Lee's, although he denies the modernity generally attributed to Tottel's *Miscellany*—it is "a drab age anthology"—and dismisses Wyatt's and Surrey's experiments with continental verse forms as insignificant. The Italian influence would have reached England anyway, without Wyatt's "scanty help." "Historically considered, Wyatt is not the father of the Golden, but of the Drab, Age."[2] But as for his view of developments within the lyric tradition during the century, it is essentially in agreement with Lee's. The only verse preceding the "Golden Age" that Lewis is willing to talk about with any enthusiasm is that in which he finds anticipations of the Petrarchans.

A second cliché assumes that the domestication of continental conventions, especially the sonnet, is central to the history of the short vernacular poem in the sixteenth century. Every beginning student of English literature learns that at the outset of the century there are Wyatt, the father of the English sonnet,

[1] *Elizabethan Sonnets*, 1 (Westminster: Archibald Constable & Company, Ltd., 1904), pp. xxxii-xxxiii.
[2] *English Literature of the Sixteenth Century, Excluding Drama* (Oxford: Clarendon Press, 1954), p. 225.

[3]

and Surrey, the polisher who smoothes out the pentameter line, and that after these two poets nothing much happens until Sidney, Spenser, and Shakespeare appear, that these "masters" are followed by a number of uninspired figures who represent the Petrarchan movement in its decline, and, finally that the Petrarchan school is replaced by Donne and the Metaphysicals.

The development of the sonnet is of course an important part of the history of the English lyric. But there are other developments than the domestication of the Italian sonnet and other influences than the Petrarchan which are at least as important and, demonstrably, more fundamental. Among those influences are the rhetorical treatises and handbooks which carry over into the English Renaissance medieval theories of style which shape the lyric tradition throughout the sixteenth century and well on into the next. There are also the strong and diverse influences from about 1580 on which encourage the writers of secular love poetry to turn to themes of divine love and which in the secular verse tradition lead to the "intellectualization" of amatory poetry.

The impact of the medieval rhetorical tradition upon the poetry of the first three-quarters of the century is enormous. The poets who wrote during that period were faced with a language which since Chaucer had, if anything, regressed, and with a verse tradition which offered little in the way of models suitable for imitation. They considered the vernacular inadequate as a literary medium, and they turned to the rhetoricians for the same reasons they turned to Petrarch, primarily in an attempt to enrich the vernacular as, in fact, Petrarch himself had done for his native tongue. Furthermore, when they turned to Petrarch, they read him in the light of the rhetorical theory in which they had all been thoroughly trained. Whatever the inadequacies they saw in the current vernacular and whatever the continental models they chose to follow, it is a medieval theory of eloquence which, at least up to 1580, informs their judgment. That theory identified literary excellence with the copious embellishment of style by means of verbal trope and grammatical scheme.

Those poets who joined ranks with the Humanists in an effort to refine the mother tongue and enrich its literature, cultivated a copious and ornate style and sought out as models those works which seemed best to satisfy their own notion of eloquence; or they imitated those characteristics of style in their models—in Petrarch usually at the expense of other characteristics—which satisfied that notion.

The point cannot be stressed enough: the initial phase of the Humanists' efforts to enrich the vernacular literature is essentially stylistic; and it is given direction by the medieval notion of *elocutio*. The minor contributors to Tottel's *Miscellany*, Surrey and in some instances Wyatt, the contributors to the later miscellanies (*A Gorgeous Gallery of Gallant Inventions* and *A Handful of Pleasant Delights*), and Thomas Watson imitate stylistic characteristics which best exemplify *elocutio*. They see and endeavor to emulate in continental and classical verse what their own rhetorical training has prepared them to see.

After 1580 rhetorical concerns continue to dominate the poetry of the Court, although the refinement of the vernacular was regarded as sufficient to make it worthy of the most elevated literary effort. It is during the eighties that the opposition to the writing of secular love poetry, which Lily B. Campbell has shown to have been present since the beginning of the century,[3] replaces medieval rhetoric as a determining influence on style and structure, as well as upon theme and intention. Neither the influence of medieval rhetoric during the first three-quarters of the century nor the consequences of the opposition to love poetry during the final quarter have been adequately assessed.

The concentration upon the Petrarchan movement and the domestication of the sonnet has also led to serious errors in judgment. Lewis' classification, which he claims is only descriptive, of the "drab" and "golden" schools is one instance. To establish the ornate style of the Petrarchans and their genteel attitudes and feelings about love as critical touchstones and to judge Wyatt's "Blame not my lute," or Ralegh's "The Lie" as inferior because they are written in a style that is deliberately

---

[3] *Divine Poetry and Drama in Sixteenth Century England* (Berkeley & Los Angeles: University of California Press, 1959).

[5]

lacking ornamentation and that avoids with equal deliberation the sentiments of the courtly "golden" school, is more than an error of critical judgment. It is to ignore the presence in the sixteenth century of two well-established traditions of the short vernacular poem which are distinguished by differences of purpose and method. I am referring to the plain and eloquent traditions which had existed side by side since well before Chaucer.

The verse representative of these two traditions is the embodiment of completely different concerns. From the beginning the plain stylists were concerned primarily with matter. The earliest among them were writers of short didactic verse; but in the sixteenth century the plain stylists include contemplative poets as well. The eloquent style, originating in the discussions of *elocutio* by the medieval rhetoricians, appears to have been cultivated in the beginning as a class distinction. It is the "literary" style replacing French in the medieval English Court. It cultivates embellishment and mannerisms as social graces. It persists as a courtly attainment well into the sixteenth century; but it assumes a new and distinct importance. Its excesses are unmistakable. But its contributions to the verse tradition parallel those of the Ciceronians' and the Euphuists' to the prose vernacular. Nicholas Grimald and the other minor contributors to Tottel's *Miscellany*, and Surrey, too, experimented with the schemes of *dispositio* defined and illustrated in such texts as Richard Rainolde's *Foundacion of Rhetorike* and Thomas Wilson's *The Arte of Rhetorique* and thus introduced structural devices and principles of organization that greatly extended the possibilities of English verse.

A good many things have happened to English verse between Surrey's elegy on the death of Wyatt beginning "W[yatt] resteth here, that quick could never rest" and Milton's "Lycidas," or between Wyatt's "Ffarewell Love, and all thy lawes forever" and one of Donne's *Holy Sonnets*; and they include developments on the levels of syntax, style, and structure which cannot be explained by any account of the Renaissance lyric which confines itself to a history of the domestication of continental Petrarchism. Those developments are best approached,

I believe, by examining the two traditional styles: the plain and the eloquent.

I shall begin, then, by considering in the first chapter the presence of the two traditional styles in the medieval lyric and by identifying some of the conventions common to each which the Tudor poets continue to use. I expect also to indicate in this initial chapter some of the structural and stylistic inadequacies in medieval verse which the Tudor poets had somehow to overcome if they were to advance the cause—and it is a cause which they support with chauvinistic fervor—of English poetry and the "mother tongue."

The chapters which follow cover the contributors to Tottel's *Miscellany*, Wyatt, and the mid-century poets, and trace the development of the two traditional styles up to the publication of *Astrophil and Stella*. The focus in these chapters is essentially upon style and structure, although I have also provided, especially in the chapter on Wyatt, a full critical account of individual poems whose virtues are such that they demand it. In later chapters the focus shifts somewhat from matters of style and structure to content and attitude. This shift has been necessary in order to account for the modifications that both styles undergo in the late stages of their development. The position a given poet takes in the controversy during the last quarter-century over the nature of love, for instance, will always be reflected in his choice of one of the two traditional styles. Donne, whose attitudes are mainly anticourtly, assumes conventions of the plain style, adapting them to the purposes of mockery and satire in such poems as "The Indifferent" and "Communitie," or in *The Holy Sonnets* to the purpose of religious meditation. In Greville the evolution of a style reflects shifts and changes in thought and attitude about courtly notions of love.

My treatment of the Renaissance lyric in terms of the rhetorical tradition will doubtless invite comparisons with Rosemond Tuve's *Elizabethan and Metaphysical Imagery*,[4] but the reader will find that for the most part my concerns are distinct from Professor Tuve's. Her chief concern was to show that Meta-

[4] Chicago: University of Chicago Press, 1947.

physical poetry does not represent a revolution in Renaissance poetics by demonstrating that the differences between the verse of the Spenserians and that of the Metaphysicals can be mainly accounted for by the Renaissance idea of stylistic decorum:

> It can properly be claimed for the Metaphysical poets, I think, that exactly this kind of keeping poetic decorum [i.e. that decorum *demands in the proper situations* homely, displeasing, harsh images], when "abbasing a matter," is responsible for most of their rough or homely images—ironic and self-depreciating, unpleasing, or just surprisingly down-to-earth. They may make unorthodox evaluations of men and things; I find little that is unorthodox in this respect about their images or their poetic. At least I can find few if any "low" images which can be questioned as out of line with the accepted requirements of decorum, in Donne, King, Carew, Suckling, Marvell, the Herberts.[5]

There is no reason to quarrel with this conclusion; it is supported by vigorous and thorough scholarship. On the other hand, one wonders why the poets mentioned by Professor Tuve so often engaged in "abbasing a matter," why they so often write, as Miss Tuve elsewhere remarks (p. 198), in genres requiring a low or middle style and show such sustained interest in the reflective lyric. It is such questions as these which I have gone on to consider. Their answers, I believe, are to be found in a growing dissatisfaction during the nineties with the Court as the intellectual center in London, in the opposition to courtly attitudes and sentiments as the accepted norms of a fashionable kind of poetry, and in the plain-stylists' concern to reexamine the various kinds of assumptions informing those attitudes and sentiments.

[5] P. 197.

CHAPTER I

The Medieval Lyric

THE ORIGINS OF THE plain and eloquent styles are to be found in the *didactic* and *courtly* verse of the Middle Ages. *Didactic* designates those poems that were written specifically to teach and persuade an unsophisticated audience of the desirability of Christian conduct. *Courtly* refers to those poems in which composition on every level is calculated to approach a stylistic ideal inherited from late-classical rhetoric, an ideal cultivated by the aristocracy as decorously "polite," "literary," and "noble." The medieval traditions of the *didactic* and *courtly* lyric establish habits of composition that can be traced continuously to the end of the sixteenth century. Together, they constitute the major portion of the medieval legacy of the Renaissance lyric.

Didactic Verse and Plain Style

Didactic verse in the fifteenth century either expands a "commonplace" (that is, a generalized moral truth or "sentence" which, according to Richard Rainolde, "doeth agree vniuersally to all menne"[1] or elaborates or paraphrases Christian doctrine. Its purpose is the instruction of a parochial audience in the general principles of religion, and it is written in what was known currently as the "rude," "barren," or "plain" style—the style accepted by the Humanists as best suited to the serious treatment of ideas, even when in the early sixteenth century they were most critical of the shortcomings of the vernacular as adequate to the demands of literary expression. The language

---

[1] "A Common place is a Oracion, dilatyng and amplifiyng good or euill, whiche is incidente or lodged in any man. This Oracion is called a common place, because the matter conteined in it, doeth agree vniuersally to all menne, whiche are partakers of it, and giltie of the same." *The Foundacion of Rhetorike*, ed., Francis Johnson, Scholars' Facsimiles & Reprints, etc. (New York: Edwards Brothers, Inc., 1945), Fol. xxxiij[r].

is plain, generalized, aphoristic, and frequently colloquial. The syntax is primitive, often disordered, and the development of subject proceeds almost entirely through the use of typical illustrations and examples. Occasionally the didactic poet uses allegory, personification, simile, and simple antithesis, devices advocated by the rhetoricians for teaching those upon whom logical distinctions and elaborate arguments would be wasted; but by and large he relies chiefly on the aphoristic phrase and the homely proverb. The only significant difference between commonplace and doctrinal verse is structural. In the former, structure depends ultimately on the principle of classification, whereas in the latter it depends on the logic implicit in the doctrine being paraphrased. Both kinds of verse show varying degrees of structural complexity, from the barest exigencies of coherence to relatively advanced uses of refrain and narrative framework. The chief function of structure, however, is always determined by the simple pedagogical practices of repetition and dilation.

"The Perversities of the Age" is typical of the simplest treatment of the commonplace:

> Wise men bene but scorned,
> & wedowz eke foryerned,
> Grete men arn bot glosid,
> & smale men arn borne doun & myslosed,
> lordis wex euer blynd,
> ffrendis ben vnkynde,
> dethe is oute of mynde,
> Treuth may no man fynde.[2]

The poem is simply a series of aphorisms dilating the commonplace stated in the title. The order of the lines is determined only by the requirements of rhyme. The same primitive technique is frequently used for illustrative purposes in longer poems, as in "Counsels of Prudence and Patience" (No. 183):

[2] No. 175 in Carleton Brown's *Religious Lyrics of the Fifteenth Century* (Oxford: Clarendon Press, 1939). Poems cited in this section are from Brown's collection, unless otherwise indicated.

And thy luffe be yn a place,
Haue hyt in mynde & holde the styll;
A foles bolt ys sone schote in case,
Whoo speketh mykyll sum he most spylle;
Lette neuere thy luffe be on an hylle,
Ner thy councell at the crosse by cryde;
Lette but fewe mene wytte thy wylle,
And euere more for the better A-byde.

(St. 5)[3]

Occasionally, the commonplace is dilated more discursively, as in "See Much, Say Little, and Learn to Suffer in Time" (No. 181):

See much, sey lytill, and lerne to suffre in tyme;
empreynt thes thre yn thy remembraunce.
lyke as the mone chaungyth a-for the prime
so faryth thes world, replete with variaunce.
Oft lewyd langage causyth grete distaunce,
Werfor wyse Catoun seyth to old & yong:
'the fyrst chefe vertu is to kepe owr tong.'

Werfore, wold god thes fals tongys all—
meuyng and clappyng lyk to the leue of apse,
Woys dayly venym more byttur is than gall—
Were boundyn euerchon with a claps[e]!
Tyl trowth and temperance lust them to [vnhapse];
for fals detraccioun, lesyng & dysclaunder
Hath slay mor peple than dud kyng Alysa[under].

Yf yn thes lyf thu woll encrese and eche
thyn worldly Ioy, thyn ese, and thyn wellfar[e],
Be wele avysyd at all tymes of thy [speche],
and saue the sure fro satan & hyse [snare].
Oft yll reportis engenderyth sorw[e] and [c]are;
Were-for in spekyng at no tyme [is] he ydill
That can hys tong at all tyme wysly bridill.

---

[3] I have modernized the *thorn* whenever it appears.

A lytell spark may set a towne a-fyre,
But wen it brennyth it is nought lyghly quey[nt].
On word myspoken may bryng the yn the myre
So depe y-wyss till thu theryn be draynt.
A fals tong may florysch weel & peynt
as for a cesoun, but euer the end ys schame;
And wo is hym hoys tong h[ath lost hys name].

lytill mellyng causyth [meche reste];
Ouer besy was [neuer] yit commend[able],
loke were thu art yn dowt, and deme the [beste];
Dele nogth with dowblenesse, ne be nogth desceyuable;
Rechelesse & racle [are] oft tymys repreuable;
Werfor, thysylf and thu wollt kepe fro crime,
See much, sey lytill & lerne to suffyre yn tyme[e].

The introduction of the threefold topic in the opening stanza suggests that the method of dilation to be used will be the one found frequently in medieval pulpit oratory, that of defining each term of the commonplace and then expanding each term by example and illustration in the order in which they are originally stated. Instead, each of the stanzas is devoted to the dangers of "fals tongys." There is no reason for the order of the stanzas. The writer has made no attempt to establish a principle of progression in terms of which the relation of stanzaic units to the entire poem or of particular details to each other might have been given meaning. Unity in such a poem depends upon the obvious relationship of the particular examples to the commonplace.

There are other more or less primitive methods of providing didactic verse with structure. "Virtues Exiled—Vices Enthroned" (No. 176), for instance, illustrates an enumerative method. The first stanza catalogues some ten personified virtues which have been "exiled," and the second, the vices which have been subsequently "enthroned":

Paciencia is plukytt that mony men hyme Lothys,
ffides is fybled & goys in torynde clothys,
Caritas is lowkyde & knokytt full smawyll,
. . . . (ll. 3-5)

ffraus is fykyll as a fox, & reuys in this lande,
ffuror is hys freynde, as I vndyrstand,
Decepcio is his chamerlande, haif heire-of no dowtte
Detraccio is of his cownsell—I be-schrew that rowtte!
ffalsum Iudicium is a lordschype of hys,
Violencia berys hys swerde, he may noght mysse,
Inuidia is als vmpeire qwen thai be-gyne to stryfe.

(ll. 13-19)

Personified abstractions such as these, especially the depiction of the court of Fraud and the governing tyrant, are too familiar to require much comment. Though the allegorizing provides an additional thread of coherence, the technique is essentially enumerative.

A more sophisticated structural technique than the catalogue, though related to it, is present in the numerous poems which in varying ways employ categories set up by theological doctrine, by the mystical number "3," or by some arbitrary principle of order. The use of theological doctrine as a structural principle occurs, for example, in "Death, the Soul's Friend" (No. 163), a poem instructing the reader in the progressive steps of reflection necessary for Christian resignation. The stanzas recommend in the following order that man think upon: (1) God as first and final cause, (2) the consequences of man's fall from grace and the bliss for which he was created, (3) man's wretched state, (4) the immediacy of death, (5) death as a consequence of Providence, (6) death as the end of woe, and finally (7) death as the birth of a new life. Here stanzaic progression is controlled by the logic implicit in a Christian habit of reflection. Each stanza corresponds to a step in that habit. In "Three Lessons to Make Ready for Death" (No. 155) the three steps of penitence provide a similar scheme:

In my bed liying on cristis day, half slepyng,
Sighhis wondrous hevyng, A voice I hard thus spekyng:

WAke, man, slepe not, rise vp and thynk that erth thou
art;
And that erth thou shal be, whan the hath cayht deth
smart.

Com to churche, & serve thy maker with dredefull hart,
lest that thou repent the when thou art owte of quart.

Remember that thou shall dye,
ffor this world yn certentee
Hath nothyng save deth truele.
Therfore yn thy mynde vse this lessone:
Liffe so that deth take the yn sesone.

ffor deth to make the ripe, I shal teche the thynges three,
Which and thou vse, owte of sesone thou can not dye.
The furst is a knowledge of the vij synnes dedlye
hoole with other to make to they ffader gostlye.

Secoundly, that thy conscience dayly be well soght
Of wronges to thy neighbor done both in dede and thought,
And that thereof satisfaccioun hastly be broght;
ffor ellis thou shall leese that which, bledying, thy lord
    boght.

The third lessone vse til thy mouth stopp the cold clay:
ffor thy synnes both wepe & weyle—bere this well away!
In harte be meke and contrite, and than thou shall play
In Blys with hym that of A mayde was borne this Day.

The first two stanzas establish the dream allegory convention
and introduce the theme: the immediate need to repent. The
third stanza advises that the reader look to his mortality so as
to be "ripe for death."[4] The rest of the poem paraphrases the
doctrine of penance in simplified terms for a parochial audience.
The fourth stanza counsels the reader to acquire a full knowledge of both mortal and venial sins, a preliminary requirement
for repentance. The fifth and sixth stanzas treat respectively
"confession" and "contrition," the two steps which are necessary for "satisfaction." Unimpressive though it may be, the
poem marks the beginning of a tradition of penitential meditation in English poetry which culminates in the great penitential

[4] Cf. Edgar's advice to Gloucester in *King Lear*, ". . . Men must
endure/ Their going hence even as their coming hither:/ Ripeness is
all . . . ."

lyrics of Sidney, Greville, Jonson, and Donne,[5] poems in which the doctrine treated here didactically functions as an aid to self-analysis and as a structural principle within the individual poem.

"The Testament of a Christian" (No. 162), "A Balade by Squire Halsham" (No. 171), "A Series of Triads" (No. 177), and "Three Things Against Nature" (No. 118) also employ doctrinal structures. "A Balade by Squire Halsham" is a rather ingenious treatment of the theme of the variability of fortune:

> The worlde so wide, the'aire so remuable,
> The sely man so litel of stature,
> The grove and grounde and clothinge so mutable,
> The fire so hoote and subtil of nature,
> The water neuer in oon—what creature
> That made is of these foure, thus flyttyng,
> May stedfast be as here in his lyving?
>
> The more I goo the ferther I am behinde,
> The ferther behinde the ner my wayes ende,
> The more I seche the worse kan I fynde,
> The lighter leve the lother for to wende,
> The bet y serve the more al out of mynde,
> Is thys fortune, not I, or infortune?
> Though I go lowse, tyed am I with a Lune.

The four elements provide the scheme of dilation in the first stanza, though there appears to be no particular reason for the order in which they are introduced. In the second stanza grammatical schemes of antitheses and *gradatio* provide the structure. The poem exhibits, incidentally, a consciousness of style that is unusual in the didactic poetry of the period. The rhyme royal stanza, the elaboration of change in terms of the four elements, and the grammatical schemes in the second stanza put one in mind of the stylistic exercises frequently found in the sixteenth-century miscellanies. The other poems mentioned above as illustrating similar schemes of organization

---

[5] For additional examples of the early penitential lyric see F. A. Patterson, *The Middle English Penitential Lyric* (New York: Columbia University Press, 1942).

lack this stylistic ingenuity. "The Testament of a Christian" is in the nature of a will in which the poet bequeaths in successive stanzas his body to the earth, his sins to the devil, his goods to the world, and his soul to heaven. "A Series of Triads" is a long sermonizing piece developing: (1) "iij poyntis of myscheff," (2) "iij poyntis" of "worship," and (3) "iij degreis" of "word kepis." Each member of each triad is treated as a commonplace and is developed in the same ways discussed earlier.

None of the poems shows any particular concern for style; and this is true of the didactic poets generally. Unlike the eloquent poets, they are indifferent to the crudeness of the vernacular; it is adequate to their purposes. Occasionally, as in Squire Halsham's "Balade" they use techniques which are part of the stock in trade of the eloquent poets. But the possibilities for paradox that are inherent in the subjects of change and fortune are obvious, and when the didactic poets are concerned with stressing the Christian implications of such subjects, antithetical statement is simply the most useful to their purpose. Occasionally, there are exceptions; the punning on "God" and "good" in "A Song of 'Goods,'" for instance, suggests a concern beyond the didactic. But by and large the didactic poet is a teacher whose only concern is with stating as clearly and emphatically as he can the fundamental principles of Christian living.

Another structural technique used to develop the commonplace, is the *summary refrain,* which made possible a closer mode of organization than did any of the methods so far discussed. The device was not monopolized in the fifteenth century by the didactic poets. It appears in both the devotional and the courtly poetry. In the well-known *Quia Amore Langueo,* for instance, a Latin refrain serves within a narrative framework both as a unifying principle and as a means of emphasis. Nor was its use confined to the fifteenth century. It appears frequently in the work of the sixteenth and seventeenth-century poets in revised and various guises and for a variety of purposes. One of Wyatt's contributions to the lyric was his use of the refrain in modified form to establish logical progession between stanzas.

The simplest use of the summary refrain is illustrated in "Think Before You Speak" (No. 182). The opening stanza, a formulary prayer, introduces the subject in the most general terms:

> Almyghty godde, conserue vs fram care!
>   Where ys thys worle A-way y-wente?
> A mane that schold speke had nede to be ware,
>   ffor lytyl thynge he may be schente;
> Tonggys beth y-turne to lyther entente,
>   Hertys they beth bothe fykel and felle.
> Man, be-ware leste thow repente,
>   Whate euer thow sey, Avyse the welle!

The general observation on the sinful state of the world stated in lines two through four and illustrated by the aphorisms in the two succeeding lines is the occasion for the poem. The concluding line, the refrain, introduces the commonplace, that is, the lesson to be taught: "Whate euer thow sey, Avyse the welle!" Succeeding stanzas deal specifically with some of the disastrous consequences of failing to heed the advice summed up by the commonplace. A loose tongue can only be a source of irreparable harm: some whom you have supposed to be your friends and whom you have therefore taken into your confidence may eventually use your words against you; others may betray your confidence when they next visit a tavern; in short, do not speak in haste unless you are willing to accept the consequences. The fifth stanza moves into a new set of particulars, backbiting, flattery, and slander; and the sixth generalizes again on the effects of a "venemys tonge." The poem then concludes with a stanza of instruction in verbal discretion, and a closing prayer:

> Yf that thow wolte speke A-ryght,
>   Ssyx thynggis thow moste obserue then:
> What thow spekyst, & of what wyght,
>   Whare, to wham, whye and whenne.

Thow noost how soone thow schalt go henne;
As lome to meke, as serpent felle;
In euery place, A-monge all men,
Whate euer thow sey, A-vyse the welle!

Almyghty god yn personys thre,
With herte mylde, mekly y praye,
Graunte me grace thy seruant to be
Yn woorde and dede euer and aye!
Mary, modere, blessyd maye,
Quene of hevyn, Imperes of helle,
Sende me grace both nyght and daye—
Whate euer thow sey, A-vyse the welle!

The refrain technique, represented here in its simplest form, answers to the pedagogical purpose by emphasizing the lesson to be remembered at the same time that it establishes unity in a fairly long poem. There is also some order of progression apparent between stanzas, an order of increasing particularity. Stanzas three, four, and five dilate the general advice in stanza two (to be wary of confiding in friends), and the two concluding stanzas obviously constitute a summary of all that has gone before. But it is the refrain which is chiefly responsible for what unity is present in the poem.

Frequently, the summary refrain is combined with narrative framework to assure additional coherence and unity. The framework most commonly employed is that of the *chanson d'aventure*.[6] The poet begins by relating an account of a walk in the country during which he encounters a person whose lament, either overheard or addressed directly to the poet, he then relates and comments upon. *Narrative framework*, like other methods—allegory, personification, and fable—meets the important didactic requirement that the abstract be presented concretely. The concrete appeals directly through the imagination to the emotions, whereas the abstract must first be under-

[6] For discussions of the source of the convention in French secular verse, see E. K. Chambers, *English Literature at the Close of the Middle Ages* (Oxford: Clarendon Press, 1945), pp. 66-121, *passim*; F. A. Patterson, *The Middle English Penitential Lyric*, pp. 29-45.

stood before it becomes a principle of action. Furthermore, narrative framework simplifies the poet's problems of progression, since narrative establishes the sequence of events according to an established time scheme. Numerous examples of narrative framework applied to a variety of purposes appear in Patterson's *The Middle English Penitential Lyric* and in Brown's *Religious Lyrics of the Fifteenth Century*.[7]

In the verse I have been discussing structure, style, and language are controlled exclusively by an intent to teach. The methods of composition illustrated vary from simple paraphrase and proverbial dilation to increasingly complex and often combined methods of repetition, enumeration, doctrine, and narration. In every instance these methods were calculated to drive home truths in minds unequipped to cope with the logical subtleties of Christian doctrine. The didactic poets were concerned with preserving unity only by way of formulary beginnings and conclusions, the summary refrain and narrative framework. The possibilities of logical development were not to their purposes. They show little concern for principles of order which would make the progression between statement or stanzas meaningful. They are satisfied, instead, to expand generalities by more or less random example and illustration. They are singularly uninterested in stylistic refinement and show only an occasional indebtedness to the current rhetorical treatises on the art of *elocutio*. The most distinctive characteristics of early didactic verse are, in fact, its lack of style and the plainness of its language. These are the characteristics which in the style-conscious late Middle Ages and throughout the first three-quarters of the sixteenth century are regarded as nonliterary—the characteristics which distinguish the "uneloquent," "barren," "base," "home-spun," "barbarous," or "plain" style from the "eloquent," "weighty," or "courtly" style.

Poems in the plain style occur, however, from time to time in both the fourteenth and fifteenth centuries which disclose con-

---

[7] Brown's collection provides the most interesting examples. See especially "The Day of Life—Night Comes Soon" (No. 147), "Medicines to Cure the Seven Deadly Sins" (No. 178), and "Measure Is the Best of All Things" (No. 186).

cerns beyond the didactic. They are distinguished by a concern for the commonplaces of human experience which is intensely personal and nondidactic. Whereas the didactic poem, for instance, ordinarily pays lip-service to mortality as a truism, this other kind of poem, I shall call it contemplative, is controlled by an awareness that mortality has personal as well as general implications and that they must be faced and somehow accepted. This difference of intention is apparent in style and in the qualifications and adjustments of feeling that are present on the level of connotation.

Sometimes the personal, or contemplative, concern will emerge in a stanza in an otherwise thoroughly dull piece of didactic verse, as in "Farewell, this World is but a Cherry Fair" (Brown, No. 149). The second stanza and the first part of the third shift from the method of the preacher—the recitation in this instance of the tenets of Christian resignation—to the method of personal reflection, a pondering of the significance which those tenets have for the individual and a realization of that significance which is commensurate with understanding:

> This lyfe, I see, is but a cheyre feyre;
> All thyngis passene and so most I algate.
> To-day I sat full ryall in a cheyere,
> Tyll sotell deth knokyd at my gate,
> And on-avysed he seyd to me, chek-mate!
> lo! how sotell he maketh a devors—
> and wormys to fede, he hath here leyd my cors.
>
> Speke softe, ye folk, for I am leyd aslepe!
> I haue my dreme, in trust is moche treson.
> ffram dethes hold feyne wold I make a lepe,
> But my wysdom is turnyd into feble resoun.

(ll. 8-18)

The same is true of "A Mirror for Yong Ladies at their Toilet" (Brown, No. 152). Death, represented by a death's-head, speaks:

[20]

Maist thou now be glade, with all thi fresshe aray,
One me to loke that wyll dystene thi face.
Rew one thy-self and all thi synne vprace!
Sone shalte thu flytte and seche another place,
Shorte is thy sesoun here, thogh thou go gay.

O maset wriche, I marke the with my mace.
Lyfte vp thy ieye, be-holde now, and assay!
Yche loke one me aught to put the in affray;
I wyll not spare the, for thou arte my pray.
Take hede, and turne fro synne while thu hast space.

O thoughte, welthe heele to this, thaught the say nay.
My tyme muste nedis comme as I manace;
Be lenghte one lyfe may lepe oute of my lace.
I smyte, I sle, I woll graunte no mane grace.
A-ryse! a-wake! amend here while thou may.

In this poem, as in the one previously quoted, there is a consciousness of style which is not common in the purely didactic
lyric. It is apparent in the adherence to a fairly consistent
metrical norm and in the lack of excessive illustration. There
is also a degree of complexity in the consistent adherence to the
fundamental figure used to develop the theme which is beyond
the requirements of instructional verse.

Neither of the poems cited is really successful, but they do
illustrate the distinction between didactic and personal concerns. It is a distinction that rests neither on subject matter nor
style, but rather on the strategies of style which are employed
to realize intention. Dunbar's "Lament for the Makaris" and
Chaucer's "Flee fro the Prees and dwelle with soothfastnesse,"
both of which have been commonly identified as didactic, are
excellent examples of the case in point. Both poems are written
in the plain style and are about moral subjects, but neither
poem is didactic, save perhaps in the sense that any poem that
deals with moral experience may be so interpreted.[8]

[8] It has been commonly assumed that certain areas of experience are
intrinsically prosaic, while others are intrinsically lyrical. The assumption underlies Arthur K. Moore's remark that "an age which wrote

Dunbar's poem[9] is a statement of his inability to resign himself to death. Its structural principle is classificatory, the refrain technique being used to reinforce the unity implicit in classification. The opening stanza states briefly the conditions—the infirmities of old age—that have forced the poet to be aware of and to fear death. The second stanza introduces the commonplace to which he must resign himself if he is to overcome his fear: "Our plesance heir is all vainglory/ This fals warld bot transitory." The next twenty-one stanzas demonstrate the inclusiveness of the commonplace and thus point up to the poet the futility of fearing death and refusing to recognize it as inevitable. Stanzas three through ten are general: wealth, power, political status, learning, etc., are useless against death. Stanzas eleven through twenty-one consider specific writers and poets whom death has overtaken and thus lead directly to the concluding stanzas in which the commonplace is applied directly to the poet's situation, and he is forced to recognize the inevitable logic of the syllogism which is at the core of the poem: All men must die; Dunbar is a man; ergo . . . .[10]

> Sen he hes all my brether tane,
> He will nocht lat me lif alane,
> On forse I man his nixt pray be;
> *Timor mortis conturbat me.*

---

prose with a cramped hand used metre of necessity for commonplace purposes" and leads him to dismiss Chaucer's moral lyrics with a casual word of praise: They "read rather well, even if the tone is usually homiletical. Nevertheless . . . though phrased with dignity and economy," they "are in large part pious essays trimmed to fit the ballade framework and are lyrical only in a limited sense." *The Secular Lyric in Middle English* (Lexington: University of Kentucky Press, 1951), p. 130.

[9] In *The Poems of William Dunbar*, ed., John Small (Edinburgh: The Scottish Text Society, 1885-1893), 3 vols.

[10] J. V. Cunningham has an excellent, concise account of the poem's logical structure in "Logic and Lyric: Marvell, Dunbar, and Nashe," *Modern Philology*, LI (August 1953), 33-41. The essay is reprinted in *Tradition and Poetic Structure* (Denver: Alan Swallow, 1960), pp. 40-58.

The only choice left is resignation:

> Sen for the deid remeid is none,
> Best is that we for dede dispone,
> Eftir our deid that lif may we;
> *Timor mortis conturbat me.*

The refrain, besides keeping the subject of the poem always foremost in the reader's mind and maintaining the predominant tone of the poem from beginning to end, is essential also for the effectiveness of the climactic conclusion. Up to the concluding stanzas, the contents of each stanza justify the content of the refrain; that is, each stanza offers good reasons for fearing death. But in the last two stanzas the function of the refrain is subtly changed. In the next to last stanza its function is to qualify; it makes clear that the poet is unable to adjust his emotions to what his mind has embraced as an inevitable conclusion of the logic of Providence. The effect in the closing stanza is similar. Having no other recourse but to his Christian faith, the poet finds that faith is not enough—his fear of death still lingers. These strategies obviously do not emerge out of any desire to instruct. They are developed in the interest of meditation that has for its purpose the exploration of the implications that death has for the author. The poem is at once both the instrument of that meditation and the statement of its results.

Chaucer's "Flee fro the prees" is similar in purpose, despite the fact that the "Envoy" states that the poem is for the instruction of Sir Philip la Vache.[11] It is a summary statement of a moral position, a statement of personal conviction; and because Chaucer is concerned with the precise statement of that position, he employs the style that is best suited to "conveyen his mateere." He has used the ballade convention and the rhyme-royal stanza, which he has used elsewhere for eloquent purposes, but he has also deliberately adopted the plain and sententious style of the didacticists. The differences of intention as they are reflected in style can be seen by comparing the open-

---

[11] *The Complete Works of Geoffrey Chaucer*, ed., F. N. Robinson (Boston: Houghton Mifflin Co., 1933), p. 631.

ing stanzas of "Flee fro the prees" and "The Bill of Complaint"
in "The Complaint unto Pity." The latter begins:

> Humblest of herte, highest of reverence,
> Benygne flour, coroune of vertues alle,
> Sheweth unto youre rial excellence
> Your servaunt, yf I durste me so calle,
> Hys mortal harm, in which he is yfalle;
> And noght al oonly for his evel fare,
> But for your renoun, as he shal declare.
>
> (ll. 1-7)

This is the manner of decorous address common to the conventional *salutatio* in the courtly verse epistle. The language
decorates the content; nothing important is lost in paraphrase.
On the other hand, the style of the opening stanza of "Flee fro
the prees" is wholly dedicated to the straightforward statement
of the "mateere."

> Flee fro the prees, and dwelle with sothfastnesse,
> Suffyce unto thy good, though it be smal;
> For hord hath hate, and climbing tikelnesse,
> Prees hath envye, and wele blent overal;
> Savour no more than thee bihove shal;
> Reule wel thyself, that other folk canst rede;
> And trouthe thee shal delivere, it is no drede.
>
> (ll. 1-7)

It is the didactic style, polished and pared of excessive pedagogical amplification in the interest of the precise statement of a
personal conviction—the realization in language of a contemplative intention.[12]

The Literary or Eloquent Lyric

The occasions for eloquent verse in the fifteenth century
appear to have been numerous. It was written on request to
commemorate public occasions or the deaths of nobles. It also

---

[12] Such poems are "contemplative" in two senses. They represent an
act of contemplation and they are informed by the medieval Contemplative Ideal.

appears frequently in the form of elaborate and sometimes obsequious compliment. But it appears most pervasively in the amorous poetry which was then fashionable in court society. Whatever its specific occasion, the eloquent lyric is controlled by a rigid notion of style. It seeks originality through ingenious variation, emphasis through copiousness, and elegance through the exploitation of the schemes and tropes of the textbook rhetorics.[13] It employs almost exclusively techniques of dilation and ornamentation culled from handbooks on style which treated both poetry and rhetoric only as *elocutio*.[14] Thus for the educated, the eloquent or "noble" style was the only standard of literary excellence. Hoccleve in "A Dedication for a *De Regimine Principum*" (No. 98)[15] makes conventional excuses for the poverty of his style and his "raw sentance" in terms of stylistic eloquence:

> I dreede lest that my maistir Massy,
>   That is of fructuous intelligence,

[13] For discussions of continental influences and the development of the literary lyric after Chaucer, see E. K. Chambers, "Some Aspects of Mediaeval Lyric," in *Early English Lyrics*, eds., E. K. Chambers and F. Sidgwick (London: Sidgwick and Jackson, Ltd., 1921); and F. A. Patterson, *The Middle English Penitential Lyric*.

[14] C. S. Baldwin discusses the confusion of poetry and rhetoric in the Middle Ages and the consequent preoccupation with style as an end in itself in *Medieval Rhetoric and Poetic* (New York: Macmillan, 1928). "At the fall of Rome the Trivium was dominated by *rhetorica*; in the Carolingian period, by *grammatica*; in the high middle age, by *dialectica*" (p. 151). As a result *dialectica* took over all of the classical divisions of *rhetorica*, save *elocutio*. "*Poetria* . . . meant generally the study of style, and specifically the study of stylistic decoration. The lore for this was rhetoric, partly indeed by misapplication, partly from the vagueness of the boundary in Latin tradition. The 'colors of rhetoric,' not always clearly distinguished . . . were faithfully recited as a sort of Greek ritual of poetic" (p. 195).

See also Donald L. Clark, *Rhetoric and Poetic in the Renaissance* (New York: Columbia University Press, 1922).

[15] Rossell Robbins, *Secular Lyrics of the XIVth and XVth Centuries* (Oxford: Clarendon Press, 1952). Poems cited in this section are from Robbins, unless otherwise indicated.

Whan he beholdith how vunconnyngly
My book is metrid, how raw my sentence,
How feeble eek been my coulours, his prudence
Shal sore encombrid been my folie;

(St. 2)

. . . .

For rethorik hath hid fro me the keye
Of his tresor, nat deyneth hir nobleye
Dele with noon so ignorant as me.

(St. 3, ll. 7-9)

Chaucer's Franklin makes a similar excuse; he claims that he
lacks the art of eloquence because he is generally lacking in
learning:

But, sires, by cause I am a burel man,
At my bigynnyng first I yow biseche,
Have me excused of my rude speche.
I lerned nevere rethorik, certeyn;
Thyng that I speke, it moot be bare and pleyn.
I sleep never on the Mount of Pernaso,
Ne lerned Marcus Tullius Scithero.
Colours ne knowe I none, withouten drede,
But swiche colours as growen in the mede,
Or elles swiche as men dye or peynte.
Colours of rethoryk been to me queynte.

(*The Franklin's Prologue*, ll. 8-18)[16]

The eloquent style is the learned style, the style garnished with
the colors of rhetoric and fit for addressing the nobility. The
plain style, though written in the language of the people, is
nevertheless adequate for the straightforward handling of the
truth. Chaucer's Harry Bailley makes the distinction between
the plain and the eloquent styles clear when he advises the clerk
to

---

[16] His audience learns shortly that his ignorance of "rethorik" and
its "Coulours" is only a pretense. He tells a tale that is burdened down
with elaborate ornamentation and eloquent digression.

Telle us som murie thyng of aventures.
Youre termes, youre colours, and your figures,
Keepe hem in stoor til so be that ye endite
Heigh style, as whan that men to kynges write.
Speketh so pleyn at this tyme, we yow preye,
That we may understonde what ye seye.
                    (*The Clerk's Prologue*, ll. 14-20)

The "heigh style" is decorative and irrelevant if one is concerned only to "conveyen his mateere." This the Clerk makes
clear when, in response to Harry Bailley's instructions to avoid
the high style, he promises to tell a tale learned from Petrarch
("The lauriat poete . . . whos rethorike sweet/ Enlumyned
al Ytaille of poetrie") in plain English:

        But forth to tellen of this worthy man
        That taughte me this tale, as I began,
        I seye that first with heigh stile he enditeth,
        Er he the body of his tale writeth,
        A prohemye . . .
        The which a long thyng were to devyse.
        And trewely, as to my juggement,
        Me thynketh it a thyng impertinent,
        Save that he wole conveyen his mateere;
        But this his tale, which that ye may heere.
                            (ll. 39-56 *passim*)

The anonymous author of "The Lover's Mocking Reply"
(No. 209) has a similar notion of eloquence as a matter of
stylistic refinement:

    The ynglysch of Chaucere was nat in youre mynd,
        Ne tullyus termys wyth so gret elloquence,
    But ye, as vuncurtes and Crabbed of kynde,
        Rolled hem on a hepe, it semyth by the sentence.
                            (ll. 8-11)

Since his lady has not written to him eloquently and has not
sought the aid of Cicero's figures or the style of Chaucer as a
model, the poet writes that he will reply in kind and write the

[27]

truth plainly: "And so dare I boldly withoute ony offence/ Answere to your letter, as fallyth to the purpose." (ll. 12-13)

The poetry written according to the medieval conception of eloquence is, as A. K. Moore remarks, among "the worst ever caught up in the record of English literature."[17] The amorous courtly verses are usually highly formulary developments of the commonplaces of courtly love: pledges of service; pleas for mercy and grace; detailed and stereotyped descriptions of the physical and spiritual attributes of the beloved; and plaints, apostrophes, and schematized descriptions of the lover's suffering emotions. The fifteenth-century love poet who writes within the eloquent tradition makes no attempt to look into the causes of his suffering, nor does he show any concern for the heretical implications of courtly love. He accepts its doctrines uncritically as suitable for the exercise of style. The civilized poet was expected to show that he was at home in the current fashion. The conventions of the courtly lyric are not in themselves responsible for the lifeless love poetry which they frequently produced. Wyatt, for instance, wrote a good many successful poems about the commonplaces of courtly love. It is, rather, the stylistic standard of eloquence functioning as intention which is at fault.

By accepting the analytical distinction between style and content as a real distinction—a distinction for which medieval rhetoricians were to blame—the courtly poets deny style its purpose. Style embodies perception and feeling. It is the means by which the good poet achieves the fine adjustments of attitude and feeling that he feels are proper to his subject. To some extent the educated writers of the fifteenth century recognized this in accepting the ancient principle of stylistic decorum. They agreed with the principle that style had to be suitable to its subject. But the principle of stylistic decorum is descriptive and highly generalized; and though of value, as a general precept, it does not, as a rule of composition, assure its adherents of success. The principle was derived inductively from the analysis of writing in which it appeared as an inherent quality of the work itself. When it was formulated analytically, it had to be

---

[17] *The Secular Lyric in Middle English*, p. 37.

stated in terms of a theoretical distinction between style and content. The distinction is not a real distinction, but it became such. It became a convention based on descriptive analysis without concern for the real causes out of which it emerged. When style as decoration is substituted for style as an instrument of definition and qualification, genteel platitudes can be the only result.

Stylistic preoccupations in courtly poetry resulted in a lack of variety in the selection and treatment of subject and the tendency to regard language and structure as extrinsic and unrelated to content. The subject exists only as the occasion for the poem. Popularity is its only requirement. The boring recurrence of the platitudes of courtly love, dedication, and eulogy is the result. Structure is employed merely as a supporting framework for verbal embellishment. It rarely appears as a means of ordering insights. And language as ornament, selected and rigidly controlled by the notion of eloquence, is reduced to lifeless poetic diction. These habits of composition are easily recognized.

The victim of unrequited love found the catalogue a convenient way to display his "bitter bale," "madness," "woe," and "grief." He found it also a means of describing copiously the virtues and physical charms of his beloved. Seven stanzas are devoted to the lady's charms in "A Catalogue of Delights" (No. 127):

> Her heer is yelou as the gold,
> Her forhed shapyn as it shuld
>   with all the feturs thereabout,
> Her Eris ben comly & round,
> Her browes with bewte bene bound;
>   wel wer hym that wynne her mouth.
>
> Her lovely yen of colour gray,
> Her rudy is like the rose yn may
>   with leris white as any milk,
> Her Nose is set right womanly,
> With mouth & tethe bothe so goodly,
>   her lippes soft as any silk;
>
>   (St. 4-5)

Four stanzas later the poet has finally gotten down to the lady's fingers, at which point decorum triumphs over copiousness, and the poet turns his attention to his own feelings:

> her armes bene small, her hondes swete,
> with fyngurs long with nayles mete;
>   All of plesur she is wrout;
> All other feturs of her, I-wisse,
> Bene shapyn wel, no thyng amysse—
>   so fair a wight know I nout.
>
> Allas, my sorow now doth avaunce
> ffor this garison of plesaunce,
>   No mervayl I trow that it be;
> In her Erthly no faute is found;
> But only daunger hath her bound
>   that she shall shaw no mercye.
>
> (St. 9-10)

The method and the description are equally trite, and it is not surprising to find both parodied in poems like "The Lover's Mocking Reply" (No. 209):

> Youre Camusyd nose, with nose-thryllys brode,
>   Vnto the chyrch a noble Instrument
> To quenche tapers brennying afore the roode,
>   ys best apropred at myne avysament;
>   your leud lokyng, doble of entent,
>   wyth courtly loke al of saferon hew,
>   That neuer wol fayle—the colour is so trew!
>
> (St. 4)

All of the structural forms used by the didactic poets appear also in the courtly poets. Even doctrinal framework was modified to support the adornments of the courtly love conventions. Charles d'Orleans' "A Confession of Love" (No. 185), for instance, is a parody of a public confession:[18]

---

[18] For examples of this original form see Patterson's *Middle English Penitential Lyric*, pp. 47-50.

My gostly fadir, y me confesse,
 ffirst to god and then to yow
That at a wyndow (wot ye how)
I stale a cosse of gret swetnes,
Which don was out avisynes;
 But his is doon, not vndoon, now—
My gostly [fadir, y me confesse,]
 First to [god and then to yow,]
But y restore it shall dowtles
 Ageyn, if so be that y mow;
And that, god, y make a vow,
And ellis y axe foryefnes—
My gostly [fadir, y me confesse,]
 First to [god and then to yow.]

The courtly poets also developed a scheme of arrangement in one of their favorite genres, the love epistle, which according to Robbins was "the main conventional form during the fifteenth century."[19] Its popularity was natural at a time when letter writing flourished as an art. As a means of teaching style, letter writing (*dictamen*) ranked with the disciplines of rhetoric and poetic. C. S. Baldwin, in his discussion of its pedagogical importance, concludes that "*Dictamen* was . . . practical in actual teaching. Besides giving exercises in correctness, it compelled attention to elegance."[20] No one has noticed how closely the authors of love epistles followed the precepts set down in the manuals of *Ars Dictaminis*.

According to Baldwin the manuals of letter writing, in addition to stressing eloquent style, preserved the Classical divisions of an oration:

> . . . ancient lore was immediately and practically applicable. It [the art of letter writing] did not, as in the *poetriae*, have to be perverted. . . . Immediately adaptable were the five parts of a speech. The exordium is always cardinal in a letter as *benevolentiae captatio*. *Narratio* applies exactly in its proper sense of statement of the facts.

[19] *Secular Lyrics of the XIVth and XVth Centuries*, Notes, p. 286.
[20] *Medieval Rhetoric and Poetic*, p. 215.

Petitio, though it has less scope, is quite pertinent. *Conclu-sio*, though varying most from its ancient function, has some general correspondence. In a word, the classical doctrine for the parts of a speech applied to a letter by mere reduction of scale.[21]

There is almost always evidence in the verse epistles of the conscious application of *dispositio*. It is also more than likely that the numerous "plaints" and "pleas" in the courtly tradition were sometimes written according to the specific instruction in the letter writing manuals on how to construct an *exordium*, *narratio*, or *petitio*. The verse epistles proper do not always disclose all five parts of *dispositio*; *narratio* is frequently omitted or merely implied. "A Letter to His Heart's Joy" (No. 189), one of the occasional examples short enough to be quoted in full, exhibits all five divisions.

> Myn hertys Ioy, and all myn hole plesaunce,
> Whom that I serue and shall do faythfully
> Wyth trew entent and humble obseruaunce,
> Yow for to plese in that I can treuly,
> Besechyng yow thys lytell byll and I
> May hertly, wyth symplesse and drede,
> Be recomawndyd to your goodlyhede.

> And yf ye lyst haue knowlech of my qwert,
> I am in hele—god thankyd mot he be—
> As of body, but treuly not in hert,
> Nor nought shal be to tyme I may you se;
> But thynke that I as treuly wyll be he
> That for your ese shall do my payn and myght,
> As thogh that I were dayly in your syght.

> I wryte to yow no more for lak of space,
> But I beseche the only trinite
> Yow kepe and saue be support of hys grace,
> And be your sheld from all aduersyte.
> Go lytill byll, and say thou were wyth me

---

[21] *Ibid.*, pp. 214-15.

> Of verey trouth, as thou canst wele remembre,
> At myn vpryst, the fyft day of Decembre.

In keeping with the required convention of the lover's servility to his mistress, the poet establishes the humble tone of his letter in the salutation and the beginning of the exordium. Exordium and narration merge in the second stanza where the statement of the facts is also construed as a compliment to the author's mistress. The petition in this particular poem—a prayer on the lady's behalf—is but one of various applications common in the epistles; and the conclusion is of course a ballade stereotype.

"A Letter to His Heart's Sovereign" (No. 191) develops the five-part structure more copiously. The salutation, taking up the whole first stanza, again establishes a servile tone. The second and third stanzas develop the complimentary exordium and present the facts of narration which are finally summarily stated in the fourth stanza. The fourth stanza also contains the petition:

> And of one thyng ye be full sure:
>   I lyst to loue yow euyn as my lyfe,
> And at all tymes your owne seruiture
> So that betwene shalbe no stryfe
> As hyt ys reson duryng my lyfe;
>   Wherfore, fayr loue, haue me in mynd,
>   And to yowre trew loue neuer be vnkynd.

The conclusion is a brief formulary appendage of polite compliment ending with the already trite "dieing" lover:

> The throwes of loue doth my hert so chase
>   That, truly and god, ther ys no remedy
> Without your comfort, but mercylese to dy.
>   (St. 5, ll. 5-7)

The "epistles" discussed above are typical of the many available examples illustrating how the formulas for letter writing were used for stylistic purposes.[22] Letter writing manuals continued to be used to supplement rhetorical training in the

---

[22] See Robbins Nos. 129, 130, 131, 146, 149, 161, 188, 208, 209.

Renaissance, and the vogue of the love epistle, as might be expected, continued. This is particularly evident among the minor writers in miscellanies such as *A Gorgeous Gallery of Gallant Inventions*.

By way of summary, the best that can be said of the intentions and techniques responsible for the literary lyric is that they reflect a growing consciousness of style among the educated and they establish some stylistic conventions that prove useful to later poets. On the other hand, they are also responsible for the poetic diction of courtly love which is still fashionable among most of the mid-sixteenth-century poets. The verse exercises in eloquence discussed mark the beginning of a verse tradition which flourishes to the end of the sixteenth century—a tradition which, although it discloses various refinements on every level of composition and certain shifts in emphasis from one element of style to another, is nevertheless dominated from its inception to its eventual collapse by the post-classical notion of style. It is in terms of that notion that the decorative style is mistakenly identified throughout the greater part of the sixteenth century with the Latin classical tradition and hence championed as the truly literary style. It is also in terms of that notion that the literary style comes to be considered the courtly style, a style to be pursued as a courtly accomplishment, a courtly grace distinguishing the truly refined courtier from the pedant.

By the turn of the century the two styles are well established. Examples of the plain and eloquent styles can be found side by side in the works of both Dunbar and Skelton. There can be no question as to whether or not the appearance of the two styles in the works of these poets is deliberate. They observe the same distinction between the two styles on the basis of intention that Chaucer observed. Dunbar is mainly a devout, moral poet who writes plainly of virtue and sin and of the various requirements of his religion. Such didactic pieces as "I Cry the Mercy, and Lasar to Repent" (9) and "To Dwell in Court my Friend" (20), or the contemplative pieces "Meditatioun in Wyntir" (69) and "My Heid Did 3ak 3esternich" (78) are written in the style of the "Lament for the Makaris."[23] But he is also able, when the occasion demands it, to phrase a formal compliment in the fashionable literary style. It is the style, for instance, which he feels is appropriate for addressing the Virgin in "Roiss Mary most of vertew virginall" (86):[24]

Roiss Mary most of vertew virginall.
　　Fresche flowr on quhom the hevynnis dewe doun fell.
O gemme joynit in joye anglicall,
　　In quhom Jhesu rejosit wes to dwell.
　　Rute of refute, of mercy spring and well,
Of ladyis chois as is of letteris A,
　　Empress of hevyne, of paradyss, and hell,
O mater Jhesu, salue Maria!

(ll. 1-8)

It is also the style of his infrequent courtly love verses, as in "Quhone He List to Feyne" (74):

　　My hartis tresure, and swete assured so,
　　　　The finale endar of my lyfe for ever;
　　The creuell brekar of my hart in tuo,
　　　　To go to deathe, this I deservit never:
　　O man-slayar! quhill saule and life dissever;
　　Stynt of your slauchter; Allace! your man am I,
　　A thowsand tymes that dois yow mercy cry.

(ll. 1-7)

It is the style which Dunbar accepts as the "ornate stilis so perfyte," the mark of literary refinement for which Chaucer, Gower, and Lydgate are remembered:[25]

　　O reuerend Chaucere, rose of rethoris all,
　　As in oure tong ane flour imperiall,
　　　　That raise in Britane ewir, quho redis rycht,
　　Thou beris of makaris the tryumph riall;
　　Thy fresch anamalit termes celicall

[23] Dunbar's poems are cited from *The Poems of William Dunbar*, ed., John Small.
[24] See also Nos. 85, 87, 89.
[25] "The Goldyn Targe," l. 68.

This mater coud illumynit haue full brycht:
Was thou noucht of oure Inglisch all the lycht,
   Surmounting ewiry tong terrestriall,
    Alls fer as Mayes morow dois mydnycht?

O morall Gower, and Ludgate laureate,
Your sugurit lippis and tongis aureate,
   Bene to oure eris cause of grete delyte;
Your angel mouthis most mellifluate
Our rude langage has clere illumynate,
   And faire our-gilt oure speche, that imperfyte
   Stude, or your goldyn pennis schupe to wryte;
This Ile before was bare, and desolate
   Off rethorike, or lusty fresch endyte.
       ("The Goldyn Targe," ll. 253-70)

Skelton, like Dunbar, writes only infrequently in the eloquent tradition. His interests were mainly in satire, moral instruction, and contemplation. In fact, in "The Garland of Laurel" the question as to whether he is deserving of fame is raised (ironically) since he has not followed the prescribed custom of praise:

  . . . sith he hath tasted of the sugared potion
    Of Helicones well, refreshed with your grace,
  And will not endeavour himself to purchase
    The favour of ladies with wordes elect,
    It is fittinge that ye must him correct.
     (The Queen of Fame to Dame Pallas)[26]

His infrequent use of the ornate style is limited to the early elegies, "On the Death of . . . King Edward the Fourth" and "Upon the Dolorous Death . . . of the Most Honourable Earl of Northumberland" and to several of the complimentary verses at the close of "The Garland of Laurel," verses written according to "Occupation's" instructions:[27]

[26] *The Complete Poems of John Skelton*, ed., Philip Henderson (London: J. M. Dent and Sons Ltd., 1948), p. 349.
[27] See *"To the right noble* Countess of Surrey," *"To my Lady* Elizabeth Howard," and *"To my Lady* Anne Dacre *of the South," Poems*, pp. 374-78.

Behold and see in your advertisement
  How these ladies and gentlewomen all
For your pleasure do their endeavourment,
    And for your sake how fast to work they fall:
    To your remembrance wherefore ye must call
In goodly wordes pleasantly comprised
That for them some goodly conceit be devised,

With proper captations of benevolence,
  Ornately polished after your faculty,
Sith ye must needs aforce it by pretence
  Of your profession unto humanity,
  Commencing your process after their degree,
To each of them rendering thankes commendable,
With sentence fructuous and termes convenable.

               (*Poems*, pp. 373-74)

Skelton's preferred mode, however, is the unadorned style.[28]

The limitations of both styles at the end of the fifteenth century are not difficult to assess. The eloquent poetic encouraged a kind of writing which we now discourage as "inflated" or "literary." Furthermore, its adherents, who might otherwise have commenced the process of refinement initiated in the next century by the Humanists, are limited by the state of the vernacular itself and by the paucity of literary models suitable for imitation. The plain style also suffers at this early date from the state of the vernacular and the lack of a native verse tradition. It suffers especially from a chaotic syntax and from an excessive moralizing, often expressed in the most hackneyed of aphorisms. Even its chief virtue—realistic plain statement often accomplished with aphoristic conciseness—worked against the refinement of syntax and the development of means other than the enumeration of concrete examples for qualifying and demonstrating the moral truths it treats.

    Until the plain style develops a firmer syntax and structures

[28] See, for example, "Upon a Dead Man's Head" (Sent to him from an honourable gentlewoman for a token, he devised this ghostly meditation in English convenable, in sentence commendable, lamentable, lacrimable, profitable for a soul)."

more flexible than those afforded by the refrain and common-place techniques, its possibilities as a medium of reflection or introspective analysis are severely limited. The superiority of Ben Jonson's "To Heaven," Donne's "Thou hast made me, and shall thy work decay," or George Herbert's "Church Monuments" to Dunbar's "Lament for the Makeris" or Skelton's "Upon a Dead Man's Head" is not, necessarily, a matter of talent or intelligence. It is a matter of superior techniques and structures, of refined syntax and language.

Those refinements and advances in techniques will be accomplished in the first three-quarters of the sixteenth century by the eloquent poets who in search of eloquence go to the handbooks of rhetoric or to continental models and introduce refinements of language, style, and structure, thus making possible the kinds of poem which Sidney, Shakespeare, and Donne wrote.

CHAPTER II

Tottel's *Miscellany*

Rhetorical Background

The medieval assumption that style and content are distinct persisted in Renaissance literary theory. It is inherent in the special purposes that, to the end of the Renaissance, are attributed to the plain and the literary styles—the plain having a contemplative or didactic purpose, and the literary, a stylistic or eloquent one.

The movement during the first half of the sixteenth century to refine and polish the vernacular is a matter of common knowledge. The humanists were convinced that their language was incapable of the literary excellence which they associated with the Classical authors, and the means which they cultivated to make it capable of such excellence are reflected throughout the literature of the period. The desire to improve the language inspired the popular doctrine of literary imitation, summarized by Ascham in *The Scholemaster*, and the subsequent preoccupation with translation, paraphrase, and adaptation. It gave rise to the century-long quarrel over ink-horn terms and archaisms. In prose it resulted in extremes—on the one hand, in the kind of slavish imitation of Cicero that is ridiculed by Nash in *The Unfortunate Traveler*, and, on the other, in the excessive reliance on the schemes of Gorgias that is characteristic of the euphuistic style of Lyly, Gosson, and Pettie. In poetry it lay behind the attempt to introduce into English the Classical system of prosody, the imitation in accentual verse of Classical meters, and the controversy over what Ascham calls the "barbarous" and "Gothic" habit of "Ryming."[1] But the extent to which the

---

[1] See *The Scholemaster*, Arber's English Reprints (London: Constable & Co., 1869), pp. 144-48. Although the debate over rhyme during the century was not confined to end-rhyme but was extended to include both rhyme and accentual rhythms (as opposed to Classical Latin meters), Ascham has in mind chiefly end-rhyme: "The noble Lord *Th.* Earle of

lyric was implicated in the movement to refine the language has not been sufficiently appreciated. The lyric was affected as intimately as the other literary genres; for the standards by which the vernacular was judged inferior, and which therefore gave direction to the linguistic movement, also gave direction to the development of the lyric.

The movement to refine the language was primarily stylistic. R. F. Jones has shown that for approximately three-quarters of a century "the Englishman viewed his language as plain, honest, and substantial, but uneloquent":[2] "That the English language per se was considered uneloquent may be easily deduced from the adjectives most frequently used to describe it: 'rude,' 'gross,' 'barbarous,' 'vile.' "[3] Continuing, Jones demonstrates, however, that "for the most part these terms did not possess the strong connotations for the Renaissance that they hold for us," that they usually designate only the stylistic inferiority of the vernacular. English was, in short, considered as wholly adequate for dealing plainly and precisely with ideas and accepted as the medium of popular instruction. What it lacked were the qualities which the English so much admired in the Classical authors. Refinement of the language was therefore confined almost entirely to matters of style. The terms "literary" and "stylistic" continued to be synonymous, with the result that literary efforts often resulted in the same subordination of content to style that is evident in the literary lyric of the Middle Ages. On the other hand, for efforts which required the serious treatment of ideas the plain vernacular was generally deemed adequate and, indeed, preferred.

As far as literary style was concerned, those qualities which gave verse literary stature were identified by the term "eloquence." The term meant for the Renaissance precisely what

---

Surrey, first of all English men, in translating the fourth booke of *Virgill*: and *Gonsaluo Periz* . . . in translating the *Vlisses* of *Homer* out of *Greke* into *Spanish* haue both, by good iudgement, auoyded the fault of Ryming . . ." (p. 147).

[2] *The Triumph of the English Language* (Stanford: Stanford University Press, 1953), p. 18.

[3] *Ibid.*, p. 7.

it had meant in the Middle Ages.[4] Although the goal of the Tudor literary, or courtly, poet was to write eloquently by emulating the Classical poets or those continental poets whose verse reflected what he thought were Classical qualities, his literary theory had been inherited as a part of medieval rhetoric, and he sought to imitate only those qualities of style which his inherited theory brought into focus.[5] In short, his notion of the eloquent style was not derived from his reading of the Classics, but from the rhetorical theory in which he had been trained. That theory, which construed eloquence as almost exclusively a matter of copiousness and superficial decoration, was the one primarily available to the early Tudors. R. F. Jones remarks that the tradition of medieval rhetoric is the primary source of Renaissance literary theory: "Though one seeks in vain for any significant body of literary criticism in England before the Renaissance, there did come down through the Middle Ages a very definite rhetorical tradition, based upon the postclassical writers and supported by the position of rhetoric in the university curriculum. It is not strange, then, that in the absence of a critical terminology, those who might wish to comment on poetry should use rhetorical terms, and that criticism should be primarily interested in that element which is common to both rhetoric and poetic, namely, style."[6] Eleanor Sweeting observes

[4] Professor Tuve's remarks about the term "eloquence" are misleading: "The ingenious images of Metaphysical poets offer no evidence that they disagreed with Quintilian's insistence on the need for art in achieving what he defines, from the verb *eloqui*, as the production and communication to the audience of all that the speaker has conceived in his mind . . ." (*Elizabethan and Metaphysical Imagery*, pp. 32-33). Quintilian's definition is one available meaning of the term in the sixteenth century; but it is not the prevailing one in the first three-quarters of the century. Nor does the term ever lose its medieval connotations; to the end of the Renaissance it continues to suggest copious ornamentation. *Eloquent* poetry, for Donne as for Tottel's contributors, designates poetry which cultivates the schemes and tropes classified and illustrated under the heading *elocutio* in the handbooks of rhetoric.

[5] For a parallel discussion of how during the Renaissance the Classics were read with medieval habits of thought, see Madeleine Doran, *Endeavors of Art: A Study of Form in Elizabethan Tragedy* (Madison: University of Wisconsin Press, 1954), pp. 24-46.

[6] *Triumph of the English Language*, p. 1.

[41]

that the sixteenth-century poets were indebted to medieval manuals of style: "They drew upon the laws of composition preserved in mediaeval textbooks such as Geoffroi de Vinsauf's *Nova Poetria*, from whom Chaucer says he derived his knowledge of rhetoric."[7] Scholarship has established, moreover, that the handbooks most widely used in the Renaissance schools were essentially medieval. According to W. G. Crane, "The two most popular textbooks in the grammar schools were Erasmus' *De duplici copia verborum et rerum* and Aphthonius's *Progymnasmata*."[8]

Even those new texts, such as Thomas Wilson's *Arte of Rhetorique*, which offer a balanced treatment of the five parts of rhetoric, and which thus represent a return to the Classical tradition, preserve the medieval ideal of the eloquent style in their sections on *elocutio*. *Elocutio*, the third division of rhetoric, was devoted to the principal devices by which eloquence could be achieved. Thomas Wilson accepts the commonly accepted definition of the term: "Elocution getteth words to set forth inuention, and with such beautie commendeth the matter, that reason semeth to be clad in Purple, walking afore both bare and naked."[9] By its tropes one is able "to beautifie the sentence, as precious stones are set in a ring to commende the gold"; and "among all the figures of *Rhetorique*, there is no one that so much helpeth forward an Oration, and beautifieth the same with such delightfull ornaments, as doth amplification."[10] Clearly, Wilson does not consider style as the final clarification of thought. Conceiving of eloquence as something added to content, he perpetuates the dichotomy between style and content.

The dichotomy is implicit wherever the emphasis is upon

[7] *Studies in Early Tudor Criticism* (New York: Russell & Russell, 1964), p. 111.

[8] W. G. Crane, *Wit and Rhetoric in the Renaissance* (New York: Columbia University Press, 1937), p. 61. Aphthonius was medieval; Erasmus was heavily indebted to his predecessors. See George J. Engelhardt, "Medieval Vestiges in the Rhetoric of Erasmus," *PMLA*, LXIII (1948), 739-44.

[9] *The Art of Rhetorique*, 1560 (Oxford: Clarendon Press, 1909), p. 160.

[10] *Ibid.*, pp. 165, 116.

copiousness and ornamentation; and such emphasis is to be found everywhere throughout the period. W. G. Crane, summarizing the treatises on rhetoric by Cox, Sherry, and Rainolde, concludes: "The English rhetorics of the sixteenth century reflect the emphasis which the Renaissance placed on amplification and ornamentation."[11] Francis R. Johnson comments upon the consequences of this one-sided concern: "With instruction in rhetoric centered primarily on *elocutio*, defined at the time as the classification and illustration of the various figures of speech, the inevitable tendency was to regard style as the superficial ornamentation whereby the writer adorned or 'prettified' his discourse."[12] Eleanor Sweeting observes that the practises of *elocutio* were not confined to the writing of prose, but included poetry as well: "The poets and prose writers of the late fifteenth and early sixteenth centuries were preoccupied with matters of style. When they use the term 'Rhetoric' they usually signify *elocutio*, since it provided them with the means of achieving the 'aureate' style in verse and ornamental prose. . . . This conception persisted in the fifteenth and early sixteenth centuries, when there was a strong feeling for the 'high style' in Europe, and in English poetry for a time no less than elsewhere."[13]

The poets in Tottel's *Miscellany* clearly reflect their medieval training. Those contributors who are concerned with eloquence follow generally the method of composition summarized by Stephen Hawes in *The Pastime of Pleasure*. Hawes, of course, is a supporter of the Boccaccian tradition which regards poetry as an instrument of persuasion; his instructions, however, embody the notion of eloquence assumed by the literary poets. *Inventio* and *dispositio* exist only as subordinate means necessary to the eloquent intention. *Inventio* refers not to the original choice of theme, but to the discovery of a method which enables the "ymagynacyon to draw a mater/ full facundyous" (ll. 708-9), that is, to develop a theme copiously. *Dispositio* "dooth euermore dyrecte the matters founde . . . Gyuynge them place/

---

[11] *Wit and Rhetoric in the Renaissance*, p. 97.
[12] Richard Rainolde, *The Foundacion of Rhetorike*, Introduction, ix.
[13] *Studies in Early Tudor Criticism*, p. 111.

after the aspect" (ll. 834-37). In short, the poet chooses a theme and a means of expanding it copiously, establishes a convenient principle of order, and then concentrates on "swete and dylycous" rhetoric:

> And then the iii parte is elocucyon
> Whan inuencyon/ hath the purpose wrought
> And set it in ordre/ by dysposycyon
> Without this thyrde parte/ it vayleth ryght nought
> Thoughe it be founde/ and in ordre brought
> Yet elocucyon/ with the power of Mercury
> The mater exorneth/ ryght well facundyously
> In fewe wordes/ swete and sentencyous
> Depaynted with golde; harde in construccyon
> To the artyke eres/ swete and dylycyous
> The golden rethoryke/ is good refeccyon
> And to the reder/ ryght consolacyon
> As we do golde/ frome coper puryfy
> So that elocucyon/ doth ryght well claryfy
> The dulce speche/ frome the langage rude
> Tellygne the tale/ in termes eloquent
> The barbary tongue/ it doth ferre exclude
> Electynge wordes/ which are expedyent
> In latyn/ or in englysshe/ after the entent
> Encensynge out/ the aromatyke fume
> Our langage rude/ to exyle and consume.
>
> (ll. 904-24)[14]

Striving for "Golden rethoryke," the courtly poets proceeded to do what Dame Margery in Skelton's *The Boke of Phyllyp Sparrow* had claimed she was not able to do:

> I am but a yong maid,
> And cannot in effect
> My style as yet direct
> With *Englyshe* words elect.
> Our natural tonge is rude,
> And hard to be ennewed

---

[14] *The Pastime of Pleasure*, ed., W. E. Mead (*EETS*, 173; 1928).

With pollysshed termes lusty;
Our language is so rusty
So cankered and so full
Of frowards, and so dull.
That if I wold apply
To write ornately
I wot not where to find
Terms to serue my mynd.[15]

To find "terms to serve his mind," the poet went outside the native tradition to Petrarch, or back to Chaucer, seeking models of eloquent diction and techniques precisely as the Renaissance in general sought archaisms and neologisms. Petrarch was admired in the Renaissance for the same reasons that he was admired by Chaucer. His name was synonymous with eloquence, not, as is often supposed, with modernity.[16] His praise by the anonymous author of sonnets Nos. 218 and 219 in Tottel is characteristic:

O Petrarke hed and prince of poets all,
Whose liuely gift of flowyng eloquence,
Wel may we seke, but finde not how or whence
So rare a gift with thee did rise and fall,
Peace to thy bones, and glory immortall
Be to thy name. . . .

(No. 218, ll. 1-6)

With petrarke to compare there may no wight
Nor yet attain vnto so high a stile. . . .

(No. 219, ll. 1-2)

The Tudor poets saw in his work the refinement of a native

[15] *The Complete Poems*, p. 94.

[16] We are inclined to forget that Petrarch is also the representative of medieval poetics, as Renwick emphasizes: "Petrarch, the leader of an eager band of humanists, is also, it is true, one of the great modern poets of Italy, but the success of his Tuscan poetry, and the revival of its influence more than a century after his death, have somewhat obscured the fact that it belongs to a pre-Renaissance tradition." *Edmund Spenser, An Essay on Renaissance Poetry* (London: Edward Arnold & Co., 1925), p. 10.

[45]

vernacular and must have felt, therefore, that he afforded them models not so far removed from their own tongue as those afforded by Classical poets. They translated and adapted his sonnets because he represented to them the eloquence that could be achieved in a vernacular tongue.

Renaissance commentary on the early Tudor lyricists also illustrates the preoccupation with style. Poets are praised to the extent that they have beautified the mother tongue. Jonson praises Wyatt and Surrey as "for their times admirable: and the more, because they began Eloquence with us."[17] Churchyard calls Surrey "a Tullie for his tong"; Turbervile praises him for his refinement of the vernacular: "Our mother tongue by him hath got such light,/ As ruder speach thereby is banisht quight."[18] Puttenham, whose views are more commonplace than original, sums up the popular attitude toward Wyatt and Surrey and the "new company of courtly makers." His main concern is with their contribution to the general improvement of the English tongue: ". . . Sir *Thomas Wyat* th'elder and *Henry* Earle of Surrey were the two chieftains, who hauing trauailed into Italie, and there tasted the sweete and stately measures and stile of the Italian Poesie as nouices newly crept out of the schooles of *Dante Arioste* and Petrarch, they greatly pollished our rude and homely maner of vulgar Poesie, from that it had bene before, and for that cause may justly be sayd the first reformers of our English meetre and stile."[19] These are the same reasons for which Dunbar and Skelton praise Chaucer. Neither Wyatt nor Surrey is praised for freeing the poetic imagination from the bonds of medievalism. They are "reformers," not revolutionaries. They are "the two chief lanternes of light to all others that have employed their pennes vpon the English Poesie," not because they captured the spirit of the Italian Renaissance, but because they learned from Petrarch how to achieve the "high style" in the vernacular: "Their conceits were

[17] *Discoveries*, ed., Herford and Simpson, Vol. VIII, p. 591.
[18] *The Arte of English Poesie*, eds., Gladys D. Willcock and Alice Walker (Cambridge: University Press, 1936), p. 62.
[19] *Ibid.*, p. 62.

loftie, their stiles stately, their termes proper, in all imitating very naturally and studiously their Maister Francis Petrarch."[20]

Tottel, himself, makes quite clear in his preface that the courtly lyric was read for its stylistic beauties:

> That to haue wel written in verse, yea & in small parcelles, deserueth great praise, the workes of diuers Latines, Italians, and other, doe proue sufficiently. That our tong is able in that kynde to do as praiseworthely as the rest, the honorable stile of the noble earle of Surrey, and the weightinesse of the depewitted Sir Thomas Wyat *the* elders verse, with seueral graces in sondry good Englishe writers, doe show abundantly. It resteth nowe (gentle reder) that thou thinke it not euill doon, to publish, to the honor of the Englishe tong, and for profit of the studious of Englishe eloquence, those workes which the vngentle horders vp of such treasure haue heretofore enuied thee. And for this point (good reder) thine own profit and pleasure, in these presently, and in moe hereafter, shal answere for my defence. If parhappes some mislike the statelinesse of stile remoued from the rude skill of common eares: I aske help of the learned to defend their learned frendes, the authors of this work: And I exhort, the vnlearned, by reding to learne to be more skilfull and to purge that swinelike grossenesse, that maketh the swete maierome not to smell to their delight.[21]

He is publishing his collection "to the honor of the English tong, and for profit of the studious of Englishe eloquence." Save for the passing reference to "the weightinesse of the depewitted Sir Thomas Wyat the elders verse," he expresses no interest in the content of the verse he has collected and confines his comments to a defense of English eloquence. The stately style of his collection is equal to that of any revealed in the works of "diuers Latines, Italians, and other." It affords profit as well as pleasure, for it may "purge" the unlearned of their "swinelike grossenesse" and serve as a standard for the learned who wish to master the high style.

[20] *Ibid.*
[21] Tottel's *Miscellany*, "The Printer to the Reader," p. 2.

It is apparent, then, that the courtly lyric was read, as well as written, according to the notion of eloquence inherited from the preceding age, and that the Tudor poets were praised chiefly for their contributions to the English language. Surrey, by imitating Petrarch, achieved a style which to his successors seemed most nearly to approach the accepted standard of excellence. He took his place beside Petrarch as a master of eloquence worthy of imitation. Wyatt is also praised as one of the first refiners of the language, but he is praised in this connection for his Petrarchan translations and not for his most representative work in the plain style.

The notion of poetry as essentially a stylistic discipline was not, however, the only notion accepted in the Renaissance. The plain style continues to be used by didactic and contemplative poets on through the century.[22] And there was also another uninterrupted tradition, emerging out of the confusion of rhetoric with poetry in the Middle Ages: the tradition which preserved in the Renaissance the notion of poetry as a means of inculcating virtue, but which at the same time stressed style as a persuasive element.[23] It is reflected in Roger Ascham's condemnation of the "lascivious [Latin] poets who wrote epistles and ditties of love." Rainolde's and Wilson's view of the moral uses of poetry also appears to derive from the same tradition. Rainolde, for instance, when discussing the use of fables, affirms their value by pointing out that "both Poetes and Oratours doe applie theim to their use. For fables dooe contain goodlie admonicion, vertuous preceptes of life." And he praises Ovid for "diuers fables, wherein he giueth admonicion, and godly counsaile."[24] Wilson also praises poetry for the truth it preserves: "For vndoubtedly there is no one tale among all the Poetes, but vnder the same is comprehended some thing that parteineth, either to the amendment of maners, to the knowledge of the trueth, to the setting forth of Natures work, or else the vnder-

---

[22] Aristotle in his treatise on rhetoric defines the proper function of the plain style as teaching. It is also the style best suited to contemplation.

[23] See Donald L. Clark, *Rhetoric and Poetry in the Renaissance.*

[24] *The Foundacion of Rhetorike,* Fol. iij^v.

standing of some notable thing done."[25] Although the tradition
of poetry as a means for inculcating truth stressed the importance of content and viewed style as the means of making the
content palatable, it preserved the dichotomy between content
and style.[26]

Finally, there is a third view of eloquence which, before
Sidney, is available in Ascham. This is the notion of style as the
final qualification of content and not merely as ornament decorously superimposed. Ascham distinguishes between the rude
and eloquent styles in terms of adequacy of expression, rather
than in terms of intention. Though "the rudenes of common
and mother tonges, is no bar for wise speaking," nevertheless,
"all soch Authors, as be fullest of good matter and right iudgement in doctrine, be likewise alwayes, most proper in wordes,
most apte in sentence, most plaine and pure in vttering the
same."[27] Eloquence is "plaine and sensible vtterance for the
best and de[e]pest reasons." "They be not wise, therefore that
say, what care I for a mans wordes and vtterance, if his matter
and reasons be good. . . . For good and choice meates, be no
more requisite for helthie bodies, than proper and apte words

[25] *The Arte of Rhetorique*, p. 195.

[26] Both rhetoric proper and poetry as a branch of rhetoric are, as
means of persuasion, founded on Aristotelian psychology as it was
incorporated in medieval scholasticism. See Aquinas "On the Voluntary
and the Involuntary." To achieve his end, the orator or poet appeals
to the emotions of his audience by way of the imagination; and since
the imagination is a sense faculty capable of comprehending only the
particular, he makes his appeal in a language that is least removed
from sensory impression. Hence his concern with figurative speech and
concrete example. Aristotle observes: "What they [the members of a
common audience] like in the diction is metaphor—metaphors not far-
fetched, for such are hard to grasp, nor obvious, for such leave no
impression . . . they like words that set an event before their eyes; for
they must see the thing occurring now, not hear of it as in the future."
(*The Rhetoric of Aristotle*, ed., Lane Cooper, p. 146.) Longinus affirms
that the great poet "lays hold on your spirit and leads you through the
places and turns hearing into sight" by "imaginative pictures (the name
by which some people call poetic images)." (*On the Sublime.*) Sidney's
discussion of imagery in *The Defense of Poesy* is the first explicit
development of this psychology in English literary criticism.

[27] *The Scholemaster*, ed., Edward Arber, p. 117.

be for good matters, and also plaine and sensible vtterance for the best and de[e]pest reasons: in which two pointes standeth perfite eloquence, one of the fairest and rarest giftes that God doth geue to man."[28] Eloquence, then, cannot be gained by stylistic means alone. "He that wyll wryte well in any tongue, muste folowe thys councel of Aristotle, to speake as the common people do, to thinke as wise men do."[29] Though most of Ascham's criticism of the English poets pertains to their use of "Gothic" rhyme, it also contains implicit criticism of their pre-occupation with style at the expense of content: ". . . they haue in more reuerence, the triumphes of Petrarche: than the Genesis of Moses."[30] The vernacular has undergone sufficient refine-ment and now should be put to worthwhile tasks: ". . . now, the ripest of tonge, be readiest to write: And many dayly in setting out bookes and bal[l]ettes make great shew of blossomes and buddes, in whom is neither, roote of learning, nor frute of wisdome at all. Some that make *Chaucer* in English and *Petrarch* in *Italian*, their Gods in verses, and yet be not able to make trew difference, what is a fault, and what is a iust prayse, in those two worthie wits, will moch mislike this my writyng."[31]

The notion of eloquence as copious ornament, however, pre-vailed long after the vernacular "was readiest to write"; and though the notion of poetry as a means of moral teaching

[28] *Ibid.*, pp. 117-18.

[29] *Toxophilus* as quoted in *ibid.*, Introduction, p. 5.

[30] *The Scholemaster*, p. 82.

[31] *Ibid.*, p. 146. Thomas Elyot earlier had opposed the emphasis upon eloquence at the expense of matter: ". . . who that hath nothinge but langage only may be no more praised than a popinjay, a pye, or a stare, whan they speke featly. There be many nowe a dayes in famouse scholes and uniuersities whiche be so moche gyuen to the studie of tonges onely, that, whan they write epistles, they seme to the reder that, like to a trumpet, they make a soune without any purpose, where unto men do herken more for the noyse than for any delectation that therby is meued. Wherefore they be moche abused that suppose eloquence to be only in wordes or coulours of Rhetorike, for, as Tulli saith, what is so furious or mad a thinge as a vaine soune of wordes of the best sort and most ornate, contayning neither connynge nor sentence?" *The Boke Named The Gouernour*, ed., Henry Stephen Croft (London: Kegan Paul, Trench, & Co., 1883), I, 116.

gained in favor after 1570, the distinction between content and style remained. Stylistic eloquence remained the literary ideal of courtly verse. As a principle of composition and the critical standard accepted by most rhetoricians and pedagogues, it explains why the "sweet and sonorous style of Surrey prevailed," while "the plain, vigorous style of Wyatt," though not forgotten, "was submerged."[32] Eloquence was a social grace as much honored as wisdom itself.

It is inaccurate, then, to claim, as literary historians in the past customarily have, that Tottel's *Miscellany* is revolutionary. Its courtly verse embodies a poetic inherited from medieval rhetoric. It stresses as a literary value copious decoration. It controlled the eloquent poet's methods of composition, determined for him which foreign authors were most suitable for imitation, and functioned as the standard by which his contemporaries and immediate successors evaluated his verse. These conclusions are fully borne out by an analysis of the *Miscellany* itself.

The Eloquent Lyric

Although many of the courtly poems in Tottel's *Miscellany* carry on the old tradition of eloquent verse by retaining the themes and structures of the medieval lyric and by assimilating foreign borrowings as stylistic embellishment, there is a substantial body of verse in the collection which discloses a significantly new habit of verse composition. It consists of poems which show for the first time in English a full-scale attempt to extend the possibilities of the short poem by adapting the various themes and modes of *dispositio* that are outlined and illustrated in the handbooks of rhetoric currently in use in the schools. These poems may be said to reflect, therefore, the initial influence of humanism on the English lyric. It must be stressed, however, that they in no way reveal any real changes in the conception of the eloquent poem. The new techniques they introduce have been assimilated with the old ones. Their novelty and importance rest in the fact that they introduce the habit of going to

[32] See Hallet Smith, "The Art of Sir Thomas Wyatt," *The Huntington Library Quarterly*, IX (May 1946), 249-71.

the handbooks of rhetoric for new ways of discovering and organizing what is to be said about a given theme.

Various kinds of rhetorical texts were available to the student in the English grammar schools.[33] To satisfy the requirement of copiousness he had recourse to numerous commonplace books.[34] To assure his style of the necessary ornamentation he could consult the various compilations of the figures of speech and grammatical tropes, such as Susenbrotus' *Epitome troporum ac schematum*, Richard Sherry's *A Treatise of Schemes & Tropes*, or Thomas Wilson's section on *elocutio* in *The Arte of Rhetorique*. And for the rules and formulas for discovering and arranging matter he could turn to the exercises devised by Hermogenes and Aphthonius and later adapted by Richard Rainolde in *The Foundacion of Rhetorike* (1563). It would be easy to show the indebtedness of Tottel's contributors to the commonplace books and the compilations of the figures of speech; but my present concern is with structure and arrangement—hence, with those exercises which, according to Francis Johnson, "provided [the student] with patterns for a well-framed skeleton to support the robust body that was the goal of the copious style."[35]

The great majority of those patterns, or modes of *dispositio*, were inherited by the Tudors from the Middle Ages as part of post-Classical rhetoric. Johnson remarks that the old exercises of the *Progymnasmata* were the only ones available that were concise and simple enough for use in the upper forms of the grammar schools. Those new texts, such as Wilson's, wherein the balanced Classical treatment of all the parts of rhetoric had been restored "lacked the neatly arranged rules, formulas, and

---

[33] The remainder of this paragraph summarizes materials discussed by Francis R. Johnson in the Introduction to his edition of Richard Rainolde's *A Boke called the Foundacion of Rhetoric*.

[34] Among the English collections based upon Erasmus, Johnson lists: Richard Taverner's *Proverbes Or adagies with newe addicions gathered out of the Chiliades of Erasmus* (London, 1539); *The garden of wysdom* (London, 1539); Nicholas Udall's *Apothegemes, that is to saie, proper . . . saynges* (1542); and William Baldwin's *A treatise of Moral Philosophy* (1547).

[35] Introduction, ix.

illustrative models so prized by the average schoolmaster." Consequently, ". . . the inferior later tradition of ancient rhetoric supplied the manuals that guided the beginning students in gathering and organizing the materials for their first themes. Just as Hermogones' rules for composing the various types of elementary exercises had, in Priscian's translation, won the favor of the Middle Ages, so Aphthonius' very similar and somewhat expanded treatment came, during the sixteenth and seventeenth centuries, to be the general choice of schoolmasters."[36]

The "gentleman poets" who contributed to Tottel's *Miscellany* also found some of these exercises valuable in the composition of eloquent verse, and their use of these exercises is again indicative of the growing concern over the inadequacy of the vernacular as a medium of literary expression. They went to the handbooks of rhetoric for the same reason they went to Italian and French verse. And their introduction into English verse of the modes of *dispositio* advanced by the rhetoricians is as important to the lyric at this stage of its development as the introduction of the sonnet.

At least twenty poems in Tottel's *Miscellany* show the deliberate cultivation of the methods of praise and dispraise outlined by Aphthonius and adopted by Cox, Rainolde, and Wilson. Some, such as Surrey's sonnet "Of Sardanopolis" (No. 32) or Grimald's praise of laws (No. 153), merely suggest in choice of subject and attitude a dependence on the general disciplines of deliberative oratory and show no attempt to follow literally the schemes of organization prescribed in the rhetorics as most expedient for purposes of praise or dispraise. Others, such as Nos. 144 and 145 by Grimald, are only brief notes of salutation based upon commonplaces suggested by the handbooks as convenient and fitting topics of compliment. Still others—Surrey's sonnet to Geraldine (No. 8), the longest of his elegies on Wyatt (No. 31), Grimald's praise of a garden (No. 155) and of friendship (No. 154)—follow rhetorical instructions to the letter.

---

[36] *Ibid.*, x. The ensuing discussion of the influence of Aphthonius' exercises on the eloquent lyric in Tottel cites Rainolde's English adaptation.

The rhetoricians agree that the methods of praise and dispraise are applicable to the whole field of demonstrative oratory.[37] Leonard Cox in *The Art or crafte of Rhetoryke* (1532) classifies all forms of "oracion Demonstrative" as either praise or dispraise. "There ben thre maners of oracions Demonstrative. . . . The first conteynethe the prayse or dysprayse of persones . . . The seconde kynde of an oracion demonstrative is: where in is praysed or dyspraysed/ not the persone but the dede. . . . The thyrd kynde is: wherein is lauded or blamed nother person nor dede/ but some other thing as vertue/ vice/ justice/ iniure/ charite/ envie/ pacience/ wrathe/ and suche lyke." (Fol. ii) Rainolde and Wilson offer equally inclusive classifications. Rainolde identifies as suitable for such treatment "All thynges that maie be seen, with the iye of man, touched, or with any other sence apprehended." (Fol. xxxii) Also "Any vertue maie be praised, as wisedome, rightousnes, fortitude, magnanimitee, temperaunce, liberalitee, with all other." Wilson accepts Cox's classification:

> The Oration demonstratiue standeth either in praise, or dispraise of some one man, or of some one thing, or of some one deed doen.
>
> *The kind Demonstratiue, wherein cheefly it standeth.*
>
> THere are diuers things which are praised and dispraised, as men, Countries, Cities, Places, Beastes, Hilles, Riuers, Houses, Castles, deedes doen by worthy men, and pollicies euented by great Warriors, but most commonly men are praised for diuers respects, before any of the other thinges are taken in hande.
>
> (p. 11)

In Tottel the majority of poems employing methods of praise fall into the two subdivisions of the praise of men: of the living (poems of compliment), and of the deceased (elegies of la-

---

[37] Rhetorical theory from Aristotle on held praise and dispraise to be the chief function of deliberative oratory.

ment). The simplest form of praise, verse of complimentary
salutation, is represented by Grimald's Nos. 139-147. Nos.
142, 145, and 146 are occasional poems sent as notes of greet-
ing on New Year's Day. Nos. 143 and 144 apparently served
a similar purpose, being sent in remembrance of the receivers'
birthdays. The display of learning in No. 142 is stylistically
characteristic of the others:

> Now flaming Phebus, passing through his heauenly
>   region hye,
> The vttrest Ethiopian folk with feruent beams doth frye:
> And with the soon, the yere also his secret race doth
>   roon:
> And Ianus, with his double face, hath it again begoon:
> O thou, that art the hed of all, whom mooneths, and
>   yeres obey:
> At whose commaund bee bothe the sterres, and surges of
>   the sea:
> By powr diuine, now prosper vs this yere with good
>   success:
> This well to lead, and many mo, vs with thy fauour
>   blesse.
> Graunt, with sound soll in body sound that here we
>   dayly go:
> And, after, in that conntrey lyue, whence bannisht is
>   all wo:
> Where hoonger, thirst, and sory age, and sicknesse may
>   not mell:
> No sense perceius, no hert bethinks the ioyes, that
>   there do dwel.

Nos. 140 and 141 are written in the same style, but reveal a
specific debt to the rhetoricians in both the attributes singled
out for praise and their arrangement. According to Cox, Wilson, and Rainolde praise of persons, living or deceased, may
be devoted to all or any of the following topics. The following
are Rainolde's instructions:

> First, for the enteryng of the matter, you shall
> place a *exordium*, or beginnyng.

The seconde place, you shall bryng to his praise,
Genus eius, that is to saie: Of what kinde he came of,
whiche dooeth consiste in fower poinctes

    Of what nacion.

    Of what countree

    Of what auncetours.

    Of what parentes.

After that you shall declare, his educacion; the
educacion is conteined in three poinctes:

    Institucion

In   Arte

    Lawes

Then put there to that, whiche is the chief grounde
of all praise: his actes doen, which doe procede out
of the giftes, and excellencies of the minde, as the
fortitude of the mynde, wisedome, and magnanimitee.

Of the bodie, as a beautifull face, amiable
countenaunce, swiftnesse, the might and strength of
the same.

The excellencies of fortune, as his dignitee, power,
authoritee, riches, substaunce, frendes.

In the fifte place use a comparison, wherein
that whiche you praise, maie be aduaunced to the
vttermoste.

Laste of all, use the *Epilogus,* or conclusion.[38]

There can be no doubt that Grimald's two poems quoted below
have been composed with similar instructions in mind.

No. 140

WHat cause, what reason moueth me: what fansy fils
    my brains

That you I minde of virgins al, whom Britan soile
    sustains

Bothe when to lady Mnemosynes dere daughters I
    resort,

And eke when I the season slow deceaue, with
    glad disport?

[38] *Foundacion of Rhetorike,* Fol. xl[r].

What force, what power haue you so great, what charms
    have you late found
To pluck, to draw, to rauish hartes, & stirre out of
    ther stownd?
To you, I trow, Ioues daughter hath the louely
    gyrdle lent,
That Cestos hight: wherein there bee all maner
    graces blent,
Allurementes of conceits, of wordes the pleasurable
    taste:
That same, I gesse, hath she giuen you, and girt
    about your waste
Beset with sute of precious pearl, as bright as
    sunny day.
But what? I am beguilde, and gone (I wene) out of
    the way.
These causes lo do not so much present your image
    prest,
That will I, nill I, night and day, you lodge within
    this brest:
Those gifts of your right worthy minde, those
    golden gifts of mind
Of my fast fixed fansiefourm first moouing cause I
    finde:
Loue of the one, and threefold powr: faith sacred,
    sound, sincere:
A modest maydens mood: an hert, from clowd of enuy
    clere:
Wit, fed with Pallas food diuine: will, led with
    louely lore:
Memorie, conteining lessons great of ladies fiue,
    and fowr:
Woords, sweeter, than the sugar sweet, with heauenly
    nectar drest:
Nothing but coomly can they carp, and wonders well
    exprest.

Such damsels did the auncient world, for Poets penns,
    suffise:
Which, now a dayes, welnye as rare, as Poets fyne,
    aryse.
Wherfore, by gracious gifts of god, you more than
    thrise yblest:
And I welblest myself suppose: whom chastefull loue
    imprest,
In frendships lace, with such a lasse, doth knit,
    and fast combine:
Which lace no threatning fortune shall, no length
    of tyme vntwine:
And I that daye, with gem snowwhite, will mark, &
    eke depaint
With pricely pen: which, Awdley, first gan mee with
    you acquaint.

No. 141

DEserts of Nymphs, that auncient Poets showe,
  A r not so kouth, as hers: whose present face,
M ore, than my Muse, may cause the world to knowe
A nature nobly giuen: of woorthy race:
S o trayned vp, as honour did bestowe.
C yllene, in sugerd speech, gaue her a grace.
E xcell in song Apollo made his dere,
N o fingerfeat Minerue hid from her sight.
E xprest in look, she hath so souerain chere,
  A s Cyprian once breathed on the Spartan bright.
W it, wisdom, will, woord, woork, and all, I ween,
D are no mans pen presume to paint outright.
L o luster and light: which if old tyme had seen,
E nthroned, shyne she should, with goddesse Fame.
Y eeld, Enuie, these due prayses to this dame.

In No. 140 the opening six lines constitute the *exordium* in
the form of two rhetorical questions as to the cause of the poet's
admiration and poetic inspiration (the "matter" to be "en-
tered"). The next five lines, containing the ornate description
of the girdle, suggest that the lady's physical and social graces

are the cause of his admiration. But these are not the fundamental causes; the poet admits he has digressed:

> But what? I am beguilde, and gone (I wene) out of
>   the way.
> These causes lo do not so much present your image
>   prest,
> That will I, nill I, night and day, you lodge
>   within this brest:³⁹

The "first moouing cause" is "Those gifts of your right worthy
mind." These are then catalogued: modesty, lack of envy, wit,
will guided by learning, memory well stocked by the Muses,
and eloquent or sugared speech. Having catalogued the virtues
which form "the chief grounde of all praise," the poet next
introduces, according to precept, a brief comparison before the
conclusion. No. 141 is less ambitious than the poem just discussed, but it is equally indebted to rhetorical precept. Grimald
is content here simply to catalogue Mistress Awdley's virtues
and accomplishments. He manages to include each of the six
"places" which according to the rhetoricians make up the
biographical method of praise: (1) the *exordium*, lines 1-3;
(2) *Genus eius*, line 4; (3) education, line 5; (4) acts done
"which doe proced out of the giftes, and excellencies of the
minde," lines 6 through 14; (5) comparison, lines 9 and 10;
and (6) Epilogus, line 15.⁴⁰

---

³⁹ Thomas Wilson identifies the admission of digression as a specific
figure of speech: "*Of comming againe to the matter.*" "When we haue
made a digression, wee may declare our returne, and shew that whereas
we haue roued a litle, we will now keepe vs within our boundes. In this
kinde of digression, it is wisedome not to wander ouer farre, for feare
we shall wearie the hearers, before we come to the matter againe"
(p. 182).

⁴⁰ Grimald uses the same techniques in No. 139. The lady's accomplishments are catalogued: "While latine you, and french frequent:
while English tales you tell:/ Italian whiles, and Spanish you do hear,
and know ful well: . . ." (ll. 7-8) And a few lines later he discusses
the "worthy feates that now so much set forth your noble name."
(l. 13) It also should be noted that the poem is conceived in the form
of an epistle complete with *exordium, narratio, salutatio, petitio,* and
conclusio.

One might expect to find Grimald adhering closely to the precepts of rhetoric in his verse, since he was a teacher of rhetoric. But the topics and schemes he employs continue to be exploited throughout the century, and by poets whose reputations in their own times as well as in our own were much greater than his. They form a poetic convention employed by Greville, Googe, Turbervile—as late as Milton and at least as early as Surrey.[41] Surrey's well-known sonnet to Geraldine, which seems to have been the source of the Renaissance myth concerning his famous love, follows exactly the biographical method of praise:

> From Tuskane came my Ladies worthy race:
> Faire Florence was sometyme her auncient seate:
> The Western yle, whose pleasaunt shore dothe face
> Wilde Cambers clifs, did geue her liuely heate:
> Fostered she was with milke of Irishe brest:
> Her sire, an Erle: her dame, of princes blood.
> From tender yeres, in Britain she doth rest,
> With kinges childe, where she tasteth costly food.
> Honsdon did first present her to mine yien:
> Bright is her hewe, and Geraldine she hight.
> Hampton me taught to wishe her first for mine:
> And Windsor, alas, dothe chase me from her sight.
> Her beauty of kind her vertues from aboue.
> Happy is he, that can obtaine her loue.

It is impossible to take seriously the concluding line in which Surrey suggests that he desires the love of the nine-year-old child. He is obviously directing his intentions to her parents. Thomas Wilson suggests the importance of lineage in an aristocratic society in his treatment of the biographical method of praise:

> The house whereof a noble personage came, declares
> the state and natures of his auncesters, his alliance, and
> his kinffolke. So that such worthie feates as they haue

---

[41] See, for example, Milton's Sonnet IX, beginning "Daughter to that good Earl, once President."

heretofore done, & al such honors as they haue had for such their good seruice, redounds wholy to the encrease and amplifying of his honor, that is now liuing.

The Realme declares the nature of the people. So that some Countrey bringeth more honor with it, then an other doeth. . . .

The Shire or Towne helpeth somewhat, towardes the encrease of honor: As it is much better to bee borne in Paris, then in Picardie: in London then in Lincolne. . . .

. . . .

Now, for the bringing vp of a noble personage, his nurse must bee considered, his play fellowes obserued, his teacher and other his seruants called in remembraunces.[42]

It is of course impossible that Surrey had ever seen Wilson's treatise, which first appeared in 1553, but the parallels between the poem and the passages from Wilson are indicative of a common tradition which was familiar to both men.

The closeness with which Surrey and Grimald follow rhetorical precept does not necessarily mean that they were only experimenting in verse with techniques commonly used in prose; it means, rather, that they were endeavoring to introduce into verse schemes and topics which would be valuable as disciplines for the discovery and arrangement of material suitable to the purposes of eulogy. The poems produced as a result are often awkward and mechanical in their strict adherence to rhetorical instructions, but I believe that their importance justifies the close attention I have given them. Ways of discovering what to say about a given subject and ways of making coherent the material discovered were precisely what the verse tradition was then most urgently in need of. Before the poets went to the handbooks of rhetoric, they were more or less limited in the composition of a long poem to conventions of narrative. In the rhetoricians Grimald and Surrey and their contemporaries found new structures, such as those implicit in the topics of praise, which were equally suited to the confines of the sonnet or to a poem of several hundred lines.

[42] *Arte of Rhetorique*, pp. 12-13.

The same methods used for praising the living are also used in the elegy of lament. Of the twenty-odd elegies in Tottel commemorating the death of friends and famous personages, Grimald contributed eight and Surrey five. These two men, therefore, can be said to be chiefly responsible for the vogue of the elegy and its characteristic conventions among the imitators of Tottel's *Miscellany* during the third quarter of the century. Grimald's poems are undistinguished but interesting nevertheless for the care with which they follow rhetorical models. Many of them lead one to suspect that he had Wilson's or some other rhetorician's text before him while writing. It is Wilson, for instance, who identifies the two methods of comforting the bereaved which Grimald most frequently uses: "They [the Wise] use two waies of cherishing the troubled mindes. The one is, when we shewe that in some cases, and for some causes, either they should not lament at all, or els be sorie very little: the other is when we graunt that they haue iust cause to be sad, and therefore we are sad also in their behalfe, and would remedie the mater if it could be, and thus entering into felowshipe of sorowe, we seeke by a little and litle to mitigate their greefe."[43] Continuing, Wilson affirms that "Those harmes should be moderatly borne, which must needes happen to euery one, that haue chaunced to any one. As Death, which spareth none, neither king nor Keisar, neither poore nor riche." Wilson then provides an "example of comfort," expanding the following Christian commonplaces: "The cause why God taketh away the most worthiest"; "Where necessitie ruleth, sorowe is needelesse"; "The folly of such as sorrow the want of their freendes"; "Death common to all"; "Euill to liue among the euill"; "To die happely, is great happinesse"; "Life, the right way to death. Death purchaseth rest."; "Death more frendly, the soner it commeth."; "Lent goods must be restored at the owners will."; "Immoderat sorowe, not naturall."; "Time, a remedie for fooles to take awaie their sorowe."; "The great miserie of this worlde, makes weariness of life."; "Trees, not cursed, because Apples fall from them."; "Ripe things last not long."; and "Pacience praise worthy in aduersitie."[44]

Grimald's two "epitaphs" on Sir James Wilford, Nos. 156

[43] *Arte of Rhetorique*, pp. 65-66.   [44] *Ibid.*, pp. 66-86, *passim*.

and 157, represent the "two waies of cherishing the troubled mindes" distinguished by Wilson. No. 156 illustrates the second way: "when we graunt that they haue iust cause to be sad, and therefore we are sad also in their behalfe." After recording Wilford's feats as a soldier, the poem concludes with the statement that all of England mourns his death:

> Crye Musselborough: prayse Haddington thy lord,
> From thee that held both Scots, and frekes of Fraunce:
> Farewel, may England say, hard is my chaunce.

No. 157 consists of an elaborate hyperbole emphasizing how greatly Wilford's death is mourned:

> For Wilford wept first men, then ayr also,
> For Wilford felt the wayters wayfull wo.
> The men so wept: that bookes, abrode which bee,
> Of moornyng meeters full a man may see.
> So wayld the ayr: that, clowds consumde, remaynd
> No dropes, but drouth the parched erth sustaynd.
> So greeted floods; that, where ther rode before
> A ship, a car may go safe on the shore.
> Left were no mo, but heauen, and erth, to make,
> Throughout the world, this greef his rigor take.

But all this wail and woe is foolish, ". . . sins the heauen this Wilfords gost dothe keep,/ And earth, his corps: saye mee, why shold they weep?" Nos. 158 and 160 through 163 illustrate either one or the other of the two methods of consolation distinguished by Wilson. They show also that Grimald was familiar with a number of the Christian commonplaces expanded by Wilson in his sample oration. No. 158 develops "Lent goods must be restored at the owner's will" and "To die happely is great happiness":

> For with good will I dare well saye, her waye to
>   him she sped:
> Who claymed, that he bought: and took that erst
>   he gaue:
> More meet than any worldly wight, such heauenly
>   gems to haue.

(ll. 8-10)

Nos. 160 and 161 develop "death purchaseth rest" and "the great miserie of this worlde, makes weariness of life." And Nos. 162 and 163 dilate "death common to all" and "to die happely is great happiness."

Christian commonplaces are also evident in the anonymous elegies, Nos. 169, 205, and 248. In No. 169 "master Deuerox's" lineage, virtues, and services to the king are enumerated:

> His birth of auncient blood: his parents of great fame:
> And yet in vertue farre before the formost of the same.
> His king, and countrye bothe he serued to so great gaine:
> That with the Brutes record doth rest, and euer shall
>   remain.
> No man in warre so mete, an enterprise to take:
> No man in peace that pleasurd more of enmies frends
>   to make.
> A Cato for his counsell: his head was surely such.
>
>   (ll. 11-17)

The conclusion of the poem cites commonplaces which are also listed by Wilson:

> A man sent vs from God, his life did well declare:
> And now sent for by god again, to teach vs what we are.
> Death, and the graue, that shall accompany all that
>   liue,
> Hath brought him heuen, though somewhat sone,
>   which life could neuer geue
> God graunt well all, that shall professe as he
>   profest:
> To liue so well, to dye no worse: and send his soule
>   good rest.
>
>   (ll. 21-27)

No. 205 also recapitulates the subject's virtues, deeds, and education. The final consolation is again one listed by Wilson:

> Thus long he liued loued of all as one mislikt of none,
> And where he went who cald him not the gentle Peragon.

But course of kinde doth cause eche frute to fall when
    it is ripe,
And spitefull death will suffer none to scape his
    greuous gripe.   (ll. 17-20)

The parallel passage in *The Arte of Rhetorique*: "Among fruite
we see some apples are sone ripe, and fal from the Tree in the
middest of Sommer, other be still greene and tary til Winter,
and hereupon are commonly called Winter fruite: euen so it is
with man, some die young some die old, and some die in their
midle age." (p. 83) No. 248 offers similar parallels with
Wilson:

But now (vnthanke to our desert be geuen,
Which merite not a heauens gift to kepe)
Thou must with me bewaile that fate hath reuen,
From earth a iewell laied in earth to slepe.
                        (ll. 5-8)

He forgetteth much his duetie, that boroweth
a Iewell of the Kings Maiestie, and will not
restore it with good will, when it shall
please his Grace to cal for it.
                     (Wilson, p. 75)

Well sayd therfore a heauens gift she was,
Because the best are sonest hence bereft:
And though her selfe to heauen hence did passe,
Her spoyle to earth from whence it came she left.
                       (ll. 17-20)

Assuredly, whom God loueth best, those he taketh
sonest according to the saying of Salomon:
The righteous . . . is sodainly taken away, to the
intent, that wickedness should not alter his vnder-
standing, and that hypocrisie should not begile his
soule.   (Wilson, p. 73)

These poems initiate what eventually becomes a rich tradition
of Christian elegy. By borrowing from the rhetoricians the two
ways of assuaging grief mentioned by Wilson, they introduce

an affective purpose into consolatory verse which distinguishes
the genre as specifically Christian and identifies the poet's role
with that of the Christian rhetorician. He must square the fact
of death with the idea of an infinitely just and merciful deity
in order to persuade those who grieve the deceased that, as
Claudius reminds Hamlet, it is natural "for some term/ To do
obsequious sorrow. But to persevere/ In obstinate condolement
is a course/ Of impious stubbornness." The writer of Christian
consolation must, in short, justify the ways of God to man in
order to bring the grief-stricken to an acceptance of God's will.
Spenser in all but one of his elegies commemorating Sidney's
death assumes that obligation (in "To praise thy life, or waile
thy worthy death," he also follows the biographical topics),
concluding each, in a way which violates the Classical conventions of pastoral, with an affirmation of Sidney's immortality. Milton, too, assumes the burden in "On the Death of a
Fair Infant," and "Lycidas." In "Lycidas" an awareness of
how that affective burden imposes a principle of order upon the
materials presented within the pastoral convention is essential
to an understanding of how the pastoral elements operate.

What one finds in these early attempts at consolation, clumsy
though they often are, is a confluence of the plain and the
eloquent traditions. The writers' intention in these poems is
didactic and sometimes contemplative, and to realize that intention they have appropriated eloquent techniques from the
rhetorical treatises. Perhaps the best examples of this practice
of borrowing that can be found in Tottel's collection are two
elegies by Surrey: the longest and certainly the best of his three
elegies on Wyatt (No. 31) and his elegy commemorating the
death of his childhood friend, the Duke of Richmond (No. 15).

> W. resteth here, that quick could neuer rest:
> Whose heauenly giftes encreased by disdayn,
> And vertue sank the deper in his brest.
> Such profit he by enuy could obtain.
>
> A hed, where wisdom misteries did frame:
> Whose hammers bet styll in that liuely brayn,
> As on a stithe: where that some work of fame
> Was dayly wrought, to turne to Britaines gayn.

A visage, stern, and myld: where bothe did grow,
Vice to contemne, in vertue to reioyce:
Amid great stormes, whom grace assured so,
To lyue vpright, and smile at fortunes choyce.

A hand, that taught, what might be sayd in ryme:
That reft Chaucer the glory of his wit:
A mark, the which (vnparfited, for time)
Some may approche, but neuer none shall hit.

A toung, that serued in forein realmes his king:
Whose courteous talke to vertue did enflame.
Eche noble hart: a worthy guide to bring
Our English youth, by trauail, vnto fame.

An eye, whose iudgement none affect could blinde,
Frendes to allure, and foes to reconcile:
Whose persing loke did represent a mynde
With vertue fraught, reposed, voyd of gyle.

A hart, where drede was neuer so imprest,
To hyde the thought, that might the trouth auance:
In neyther fortune loft, nor yet represt,
To swell in wealth, or yeld vnto mischance.

A valiant corps, where force, and beawty met:
Happy, alas, to happy, but for foes:
Liued, and ran the race, that nature set:
Of manhodes' shape, where she the molde did lose.

But to the heauens that simple soule is fled:
Which left with such, as couet Christ to know,
Witnesse of faith, the neuer shall be ded:
Sent for our helth, but not receiued so.
Thus, for our gilte, this iewel haue we lost:
The earth his bones, the heauens possesse his gost.

The poem begins and concludes with two of the consolatory commonplaces listed by Wilson: the deceased has found in heaven the rest which life did not permit him; he has been taken away for man's sins.[45] The affective purpose of elegy

[45] Wilson, in his sample oration to Lady Suffolk on the death of her sons, writes: "But wherefore did GOD take two such awaie, and at that time? Surely, to tell the principall cause, wee may by all likenesse

identified by Wilson—that of assuaging grief by affirming Divine Justice—is not present, but the idea of Divine Justice is present as the controlling idea. By Wyatt's death God has punished us "for our guilt." Also evident is the most important of the six "places" identified by Wilson as constituting the biographical method; in concentrating on Wyatt's virtues as a man, Surrey has concentrated on "his actes doen, which doe procede out of the giftes, and excellencies of the mind." Evidence in the poem, therefore, that Surrey had been to school with the rhetoricians is considerable. But the style, the seriousness of intent, and the moral tone of the poem are just as surely signs of the plain style. By avoiding rhetorical descriptions of grief and enumerating Wyatt's accomplishments and his unyielding commitment to virtue in a language that is plain, the poem conveys a real sense of loss and an equally convincing arraignment of a society in which compromise and expedience are the rule.

One indication of the poem's success is the fact that even after we recognize the commonplaces in the poem they do not bother us. For instance, the opening twelve lines of the poem develop a commonplace about Christian patience: The patient man welcomes adversity because he recognizes that it is a gift from God which he may use to prove and strengthen his virtue and faith. Also evident are traces of a familiar emblem—the storm-tossed ship representing the patient man enduring life's adversities. But neither these commonplaces nor those earlier identified as consolatory weaken the poem. They have been made the occasion for serious reflection; they are not a substitute for it.

The superiority in this instance of the plain style over the eloquent can perhaps be more fully appreciated by selecting for comparison with No. 31 another of Surrey's elegies to Wyatt, No. 30, a sonnet which clearly bears the marks of the eloquent tradition.

---

affirme, that they were taken away from vs for our wretched sinnes, and most vile naughtinesse of life, that thereby wee being warned, might be as ready for God, as they now presently were, and amend our liues in time, whom God will call, what time wee know not" (pp. 68-69).

Dyuers thy death doe diuersly bemone.
Some, that in presence of thy liuelyhed
Lurked, whose brestes enuy with hate had swolne,
Yeld Ceasars teares vpon Pompeius hed.
Some, that watched with the murdrers knife,
With egre thirst to drink thy giltlesse blood,
Whose practise brake by happy ende of lyfe,
Wepe enuious teares to heare thy fame so good.
But I, that knew what harbred in that hed:
What vertues rare were temperd in that brest:
Honour the place, that such a iewell bred,
And kisse the ground, whereas thy corse doth rest,
With vapord eyes: from whence such streames auayl,
As Pyramus dyd on Thisbes brest bewail.

The "invention," consisting of a contrast between unjust and "just causes" for sorrow, might conceivably have produced a more satisfactory poem if it had been realized through the use of precise detail. But the brevity of the sonnet form here works against that kind of particularity and forces the poet to rely upon general statement, hyperbole, classical allusion, and the elevated connotations of the eloquent manner. The result is a tone of lament which is supported only in the most general way by the content. One needs to be told more than that Wyatt was good and that he was hated and envied before one can take seriously the concluding declaration of sorrow. This reliance upon verbal assertion and a convention of heightened, or "literary," rhetoric (introduced here immediately by the obvious alliteration of the opening line) is a characteristic weakness of the elegies in the works of the next generation of poets, especially in the works of Googe and Turbervile.

Traces of the literary manner are even evident in what is probably the best elegy in the entire *Miscellany*, Surrey's poem on the death of Richmond. The opening lines bear evidence of the defect in the radical departure in the first line-and-a-half from normal word order, in the poet's extravagant claim that the years he spent at Windsor as a child were spent "In greater feast than Priam's sonnes at Troy," and in the way in which

manner prevails over matter in the easy "sweet-sour" antithesis
of the line following:

> SO cruell prison how coulde betide, alas,
> As proude Windsor? where I in lust and ioye,
> With a kinges sonne, my childishe yeres did passe,
> In greater feast than Priams sonnes of Troy:
> Where eche swete place returns a taste full sower.
>
> (ll. 1-5)

But the literary manner of these opening lines is dropped, and
the details (suggested by the biographical topic of childhood)
which Surrey recalls from those Windsor days are presented
with a simplicity that is extremely effective. The diction is plain
and the word order close to that of good prose:

> The large grene courtes where we were wont to houe,
> With eyes cast vp into the maydens tower,
> And easie sighes, suche as folke drawe in loue;
> The stately seates, the ladies bright of hewe:
> The daunces shorte, longe tales of great delight:
> With wordes and lokes, that tygers coulde but rewe,
> Where eche of vs did pleade the others right:
> The palme play, where, dispoyled for the game,
> With dazed eies oft we by gleames of loue,
> Haue mist the ball, and got sight of our dame,
> To baite her eyes, whiche kept the leads aboue:
> The grauell grounde, with sleues tyed on the helme:
> On fomynge horse, with swordes and frendlye hartes:
> With cheare, as though one should another whelme:
> Where we haue fought, and chased oft with dartes,
> With siluer droppes the meade yet spred for ruthe,
> In actiue games of nimblenes, and strength.
>
> (ll. 6-22)

The reminiscences of adolescent days spent in such innocent
pleasures are fittingly concluded by a short section in which
Surrey recalls the evenings and the nighttime confidences that
he and Richmond had once exchanged:

The secrete thoughtes imparted with such trust:
The wanton talke, the diuers change of play:
The frendship sworne, eche promise kept so iust:
Wherwith we past the winter night away.

(ll. 37-40)

Unfortunately, the final lines resume the eloquent manner. The sudden shift from a language which is styleless in its simplicity, and therefore fresh, to the diction of eloquence is curious and interesting in what it reveals about the state of English verse at this early date. The shift coincides exactly with the poet's shift from his reminiscence over the particular details of how he and his friend once passed their time to his consideration of how he now feels:

And, with this thought, the bloud forsakes the face,
The teares berayne my chekes of deadly hewe:
The whiche as sone as sobbyng sighes (alas)
Vpsupped haue, thus I my plaint renewe:
O place of blisse, renuer of my woes,
Geue me accompt, where is my noble fere:
Whom in thy walles thou doest eche night enclose,
To other leefe, but vnto me most dere.
Eccho (alas) that dothe my sorow rewe,
Returns therto a hollow sounde of playnte.
Thus I alone, where all my fredome grewe,
In prison pyne, with bondage and restrainte,
And with remembrance of the greater greefe
To banishe the lesse, I find my chief releefe.

(ll. 41-55)

The sudden shift in manner is an indication of the general inadequacy at this early date of the vernacular. It is simply not up to the demands Surrey places upon it. He wants to describe his grief, and he is forced to turn to the diction and phraseology of the courtly love poets; specifically, to the verse in which the lover describes the melancholia of unrequited love. The borrowed phraseology is unmistakable: "sobbyng sighes (alas)," "teares berayne my chekes," "O place of blisse, renuer of my woes," and so on.

The use of rhetorical methods of praise by Tottel's contributors is not the only indication of their indebtedness to the rhetoricians for means of discovering and arranging matter. Nos. 131 and 132, both apparently by Grimald,[46] argue the "thesis," whether it is good to marry, a subject of written debate popularized by Erasmus, cited as a suitable subject for the exercise of thesis by Rainolde, and later forming the substance of Shakespeare's "marriage sonnets."[47] Grimald's treatment of the question is purely sophistic. His arguments hinge on questions of possibility and probability—two of the four points which the rhetoricians agree must be established in deliberative oratory.[48] No. 131 argues that happiness in marriage is impossible, and No. 132 attempts to answer the argument by proving that not only is happiness in marriage possible but that marriage is profitable and virtuous. No. 131 poses a dilemma: your wife will either be ugly or common; or she will be beautiful. But in either case she will afford you no pleasure.[49] It is impossible that an ugly wife would please you; and since it is

[46] For Grimald's authorship of these poems see Tottel's *Miscellany*, II, 77.

[47] See Wilson, *Arte of Rhetorique* for a translation of a letter by Erasmus advising a young man to marry. Wilson cites the letter as an example of deliberative oratory, pp. 39-63.

[48] The two poems probably represent the practice of "mooting" which Thomas Elyot describes in *The Governour*: ". . . in the lernyng of the lawes of this realme, there is at this daye an exercise, wherin is a maner, a shadowe, or figure of the auncient rhetorike. I meane the pleadynge used in courte and Chauncery called motes; where fyrst a case is appoynted to be moted by certayne yonge men, contaynyng some doubtefull controuersie, which is in stede of the heed of a declamation called *theme*. The case beinge knowen, they whiche be appoynted to mote, do examine the case, and inuestigate what they therin can espie, whiche may make a contention, wherof may ryse a question to be argued . . .

"Also they consider what plees on euery parte ought to be made, and howe the case maye be reasoned . . ." I, 148-49.

[49] Wilson lists "the reasons, which are commonly vsed to enlarge such matters" in deliberative oratory: "The thing is honest. Profitable. Pleasaunt." (p. 29)

improbable that she will remain true to you if she is beautiful, her beauty will only prove a source of unrest. Moreover, if you have children, you are simply bringing upon yourself more woe. The second poem meets these arguments by admitting that a "fair" wife is preferred, but that beauty is not all one should look for in a woman, and that the question of children is irrelevant. Moreover, since all pleasures are accompanied by displeasures, the question of pleasure in marrying is also irrelevant. The deciding point is whether marriage is on "vertues path."

The frequent recurrence of such exercises in later miscellanies suggests that they were commonly practiced in the schools. Undoubtedly, they helped to develop the potentialities for closely reasoned analysis and argument within the short poem—the kind of analysis and argument present in the sonnets of Sidney and Shakespeare and in the short poems of Greville, Donne, and Jonson. As Grimald's two examples indicate, the exercise of developing a refutation or confirmation within the confines of short verse forms forced the writer not only to order his argument carefully, but also to work out a syntax capable of carrying it.

Ethopoeia, "a certaine Oracion made by voice, and lamenttable imitacion, vpon the state of any one," is also present in Tottel.[50] Nos. 17 (Surrey), 166 (Grimald), 222, and 299 resemble exercises in ethopoeia. Surrey in No. 17 imagines how a woman might feel and what she might say while awaiting the

---

[50] Richard Rainolde, Fol. xlix[v]. Rainolde divides *ethopoeia* into three kinds:

"The firste, a imitacion passiue, which expresseth the affection, to whom it parteineth: which altogether expresseth the mocion of the mynde, as what patheticall and dolefull oracion, Hecuba the Quene made, the citee of Troie destroied, her housbande, her children slaine.

"The second is called a morall imitacio[n], the whiche doeth set forthe onely, the maners of any one.

"The thirde is a mixt, the whiche setteth forthe, bothe the maners and the affection, as how, and after what sorte, Achilles spake vpon Patroclus, he beyng dedde, when for his sake, he determined to fight: the determinacion of hym sheweth the maner. The frende slaine, the affection." (Fol. xlix[r])

return of her lover. It is an example of what Rainolde identifies as "imitacion passiue." No. 222 is similar. No. 166, on the other hand, is an example of "imitacion mixed" in which Grimald imagines what Cicero's actions, as well as his thoughts and feelings, might have been at the time of his death.

No. 299 is of special interest, since it seems to have been conceived to move pity according to methods suggested by Thomas Wilson. Wilson observes that "we may exhort men to take pitie of the fatherless, the widowe, & the oppressed innocent, if we set before their eyes, the lamentable afflictions, the tyrannous wrongs, the miserable calamities, which these poore wretches doe sustaine." The exhortation of pity, to be most effective, must concentrate on the following: ". . . the waight of the matter must be set forth, as though they [men] sawe it plaine before their eyes, the report must be such, and the offence made so hainous, that the like hath not bene seen heretofore, and all the circumstaunce must thus be heaped together: The naughtinesse of his nature that did the deede, the cruell ordering, the wicked dealing, and malicious handling, the tyme, the place, the maner of his doing, and the wickednesse of his will to haue done more."[51] Wilson is referring to *ethopoeia* when he discusses the figure most effective in setting the matter "before the eyes of men"—the figure wherein "wee imagine a talke, for some one to speake, and according to his person, we frame the Oration."[52] The anonymous author of No. 299 may or may not have been familiar with *The Arte of Rhetorique*, but there is no doubt as to what his intentions were in writing the poem, or as to the techniques he employed. He was exhorting men to pity through the use of *ethopoeia*:

> A Cruell Tiger all with teeth bebled,
> A bloody tirantes hand in eche degre,
> A lecher that by wretched lust was led,
> (Alas) deflowred my virginitee.

[51] *Arte of Rhetorique*, p. 131.
[52] *Ibid.*, p. 179.

And not contented with this villanie,
Nor with thoutragious terrour of the dede,
With bloody thirst of greater crueltie:
Fearing his haynous gilt should be bewrayed,
By crying death and vengeance openly,
His violent hand forthwith alas he layed
Vpon my guiltles sely childe and me,
And like the wretch whom no horrour dismayde,
Drownde in the sinke of depe iniquitie:
Misusing me the mother for a time,
Hath slaine vs both for cloking of his crime.

The closeness of the parallel is obvious. Wilson's instructions are clearly illustrated in the poem: the "tyrannous wrongs," and the "miserable calamities" sustained by the "oppressed innocent"; the "hainous offence" and the "circumstaunce"; the "naughtinesse" of the offender's nature, his "wicked dealing," "malicious handling" and his "will to haue done more." But of chief importance is the fact that the poem illustrates again how verse composition in the Tudor period was dominated by rhetorical experimentation.

There are many other poems in Tottel's *Miscellany* indicating how extensively the contributors experimented with rhetorical modes. No. 241, in which the loves of Apollo and Jove are briefly recounted, suggests an exercise in "Narracioun." Nos. 273 and 172 also employ narration, but in conjunction with comparison. The former retells the tale of Troilus and Cressida that the poet may compare Troilus' miseries with his own; and in the latter the tale of Pigmalion is retold for a similar purpose. Commonplace, Chria, and Fable are also represented; but they are didactic modes by definition and therefore will be discussed later. Comparison (by which the Renaissance understood also contrast) also appears frequently, usually in the form of similes heaped together and occasionally, as in No. 28, as a means of praising a virtue.

It should be clear that the literary lyric in Tottel is medieval in conception and predominantly medieval in technique. Having appeared in English well before Chaucer, the eloquent lyric was

[75]

inherited by the Renaissance along with the post or late-Classical rhetorical theory which had first given it direction. Its purpose remains principally stylistic. Structure, language, and versification remain subordinate to style. What is new in the way of technique, besides obvious improvements in verse and language, is absorbed by the prevailing theory which is medieval: or it is already a part of that prevailing theory (as in Aphthonius' *Progymnasmata*) that is being used for the first time in the composing of verse. Some of these innovations—for instance, the sonnet and a number of the various structural schemes derived from the handbooks of rhetoric—are of considerable importance. We shall see eventually how they extended the possibilities of the short poem and in general extended the possibilities of English verse as a medium for the serious expression of ideas.[53] But in no way can they be said to indicate the beginning of a revolution in poetics. The lyric was affected primarily, as were all literary genres, by the general movement to make the English language capable of literary excellence. That movement, and the lyric as it was implicated in that movement, was given direction by the critical theory inherited from the preceding age, theory which identified literary excellence with copious treatment, learned and mellifluous ornament, and ingenious invention.

The Plain Lyric in Tottel's Miscellany

Richard F. Jones has demonstrated that the Renaissance seldom questioned the value of the "rude" vernacular as an adequate medium for the expression of ideas, that in fact "the Englishman viewed his language as plain, honest and substantial."[54] The soundness of Jones' conclusions is borne out by numerous poems in Tottel's *Miscellany* in which the medieval tradition of the plain style is as clearly identified as the eloquent.

---

[53] The adaptation of eloquent conventions to serious purposes, as I shall eventually show, constitutes one of the most important means by which the Tudor poets steadily refined the plain style, extending its range and adding to its precision.

[54] *The Triumph of the English Language*, p. 11.

Among the most interesting is Surrey's No. 34, a poem which has generally been regarded as obscure:[55]

> The stormes are past these cloudes are ouerblowne,
> And humble chere great rygour hath represt:
> For the defaute is set a paine foreknowne,
> And pacience graft in a determed brest.
> And in the hart where heapes of griefes were growne,
> The swete reuenge hath planted mirth and rest,
> No company so pleasant as myne owne.
> Thraldom at large hath made this prison fre,
> Danger well past remembred workes delight:
> Of lingring doutes such hope is sprong pardie,
> That nought I finde displeasaunt in my sight:
> But when my glasse presented vnto me,
> The cureless wound that bledeth day and nyght,
> To think (alas) such hap should graunted be
> Vnto a wretch that hath no hart to fight,
> To spill that blood that hath so oft bene shed,
> For Britannes sake (alas) and now is ded.

Some clarification of the difficulties in the poem is possibly provided by the conclusion reached by Surrey in his elegy on the death of Richmond. There he had said that the pain of remembering Richmond's death has made his own imprisonment at Windsor seem inconsequential:

> Thus I alone, where all my fredome grewe,
> In prison pyne, with bondage and restrainte,
> And with remembrance of the greater greefe
> To banishe the lesse, I find my chief releefe.

It may be that Surrey is here developing a variation of that notion. Perhaps he is in prison at Windsor, either awaiting his execution in 1547 or, possibly, serving his first term of imprisonment in Windsor in 1536.[56] He has received his sentence for

[55] Hyder Rollins acknowledges Nott's suggestion that a line is missing after line seven, but claims that Nott's addition, "Who lives in privacy, is only blest," is no help: "Even then the syntax and meaning of the whole passage remain obscure." Tottel's *Miscellany*, II, 159.

[56] Rollins believes the poem to have been written during this final

his "defaute" and resigned himself to endure it patiently, with the result that what was intended as punishment has been turned into "swete revenge." For in patience he has found "mirth and rest," pleasure in his own company, and even a kind of freedom. Now nothing causes him disquiet. Memories of the past delight him. He finds nothing "displeasaunt in my sight"— with a single exception: "The cureless wound that bleedeth day and night." Nott suggests that "the cureless wound" is a personal reference to Surrey's pride, but this is unsatisfactory. It cannot be accepted as a personal reference, unless one is willing to admit that the poet refers also to himself in the next line as "a wretch that hath no hart to fight," and that he considers himself already dead. Furthermore such a reading ignores the fact that Surrey claims he has achieved patience which by definition presupposes humility. Nott assumes that the "cureless wound" is figurative; but the line, "The cureless wound that bledeth day and nyght," is a literal description of consumption. The Duke of Richmond died of consumption; furthermore, he died in 1536, the same year in which Surrey was first imprisoned at Windsor.

But a difficulty persists. Such a reading requires that the "glass" revealing the "cureless wound" be interpreted as designating the memory, and there is no literary precedent of which I am aware to justify such an interpretation. On the contrary, mirrors in English literary traditions of the sixteenth century most commonly designate examination of self (witness, for instance, the deposition scene in *Richard II*); hence, the "glass" here suggests strongly that the "cureless wound" is Surrey's—some unrevealed source of guilt with which he cannot make his peace.

Other poems in the collection disclose the use of the plain style for reflective and didactic purposes, sometimes in a version

---

period: "Nott . . . points out that Surrey's son, Henry Howard, Earl of Northampton, asserted this to be the last poem Surrey wrote; but he is inclined to refer its composition to an earlier period of imprisonment . . . There is, however, no urgent reason for disputing Northampton's statement."

close to the medieval, at other times in a version refined by the same rhetorical methods cultivated by the eloquent stylists.

The author of No. 177 is content to amplify and illustrate a moral commonplace after the fashion of his medieval predecessors:

> O Euyll tonges, which clap at euery winde:
> Ye slea the quick, and eke the dead defame:
> Those that liue well, som faute in them ye fynde.
> Ye take no thought, in slaundring theyr good name.
> Ye put iust men oft times to open shame.
> Ye ryng so loude, ye sound vnto the skyes:
> And yet in proofe ye sowe nothyng, but lyes.
>
>   Ye make great warre, where peace hath been of long,
> Ye bring rich realmes to ruine, and decay.
> Ye pluck down right: ye doe enhaunce the wrong.
> Ye turne swete myrth to wo, and welaway
> Of mishiefes all ye are the grounde, I say.
> Happy is he, that liues on such a sort:
> That nedes not feare such tonges of false report.

The poet's intent here is clearly didactic. He shows little interest in the personal implications which his subject might have for him. He offers simply a loosely ordered series of typical examples illustrating the effects of slander, and is content to conclude with a formulary and obviously didactic statement suggestive of pulpit literature.

Other examples in Tottel of the didactic lyric, like their medieval predecessors, disclose a variety of structures. The simplest structures appear in the numerous poems, similar to No. 177, which merely expand by example commonplaces of long standing. No. 286, for instance, expands the commonplace that is developed in "See much, sey lytill, and Lerne to Suffer in Time" (Robbins, No. 181). After a stereotyped beginning, which introduces the commonplace as worthwhile advice to those "Who list to lead a quiet life," some thirty proverbs are listed only in the loosest order. The following lines are sufficient to illustrate the proverbial method of expansion:

Holde backe thy tong at meat and meale,
Speake but few wordes, bestrow them well.
By wordes the wise thou shalt espye,
By wordes a foole sone shalt thou trye.
A wise man can his tong make cease,
A foole can neuer holde his peace.
Who loueth rest of wordes beware.
Who loueth wordes, is sure of care.

(ll. 5-12)

No. 183, "Of the wretchednes in this world," lists a number of obvious particulars and concludes with the commonplace that resignation is the only means of accepting existence in a miserable world. No. 225, "When aduersitie is once fallen, it is to late to beware," is a highly repetitive treatment of the familiar medieval theme, "beware of had I wist." There are also examples of doctrinal structure. Nos. 184 and 270 employ, respectively, the doctrines of penance and of the Christian psychology of reason, will, and the emotions. No. 180, "Of the mutabilities of the world," employs the structure of the medieval dream narrative:

BY fortune as I lay in bed, my fortune was to fynde
Such fansies, as my carefull thought had brought
    into my minde
And when eche one was gone to rest, full soft in
    bed to lye:
I would haue slept: but then the watch did folow
    still myne eye.
And sodeinly I saw a sea of wofull sorowes prest:
Whose wicket wayes of sharp repulse bred mine
    vnquiet rest.

(ll. 1-6)

The rest of the poem then enumerates the details of mutability, employing personification and metaphor for the purpose of instruction.

Each of these techniques continues to be employed by Googe, Turbervile, and the contributors to *The Paradise of Dainty*

Devices (1576, 1580), when those poets are not writing eloquent verse. Turbervile's "To one of little wit" and Googe's
"Of Friendship," for instance, are in the tradition of No. 285,
which is short enough to quote in full:

> DO all your dedes by good aduise,
> Cast in your mind alwaies the end.
> Wit bought is of to dere a price.
> The tried, trust, and take as frend,
> For frendes I finde there be but two:
> Of countenance, and of effect.
> Of thone sort there be inow:
> But few ben of the tother sect.
> Beware also the venym swete
> Of crafty wordes and flattery.
> For to deceiue they be most mete,
> That best can play hypocrisy.
> Let wisdome rule your dede and thought:
> So shall your workes be wisely wrought.

In a similar way No. 284 anticipates Ralegh's "The Lie," although Ralegh's poem contains the added structural device of
the summary refrain. The author introduces the theme, "much
is amisse," in the opening four-line stanza and then proceeds to
justify his assertion by devoting a stanza each to what is "amisse"
in duty, learning, political power, law, and so on.

There is also some indication in Tottel that the didactic poets
also consulted the handbooks of rhetoric and thus added new
techniques to those they had inherited from the Middle Ages.
Grimald's No. 135, on "Marcus Catoes comparison of mans life
with yron," suggests an exercise in *chria*;[57] and his poems in
praise of mirth (No. 138) and friendship (No. 154) follow
closely the methods of "comparison" discussed by the rhetoricians. The use of "fable" is of course illustrated by Wyatt's first
satire addressed to John Poins (No. 124) and by the anonymous
No. 279. The structure of the latter closely follows Rainolde's

[57] *Chria* designates a theme which is based upon some act or saying
of a famous person.

instructions on how to develop an oration by means of fable. Those instructions are as follows:

These notes must be obserued, to make an oracion by a Fable.

1. Firste, ye shall recite the fable, as the authour telleth it.
2. There in the seconde place, you shall praise the authoure who made the fable . . . .
3. Then thirdlie place the morall, which is the interpretacion ancred to the Fable, for the fable was inuented for the moralles sake.
4. Then orderlie in the fowerth place, declare the nature of thynges conteined in the Fable, either of man, fishe, foule. . . .
5. In the fifthe place, sette forthe the thynges, reasonyng one with another. . . .
6. Then in the vi. place, make a similitude of the like matter.
7. Then in the seuenth place, induce an exa[m]ple for the same matter to bee proued by.
8. Laste of all make the Epilogus, whiche is called the conclusion. . . .[58]

Tottel's editor entitles the poem "Of the troubled common welth restored to quiet by the mighty power of god," but the poem is really a statement of the need for man to put his trust only in God. The poet, in retelling the tale of the Trojan horse, has not followed the instructions to the letter. He has not praised the author as Rainolde and Aphthonius suggest; and he has combined places one, three, and four (ll. 1-18). But the remaining "places" are all included. Stanzas four, five and six are devoted to "the setting forthe of thynges, reasonyng one with an other"; that is, to the developing of the moral that misplaced trust is disastrous:

But all to long such wisdome was in store,
To late came out the name of traytour than,
When that their king the aultar lay before
Slain there alas, that worthy noble man.

[58] *The Foundacion of Rhetorike*, Fol. iii[v].

Ilium on flame, the matrons crying out,
And all the stretes in streames of blood about.
 But such was fate, or such was simple trust,
That king and all should thus to ruine roon . . .
      (ll. 19-26)

Next, appears "a similitude of the like matter," in which the poet compares the catastrophe at Troy with a contemporary catastrophe. Two stanzas are used to expand the lines, "Like to our time, wherin hath broken out,/ The hidden harme that we suspected least" (ll. 27-28), after which another four stanzas expand the contrary and proper alternative to the topic of "misplaced trust"—that is, to the topic of faith and trust in God. The following lines establish the basis of the contrast:

Of treason marke the nature and the kinde,
A face it beares of all humilitie.
Truth is the cloke, and frendship of the minde,
And depe it goes, and worketh secretly. . . .

. . . .

 But he on hye that secretly beholdes
The state of thinges: and times hath in his hand. . . .[59]

All of the didactic poems in Tottel's *Miscellany*, as we have seen, have certain characteristics in common; and they are the same characteristics which are typical of the didactic lyric in the fourteenth and fifteenth centuries. They expand Christian commonplaces by medieval methods of qualification, arrangement, and illustration. Though they reflect various refinements of structure and style, they are written in the "rude," as opposed to the "sugared," style: the language is plain, tending toward the proverbial; syntax is simple and aphoristic. Generally, the plainness and directness of the didactic style is reinforced by a somewhat heavy and unvaried rhythm. The didactic poet was simply not interested in original invention, learned

---

[59] Rainolde makes no mention of the drawing out of contraries in his preliminary discussion of the eight places which comprise an oration made up of a fable. But in both of the sample orations which immediately follow he heads the seventh place "Of contraries." See Fol. xii^r, xix^v.

allusion, or ornamental figures; they were irrelevant to his purpose. Nor was he interested in the personal exploration of the truisms of which he wrote. He was concerned only with impressing his reader with the importance of ideas that were of ethical concern to all Christians.

Except for Wyatt, the contributors to Tottel's *Miscellany* who write in the plain style are heavily didactic. There occur only occasionally among their works poems of genuine merit. Vaux's "I lothe that I did loue" (No. 212), from which Shakespeare borrowed and adapted three stanzas for the grave digger's song in *Hamlet* (v. i. 69ff.), is sufficiently well-known to need little comment. Its effectiveness is the result of the songlike rhythm and the realistic description of old age:

> The wrincles in my brow,
> The furrowes in my face:
> Say limpyng age will hedge him now,
> Where youth must geue him place.
> The harbinger of death,
> To me I see him ride:
> The cough, the colde, the gaspyng breath,
> Dothe bid me to prouide.
> A pikeax and a spade,
> And eke a shrowdyng shete,
> A house of claye for to be made,
> For such a gest must mete.
>
> (St. 6-8)

"Brittle beautie, that nature made so fraile" (No. 9), along with Wyatt's "Farewell, Loue, and all thy laws for euer" (No. 99),[60] is one of the first of a series of repentance sonnets to appear which includes Sidney's "Leave me O love which reachest but to dust," "Thou blind man's mark, thou fool's self-chosen snare," and Shakespeare's "Th' expense of spirit in a waste of shame." No. 297 is not only the best of the three

[60] Tottel ascribes No. 9 to Surrey, but Rollins thinks it more likely that Vaux was the author. Certainly the rough rhythm and the particular use of antithesis are more characteristic of Vaux.

Tottel poems, but is also of particular interest, since rhythmically it looks forward to Googe and Gascoigne. The subject is again commonplace, and there is nothing new in the way in which it is developed. But the attention given to the possibilities of rhythmic variation set the poem off from didactic treatments of the same and related themes:

> VAine is the fleting welth
> Whereon the world stayes:
> Sithe stalking time by priuy stelth,
> Encrocheth on our dayes.
>   And elde which creepeth fast,
> To taynte vs with her wounde:
> Will turne eche blysse vnto a blast,
>   Which lasteth but a stounde.
>   Of youth the lusty floure,
> Which whylome stoode in price:
> Shall vanish quite within an houre,
> As fire consumes the ice.
>   Where is become that wight,
> For whose sake Troy towne:
> Withstode the grekes till ten yeres fight,
> Had rasde their walles adowne.
>   Did not the wormes consume,
> Her caryon to the dust?
> Did dredfull death forbeare his fume
> For beauty, pride, or lust?

There is nothing in the method by which the commonplace is developed that is not to be found in fifteenth-century didactic verse. The truism is first stated as an inevitable consequence of mortality; then, after the generalized statement that age is the destroyer of pleasures, youth and beauty are developed as qualifying examples of the truism. What is new is the realization of the possibilities inhering in the elements of style for the qualification of feeling. It is the personal feeling defined by the connotative elements of style, particularly by the rhythm, which reveals the poet's own understanding, evaluation, and consequent attitude toward the truism. There is nothing original in the stylistic conventions employed. The allusions are familiar, the language is plain, and the structure is, as has been shown, common in both the didactic and eloquent lyric. But these conventions are put to contemplative use; the poem contains neither allusions for the sake of ornament, nor excessive and repetitious expansion for persuasive emphasis.[61] The rough song rhythm is effectively employed for rhetorical stress and to reinforce the dignity of the feeling of resignation to an unalterable fact of human existence. The initial foot in the opening line of stanzas one and four, for instance, is inverted to stress, respectively, an important statement and question; and in the second line of the first and fourth stanzas consecutive heavy accents are used for a similar purpose. But these are only obvious characteristics. The poem should be read and studied carefully if its stylistic subtleties are to be comprehended. They are subtleties more fully realized by Sir Thomas Wyatt.

[61] The poem should be compared with didactic treatments of the same theme in poems discussed in Chapter I and earlier in this chapter.

CHAPTER III

Sir Thomas Wyatt

WYATT APPEARS TO HAVE BEEN constitutionally at odds with the values and mores of court society.[1] If we are to judge from the tone of his poetry he found the empty rhetoric of courtly verse and the mock subservience of the courtly lover about equally offensive. His opposition to both is expressed in the plain style stripped of its didactic excesses and employed with a flexibility it had never before achieved.

Whatever Wyatt introduced in the way of new techniques or of refinements in native techniques was determined by his intellectual interests rather than by a chauvinistic desire to refine the vernacular. His poetry is mainly in the tradition of the plain style, the style which, as we have seen, from Chaucer on was considered adequate for the expression of ideas.[2] The language

---

[1] Wyatt's poetry poses problems which lie outside the scope of this study. The problems involved in scanning his verse have received a good deal of attention. See Alan Swallow, "The Pentameter Lines in Skelton and Wyatt," *Modern Philology*, XLVIII (August 1950), 1-11; Hallett Smith, "The Art of Sir Thomas Wyatt," *The Huntington Library Quarterly*, IX (August 1946), 323-355; and D. W. Harding, "The Rhythmical Intention in Wyatt's Poetry," *Scrutiny*, XIV (December 1946), 90-102. The question of precisely how and to what extent his works are indebted to the song tradition, a question which involves the problem of how the Renaissance lyric in general was affected by music has been studied by John Stevens in his excellent book *Music and Poetry in the Early Tudor Court* (London: Methuen and Co., 1961).

[2] Hallett Smith observes that "the conversational and spoken has influenced Wyatt's style, away from the aureate and elaborate, toward the language that is plain, is English, on the tongues of men." ("The Art of Sir Thomas Wyatt," *HLQ*, pp. 340-41). C. S. Lewis notes, somewhat reluctantly, that Wyatt's best poems "never go beyond the resources of drab poetry," that they display "little sensuous imagery and no poetic diction" (*English Literature of the Sixteenth Century*, p. 231). According to Lewis, Wyatt is a good poet in spite of his limited resources: "Clearly, we are not dealing with an incantatory or evocative poet. We are in fact dealing with a Drab poet—provided we remember that 'Drab' is not a pejorative term. All Wyatt's weaknesses, and nearly

of his poetry is the same language, for instance, that he employs
in his letters to his son and in his defense against Bonner's accusations of misconduct while representing the Crown in Spain.
In verse as in prose, his main preoccupation was with matter;
he saw little reason to emulate, in the cause of a decadent
rhetorical theory, the superficial characteristics of Latin and
continental authors.[3] Even in his attempts at fashionable verse,
he rarely pursues copiousness for its own sake, or the kind of
learned and ornamental diction typical of the eloquent style. He
is more inclined in such poems toward ingenuity of invention
than toward purely verbal ornament.

There is, moreover, good reason to suspect that Wyatt ob-
jected on moral grounds to the ornate, the sophistic, and the
mechanically clever. In the satire addressed to John Poyns,[4]
which he wrote after retiring from Court, he says that he has
not been able to master the kind of eloquence required at Court.
He has not been able to praise the unworthy: "My Poynz, I
cannot frame me tune to fayne,/ To cloke the trothe for praisse
withowt desart,/ Of them that lyst all vice for to retayne." (ll.
19-21) Nor can he admire the followers of Venus and Bacchus
or convincingly assume the role of lover:

> I cannot honour them that settes their part
> > With Venus and Baccus all theire lyf long;
> > Nor holld my pece of them allthoo I smart.
> I cannot crowche nor knelle to do so grete a wrong,

---

all his strengths, are connected with his unadorned style. . . . He has no
splendors that dazzle you and no enchantments that disarm criticism."
(*Ibid.*, 227) Stevens, too, notices the plainness of Wyatt's songs and
makes the interesting observation that the literary distinction between
the two styles is also "reflected in the musical settings" (*Music and
Poetry in the Early Tudor Court*, p. 16).

[3] Patricia Thomson in *Sir Thomas Wyatt and His Background* (London: Routledge & Kegan Paul, 1964) stresses Wyatt's plainness. She finds
a "colloquial plainness" characteristic of his prose and a lack of aureation typical of his poetry (pp. 100-03, 180ff).

[4] Quotations from Wyatt are from *Collected Poems*, ed., Kenneth
Muir (Cambridge, Mass.: Harvard University Press, 1949).

To worship them, lyke gode on erthe alone,
That ar as wollffes thes sely lambes among.
I cannot with my wordes complayne and mone,
　　And suffer nought; nor smart wythout complaynt,
　　Nor torne the worde that from my mouthe is gone.
I cannot speke and loke lyke a saynct,
　　Vse wiles for witt and make deceyt a pleasure,
　　And call crafft counsell, for proffet styll to paint.
　　　　　　　　　　　(ll. 22-33)

He has only disgust for the art of dissimulation which in court parlance goes by the name of eloquence:

I am not he suche eloquence to boste,
　　To make the crow singing as the swane,
　　Nor call the lyon of cowarde bestes the moste
That cannot take a mows as the cat can:
　　And he that dithe for hungar of the golld
　　Call him Alessaundre; and say that Pan
Passithe Apollo in musike manyfolld;
　　Praysse Syr Thopas for a nobyll talle,
　　And skorne the story that the knyght tolld.
　　　　　　　　　　　(ll. 43-51)

He refuses on moral grounds to adapt to sophistic use the "colours" of rhetoric:

None of these poyntes would ever frame in me;
　　My wit is nought—I cannot lerne the waye.
　　And much the lesse of thinges that greater be,
That asken helpe of colours of devise
　　To joyne the mene with eche extremitie,
With the neryst vertue to cloke alwaye the vise:
　　.　.　.　.　.　.　.　.
And say that Favell hath a goodly grace
　　In eloquence; and crueltie to name
　　Zele of justice and chaunge in tyme and place;
And he that sufferth offence withoute blame

Call him pitefull; and him true and playn
That raileth rekles to every mans shame.
Say he is rude that cannot lye and fayn;
 The letcher a lover; and tirannye
 To be the right of a prynces reigne.
I cannot, I. No, no, it will not be.[5]

(ll. 56-76)

There are numerous other poems in which Wyatt frankly states
his opposition to equivocation, several of which refer specifically
to verbal sophistry. Sophistry is condemned in the epigram en-
titled by Tottel's editor "Of dissembling wordes":

Through out the world, if it wer sought,
Faire wordes ynough a man shall finde:
They be good chepe, they cost right nought.
Their substance is but onely winde:
 But well to say and so to mene,
 That swete acord is seldom sene.

It is condemned also in the satire, "A spending hand that alway
powreth owte." Wyatt is offering Brian advice on how to win
success:

Thou knowst well first who so can seke to plese
Shall pourchase frendes where trowght shall but
 offend.
Ffle therefore trueth: it is boeth welth and ese.
 For tho that trouth of every man hath prayse,
 Full nere that wynd goeth trouth in great misese.
Vse vertu as it goeth now a dayes:
 In word alone to make thy langage swete,
 And of the dede yet do not as thou sayse. . . .

(ll. 32-39)

[5] The words "rude" and "playn" in context clearly allude to the uneloquent style. Stevens, in his discussion of the two styles of lyric, distinguishes "the ornate style usually called aureate" from "the style which
Caxton would have called 'plain' rather than 'curious' on the one hand,
or 'rude' on the other" (*ibid.*, 13).

Wyatt prefers plain and unadorned statement, the proverbial and the aphoristic, which because it concerns itself only with the truth is assured permanence:

A spending hand that alway powreth owte
   Had nede to have a bringer in as fast,
   And on the stone that still doeth tourne abowte
There groweth no mosse: these proverbes yet do
      last.
   Reason hath set theim in so sure a place
   That lenght of yeres their force can never wast.
           ("A Spending hand," ll. 1-6)

There is, consequently, no need to defend Wyatt's use of the plain style by suggesting that as a song writer he expected the music to provide the necessary ornament, or to apologize for the fact that he is neither "evocative" nor "encantatory."[6] He regarded ornament as superfluous. It is also erroneous to assume that his "primary interest is in form, rather than in content," and that historically "the important thing is that in his work the early Tudor found examples of a large variety of verse forms, coldly but carefully worked out."[7] His experimentations with "form" (or, more precisely, with verse and stanzaic arrangement) were mainly in the interest of "content."

Wyatt did indeed write a good deal of fashionable verse. He began to write as a member of the Court, who was probably anxious to indulge court tastes. The results are a number of songs, formal complaints, laments, and pleas in which his only interest appears to be in expressing fashionable modes of amorous feeling in equally fashionable literary conventions. In such poems as "When first myne eyes did view and marke," "For want of will, in wo I playne," "The flamyng sighes that boile within my brest," and "Passe forth, my wonted cryes," he is content to identify himself with the "Courtly Lover" prototype, to show that he, too, is a victim of the "malady" by describing its symptoms in the stock terminology of the Code.[8] The fashionable is

[6] Lewis, *English Literature in the Sixteenth Century*, p. 227.
[7] John M. Berdan, *Early Tudor Poetry, 1485-1547* (New York: Macmillan Co., 1920), p. 484.
[8] See also "Your lokes so often cast"; "The Joye so short, alas, the

here the selective principle; theme, diction, convention, and feelings are predetermined. If these poems show any concern for originality, it is only with reference to *inventio* or in variations of verse, stanza, and rhyme. For the rest, they are mainly clichés, categories of apostrophes and antitheses, and hyperboles of self-pity supported by the simplest and most mechanical of structures. In their emotional burden they are undistinguished from their hackneyed prototypes. "For want of will," for instance, is lacking even in mechanical ingenuity. It simply lists the paradoxes of unrequited love in the most threadbare imagery:

> I dye, though not incontinent,
>> By processe yet consumingly
> As waste of fire, which doth relent,
>> If you as wilfull wyll denye.
>> Wherfore cease of such crueltye,
> And take me wholy in your grace,
> Which lacketh will to change his place.
>
> (St. 4)

"When first mine eyes did view and mark" is little better. It is a variation, structurally, of the catalogue of charms, employed to describe the successive stages of the "malady." Love begins in the senses (St. 1), proceeds to a confession (St. 2), and then to the frustration that accompanies rejection (St. 3). The concluding stanza summarizes the venture with a generalizing statement of how reason has been, with the aid of fancy, enslaved by desire:

> When first mine eyes did view and marke,
>> Thy faire beawtie to beholde;
> And when mine eares listned to hark
>> The pleasant wordes that thou me tolde:

---

paine so nere"; "My loue ys lyke vnto th' eternall fyre"; "Sum tyme I syghe, sumtyme I syng"; "The restfull place"; "Revyver of my smarte"; "Suffryng in sorow in hope to attayn"; "If waker care, if sodayne pale Colour"; and "Lyke as the Swanne towardis her dethe."

I would as then I had been free
From eares to heare, and eyes to see.

And when my lips gan first to moue,
    Wherby my hart to thee was knowne;
And when my tong did talk of loue
    To thee that hast true loue down throwne:
I would my lips and tong also
Had then bene dum, no deale to go.

And when my handes haue handled ought
    That thee hath kept in memorie;
And when my fete haue gone, and sought
    To finde and geat thy company:
I would eche hand a foote had bene,
And I eche foote a hand had sene.

And when in mynde I did consent
    To folow this my fansies will;
And when my hart did first relent
    To tast such bayt, my life to spyll:
I would my hart had bene as thyne,
Or els thy hart had bene as mine.

This is the poetry of a "gentleman versifier," rhythmically
better and less ornate than the average courtly lyric in Tottel,
but inspired, nonetheless, by the same fashions.

John Stevens finds equally unsatisfying and conventional another group of Wyatt's songs, the "balets": " 'Barrenness,'
'monotony,' 'superficiality'—these are the terms that will come
to the minds of most of those who have read Wyatt's balets
in extenso, however greatly they admire his craftsmanship."
They belong, he continues, to "a tradition of *vers de societé*
which can be traced back at least a hundred and fifty years."[9]
There is no quarreling with Stevens' conclusion. Many of the
balets are just as dull as he claims them to be, and they are, as
he says, dull because they are examples of *vers de societé*. But
there are occasional exceptions, songs in which love is ex-

[9] *Music and Poetry in the Early Tudor Court*, pp. 149, 150.

amined with a critical detachment that distinguishes them from the more purely conventional examples in Wyatt and in the tradition of anonymous love lyric which lies behind them.

Wyatt's desire to satisfy the conventional led eventually to his most significantly original contribution to the poetry of his time. He turned to the Italian sonnet for new ways of handling courtly themes, and finding in Petrarch poems precisely suited to the tastes of literary Englishmen, he translated and adapted them. It is only on this hypothesis—that fashion dictated, at least initially, his selections from Petrarch—that one can account for his choice of certain translations, which as Lewis remarks are among the worst of Petrarch. But though he began translating in the interest of peripheral ornament, it can be demonstrated that his interest shifts. He becomes interested in the Petrarchan conceit as something more than a novel invention. He sees it as a means of analyzing feeling and organizing a poem. The results in his best translations are a combination of effects. As his interest shifts from the conceit, itself, to the emotion associated with it, the conceit becomes, as it often does in Donne, a means for examining the emotion, a means rather than an end, and contributes in this function to the originality of the emotion by altering and qualifying it. Whereas in the translations controlled by stylistic concern emotion remains conventional, in the serious translations there is an emerging preoccupation with the quality of emotion and a subordination of the conceit to this new concern.

This change of intention and its consequences have generally been overlooked.[10] It has been generally assumed that Wyatt

---

[10] It should be acknowledged that Hallett Smith, however, concludes from his study of Wyatt's revisions and from an excellent comparison of "The longe love, that in my thought doeth harbar" and Surrey's "Love, that liveth, and reigneth in my thought," that "Wyatt was interested primarily in compression, the tightening up of the idea, the insertion of additional adjectives . . . but most of all in the general strategy of the poem" (p. 328). He differs from Surrey in that his chief interest is in "rhetorical and logical changes in the development of the poem" for the sake of "deepening the idea" by the resulting "change of tone."
Alan Swallow also recognizes Wyatt's seriousness of intention and comments upon his use of metaphor in the interest of "dramatic struc-

was simply interested in importing, by way of translation, the sonnet form.[11] But what actually occurs in these poems is crucial to an understanding of Wyatt, and since it amounts to one of the most important developments in the Tudor tradition of the lyric, it is worth considering in detail. Such a consideration is hindered by the impossibility of dating the translations precisely; but it is not necessary to suppose that the development which they show of both structural and emotional complexity requires a strictly chronological order. What is important is that this development occurs and that its occurrence is commensurate with a shift in intention. Among those translations which show an interest mainly in new and ingenious ways of expanding stereotyped themes, "I fynde no peace and all my warr is done" is a most obvious example. Although one can only conjecture as to why Wyatt chose to translate this poem, it probably caught his eye because its attitude and antithetical method were familiar to him. The poem is simply a series of variations on the fundamental paradox stated in the closing line. The lack of any clear structural principle which might have given the catalogue some direction eliminates any chance for development of the conventional state of feeling that is assumed in the beginning. The method is descriptive rather than psychological.

"The lyvely sperkes that issue from those Iyes," "Like to

---

ture," his "dependence upon metaphor, conceit, and word-play" as "methods of giving tension to the language of the poem," and his "precise control" in the variation of stanzaic pattern and meter "as a part of the sensibility communicated in the poem." (Introduction, *Some Poems of Sir Thomas Wyatt* [New York: Swallow Press, 1949], xviii).

[11] Kenneth Muir comments on the distorted historical importance given these importations: "[Critics] have been obsessed by his historical importance as the importer of the sonnet and as the *fons et origo* of all Elizabethan poetry. It is worth remembering in this connection that about twenty-five years elapsed between the publication of Wyatt's poems and the writing of the first Elizabethan sonnet-sequence, *Astrophel and Stella*. Sidney may have been encouraged by the experiments of Surrey in the sonnet form, but both he and Spenser went to foreign models. The sonnet was virtually reintroduced into England two generations after Wyatt's first translations from Petrarch" (*The Collected Poems of Sir Thomas Wyatt*, xviii).

these vnmesurable montayns" (adapted from Sannazaro), and "Resound my voyse, ye wodes that here me plain" also show Wyatt's dedication to convention for its own sake. There is, however, one difference. In each of these poems a conceit provides a structural principle. In "The lively sparks" it is a metaphor, originating probably in Ovid, that had been familiar among English poets since Chaucer. In the other two poems a state of personal feeling is portrayed by a series of details selected from natural landscape, with comparison, therefore, providing the structure. "Resound my voyse," may have suggested to Surrey the conceit of establishing a classification and then excluding one particular from that classification.[12] The poem is also, incidentally, one of the few in which Wyatt assumes the inflated rhetorical tone—one is tempted to call it Latinate—which is cultivated so assiduously by contributors to Tottel's and succeeding miscellanies. It begins with a high-flown invocation to the woods, hills, and valleys:

> Resound my voyse, ye wodes that here me plain,
>   Boeth hilles and vales causing reflexion;
> And Ryvers eke record ye of my pain,
>   Which have ye oft forced by compassion
>   As judges to here myn exclamation;
> Emong whome pitie I fynde doeth remayn:
> Where I it seke, Alas, there is disdain.

The lover continues his lamentation by recording how his grief has been sufficient to cause nature to take up his lament:

> Oft ye Revers, to here my wofull sounde,
>   Have stopt your course and, plainly to
>   expresse,
> Many a tere by moystor of the grounde
>   The erth hath wept to here my hevenes;
>   Which causeles to suffre without redresse
> The howgy okes have rored in the wynde:
> Eche thing me thought complayning in their
>   kynde.

[12] "The Soote Season, that bud and blome furth bringes" (*Tottel*, No. 2).

[96]

Only his mistress remains coldly indifferent:

> Why then, helas, doeth not she on me rew?
>   Or is her hert so herd that no pitie
> May in it synke, my joye for to renew?
>   O stony hert ho hath thus joyned the?
>   So cruell that art, cloked with beaultie,
> No grace to me from the there may procede,
> But as rewarded deth for to be my mede.

The possibility of development is there in the invention, but it is not realized. The grief remains stereotyped because it is occasioned by a stock situation.

Each of the poems so far cited illustrates how the preoccupation with a certain notion of style has eliminated the development or particularization of feeling. This preoccupation is the obvious source of weakness in all fashionable Tudor verse. When a poem exists for the sake of ingenuity and ornament, when feeling in a poem is assumed and described rather than examined, the effect of the poem can be only static—the feeling at the end of the poem must remain qualitatively the same as it was at the beginning. Qualification and control of feeling in poetry can only proceed from an attempt to understand feeling in the light of what has occasioned it. But this was not the gentleman poet's concern; he sought only to portray those feelings that were expected of the courtier.

Wyatt's interests in courtly love, however, go beyond those of the *poseur* who is content to please his audience with ingenious trifles. His mature concern is to explore the psychological and moral implications of courtly love. It is out of such psychological explorations that he develops a new use for the Petrarchan conceit. One sees something of this new development in "Som fowles there be that have so perfaict sight." Wyatt's interest here is probably in Petrarch's sophisticated use of analogy and classification. The logic of the structure apparently interested Wyatt especially, for he translated other sonnets by Petrarch and composed several of his own in which the same technique is evident.[13] The *octave* establishes three classes, the principle of division being reaction to light, and then, tentatively, identifies the lover as a member of the third:

> Som fowles there be that have so perfaict sight,
>   Agayn the Sonne their Iyes for to defend,
>   And som bicause the light doeth theim offend,
>   Do never pere but in the darke or nyght.
> Other reioyse that se the fyer bright
>   And wene to play in it as they do pretend,
>   And fynde the contrary of it that they intend.
>   Alas, of that sort I may be by right.

The sestet then develops the analogy suggested in the final line of the octave and thus expands a familiar paradox:

> For to withstond her loke I ame not able;
>   And yet can I not hide me in no darke place,
>   Remembrance so foloweth me of that face,
> So that with tery yen swolne and vnstable,
>   My destyne to behold her doeth me lede;
>   Yet do I knowe I runne into the glede.

But the strategy of the sestet is not only to expand the paradox; it is also to imply that the lover has consciously surrendered his freedom. He is not, after all, one of those creatures who "reioyse that se the fyer bright/ And wene to play in it as they do pretend,/ And fynde the contrary of it that they intend," for he is a being capable of rationality and is therefore not only aware of the consequences, but responsible for them. In short, the sonnet reveals an awareness of what in the Christian view are sinful implications of the surrender of reason to desire, a surrender which the courtly lover is eager to confess as proof of his sincerity or to cite as an excuse for describing the torments of his unrequited love. Wyatt has discarded the dead jargon of fashionable love poetry in favor of plain style and

[13] Cf. "Caesar, when that the traytor of Egipt" (from Petrarch) and "Dyvers dothe vse as I have hard and kno" (original).

employed Petrarch's conceit as a means to examine (though admittedly its machinery is excessive) a theme which in other translations he treated for purely conventional reasons.

Wyatt's shift from acceptance of metaphor as ornament to a genuine interest in metaphor as a means of investigation is also evident in "My galy charged with forgetfulnes" and "Who so list to hount, I knowe where is an hynde." In these poems he is unconcerned with the "wail" and "woe" of the courtly lover. He is equally unconcerned with invention as stylistic accomplishment. In "My galy" he employs Petrarch's metaphor (the lover's soul as a ship commanded in its voyage through the experience of love by passion) to explore the ethical dimensions of the lover's despair.

My galy charged with forgetfulnes
    Thorrough sharpe sees in wynter nyghtes doeth pas
    Twene Rock and Rock; and eke myn ennemy, Alas,
    That is my lorde, sterith with cruelnes;
And every owre a thought in redines,
    As tho that deth were light in suche a case.
    An endles wynd doeth tere the sayll apase
    Of forced sightes and trusty ferefulnes.
A rayn of teris, a clowde of derk disdain,
    Hath done the wered cordes great hinderaunce;
    Wrethed with errour and eke with ignoraunce.
The starres be hid that led me to this pain;
    Drowned is reason that should me consort,
    And I remain dispering of the port.

The metaphor delineates, line by line, the effects upon the victim of the rational soul's surrender to a domineering passion. The sonnet is impressive, in spite of certain difficulties in meter, because Wyatt's serious interest in the irrationality of courtly love has led to an analysis, and therefore to a qualification of a state of feeling which among the fashionable poets remains merely a subject about which to write a poem. The resulting feeling expressed in the poem is personally realized, not assumed; and to that extent the poem is an original statement.

The first quatrain establishes the fundamental metaphor and the state of feeling to be analyzed. It does not attempt to establish intense feeling by the customary rhetoric of courtly love poetry; instead, it relies on the connotation of the plain language used metaphorically to describe the lover's state. The first two lines of the second quatrain develop further the extreme to which the ruling passion dominates the lover's soul. It has made even reason its servant, forcing reason to offer up arguments which render the lover's will powerless to effect a change of intention, even though the lover fully realizes that his present course can end only in catastrophe. The second two lines of the second quatrain and the first three of the sestet, ending with a generalizing statement on the lover's moral state, describe the effects of the enslavement of reason and will in terms that are formulary: "Forced sightes," "trusty ferefulnes," "rayn of teris," etc. But partly because of the fundamental nature of the metaphor and partly because their cause has been precisely identified in the lines immediately preceding, those familiar effects have been so qualified that they are no longer the empty mannerisms feigned by the courtly lover. The concluding three lines sum up the lover's desperate state. He has even lost sight of the mistress whose eyes first tempted him into a state that is a form of madness. Capable of avoiding error and created to know truth, he has lost his moral bearings by surrendering rationality and freedom to passion. The values of the poem obviously do not inhere merely in the argument as it has been briefly paraphrased; the argument does provide, however, the terms in which a state of feeling that among other poets is but a literary affectation has been analyzed and hence redefined.

"Who so list to hunt" employs metaphor to examine feeling in much the same way as "My galy." Again what is of particular interest in this poem is the unconventional attitude toward unrequited love and the noncourtly feeling expressed:

> Who so list to hount, I knowe where is an hynde,
> But as for me, helas, I may no more:
> The vayne travaill hath weried me so sore.
> I ame of theim, that farthest commeth behinde;

Yet may I by no meanes, my weried mynde
   Drawe from the Diere: but as she fleeth afore,
   Faynting I folowe. I leve of therefore,
   Sins in a nett I seke to hold the wynde.
Who list her hount, I put him oute of dowbte,
   As well as I may spend his tyme in vain:
   And, graven with Diamonds, in letters plain
There is written her faier neck rounde abowte:
   Noli me tangere, for Cesars I ame;
   And wylde for to hold, though I seme tame.

It is difficult to isolate the excellences in this poem; good poetry
inevitably suffers when discussed in the generalities of prose.
For one thing, by avoiding the jargon of courtly love and
using the plain style, Wyatt avoids the self-pity and exaggerated
sorrow which inhere in that jargon. Also, he has committed
his style and the conceit to an exposition of the feeling of loss
that is experienced in resigning to what must be given up.
Though Petrarch is responsible for suggesting the metaphor, it
is Wyatt who develops the metaphor of the hunt,[14] using it to
examine the circumstances of the experience which have determined the quality of feeling. The opening quatrain introduces
the situation and establishes the lover's exhaustion resulting
from his futile quest. The next quatrain elaborates the initial
feeling by introducing an added complication: though aware
of the futility of the hunt, the lover is unable to give it up. He
is aware intellectually of its futility—"I leve of therefore/
Sins in a nett I seke to hold the wynde"—but he is unable to
order his feelings in accordance with what reason tells him.
This incomplete resolution carries over into the sestet where
it is revealed that the hunt is hopeless, because she belongs to
someone else. The poem begins, then, with a simple statement

---

[14] Patricia Thomson's *Sir Thomas Wyatt and His Background* (London: Routledge and Kegan Paul, 1964) contains an excellent discussion
of the ways in which Wyatt adapts Petrarch's original sonnet to his own
purpose (pp. 196-200). Calling it one of his "most un-Petrarchan,
worldly, and egotistical" translations, she proceeds to show how he
converts Petrarch's "symbolic vision of a white hind" into "a prolonged
metaphor from hunting" to "aim a blow at the foundation of the sentiment of courtly love common to Petrarch and the Petrarchans" (p. 197).

of the situation of unrequited love and of the feelings common to it, generalized but expressed with restraint. After a series of qualifications in the form of complicating circumstances, those feelings are finally at the end of the poem particularized. They are contingent upon an imperfectly resolved conflict between understanding and desire and complicated further by a forced resignation.

There is apparent, then, in Wyatt's translations a shifting of interests. In some—one assumes that these are among his earliest attempts—his efforts are controlled wholly by convention. They reflect the literary standards of his time in that they attempt nothing more than to satisfy the taste for courtly themes "newly decked out" with "dainty" and ingenious "devices" (as the editor of *A Gorgeous Gallery of Gallant Inventions* would have it). In others Wyatt is concerned with subjecting the commonplace experiences of the gentleman lover to serious examination. In these poems he drops poetic diction and subordinates conceit to subject, employing it as a means for organizing insights and defining feeling. The results are translations which are original in the best sense of the Renaissance doctrine of imitation. Historically, their importance consists in this: they introduce to the English lyric a mode of closely reasoned introspection which foregoes the mere portrayal of popular habits of feeling for the sake of close analysis. They establish a new development of structure in the English lyric, the structure which inheres in logical exposition, and anticipate by at least twenty-five years the technique which the poets of the later Renaissance employed to write some of their greatest lyrics.

Wyatt's original lyrics show a development similar to that which occurs in the translations. They are characterized by his critical attitude toward the courtly love code, particularly toward the dishonesty of the servant-mistress relationship and the undignified, self-pitying role prescribed for the lover.[15] His

[15] That these poems are early is conjectural; but my dating on the basis of style generally agrees with A. K. Foxwell's conclusions concerning the dating of Wyatt's poems. See her *Poems of Sir Thomas Wiat,* 2 vols. (New York: Russell & Russell, Inc., 1964), II.

refusal to assume the pose of the conventional lover is evident
even in poems accepted to be among his earliest, and as he
explores his subjects with an increasingly critical attitude, his
later verse deepens in seriousness and complexity.

In his simplest poems his attitude is stated in the traditional
aphoristic style, the sentientious statement often being employed
with conversational directness and developed within the plainest
of structures. These poems show no attempt at psychological
introspection. They censure the servant-mistress relationship in
the light of traditional truths that Wyatt believes should govern
human relations—truth, honesty, respect, and faithfulness.
Nevertheless, the feeling expressed and the austerity of statement often give them an effectiveness which is far from the
commonplace.[16] This is apparent, for instance, in "What
vaileth trouth":

> What vaileth trouth? or, by it, to take payn?
> To stryve by stedfastnes for to attayne?
>> To be iuste and true, and fle from dowblenes?
>> Sythens all alike, where rueleth craftines,
> Rewarded is boeth fals, and plain.
>
> Sonest he spedeth, that moost can fain;
> True meanyng hert is had in disdayn.
>> Against deceipte and dowblenes,
>>> What vaileth trouth?
>
> Deceved is he by crafty trayn
> That meaneth no gile: and doeth remayn
>> Within the trappe, withoute redresse
>> But for to love, lo, suche a maistres,
> Whose crueltie nothing can refrayn.
>>> What vaileth trouth?

The poem is a prototype for a number of Wyatt's criticisms of

---

[16] The same qualities of style distinguish Wyatt's treatment of other
subjects. See, for example: "Off Cartage he, that worthie warier";
"Tagus, fare well, that westward with thy stremes"; "In court to serue
decked with freshe aray"; "Syghes ar my foode, drynke are my teares";
and "Stond who so list vpon the Slipper toppe."

courtly love. It is simple in conception and obvious in theme, developing aphoristically the rhetorical question of the summary refrain. The same method is illustrated with only slight variations in "What no, perdy, ye may be sure!" which affirms more explicitly than "What vaileth trouth" Wyatt's refusal to acquiesce in the courtly pose:

What no, perdy, ye may be sure!
   Thinck not to make me to your lure,
   With wordes and chere so contrarieng,
   Swete and sowre contrewaing;
   To much it were still to endure,
   Trouth is trayed where craft is in vre;
   But though ye have had my hertes cure,
   Trow ye I dote withoute ending?
      What no, perdy!

Though that with pain I do procure
   For to forgett that ons was pure,
   Within my hert shall still that thing,
   Vnstable, vnsure, and wavering,
   Be in my mynde withoute recure?
      What no, perdy!

Here the gnomic style has been personalized by the use of colloquialism and direct address. Also the question and answer technique has been varied, the refrain answering in each stanza the rhetorical question preceding it.

There are a number of other instances in which Wyatt states his critical position with the same straightforwardness. Such poems as "Yf amours faith, an hert vnfayned," "My hert I gave the, not to do it payn," "Ffor to love her for her lokes lovely," "Syns so ye please to here me playn," "Accused though I be without desert," and "Madame, withouten many wordes" all reject pretense and posturing with flat demands for plain dealing. These poems are not ambitious; they are expressions on the most obvious level of the poet's contempt for the fawning deceit of the courtly code. As a consequence, the aphoristic style is wholly adequate. There is no need for elaborate argument or stylistic complexity. In fact, Wyatt's attempts in this direction, as in "Dyvers dothe vse as I have hard and kno," are unsatisfactory so long as his criticism takes the form of simple rejection:

Dyvers dothe vse as I have hard and kno,
 When that to chaunge ther ladies do beginne,
 To morne and waile, and neuer for to lynne,
 Hoping therbye to pease ther painefull woo.
And some ther be, that when it chanseth soo
 That women change and hate where love hath
  bene,
 Thei call them fals, and think with woordes
  to wynne
 The hartes of them wich otherwher dothe gro.
But as for me, though that by chaunse indede
 Change hath outworne the favor that I had,
 I will not wayle, lament, nor yet be sad;
Nor call her fals that falsley ded me fede;
 But let it passe and think it is of kinde,
 That often chaunge doth plese a womans minde.

The rhetorical organization imitated from Petrarch, here, is clearly in excess of what the content justifies. The poem says simply that it is futile for the forsaken lover to lament, to accuse his mistress of faithlessness, or to seek to win her back by the art of persuasion, because it is woman's nature to be changeable. The theme—the precariousness of love which is subject to whim—is recurrent in Wyatt. But whereas on other occasions, particularly in those poems concerned with chance or fortune, Wyatt subjects the theme to elaborate psychological analysis, here he simply states it for the sake of the classificatory machinery of the first twelve lines. It is worth noting, nonetheless, how the quatrain and sestet divisions set up by the rhyme scheme are used to mark off stages in the rhetorical progression. The structural potentialities of the form have been recognized as an aid in exposition, though the exposition itself is trivial. Later in the century such adjustment of syntax to quatrain and sestet divisions becomes an established norm used consciously as a point of departure into meaningful variations.

As Wyatt pursues his criticism of courtly love by penetrating further into the role of the lover, his verse tends toward discursiveness and logical complexity. The range of analysis is great. He may treat love in such relatively simple terms as its precariousness when subject to whim or chance. Or he may use the doctrines of Christian psychology as a means of examining the ethical implications of the code.

Typical of those poems which are concerned with psychological analysis in an elementary form are "Now must I lerne to lyve at rest," "Ffarewell, the rayne of crueltie" and "Desire, alas, my master and my foo." These are hardly more complex than the aphoristic poems already considered, but they show in a rudimentary way the emergence of an attitude colored by an ethical system. The courtly love relation is no longer judged only in terms of hypocrisy and honesty but as a manifestation of lust: to seek its gratification is to seek happiness in the transitory and, in effect, to surrender reason and freedom in the quest. The argument, stated here in simple terms, becomes elsewhere the basis for analysis of the most intricate sort, as in "It was my choyse, yt was no chaunce":

> It was my choyse, yt was no chaunce
>   That browght my hart in others holde,
> Wherby ytt hath had sufferaunce
>   Lenger, perde, then Reason wold;
> Syns I ytt bownd where ytt was free
>   Me thynkes ywys of Ryght yt shold
>   Accepted be.
>
> Acceptyd be withowte Refuse,
>   Vnles that fortune have the power
> All Ryght of love for to abuse;
>   For, as they say, one happy howre
> May more prevayle than Ryght or myght,
>   Yf fortune then lyst for to lowre,
>   What vaylyth Ryght?

What vaylyth Ryght yff this be trew?
  Then trust to chaunce and go by gesse;
Then who so lovyth may well go sew,
  Vncerten hope for hys redresse.
Yett some wolde say assueredly
  Thou mayst appele for thy relesse
              To fantasy.

To fantasy pertaynys to chose:
  All thys I knowe, for fantasy
Ffurst vnto love dyd me induse;
  But yet I knowe as stedefastly
That yff love haue no faster knott,
  So nyce a choyse slyppes sodenly:
              Yt lastyth nott.

Itt lastyth not that stondes by change;
  Fansy doth change; fortune ys frayle:
Both thes to plese the way ys strange.
  Therfore me thynkes best to prevayle:
Ther ys no way that ys so just
  As trowgh to lede, tho tother fayle,
              And therto trust.

The argument is concerned with the validity of rational action.
Wyatt argues that, since his original commitment to love was
deliberate, that is, the result of rational choice rather than an
accident of chance, he must sustain his choice in the face of
subsequent chance (or mischance). To fail to do so is to admit
that rational choice is futile. In fact, if chance outweighs
deliberation, the whole notion of morality is meaningless. All
"right of love," that is, the moral principle governing love,
would be valueless. The argument appears to have its source
in Aquinas:

> . . . every human act that proceeds from deliberate reason,
> if it be considered in the individual, must be good or evil.
>   If, however, it does not proceed from deliberate reason
> . . . such an act, properly speaking, is not moral or human,
> since an act has the character of being moral or human from

the reason. Hence it will be indifferent, as standing outside
the genus of moral acts.

(S.T. 11, Q. 18, a. 9, 329-30)

Chance would eliminate the human basis for love, reducing it
merely to animal appetite, in which case it would be better in
any set of circumstances to "trust to chance and go by guess."

Having disposed of the external provocation for altering his
choice, Wyatt considers an alternative course. He has been told
that he might petition "fantasy" for his "release." He has in
mind the Thomistic notion that the will can be dissuaded from
its original choice by concentrating, with the aid of the imagination (fantasy), on the desirability of another object:

> For, since all the soul's powers are rooted in the one essence
> of the soul, it follows of necessity that, when one power is
> intent in its act, another power becomes relaxed in its opera-
> tion, or is even altogether impeded, both because every
> power is weakened by being extended to many things (so
> that, on the contrary, through being concentrated on one
> thing, it is less able to be directed to several), and because,
> in the operations of the soul, a certain attention is requisite,
> and if this be closely fixed on one thing, less attention is
> given to another. In this way, by a kind of distraction, when
> the movement of the sensitive appetite is strengthened in
> respect of any passion whatever, the proper movement of
> the rational appetite or will must of necessity, become relaxed
> or altogether impeded.

(S. T. 11, Q. 77, a. 1, 631)

It is therefore possible that he might divert his love to someone
else by appealing to "Fantasy." He admits that fantasy first
induced him to make his original choice, though there is nothing
apologetic in this admission. In the scholastic division of the
faculties, it is the function of the imagination to present an
object of choice as desirable; its function, however, may or
may not be in accordance with reason.[17] But if love has no

----

[17] ". . . the apprehension of the imagination, being a particular apprehension, is regulated by the apprehension of reason, which is univer-

stronger bond than desire instigated by fantasy alone (as the courtly code would have it) such diversion cannot prove lasting; for here, as in the consideration of chance, love is unsupported by reason. It is, in fact, a subversion of reason, a disordering of the faculties, amounting to madness: "For the judgment and apprehension of reason is impeded because of a vehement and inordinate apprehension of the imagination and the judgment of the estimative power, as appears in those who are out of their mind." (*S.T.*, Q. 77, a. 1, 631) Thus both arguments come to the same conclusion: Wyatt must stand by his original choice, since to reject it is to reject the supremacy of reason and to deny any permanent basis for love.

The interest in the poem as an extremely sophisticated argument is deepened by its relation to literary convention. It shows how Wyatt was able to use a quite obvious convention to examine the assumptions about love out of which the convention (the pledge of service) emerged. Even the required compliment to the lady has been observed; though the argument is a refutation of the usual form of compliment, it is, nevertheless, intended as a compliment of the highest order. His commitment to love is the consequence of deliberation rather than unqualified desire. He has chosen; he has not been captured.

As one might expect from the obvious seriousness of the argument, the structure of the poem is subordinate to its content; it marks off the steps in the argument. Wyatt uses a variation of the repetitive scheme known among the rhetoricians as *gradatio* as a means of distinguishing and at the same time linking together the stages of his argument. Each stage is closed off at the end of a stanza by a dimeter line which is then picked up again

---

sal. . . . Consequently, in this respect, the act of the sensitive appetite is subject to the command of reason, and, consequently, in this respect, the movement of the sensitive appetite is hindered from being wholly subject to the command of reason.

"Moreover, it happens sometimes that the movement of the sensitive appetite is aroused suddenly in consequence of the imagination or sense. And then such a movement occurs without the command of reason, although reason could have prevented it, had it foreseen it." (*S.T.* II, Q. 17, a.7, 312.)

to introduce the next stage. It is also interesting to notice here how *gradatio* at times becomes the principle of development in the argument itself, particularly between stanzas two and three where Wyatt tests by a chain of conditional propositions the assumption that chance may be superior to choice.

Although other poems by Wyatt show a similar exploration of the same subject, there is no other poem in his work or in that of his contemporaries which approaches "It was my choice, it was no chance," in the way of logical analysis. There is, however, a stage of development, perhaps a later state, in which his exploration of the lover-mistress relationship, having been formulated in its full complexity, is resolved into summary statement. These are the key poems by which the serious tone of most of Wyatt's verse can best be understood, and in which his particular distinctions, especially his originality, can best be studied. They explain in the plainest of summary statement the ethical position which governed his attitude toward love and the values of court society. "If thou wilt mighty be, flee from the rage" discloses the doctrine upon which his belief in personal dignity depended.

> If thou wilt mighty be, flee from the rage
>   Of cruell wyll, and see thou kepe thee free
> From the foule yoke of sensuall bondage;
>   For though thy empyre stretche to Indian sea,
>   And for thy feare trembleth the fardest Thylee,
> If thy desire haue ouer thee the power,
> Subiect then art thou and no gouernour.
>
> If to be noble and high thy minde be meued,
>   Consider well thy grounde and thy beginnyng;
> For he that hath eche starre in heauen fixed,
>   And geues the Moone her hornes and her eclipsyng,
>   Alike hath made the noble in his workyng,
> So that wretched no way thou may bee,
> Except foule lust and vice do conquere thee.
>
> All were it so thou had a flood of golde
>   Vnto thy thirst, yet should it not suffice;
> And though with Indian stones, a thousande folde
>   More precious then can thy selfe deuise,

Ycharged were thy backe, thy couitise
And busye bytyng yet should neuer let
Thy wretchid life ne do thy death profet.

This is known to be a fairly late poem. It should be noticed
that with a return to summary statement, there is a corresponding return to relatively simple structure.[18] The theme—the
ordering of the passions—is viewed from a different standpoint
in each stanza and elaborated by antitheses: (1) political power/
spiritual slavery; (2) wretchedness/Godlike nobility; (3)
temporal riches/spiritual poverty. But though the poem is, in
its structure, more or less similar to Wyatt's early aphoristic
verse, it achieves a richness of feeling that Wyatt does not
approach in his aphoristic style. The difference cannot be defined
simply because it is one of tone—a difference in the connotative
use of language to which the extensive analysis of the theme in
earlier poems contributes. Stated in another way, one might say
that the language shows its derivation from a fuller awareness
of the subject than in the simple poems of an earlier period. One
can notice, particularly, how the quality of the language conveys, beyond the explicit statement, Wyatt's awareness of the
potential dignity of man. It is a quality which suggests the
profound seriousness of Hamlet's "What a piece of work is a
man."

The same theme is subjected to various treatments in the
poems which deal with chance and fortune, the best of which
are "It may be good like it who list," and "In faith I wot not
well what to say." In each of these poems the argument rests
on the assumption that the only sound basis for action—precarious and susceptible to error though it may be—is rationality.
"It may be good, like it who list," considers the assumption
itself.

It may be good, like it who list,
    But I do dowbt: who can me blame?
For oft assured yet have I myst,
    And now again I fere the same.

[18] Cf. "Ffarewell Love and all thy lawes for ever."

The wyndy wordes, the Ies quaynt game,
Of soden chaunge maketh me agast:
For dred to fall I stond not fast.

Alas! I tred an endles maze
  That seketh to accorde two contraries;
And hope still and nothing hase,
    Imprisoned in libertes;
    As oon vnhard, and still that cries;
Alwaies thursty, and yet nothing I tast;
For dred to fall I stond not fast.

Assured, I dowbt I be not sure;
  And should I trust to suche suretie
That oft hath put the prouff in vre
    And never hath found it trusty?
    Nay, sir, in faith it were great foly.
And yet my liff thus I do wast;
For dred to fall I stond not fast.

A simple medieval structure is again immediately recognizable. The refrain contains the "sentence" or theme of the poem. Each stanza qualifies it further by applying it to a different area of experience: the first, to guile and deceit; the second, to hope and desire which are at the same time both cherished and feared; and the third, climactically, to the paradoxical awareness of the difficulty of establishing certainties upon which to act, of the subsequent fear of not acting at all, and of the absolute necessity to act if existence is to be meaningful. "In faith I wot not well what to say," which also makes use of the summary refrain technique, is in the form of a direct address to fortune. The argument briefly paraphrased: Though you have attempted to lead me on by treating me well, and thus to trap me, you have failed; for

Though thou me set for a wounder,
  And sekest thy chaunce to do me payn,
Mens mynds yet may thou not order,
  And honeste, and it remayne,
    Shall shyne for all thy clowdy rayn;

In vayn thou sekest to have trapped:
Spite of thy hap hap hath well happed.

(ll. 8-14)

By exercising his intelligence, and thus avoiding the temptations that fortune has placed in his way, Wyatt has preserved his freedom and avoided any reversal of fortune:

> Cruell willes ben oft put vnder,
>   Wenyng to lowre, thou diddist smyle.
>   Lorde! how thy self thou diddist begile,
> That in thy cares wouldest me have lapped!
> But spite of thy hap hap hath well happed!

(ll. 17-21)

It was from the ethical position summarily stated in such poems as those discussed above that Wyatt could return even to the simplest of song techniques and employ them with an unprecedented sophistication and subtlety. For the simplicity to which he returns—for instance, in "Ys it possyble," "Fforget not yet," "Blame not my lute," and "What menythe thys? when I lye alone"—is not the same as the simplicity with which he began. Behind these poems lies the history of lengthy exploration, of statement and restatement, directed toward a full awareness of what the entire courtly love code implied. It is the simplicity which a first-rate poet can derive from a full realization of his subject. And it is also the kind of simplicity which one frequently encounters in the best poets of the later Renaissance—in the late plays of Shakespeare, for instance, and occasionally, in the lyrics of Ralegh, Nashe, and Jonson. Wyatt's virtues are, unfortunately, less obvious than those which are commonly amenable to critical demonstration. His songs are lacking, as C. S. Lewis has remarked, in the "splendors that dazzle" and the "enchantments that disarm." It is, rather, in the use of simple forms and simple statement that the full force of Wyatt's talent comes to bear.

Some of Wyatt's most widely anthologized songs are among this group. If they are read in the light of what this study has attempted to establish—for example, that Wyatt's departure

[113]

from and criticism of the courtly fashions are to be accounted
for by the fact that he regarded verse as a means for exploring
the moral implications of courtly behavior—their uncompromising attitude toward the fawning and groveling pose of the
enslaved lover is clear. It has seemed sufficient, therefore, to
conclude the study of Wyatt's work with an analysis of only
two of his finest songs: "Ys it possyble," because its meaning for
the contemporary reader seems to have been partly obscured by
the nature of its conceit; and "Blame not my lute," because it,
among all of his poems, states most explicitly and in the simplest
of terms his poetic intentions.

Rhetorical tradition from Aristotle to Thomas Wilson insists
that any argument which attempts to persuade men to embrace
a proposed course of action must convince the audience that the
action is desirable and that it is not only possible, but easy, to
achieve. It is on the grounds of desirability, possibility, and
probability that Wyatt considers the question of whether or not
one can expect to discover truth and constancy in the game of
courtly love in "Ys it possyble":

Ys yt possyble
That so hye debate,
So sharpe, so sore, and off suche rate,
Shuld end so sone and was begone so late?
Is it possyble?

Ys yt possyble
So cruell intent,
So hasty hete and so sone spent,
Ffrom love to hate, and thens ffor to Relent?
Is it possyble?

Ys yt possyble
That eny may fynde
Within on hart so dyverse mynd,
To change or torne as wether and wynd?
Is it possyble?

[114]

Is it possyble
To spye yt in an Iye
That tornys as oft as chance on dy?
The trothe whereoff can eny try?
Is it possyble?

It is possyble
Ffor to torne so oft,
To bryng that lowyste that wasse most aloft,
And to fall hyest yet to lyght sofft:
It is possyble.

All ys possyble,
Who so list beleve;
Trust therfore fyrst, and after preve:
As men wedd ladyes by lycence and leve,
All ys possyble.

The implication in the first three stanzas is that though such inexplicable contrariness of behavior may be sincere, it is highly improbable. It is much more likely that such diversity of mind is merely a game of pretense and deceit, a game played according to the rules of courtly "courtesy." The fourth stanza then answers the question—"Is it possible to detect any sign of true affection in such play?"—which is the theme of the poem. The answer is an ironic "yes" since Fortune and chance make all possible, if not probable. If, then, one is convinced that "love hath no faster knott" than chance, he may as well "trust to chaunce and go by guess." He may as well accept the courtly game as desirable and base his hope that he will find true affection on the grounds that at least "All ys possyble." In short, if love is governed only by chance and fortune, the degree of probability is an irrelevant consideration. Wyatt's position, on the other hand, is clear. He has in other poems insisted that love must be based on truth; here he refuses to embrace the art of courtly love on the grounds of probability, for it is not likely that true and enduring affection will be discovered in deceitful behavior.

"Blame not my lute" is a direct statement of Wyatt's con-

viction that poetry should be devoted to the straightforward
expression of truth, a task for which the plain style is best suited.

Blame not my lute for he must sownde
    Of thes or that as liketh me;
For lake of wytt the lutte is bownde
    To gyve suche tunes as plesithe me:
Tho my songes be sume what strange,
And spekes suche wordes as toche thy change,
        Blame not my lutte.

My lutte, alas, doth not ofende,
    Tho that perforus he must agre
To sownde suche teunes as I entende
    To sing to them that hereth me;
Then tho my songes be some what plain,
And tochethe some that vse to fayn,
        Blame not my lutte.

My lute and strynges may not deny,
    But as I strike they must obay;
Brake not them than soo wrongfully,
    But wryeke thy selff some wyser way:
And tho the songes whiche I endight
Do qwytt thy chainge with rightfull spight,
        Blame not my lute.

Spyght askyth spight and changing change,
    And falsyd faith must nedes be knowne;
The faute so grett, the case so strainge,
    Of right it must abrode be blown:
Then sins that by thyn own desartt
My soinges do tell how trew thou artt,
        Blame not my lute.

Blame but the selffe that hast mysdown
    And well desaruid to haue blame;
Change thou thy way, so evyll begown,
    And then my lute shall sownde that same:

But if tyll then my fyngeres play
By thy desartt their wontyd way,
   Blame not my lutte.

Farwell, vnknowne, for tho thow brake
   My strynges in spight with grett desdayn,
Yet haue I fownde owtt for thy sake
   Stringes for to strynge my lute agayne;
And yf perchance this folysh Rymyme
Do make the blushe at any tyme,
   Blame nott my lutte.

Behind this poem lies the lengthy exploration of the courtly pose—its glorification of reason enslaved by desire, its requirement that the lover publicize his servility in a language of self-pity and whining plaint, and its standard of eloquence that demands from its poets empty rhetoric and fashionable emotion. Wyatt will speak the truth "as plesithe me," even though the results are "somewhat plain" and sometimes directed to "some that use to fain."

There are other songs among Wyatt's work which deserve mention. "A, Robyn," a pastoral uncontaminated by classical trappings; "How shulde I," written in the convention of the *chanson d'aventure*; "A! my herte a! what aileth the"; "Longre to muse"; and "Love doth againe" are the work of a poet whose ear had been trained by the music of Henry's Court and whose conception of the function of language made him disinclined to pursue the kind of ornateness that appears so frequently in the songs of the Elizabethans. They show, also, how even the most stereotyped of themes can be treated effectively when plain statement is employed in the place of pretentious diction. There are other songs in which Wyatt treats serious themes playfully, as in "If chance assynd," "Lo, what it is to love," and "Who most doeth slander love." But even in songs such as these, in which his intentions are not serious, he is never tempted by the excessive rhetoric and fashionable feeling that is characteristic of his essays into "literary" verse.

We have seen that Wyatt's poetry represents a development of the English lyric beyond that which is generally recognized. Though he continues the medieval traditions of the two styles, he chooses to write, for reasons stated in "Myn owne John Poyns" and "Blame not my lute," in the plain style. Occasionally he pursues ingenuity for its own sake, but more often his concern with invention is in the interest of structure as an aid to organizing insights. Though it is true that he deserves recognition for having introduced the sonnet and other foreign verse forms into English, the important discovery he made in Petrarch was the latter's use of invention as a means of discovering insights and of controlling the quality of emotion in a given poem. It is also his interest in the ethical dimensions of experience which accounts for his originality. He was the first poet in the sixteenth century to have examined in any detail the ethical implications of the courtly love doctrine. And by examining critically the modes of feeling which other love poets were content to assume, he was able to deal with them originally. Sometimes, as in "It was my choice, it was no chance," the poem itself is the means for exploring the servant-mistress relationship. Elsewhere, as in "Blame not my lute," the poem is both a summarizing statement of such exploration and a consequent rejection of the kind of servility that the game of love demands. Overtones which indicate how seriously he pursued his analysis are apparent in even some of his slightest songs in which commonplace topics are sharply qualified in the light of Renaissance ethical psychology. He is also the first poet in sixteenth-century England to have used the plain style within the native song tradition to deal seriously with ideas. And in spite of the historical difficulties which seem to have limited his understanding of the accentual-syllabic metrical system, he deserves to be ranked among the best and most original poets of his century.

One other thing needs to be stressed. In Wyatt the plain style becomes for the first time consistently associated with an anticourtly attitude, an attitude it will continue to be identified with throughout the century. In the next generations of poets the irony of Wyatt's manner in the satires on the Court will be reasserted and sustained by Googe and Turbervile, and especially by Gascoigne and Ralegh. Even as late as Donne and George Herbert, by which time the plain style will have undergone extensive modifications, it retains its reputation for honesty and continues to be the medium of expression for those who for one reason or another are opposed to the social, ethical, and literary norms represented by the Court as the cultural center of London. Satirical, devotional, and contemplative poet, alike, will continue to use the plain style as the style of integrity. They will continue also to exploit its anticourtly associations when affirming ethical and religious commitments that involve rejection of the world, court preferment, and courtly love.

CHAPTER IV

The Early Elizabethans

THERE ARE NO ESSENTIAL CHANGES in the conception of the lyric during the first two decades of Elizabeth's reign. The distinction between the eloquent and plain styles is accepted as axiomatic. Eloquence is still cultivated as a means for refining the vernacular, as a stylistic art, and as a social grace. Eloquent or "literary" poetry is still subsumed under a rhetorical tradition which regards poetry as a branch of rhetoric and which tends still to view rhetorical discipline as the art of *elocutio*. Although Thomas Wilson moves closer than any of his predecessors to the Classical notion of rhetoric by treating its five traditional parts proportionately, Richard Sherry, Geoffrey Fenton, and George Puttenham sustain the medieval preoccupation with the tropes and schemes that constitute the discipline of *elocutio*; and it is apparent that rhetorical training in the schools during the third quarter of the century still stressed style as an end in itself. The plain style, on the other hand, continues to be viewed as it had been by Wyatt and Ascham—that is, as the style best suited to the treatment of matter.

Gascoigne defends his use of the plain style in the Prologue to *The Glasse of Government* (1575); and he admonishes those who are looking for the frills of the "enterlude" or the "pleasaunt sporte" of "*Italian* toyes" in the Petrarchan vogue to look elsewhere, since his purpose is to show "In true discourse howe hygh the vertuous clyme,/ How low they fall which lyve withouten feare/ Of God or man . . ."—a purpose best served, as he remarks in his "Councell given to master Bartholmew Withipoll," by "plaine dealing."[1]

> What? laughest thou *Batte*, bicause I write so plaine?
> Beleeve me now it is a friendly touch,

[1] *The Complete Works of George Gascoigne*, ed., John W. Cunliff (Cambridge: University Press, 1907-10); *The Glasse of Government*, II, 6; and I, 344-47.

To use fewe words where friendship doth remaine.
And for I finde, that fault hath runne to fast,
Both in thy flesh, and fancie too sometime,
Me thinks plaine dealing biddeth me to cast
This bone at first amid my dogrell rime.

. . . .

Then marke me well, and though I be not wise,
Yet in my rime, thou maist perhaps find reason.

On the other hand, when Gascoigne has the literary lyric in mind, he confines himself to discussing the means of refining style. Only at one point in his "Certayne notes of Instruction concerning the making of verse or ryme in English" does he consider content and then only in passing, with respect to stylistic decorum: ". . . as this riding rime serveth most aptly to wryte a merie tale, so Rhythme royall is fittest for a grave discourse. Ballades are beste for matters of love, and rondlettes moste apt for the beating or handlyng of an adage or common proverbe: Sonets serve as well in matters of love as of discourses: Dizaymes and Sixames for shorte Fantazies: Verlayes for an effectual proposition . . . and the long verse of twelve and fouretene sillables, although it be now adayes used in all Theames, yet in my judgement it would serve best for Psalmes and Himpnes."[2] For the rest the "Certayne notes" is devoted to those techniques of style which were requisite for the writing of courtly verse, and is consequently devoted to invention as the source of poetic originality and to the standard types of embellishment—rhyme schemes, versification, figurative language, and devices of poetic license.

Googe, also, reflects the continuing preoccupation with style in "*An Epytaphe* of *Maister* Phayre" (c. 1563). According to Googe, Phayre's most praiseworthy achievement was his successful introduction into English of the "high" or "learned" style of Virgil:

The hawtye verse, that *Maro* wrote
made Rome to wonder muche

[2] *Ibid.*, I, 473.

And meruayle none for why the Style
and waightynes was suche,
That all men iudged *Parnassus* Mownt
had clefte her selfe in twayne.

. . . .

But wonder more, maye Bryttayne great
where *Phayre* dyd florysh late,
And barreyne tong with swete accord
reduced to such estate:
That *Virgils* verse hath greater grace
in forrayne foote obtaynde
Than in his own, who whilst he lyued
eche other Poets staynde.

(ll. 1-8)[3]

Googe praises Phayre for the same reasons he praises Surrey, Grimald, and Douglas.

But the reason for the continued emphasis upon the literary style is no longer only the concern to improve the vernacular. In fact, Googe says elsewhere that English is now equal to any task; that there are now a hundred poets in England who command the eloquent style.[4] To be able to write eloquently was a courtly requisite.

One of the duties of the gentleman was to write eloquent verse when the occasion demanded, and, if he expected preferment, he naturally tried to gratify the tastes of the court circle. Turbervile, in a retraction appended to his last published volume of verse, *Tragical Tales and Other Poems* (c. 1574), reviews his duties at Court and in so doing provides a valuable commentary on the reasons and occasions for verse composition at court:

. . . I lived in place among the moe,
Where fond affection bore the cheefest sway,
And where the blinded archer with his bow
Did glaunce at sundry gallants every day:

[3] *Eglogs, Epytaphes, and Sonettes,* ed., Edward Arber (London: Constable and Company Ltd., 1910), p. 72.
[4] *Ibid.,* Preface to *The Zodiake of Life,* pp. 6-8.

And being there, although my minde were free,
Yet must I seeme love wounded eke to be.

I sawe how some did seeke their owne mishap,
And hunted dayly to devoure the hoopes
That beuty bayted, and were caught in trap,
Like wilfull wights that fed on women's lookes:
Who being once entangled in the line,
Did yelde themselves, and were content to pine.

Some other minding least to follow love,
By haunting where dame Venus darlings dwelt,
By force were forst Cupidos coales to proove,
Whose burning brands did make their minds to melt,
So as they were compeld by meere mischaunce,
As others did, to follow on the daunce.

Some eke there were that groapt but after gaine,
That faynd to frie and burne with blooming heate
Of raging love and counterfetted paine,
When they (God wot) had slender cause to treate:
But all was done to make their Ladies deeme
How greatly they their beuties did esteeme.

And then (O Gods) to vew their greeful cheeres,
And listen to their fonde lamenting cries,
To see their cheekes deepe dented in with Teares,
That day and night powred out from painful eyes,
Would make a heart of marble melt for woe,
That sawe their plights, and did their sorowes know.

And all for lacke of ruthe and due remorse,
Their cruel Ladies bore so hard a hand,
And they (poore men) constraynd to love perforce,
And fruitlesse cleane to sowe the barrain sand:
That unto me, who privie was of all,
It was a death, and grieved me to the gall.

Then for my friends (as divers loved me well)
Endite I must some light devise of love,

And in the same my friends affection tell,
Whom nothing mought from beauties bar remove:
My pen must plead the sillie Suters case,
I had my hire, so he mought purchase grace.

Some otherwhile, when beautie bred disdaine,
And feature forst a pride in hawtie brest,
So as my friend was causelesse put to paine,
And for good will might purchase slender rest:
Then must my quill to quarels flatly fall,
Yet keepe the meane twixt sweete and sower brall.

Sometimes I must commend their beauties much
That never came where any beautie lay,
Againe somwhiles my mates would have me tutch
The quicke, bicause they had received the nay:
And thus my pen, as change of matter grew,
Was forst to grief, or els for grace to sue.

Thus did I deale for others pleasure long,
(As who could well refuse to do the like?)
And for my self sometimes would write among
As he that lives with men of war must strike.
I would devise a Sonet to a dame,
And all to make my sullen humor game.

(St. 2-11)

The poet has had to pretend to be, along with the rest of the court circle, a victim of Cupid. He has had, on occasion, to "endite . . . some light devise of love" for friends who lacked eloquence to plead for themselves. He has used his pen to praise women of questionable beauty and to smoothe over lovers' quarrels. And, finally, he has been so caught up in amorous vogues that he has sometimes even devised on his own behalf "a Sonet to a dame" simply "to make game of his sullen humor."

Of course such recantations by their very nature encourage a kind of hyperbole, but even after making allowances for a margin of personal exaggeration, much of what Turbervile says can be accepted as reliable. His description, for instance, of how the code of love actually existed as a code of manners is confirmed by numerous other sources throughout the period. What is especially interesting about Turbervile's version is the way in which it confirms Wyatt's earlier charge that hypocrisy and affectation are nurtured in court society, in the writing of verse as well as in social relationships. These are precisely the vices which the proponents of the plain style from Wyatt to George Herbert proudly proclaim their own habits of plain speaking avoid.

Gascoigne deprecates the numerous trifles he has published in the same way as Turbervile. Replying in "The Epistle to the Reverend Divines" (1574) to critics who have accused him of wantonness, he declares that his intentions have been purely stylistic and for the conventional reasons, and that his verse should be read in the spirit in which it was written. He has published his work to show "that it is not unpossible eyther in Poems or in Prose to write both compendiously and perfectly in our Englishe Tongue," and also to increase his chances for preferment:[5] ". . . so was I desirous that there might remaine in publike record, some pledge or token of those giftes wherwith it hath pleased the Almightie to endue me: to the ende that thereby the virtuous might be incouraged to employ my penne in some exercise which might tend to my preferment, and to the profite of my Countrey. For many a man which may like mine outwarde presence, might yet have doubted whether the qualityes of my minde had bene correspondent to the proportion of my bodie."[6] To take such literary poetry seriously, he insists in a letter "To al yong Gentlemen," is to "take chalke for cheese." Knowing only native techniques, his critics have failed to see that in the "Areignment and divorce of a lover" and similar poems he employs foreign techniques to show how the vernacular can be refurbished by such means: ". . . I will not say how much the areignment and divorce of a Lover (being written in jeast) have bene mistaken in sad earnest. . . . Of a

[5] *Works*, I, "The Epistle to the Reverend Divines," p. 5.
[6] *Ibid*.

truth (my good gallants) there are such as having only lerned to read English, do interpret Latin, Greke, French and Italian phrases or metaphors, even according to their owne motherly conception and childish skill."[7] By his own admission, Gascoigne was not much concerned in such poems with content, but rather with the domestication of foreign techniques.

Both the eloquent and plain styles, however, disclose certain new tendencies and refinements. From tendencies present in the eloquent verse in Tottel's *Miscellany* three kinds of eloquent lyric emerge, each possessing specific requirements of subject and style: courtly verse of polite compliment and amatory decorum; learned verse, written in the "high style" and distinguished from the courtly by a new emphasis upon elaborate schemes and classical allusions; and argumentative or "sophistic" verse such as might have been suggested by Aphthonius' exercises in confirmation and refutation. The courtly, of course, had been clearly represented by Surrey and, in his Italianate verse, by Wyatt. Grimald provided examples of both the "learned" and the "argumentative," the former in his various poems of praise and the latter in such poems as Nos. 131 and 132 in which he argues the thesis, whether it is wise to marry. These types, however, were not sharply distinguished in Tottel; it is not until the sixties and seventies that they come to be recognized as virtually distinct modes and their separate requirements observed, even though some overlapping still occurs. In the tradition of the plain style there are two new tendencies apparent: among the didactic poets the old notion of poetry as an art of moral persuasion, outlined by Stephen Hawes early in the century, gains impetus, with the result that didactic verse frequently adopts eloquent techniques, particularly those developed in the argumentative genres; and among the contemplative poets eloquent techniques of structure and syntax occur more and more frequently and occasionally with brilliant results.

The Miscellanies

The early Elizabethan miscellanies show the taste of the

[7] *Ibid.*, 11.

period and the continuation of the old habits of composition. Each identifies itself with one of the two traditional styles. *A Handful of Pleasant Delights* (1566, 1584) contains polite courtly songs and a form of "learned" poem which becomes one of the most popular genres in the seventies and eighties. *The Paradise of Dainty Devices* (1576)[8] is predominantly didactic. *A Gorgeous Gallery of Gallant Inventions* (1578)[9] represents one strain of the eloquent lyric that has come to a dead end and is probably the worst collection of versified jargon and pedantry to be published in the century.

The *Handful* is usually and incorrectly described as a collection of broadside ballads of the sort hawked on the London streets. It is impossible to agree with Rollins who remarks, apparently on the strength of the fact that the collection was advertised as such, that it was published "for the delectation, not of the literary reader, but for the vulgar, who loved 'a ballad in print of life.' "[10] Neither the style nor the themes of its poems warrant such a conclusion. They give every reason to believe, in fact, that they were published for the courtier. The prefatory poem advertises the *Handful*'s contents as consisting of "pleasant songs" and "fine Histories," both of which are wholly within the courtly tradition:

> Here may you wish and haue,
> Such pleasant songs to ech new tune,
>   as lightly you can craue.
> Or if fine Histories you would reade,
>   you need not far to seek:
> Within this booke such may you haue,
>   as Ladies may wel like
> Here may you haue such pretie thinges
>   as women much desire.
>
>   ("The Printer to the Reader," ll. 6-14)

[8] Ed., Hyder E. Rollins (Cambridge, Mass.: Harvard University Press, 1927).

[9] Ed., Hyder E. Rollins (Cambridge, Mass.: Harvard University Press, 1926).

[10] *A Handful of Pleasant Delights*, ed., Hyder E. Rollins (Cambridge, Mass.: Harvard University Press, 1924), Introduction, viii-ix.

The "pleasant songs" are for those who desire "pretie things"; the "fine Histories," for those who prefer something more substantial. The themes and style of the songs are courtly, and the language, though tending toward plainness, is highly formalized. The "histories" cultivate learned allusion and diction as an embellishment of style. If its contents do consist of broadside ballads, the *Handful* supports Douglas Bush's warning that "it would be a mistake to regard the early Elizabethan ballads as a distinct stratum of verse quite different from and inferior to the 'sonets' written by the courtly poets" and to think that there was "an impassable gulf between the courtly ballads and their poor relations of the street."[11]

Some of the songs, in plainness of language, use of song metres, and ingenuity of stanzaic patterns, echo the song tradition of the Court of Henry VIII; but none approaches in quality the best of Wyatt's songs. Their language, though it avoids excessive aureation, retains the formalization of courtly diction, and their familiar themes are not treated seriously. There are "plaints" and "pleas" in poulter's measure,[12] catalogues of the paradoxical emotions of unrequited love,[13] and whimsical elaborations of the theme of love as a form of madness.[14] Structure in these songs, though undoubtedly affected by

[11] *Mythology and the Renaissance Tradition in English Poetry* (Minneapolis: University of Minnesota Press, 1932), pp. 56-57.

[12] *A proper sonet, wherin the Louer dolefully sheweth his grief to his L. & requireth pity* (pp. 22-25); *The Louer being wounded with his Ladis beutie, requireth mercy* (pp. 56-57); *The painefull plight of a Louer oppressed with the beautifull looks of his Lady* (pp. 61-63).

[13] *A Sorrowfull Sonet, made by M. George Mannington, at Cambridge Castle.* The first few lines will suffice to show how completely the author is abject to the courtly cliché:

I Waile in wo, I plunge in pain,
    with sorowing sobs, I do complain,
With wallowing waues I wish to die,
    I languish sore whereas I lie,
In feare I faint in hope I holde,
    with ruthe I runne, I was too bolde.
                (ll. 1-6)

[14] *Dame Beauties replie to the Louer late at libertie* . . . (pp. 15-19); *An excellent Song of an outcast Louer* (pp. 46-50).

the requirements of musical accompaniment, serves ultimately the purpose of copiousness. No new structural devices are apparent. The principles of organization are the familiar ones: variations of the refrain, comparison, catalogue, and narrative.

The "histories" show the first signs of any extensive movement toward classical imitation, as Douglas Bush has observed.[15] They strive, through imitation and paraphrase, to approach the excellences of classical Latin narrative, excellences still defined according to medieval precept. Ornament is still the primary concern. *A new Sonet of Pyramus and Thisbie* (pp. 35-38). *The Historie of Diana and Acteon* (pp. 25-31), and *L. Gibsons Tantara, wherin Danea welcommeth home her Lord Diophon from the war* (pp. 7-8) are exercises in paraphrase. Others, such as *The Louer being wounded with his Ladies beautie, requireth mercy* (pp. 74-75), *The lamentation of a woman being wrongfully defamed* (pp. 56-57), and *A warning for Wooers, that they be not ouer hastie, nor deceiued with womens beautie* (pp. 43-46) make extensive allusions to the Classics for the purpose of drawing analogies between the plights of mythological lovers and those of the authors'.[16] These poems show classical and, indirectly, Italian influence, but it is only of a peripheral sort. Their chief interest is in neologisms and, as sources of allusion, the classical myths.

The next miscellany to appear, *The Paradise of Dainty Devices*, was published in 1576; but its contents had been collected by Richarde Edwardes who had died ten years earlier, and in all probability the contents are contemporary with those of the *Handful*.[17] The *Paradise*, however, represents the opposed stylistic tradition; almost all of its verse is morally didactic and written in the plain style. Even its infrequent love poems are usually tinged by moral considerations.[18] Except for refinements of language and some metrical improvements, many of the poems in the collection might well have been written a

[15] *Mythology and the Renaissance*, p. 57.

[16] The poems cited all appeared in the 1566 edition.

[17] For facts of publication see Hyder E. Rollins, ed., *A Handful*, Introduction.

[18] See Nos. 79-83, 86, 87.

century earlier. They generally employ the simple structures of catalogue, repentance doctrine, narration, and summary refrain to dilate moral commonplaces.[19] They introduce nothing new in the way of technique and simply use medieval techniques, sometimes discursively in poulter's measure, hexameter, and septameter, and elsewhere aphoristically in short verse forms, to satisfy the pedagogical requirement of copiousness.[20] Occasionally a poem appears which suggests a Tottelian influence, but such occasions are infrequent. "Wantyng his desyre, he complayneth" (No. 24), which likens the lover's plight to a storm-tossed ship, may have been suggested by Wyatt's "My galy charged with forgetfulnes," although the figure was familiar in the fifteenth century. Lord Vaux's "In his extreame sycknesse" (No. 8), with its elaborate play upon the words "tosse," "turne," "change," and "stretch," may have been intended as a variation of Wyatt's "What menyth thys?"; and "Justice. Zaleuch and his Sonne" (No. 53) was probably inspired by Grimald's epigram on law (Tottel, No. 153). But the only certain indication of Tottelian influence is in "Richard Edwardes' his I may not" (No. 125), which is an unmistakable imitation of Surrey's "The Soote season, that bud and blom furth bringes."[21] Here is the second stanza of Edwardes' poem:

[19] A few titles of poems selected at random will suffice to indicate the moralistic temper of the collection: "Of perfect wisedom"; "Look or you leape"; "Of the instabilites of youth"; "He repenteth his folly"; "Our pleasures are but vanities"; "A description of the world"; "Thinks to die."

[20] Examples of the characteristic medieval didactic structural techniques in the collection are as follows. Varieties of the catalogue: Nos. 20, 25, 61, 62, 63, 95, 110. The development of commonplaces by proverbs and examples: Nos. 19, 26, 33, 96. Refrain: Nos. 48, 56. Doctrines of repentance: No. 6. Narrative framework: No. 76 (*chanson d'aventure*), No. 46 (dream allegory fused with the *chanson de mal marie*), No. 7 (personal narrative in which are cast a series of familiar proverbs).

[21] Surrey's provides the conceit as well as many of the details by which it is developed:

> The soote season, that bud and blom furth bringes,
> With grene hath clad the hill and eke the vale:
> The nightingale with fethers new she singes:

The stately Harte in Maye doth mue, his olde and
    palmed beames,
His state renewes in May, he leapes to view Appollos
    streames:
In Maie, the Bucke his horned toppes, doth hang vpon
    the pale,
In Maie, he seekes the pastures greene, in ranging
    every Dale.
In Maie, the better that he may increase his scaley
    skinne:
All thinges in May I see, they may reioyce like
    Turtle doue,
I sorrow in Maie since I may not, in May obtayne
    my loue.

But the Tottelian influence is negligible. If it discloses any
new elements of historical significance, these are to be found
in poems showing the emerging interest in Latin borrowings
or in the use of argumentation and grammatical schemes.

The classical influence is similar to that already discussed in
connection with the *Handful*, though revealing different purposes. In the "histories" it is governed by the rhetorical precept
that instruction should be made palatable. Richard Hill in
"Sundrie men, sundrie affects" (No. 34), puts the "lerned
style" to work in the interest of didacticism by illustrating a
commonplace with allusions to Diana, Minerva, and Apollo.[22]

    The turtle to make hath tolde her tale:
    Somer is come, for euery spray nowe springes,
    The hart hath hong his olde hed on the pale:
    The buck in brake his winter cote he flinges:
    The fishes flote with newe repaired scale:
    The adder all her sloughe awaye she slinges:
    And swift swalow pursueth the flyes smale:
    The busy bee her honye now she minges:
    Winter is worne that was the flowers bale:
    And thus I see among these pleasant things
    Eche care decayes, and yet my sorow springes.

[22] He uses the same technique in "Time giues experience" (No. 36).
See also Nos. 39 and 40.

And what Richard Rainolde had classified as "poetical nar-
racion" is used to illustrate a moral in several poems, probably
all by the same author—"Prudens. The historie of Damacles,
& Dionise" (No. 51), "Fortitude. A yong man of Aegipt,
and Valerian" (No. 52), "Iustice. Zaleuch and his Sonne"
(No. 53), and "Temperaunce. Spurina and the Romaine
Ladies" (No. 54). Of greater interest than the "histories" are
the two elegies, "An Epitaph vpon the death of syr William
Drury" (No. 120) and "An Epitaph vpon the death of Syr
Edward Saunders" (No. 103), which show the earliest of the
classical effects which by the end of the century were to transform the native elegy almost completely. The effects are of
two sorts. There is, first, an attempt to establish through
extensive classical allusion that gravity of tone which the sixteenth century considered proper to lamentation. In the epitaph
for Saunders the method is established at the outset by a
ponderous invocation to the muses:

> You Muses weare your mourning weeds, strike on thy
>   fatal Drome
> Sound *Triton* out the trumpe of fame, in spite of
>   Parcas dome.
> Distill Parnassus pleasant drops, possesse Pierides
>   plase.
> Appolo helpe with dolefull tune, to wayle this woful
>   case.

(ll. 1-4)

Second, though many of the old biographical topics and commonplaces listed by Wilson as befitting lament are still very
much in evidence, the topic of "deedes doen" assumes the main
position. The new emphasis is probably due to the growing
interest in classical narrative. The heroic manner of the narrative in the elegy for Drury supports this conjecture. But it
should be noticed that, though recited in heroic style, the
"doleful tale" of Drury's military feats fulfills the old rhetorical
prescription. It shows "juste cause" why his death should be
lamented and "good reason" why it should not be forever a

source of sorrow.[23] Although these influences of classical heroic
narrative upon the elegy are more pervasive in the *Gorgeous
Gallery* and in Googe and Turbervile, the *Paradise*, which
had gone through at least ten editions by 1602, probably helped
to establish the vogue of heroic narrative within the elegy.[24]

A number of poems in the *Paradise* carry on the practice
of argumentative verse which had appeared occasionally in
Tottel.[25] The worth of friendship, a favorite topic in verse
debate during the next several decades, is argued in Nos. 14,
18, 72, 104, and 109.[26] The poetic value of these poems is
negligible, but the recurrence of the argumentative method is
important: it is indicative of the direction that the most vigorous
representatives of the lyric tradition will take. Furthermore,
verse argumentation employing quite consciously the devices
of classical logic prepared the way for Sidney's reintroduction
of Petrarchism, and a similar purpose is performed by the
increasing experimentation with grammatical schemes, particularly of those involving word and phrase repetition. The
manner in which these are cultivated (as in Nos. 4, 8, 30, 43,
45, and 60) helped to refine verse syntax in much the same
way as the Euphuistic movement helped to further principles of
order in prose. The experimentation with grammatical schemes
along with verse argumentation prepared for the mature deliberative lyrics of the late Elizabethan period.

The *Gorgeous Gallery*, the last of the early Elizabethan
miscellanies, shows the extremes to which the learned style was
eventually carried. It exploits to greater excess all the worst
vogues popularized by Tottel. The verse is weighted with
allusion and copious paraphrase. The catalogue of charms is
in evidence even down to the mistress's "unnamed" parts.[27]

---

[23] See Wilson, *Arte of Rhetorique*, pp. 65-66.

[24] See Rollins ed., *Paradise*, Introduction, viii, for facts of publication.

[25] See *Tottel*, Nos. 131 and 132.

[26] Rainolde lists as a thesis to be argued: "Whether is frendship aboue
all thinges to be regarded," *Foundacion of Rhetorike*, Fol. liiij[r].

[27] See for example, "The Louer extolleth, as well the rare vertues of
his Lady beloued, as also her incomparable beautie" (p. 24). The
catalogue is sometimes embroidered by classical allusions, as in "In the

The pains and woes of lovers are also endlessly listed and expanded by hyperbole in the established fashion, or, even worse, in the labored epistolary forms that were being taught in the schools.[28] The latter, like their medieval predecessors, frequently follow the five-part formula, but they are usually five or six times the length of the medieval epistles. Classical myths are used as they were in the *Handful*; that is, they are either simply paraphrased or they are used to garnish the elegy of personal lament.[29] In short, the *Gorgeous Gallery* manages to appropriate nearly all of the worst pedantries and affectations of literary fashion.

Googe, Turbervile, and Gascoigne

BARNABE GOOGE

Most of the good poems written in the two decades following the appearance of Tottel's *Miscellany* in 1557 are to be found among the works of Barnabe Googe, George Turbervile, and George Gascoigne.[30] Of these three poets only Gascoigne continued to write verse over a period of years. Googe and Turbervile, after publishing single collections of lyrical verse which they had probably written when fresh from the university, turned to what seemed to them more important

---

prayse of the rare beauty, and manifold vertues of Mistres D." (pp. 63-64), or in "The Louer vnto his Lady beloued, of her disdaynfulness toward him" (p. 55).

[28] The miscellany's index lists at least a dozen examples of the epistolary forms. See also William Fullwood's *The Enemy of Idleness* (1567) which defines and illustrates the various formulae.

[29] See "An Epytaph vpon the death of Arthur Fletcher of Bangor Gent," pp. 52-53.

[30] Barnabe Googe, *Eglogs, Epytaphes & Sonettes*, 1563; George Turbervile, *Epitaphes, Epigrams, Songes and Sonets*, 1567; George Gascoigne, *A Hundreth sundrie Flowres bounde vp in one small Poesie*, 1572, and *The Posies of George Gascoigne Esquire. Corrected, perfected, and augmented by the Authour*, 1575. Available modern editions are: Googe, *Arber Reprints* (London: Constable and Company, 1910); Turbervile, Chalmers' *The Works of the English Poets*, II (London, 1810); Gascoigne, *Complete Works*, ed., John W. Cunliffe (Cambridge: University Press, 1910), I.

political and literary labors.[31] Generally they follow the fashionable vogues that had been established by Tottel's *Miscellany*, although Turbervile was one of the early imitators of classical epigram, and Googe worked hard, if unsuccessfully, to resurrect the Mantuan eclogue. Each also experimented with variations of the eloquent style. But mainly they follow the models they found in Tottel among the works of Surrey, Wyatt, and Grimald.[32] Gascoigne, too, shows the influence of Tottel, though to a lesser extent.

Googe appears deliberately to have set out to learn to write verse by imitating the poets in Tottel's *Miscellany*, especially Wyatt and Grimald, and his verse indicates how rigidly the early Elizabethan poet felt bound to those conventions which the *Miscellany* had established as proper for the treatment of specific subjects and themes.

Most of Googe's aphoristic poems reflect the continuation of the medieval didactic tradition. They have the effect of wise proverbs neatly expressed, but they lack the conviction of Wyatt's better epigrams, or the incisive wit of Turbervile's. "*To L. Blundeston*" is typical in these respects.

> Some men be countyd wyse that well can talke:
> And some because they can eche man begyle.
> Some forbecause they know well chese from chalke,
> And can be sure, weepe who so lyst to smyle.
> But (Blundston) hym I call the wysest wyght,
> Whom God gyues grace to rule affections ryght.[33]

The verse states the advice with about as much effect as

---

[31] Googe's major effort was to translate Palingenius' *Zodiacus Vitae*. Turbervile became ambassador to Russia, translated Ovid's *Heroides*, wrote courtesy books on falconry and venery, and contributed his *Tragical Tales and other poems* to the body of didactic "complaint verse."

[32] Turbervile's indebtedness to Tottel's poets is demonstrated by John Erskine Hawkins in *The Life and Works of George Turbervile* (University of Kansas Publications, Humanistic Studies, No. 25, 1940), pp. 70-84.

[33] See also "*Of a Ronnynge Heade*"; "*To* Alexander Neuell"; "Accuse not God, yf fancie fond"; and "*Of the blessed State of him that feeles not the force of Cupids flames.*"

Polonius' advice to Laertes. More effective is his handling of the theme of friendship which, judging by the number of poems in the *Paradise* and the *Gallery* treating it, must have been a favorite among the schoolmasters.[34]

Of Money

Gyue Money me, take Frendshyp who so lyst,
For Frends are gon come once Aduersytie,
When Money yet remayneth safe in Chest,
That quickely can the bryng from myserye,
Fayre face showe frendes, whan ryches do habounde,
Come tyme of proofe, farewell they must awaye,
Beleue me well, they are not to be founde.
If God but sende the once a lowrynge daye.
Golde neuer starts asyde, but in dystres,
Fyndes wayes enoughe, to ease thyne heuynes.

The poem shows signs of the discipline gained from the exercise of *refutatio* and may, in fact, have been written as an exercise in refutation.[35] But it shows none of the cavalier qualities that usually accompany such schoolboy assignments. As an attack upon the fawning hypocrisy of the Court, which Wyatt had also attacked in "Myn owne Iohn Poyns,"[36] and as a blunt condemnation of the fatuous and insincere praises of friendship

[34] See Hoyt Hudson's discussion of the "setting of themes" in the Renaissance schools: *The English Epigram in the Renaissance* (Princeton: Princeton University Press, 1947), pp. 145-53.

[35] Cf. Nos. 131 and 132 in Tottel's *Miscellany*, discussed in Chapter II.

[36] Googe knew and admired Wyatt's poem enough to imitate it in "To M. Henry Cobham, *of the most blessed state of Lyfe.*" Lines 9-16, in fact, probably contain an allusion to Wyatt:

> I take not I as some do take,
> To gape and fawne, for Honours hye,
> But Court and Cayser to forsake,
> And lyue at home, full quyetlye,
> *Remembrest thou? what he once sayde*
> *Who bad, Courte not in any case,*
> For Vertue is, in Courtes decayed
> And Vyce with States, hath chyefest place.
>
> [Italics mine]

of the sort collected by Richard Edwardes,[37] the poem is distinguished by the personal conviction that comes through in its unrelieved severity of statement. It is concomitant with an uncompromising honesty in attitude and language—a quality of mind which distinguishes Wyatt and for which Googe probably admired him.

Googe, however, was also intent on mastering eloquence and experimented with a good many of the conventions of the polite and learned lyric that he found in Tottel. The opening stanzas of *"To Maystresse D."* and *"Of the vnfortunate choyse of his Valentyne"* emulate the learned and rhetorical style of Grimald's praises of women:[38]

> Not from the hye *Cytherion* Hyll
>   nor from that Ladies throne
> From whens flies forth the winged boy
>   that makes some sore to grone.
>
> THe Paynes that all the Furyes fell
>   can cast from Lymbo lake,
> Eche Torment of those Hellish brains
>   wher crawleth mani a snake . . . .

"Out of Syght, out of Mind" is an exercise in *gradatio* and almost certainly an imitation of No. 16 in Tottel's collection. *"To the Tune of Appeles"* suggests a similar indebtedness; its opening stanzas echo Wyatt's "Resound my voice, ye woods that hear me plain":

> The rushyng Ryuers that do run
> The valeys sweet adourned new
> That leans their sides against the Sun
> With Flours fresh of sundry hew,
> Both Ashe and Elme, and Oke so hye,
> Do all lament my wofull crye.
>
> While winter blak, with hydious stormes

[37] *The Paradise of Dainty Devices*, was advertised as Edwardes' commonplace book.

[38] Cf. Nos. 139-147 in Tottel's *Miscellany*.

Doth spoil the ground of Sommers grene,
While springtime sweet the leaf returns
That late on tree could not be sene,
While somer burns while haruest rains
Stil styl do rage my restles paynes.

The rest of the poem is composed of familiar amatory materials,
the third and fourth stanzas developing the notion of love as
a passion consuming reason, and the fifth cataloguing the
mistress' charms:

O Nature thou that fyrst dyd frame,
My Ladyes heare of purest Golde
Her face of Crystall to the same.
Her lippes of precious Rubyes molde,
Her necke of Alablaster whyte
Surmountyng far eche other Wight.

The two concluding stanzas develop in familiar antitheses the
customary plea for pity. These poems show little concern for
invention and satisfy the requirements of eloquence either by
concentrating upon decorative language or by emulating courtly
love fashions.

On the other hand, there are other love poems in Googe's
collection that suggest an indebtedness to the Tudor song.
Occasionally in a way that recalls Wyatt they treat love in a
moral context. "*A Refusal*" suggests Wyatt's treatments of
the lover who has been badly treated by fortune:

Syth Fortune fauoures not
  and al thynges backward go,
And syth your mynd, hath so decreed,
  to make an end of woe.
Syth now is no redresse,
  but hence I must a way,
Farwele I wast no vayner wordes,
  I Hope for better day.

"*At Bonyall in Fraunce,*" "*The Harte absent,*" and "*Vnhappy
tonge why dydste thou not consent*" are also close to the Wyatt

[138]

of the native song tradition, except that Googe uses the pentameter line in place of the short-line forms. The best of these is "The Harte absent":

> SWete muse tell me, wher is my hart becom,
> For well I feele, it is from hence a way,
> My Sences all, doth sorrow so benumme:
> That absent thus, I can not lyue a Day.
> I know for troth, there is a specyall Place,
> Wher as it most, desyreth for to bee:
> For Oft it leaues, me thus in Dolfull case,
> And hether commes, at length a gayne to me?
> Woldest thou so fayne, be tolde where is thy Harte
> Sir Foole in place, wher as it shuld not be:
> Tyed vp so fast, that it can neuer starte?
> Tyll Wysdom get, agayne thy Lybertye:
> In place wher thou, as safe maist dwel swet daw?
> As may the harte, ly by the Lyons paw:
> And wher for thee, as much be sure they passe:
> As dyd the master ons for *Esops* Asse.

The treatment is formulary, but the language is unpretentious, even idiomatic, the attitude unrhetorical. What makes the poem particularly interesting is the variation of cesural length and placement. The resulting cadences are unsophisticated when compared with the cadences in the song after Sidney, but they mark the beginning of the process of refinement of the pentameter line which culminates in the sonnets of Sidney and Shakespeare.

Most of Googe's epitaphs and poems in praise of friends, on the other hand, are experiments in the high style and make use of the conventions of the "hawty verse" which Googe praises as Virgilian in "*An Epytaphe of Maister* Phayre." "*An Epytaphe of M.* Shelley" labors to sustain the "doleful" tone that is established by an astrological beginning.[39] "*An Epy-*

---

[39] For earlier examples of the astrological beginning see the discussion of Surrey and Grimald in Chapter II. See also *Ecclogues* one and eight in *Cupido Conquered* for other examples in Googe.

taphe of Lorde Sheffeldes *death"* attempts to realize the heroic convention by balanced syntax, heavy alliteration, and other devices of classical heroical narrative.

   Both poems reflect the ways in which the old biographical methods of praise were undergoing modification under the influence of Latin heroic narrative. Each attempts to present "iust cause" for lamentation and to exhort pity by the traditional methods outlined in Wilson's *Arte of Rhetorique*.[40] The "places" of praise are still present, but the "place" of "dedes doen," under the influence of epical narration has been made the main concern. Shelley was of noble heart and a loss to the kingdom; Sheffelde's death was untimely and is mourned by all who knew him:

> Farewel good Lord, thy deth bewayle
>   all suche as well the knewe,
> And euerye man laments thy case:
>   and *Googe* thy death doth rewe.
> (ll. 21-2)[41]

But, except for passing references to the other "places," Googe concentrates either on "actes doen, which doe Procede out of the giftes, and excellencies of the minde" or on physical giftes and "the might and strength of the same."[42] "Actes doen"

---

[40] See Chapter II, pp. 62-66.

[41] The elegies on Grimald and Phayre also offer commonplace reasons for lamentation. Phayre died before finishing his important work:

> The enuyous fates (O pytie great)
>   had great disdayne to se,
> That vs amongst there shuld remayn
>   so fyne a wyt as he,
> And in the mydst of all his toyle,
>   dyd force hym hence to wende,
> And leaue a Worke vnperfyt so,
>   that neuer man shall end.
> (ll. 15-18)

Grimald died before his time:

> But Fortune favours Fooles as old men say
> And lets them lyue, and take the wyse away.
> (ll. 21-22)

[42] Cf. Rainolde, *The Foundacion of Rhetorike*, Fol. xl^r.

provides the content of heroical narrations honoring Shelley the soldier and Sheffelde the sheriff. In the latter instance Googe exhorts pity by relating the incident of Sheffelde's murder, that is, by setting "the waight of the matter" (that is, "the tyrannous wrong") "plain before [men's] eyes."[43] In both instances Googe's interest is mainly in narration in the heroic style. But the style that was suitable for describing the deeds of Aeneas, the founder of a new race, is simply not suitable for describing the deeds of a Shelley or the murder of a Sheffelde, no matter how worthy of praise each may have been. It is the incongruity between the heroic style and the subject that makes these poems ring hollow. The narratives provide only the barest details, at best only a sketch of their respective actions, with the consequence that the heroic convention is unsupported.

The weaknesses in Googe's elegies, and this is true of his amorous verse as well, result from a concern with conventions as ends in themselves. There are occasional exceptions, however. In *"Of Maistres* D S," he has combined the familiar pledge-of-service formula with the biographical formula, to produce an original and very charming poem:

> Thy fyled wordes, that from thy mouth did flow
> Thy modest looke with gesture of *Diane.*
> Thy curteous mynde, and althynges framed so.
> As answered well, vnto thy vertuous fame,
> The gentlenes that at thy handes I founde
> In straungers hou[s]e, all vnaquaynted I,
> Good S. hath my Hart to the so bounde,
> That from the can it not be forced to flye,
> In pledge wherof, my seruyce here I gyue
> Yf thou so wylte to serue the whylst I lyue.

The cataloguing of the lady's spiritual and physical gifts, the confession of love, and the avowal to serve faithfully are saved from the triteness and self-pity that usually inhere in the pledge by the plain and dignified language. The poet's reference to

[43] Wilson, *Arte of Rhetorique,* p. 131.

the kindly way he has been received into a strange household by D. S. and his desire to serve only if it pleases her, set the poem beyond the customary exercise. The poem's charm lies in the way in which the convention is restrained and made to express a genuine respect for the lady.[44]

There are several other poems by Googe which show in various ways the successful fusion of the plain style and eloquent conventions. They include "*An Epytaphe of the Death of* Nicolas Grimaold," "*To Doctor* Bale" and "*To the Translation of Pallingen*." The epitaph for Grimald shows a fine control of syntax and tone:

> Beholde this fletyng world how al things fade
> Howe euery thyng doth passe and weare awaye,
> Eche state of lyfe, by comon course and trade,
> Abydes no tyme, but hath a passyng daye.
> For looke as lyfe, that pleasaunt Dame hath brought,
> The pleasaunt yeares, and dayes of lustynes,
> So death our Foe, consumeth all to nought,
> Enuyeng these, with Darte doth vs oppresse,
> And that which is, the greatest gryfe of all,
> The gredye Grype, doth no estate respect,
> But wher he comes, he makes them down to fall,
> Ne stayes he at, the hie sharpe wytted sect.
> For if that wytt, or worthy Eloquens,
> Or learnyng deape, coulde moue hym to forbeare,
> O *Grimaold* then, thou hadste not yet gon hence
> But heare hadest sene, full many an aged yeare.
> Ne had the Muses loste so fyne a Floure,
> Nor had *Minerua* wept to leaue the so,
> If wysdome myght haue fled the fatall howre,
> Thou hadste not yet ben suffred for to go,
> A thousande doltysh Geese we myght haue sparde,
> A thousande wytles heads, death might haue found
> And taken them, for whom no man had carde,
> And layde them lowe, in deepe obliuious grounde,

---

[44] See also "To Maystresse A."

But Fortune fauours Fooles as old men saye
And lets them lyue, and take the wyse awaye.

The poem begins quietly with a contemplation of the commonplace that all worldly things are transient. The commonplace
is then applied successively to mankind in general, to those
who have devoted their lives to learning, and finally to Grimald
himself. His death is a just cause for lament, for his gifts of
mind were such that were death able to spare wisdom, certainly Grimald would have been spared. But the worthiest are
often taken away before their time.[45] These topics are among
the most familiar in medieval and sixteenth-century poetry.
And yet the poem is distinguished from the elegiac exercise by
a genuine, personal grief. This is achieved by a thorough mastery of a style that is wholly dedicated to its subject. It is a
style that enables Googe to control feeling in every line of the
poem. The opening commonplace and its development, first
with respect to the world and then to mankind, establish the
general tone for the whole poem—a feeling of loss and quiet
resignation; but as the poem proceeds to restrict the application
of the truism, until finally it is focused on Grimald, the initially
established feeling is gradually particularized. Whereas initially the sadness expressed is for human mortality, by the time
Grimald is introduced it is sadness occasioned by the profound
loss of a civilized and venerable scholar. The feeling has been so
well managed that the reader is apt to miss the shift from the
detached meditative statement of the opening lines to the conversational directness of the final passage. One should notice
how feeling begins to develop from the rhetorical series which
introduces the direct address to Grimald until it emerges as
private indignation in lines 19 through 24, and is resolved finally
with the reluctant acceptance of the closing commonplace.

The same successful fusion of the plain style and eloquent
structure is apparent, though less distinctly, in "*To Doctor
Bale*" and "*To the Translation of Pallingen.*" The former is
a fine and original compliment to an aging scholar:

[45] Wilson, *Arte of Rhetorique*, p. 69.

Good aged *Bale*: that with thy hoary heares
Doste yet persyste, to turne the paynefull Booke,
O happye man, that hast obtaynde suche yeares,
And leavst not yet, on Papers pale to looke,
Gyue ouer now to beate thy weryed brayne,
And rest thy Pen that long hath laboured soore
For aged men vnfyt sure is suche paine,
And the beseems to laboure now no more,
But thou I thynke Don Platoes part will playe
With Booke in hand, to haue thy dyeng daye.

A thorough training in rhetoric lies behind the poem. Googe's familiarity with the methods of praise suggested to him a suitable way for expressing his admiration for Bale. He selects what Rainolde suggests in his adaptation of Aphthonius as suitable for the third and fifth topics when praising persons living or deceased—"excellencies of mind, as the fortitude of the mynde" and "Comparison, wherein that which you praise, maie be aduanced to the vttermoste."[46] "*To the Translation of Pallingen*," on the other hand, is more indebted to the conventional divisions within the sonnet than it is to rhetorical precept:

The labour swete, that I sustaynde in the,
(O *Pallingen*) when I tooke Pen in hande,
Doth greue me now, as ofte as I the se,
But halfe hewd out before myne eyes to stande,
For I must needes (no helpe) a whyle go toyle,
In Studyes, that no kynde of muse delyght.
And put my Plow, in grosse vntylled soyle,
And labour thus, with ouer weryed Spryght,
But yf that God, do graunt me greater yeares
And take me not from hence, before my tyme,
The Muses nyne, the pleasaunt synging feares
Shall so enflame my mynde with lust to ryme,
That *Palingen* I wyll not leaue the so,
But fynysh the accordyng to my mynd.

[46] *The Foundacion of Rhetorike*, Fol. xl^r.

[144]

And yf it be my chaunce away to go,
Let some the ende, that heare remayne behynde.

The argument of the poem is probably developed to fit the quatrain and sestet divisions that Googe found in the Petrarchan sonnets in Tottel: a general statement of reluctance at having to give up an unfinished task (ll. 1-4); the reason for having to give it up (ll. 5-8); the hope that it may be recommenced (ll. 9-14); and the concluding hope that if it may not be completed personally, it may be completed by someone else. Both "*To Doctor* Bale" and "*To the Translation of Pallingen*" are written in the old plain style but in conjunction with new principles of order that Googe discovered in the course of his rhetorical training and study of Tottel's *Miscellany*. Those principles operate both as principles of order and methods of analysis, since by establishing an order of progression they also provide a means of discovering what to say about a given subject. These two poems again illustrate the way in which the plain style was continually being improved by the adaptation of rhetorical practices.

GEORGE TURBERVILE

Almost all of Turbervile's verse is in the polite courtly style and is similar in themes and techniques to the verse in Googe and the miscellanies. Stylistically, his work varies from the plain but polite, as in "*The Louer* finding his loue flitter from wonted truth" (probably an imitation of Wyatt's "Blame not my lute"), to the weighty and grandiloquent, as in "*The Louer* hoping in May to haue had redresse of his woes" (in imitation of Richard Edwardes' May poem in *The Paradise*), "He sorrowes the long absence of his ladie P.," and "An answere to his ladie." But for amorous verse he appears generally to have preferred a polite, conversational style, embellished with native proverbs and numerous classical allusions. Structurally, he adds little that is new to the tradition. In a good many of his poems Turbervile paraphrases love stories from the Classics for purposes of illustrating amorous commonplaces or for drawing comparisons between his own and some classical lover's

[145]

griefs.[47] In his praises of women he uses the catalogue of charms and the biographical methods of praise.[48] One of these, "Of the renowned Lady, Lady Anne Countesse Warwick," is nearly identical to Surrey's sonnet to Geraldine in its adherence to the biographical topics. Here are the first two stanzas:

> An Earle was your Sire a worthie wight,
> A Countesse gave you Tet, a noble Dame,
> An Earle is your Feere, a Mars outright,
> A Countesse eke your selfe of bruted fame:
> A brother Lord your Father Earles sonne,
> Thus doth renowne in Lordes and Earles ronne.
>
> You were well knowne of Russels race a childe,
> Of Bedford's blood that now doth liue an Earle,
> Now Warwicks wife, a warlike man in fielde,
> And Venus Peere, a ritch and orient Pearle,
> Wherefore to you that Sister, Childe and Wife
> To Lorde and Earles are, I wishe long life.

Turbervile also tried his hand at various pleas, pledges, descriptions of the courtly malady, love epistles, and examples of *ethopoeia*.[49] The epistles usually show the five-part structure: salutation, exordium, narration, petition, and conclusion. It is

---

[47] "The assured Promise of a constant louer"; "Agaynst the ielous heades that alwayes haue louers in suspect"; "The Louer excuseth himselfe for renowncing his loue"; "The ventrous louer after long absence craues his ladie to meete with him"; "The Louer driven to absent him from his ladie bewwayles his estate"; "The Louer in vtter dispaire of his ladies returne in eche respect compares his estate with Troylus."

[48] "The Louer extolleth the singular beautie of his ladye"; "Verse in prayse of Lorde Henrie Howarde Erle of Surrey"; "He sorrowes the long absence of his ladie P."

[49] For an example of *ethopoeia* see "Of Dido and the truth of her death," and for the epistle: "A letter sent by Tymetes to his ladie Pyndara at the time of his departue"; "To his absent friend the louer writes of his vnquiet and restlesse state"; "The louer wisheth to be conioyned and fast linkt with his ladie neuer to sunder"; "The Louer confesseth him selfe to be in love"; "To His Loue long absent, declaring his torments."

easily demonstrated in "To His Loue, Long Absent, Declaring His Torments."

Salutation and exordium (stanzas 1-3):

> O Lingring Loue, O friend that absent are so long,
> Where so thou bee, the Gods the guide And quit thy
> Corse from wrong:
>
> And sende thee harmelesse health, and safely to
> reuart,
> How soone your selfe may deeme full well to saue a
> dying hart
>
> For since your parture I haue lead a lothsome state:
> And saue the hope of your returne nought might my
> woes abate.

Narration (stanzas 4-27):

> And will you know the time how I haue spent away?
> And doe you long in ruthfull rime my torments to
> suruay?
>
> Though but with weeping eyes I may the same recite:
> Yet naythelesse the truth herein to thee (my Friend)
> I write
>
> .   .   .   .
>
> I viewe thy secret hart, and how it longs to bee
> With him that for unfayned loue unpawnde his faith
> to thee.

Petition (stanza 28):

> For mercie then I call of you that iudge so yll,
> Whose pleasure is to garde your Friend and not your
> Foe to kyll.

Conclusion (stanzas 29-32):

> Of dreames a thousand such eche night I haue a share.
> To bannish sleepe from pining corse and nurse my
> cankred care.

Thus day and night I liue. thus night and day I die:
In death I feele no smart at all, in life great wo I trie.

Wherefore to rid my griefes and bannish all annoie
Retire from Greece and doe soiourne here with thy
Friend in Troie.

Who longs to see thy face and witnesse of thy state:
And partner be of thy delights his furious fits to bate.

Turbervile's polite verse is pretty much as he has described it in his retraction.[50] He is content to treat fashionable themes within the conventions which were available to him. It shows little that is new in structure, and its style is distinct only in that it borrows more heavily from classical narrative than the verse of any of the preceding poets, except, possibly, for Grimald's.

Turbervile's epitaphs also follow generally the methods used by Googe and the contributors to the miscellanies.[51] They are neither better nor worse than those written by his immediate predecessors and contemporaries, though none is equal to Googe's on Grimald. Several are of interest, however, in that they show a shift of interest from personal lament to moral didacticism and a corresponding shift to the plain style: in the first of his two epitaphs for Master Tufton of Kent, Turbervile treats Kent's death as an example of the commonplace that all men must die. He is not interested in lamenting Kent's death but with stressing the importance of man's need to resign himself to death. The same moral lesson is propounded in "An Epitaph Of The Lady Br" and in the first of the two epitaphs for "Maister Win Drowned In The Sea," but with one important difference in technique. Both are conceived as *ethopoeia*—the figure wherein "Wee imagine a talke, for someone to speak, and according to his talk, we frame the Oration"—

[50] Quoted on pp. 122-123.

[51] See "On the death of Dame Elyzabeth Arhundle"; "Of the death of Sir Iohn Tregonwell Knight . . ."; "Vpon the death of Sir John Horsey Knight"; "Of Maister Edwards"; "On the death of Maister Arthur Brooke." Also compare the first of the two epitaphs on Tufton with Googe's elegy on Grimald which Turbervile obviously used for his model.

and bear a close resemblance to *The Mirror for Magistrates* "complaint."

Of Maister Win Drowned in the Sea

Who so thou art that passeth by this place
And runst at random on this sliper way,
Recline thy listning eare to mee a space
Doe stay thy ship and hearken what I say:
Cast Ankor here vntill my tale be donne,
So maist thou chaunce the like mishaps to shonne.

Learne this of mee, that men doe liue to die
And Death decayes the worthiest Wightes of all,
No worldly wealth or kingdomes can supplie
Or garde their princes from the fatall fall:
One way to come vnto this life we see,
But to be rid thereof a thousand bee.

My gallant youth and frolick yeares behight
Mee longer age, and siluer haires to haue,
I thought my day would neuer come to night,
My prime prouokte me to forget my graue:
I thought by water to haue scapte the death
That now amid the Seas doe lose my breath.

Now, now the churlish chanell me doe chock
Now surging Seas conspire to breede my carke
Now fighting flouds enforce me to the rock,
Charybdis Whelps and Scyllas Dogs doe barke
Now hope of life is past, now, now I see
That W. can no more a liues man bee.

Yet I doe well affie for my desart
(When cruell death hath done the worst it may)
Of well renowned Fame to haue a part
To saue my heart from ruine and decay:
And that is all that thou or I may gaine,
And so adue, I thank thee for thy paine.

The resemblance between the complaint and Turbervile's use

of *ethopoeia* is unmistakable, although the epitaphs in question are much shorter and lack the elaborate complaint framework. Behind both is the ancient rhetorical principle that the best way to move men to act is to appeal to their emotions by way of the imagination, or as Thomas Wilson puts it—by setting forth "the waight of the matter as though they saw it plaine before their eyes."[52]

Turbervile's aphoristic poems are also in the old didactic tradition, though they show a degree of competence (the result, probably, of Turbervile's study of the classical epigram) that earlier English epigrammatists had seldom approached.[53] His epigrams are sometimes witty; but they are rarely distinguished and never profound:

Of a Tayler

Though Tayler cut thy garment out of frame,
And strie thy stuffe by sowing it amis:
Yet must we say the Tayler makes the same,
To make and marre is one with them ywis.

Of One That Had A Great Nose

Stande with thy Nose against the Sunne
    with open chaps,
And by thy teeth we shall discerne
    what 'tis oclock perhaps.

Others are moralistic and suggest Greek sources.

Of a ritch miser

A Misers minde thou hast,
    thou hast a Princes pelfe:
Which makes thee welthy to thine Heire,
    a Beggar to thy selfe.

[52] *The Arte of Rhetorique*, p. 131.
[53] For a discussion of the English epigram in the sixteenth century see Hoyt H. Hudson, *The Epigram in the English Renaissance*.

Among the best are the following:

Declaring What Vertue It Is To Stick
To Former Plighted Friendship

The sage and Siluer haired Wights doe thinke
A vertue rare not to be prowde of mind
When Fortune smiles: nor cowardly to shrink
Though chaunged Chaunce do shew hir self unkind.
But chiefest prayse is to imbrace the man
In welth and wo with whome your loue began.

Of The Clock And The Cock

Good reason thou allowe
   one letter more to mee
Than to the Cock. For Cocks doe sleepe
   when Clocks doe wake for thee.

To An Olde Gentlewoman, That
Painted Hir Face

Leaue off good Beroe now
   to sleeke thy shrivled skin,
For Hecubes face will neuer be
   as Helens hue hath bin.

Let Beautie go with youth,
   renownce the glosing Glasse,
Take Booke in hand: that seemely Rose
   is woxen withred Grasse.

Remooue thy Pecocks plumes
   thou cranck and curious Dame:
To other trulls of tender yeares
   resigne the flagge of Fame.

These three poems are early representatives of a tradition to which Greville, Donne, Jonson, and Herrick contributed. They prove the truth of Bacon's view of the aphoristic style.

> . . . the writing in aphorisms hath many excellent virtues, whereto the writing in method doth not approach.

For first it trieth a writer whether he be superficial or solid: for aphorisms, except they should be ridiculous, cannot be made but of pith and heart of sciences: for discourse of illustration is cut off; recitals of examples are cut off; descriptions of practice are cut off; so there remaineth nothing to fill the aphorisms but some good quantity of observation.[54]

GEORGE GASCOIGNE

Gascoigne is at his best in "Wodmanship," "Memories 3," and "The Constancie of a Lover." Each shows in different ways how the plain style has borrowed structures from the handbooks of rhetoric and the eloquent tradition. "Wodmanship" and "Memories 3" are the first successful long lyrics to have been written in the sixteenth century. "The Constancie of a Lover" discloses a control of style not approached by any writer of love poems after Wyatt or before Sidney.

That selfe same tonge which first did thee entreat
To linke thy liking with my lucky love:
That trustie tonge must nowe these wordes repeate,
I love thee still, my fancie cannot move.
That dreadlesse hart which durst attempt the thought
To win thy will with mine for to consent,
Maintaines that vow which love in me first wrought,
I love thee still, and never shall repent.
That happie hande which hardely did touch,
Thy tender body to my deepe delight:
Shall serve with sword to prove my passion such
As loves thee still, much more than it can write.
Thus love I still with tongue, hand, hart and all,
And when I chaunge, let vengeance on me fall.

The poem is a thoroughly conventional pledge of service developed with the aid of a variety of catalogue. But the catalogue is not used merely to assure an easy coherence; it is essential

[54] *Advancement of Learning*, Bk. II, ed., W. A. Wright (Oxford: Clarendon Press, 1900), p. 172.

to the development of the conceit. Tongue, heart, and hand are the willing servants of the speaker's love. The tongue which had originally attempted to persuade the mistress to return his affection is unable to speak cleverly; it can only repeat in the plainest of terms "I love thee still," the vow which the heart has sealed and which the hand is pledged to serve. One should note especially the subtle antitheses in the third quatrain that are used to develop the hand as at once that of lover, soldier, and poet. It is only by physical force that the gentle and respectful lover can even hope to show how deep are his feelings; as a poet he can only repeat the plainly worded vow, as he has done in the present poem. One should also notice how the vow, repeated at the end of each quatrain, suggests the refrain technique as used by Wyatt. It, too, functions in several ways: it is, as has just been shown, essential to the conceit; it is chiefly responsible for the poem's gentleness and honesty; and it sets off the shift of thought that occurs in each quatrain.

"Memories 3" and, especially, "Wodmanship" display, on the other hand, both skill and profound seriousness. The language in these poems is that of the native tradition—direct, plain, and often proverbial. It shows no signs of literary affectation; it is dedicated to the exact and forceful expression of truisms particularized by the poet's personal experience. It is the language of a tough-minded, though civilized, poet. But what is particularly relevant to this study is the structural methods used in the writing of these poems.

"Memories 3" is an elaborately developed refutation of the proverb "Spend and God will send" which develops according to a carefully plotted seven-part scheme. Each part carries the refutation through a new stage of development: (1) Introduction of theme and the method of contrast that is to be used throughout to refute it and a condemnation of those who hold the position he is concerned to refute (ll. 1-4); (2) Development of the contrast of thrift and extravagance in general terms (ll. 5-11); (3) Illustration by concrete example of the general contrast developed in the preceding lines (ll. 12-19);

(4) Anticipation and refutation, including the use of simile and example, of an argument likely to be offered by the opposition (ll. 20-31); (5) a series of proverbs summarizing what has gone before and introducing what is to follow (ll. 32-36); (6) Proverbial instructions on how to avoid poverty (ll. 37-51); (7) Concluding aphoristic couplet (ll. 52-53). Whether or not Gascoigne had a specific scheme in mind when he wrote the poem, perhaps one remembered from his school days, is not important. But it is clear that he is deliberately working to achieve development and unity by following the principles of deliberative oratory.

The problem of coherence in the long lyric was at the time the poem was written a serious one, and it is interesting to see Gascoigne turning to his rhetorical training to solve it. The rhetorical organization in "Wodmanship" is even more apparent.

Prouty has discussed "Wodmanship" as an example of the method of grounding a poem " 'upon some fine invention,' here the invention being the conceit of shooting awry."[55] He has also observed that "the real reason of the poem" is to appeal to "Lord Grey 'to traine him yet into some better trade.' "[56] Prouty overlooks a good deal. The phrase, "to miss the mark," has a much richer range of implication than Prouty's discussion suggests. Gascoigne has in mind the idea of *hamartia*, of how man fails, in varying degrees, to attain the perfection for which he was created. He fails by missing the mark—that is, through some mistake in the reasoning process that leads to judgment and hence to choice. The poem is, therefore, an ethical analysis of the failure of Gascoigne's intentions. Prouty further oversimplifies the poem when he concludes that its development and organization are controlled only by the conceit. The development, on one level, is simply an exposition of missing the mark. The poet relates how throughout his life he has proved to be a sorry marksman, first as a student of various intellectual disciplines (philosophy, law, and rhetoric), then as a courtier

[55] C. T. Prouty, *George Gascoigne, Elizabethan Courtier, Soldier, and Poet* (New York: Columbia University Press, 1942), p. 121.
[56] *Ibid.*

seeking preferment, and finally in his old age as a soldier. On this level the principle of progression is chronological. But there is another and more complex scheme of organization within the poem. It is that of the demonstrative oration which has, according to Cicero (and it is Cicero whose teachings Gascoigne says he struggled unsuccessfully to master), six parts: (1) Exordium, (2) Proposition, (3) Narration, (4) Confirmation, (5) Refutation, (6) Peroration.[57] Gascoigne follows these divisions closely, though not mechanically.

The poem is conceived as an apology or, as Gascoigne refers to it, "an excuse in verse" for his ineptness as a woodsman on the grounds that, since his poor marksmanship with the crossbow is but one comparatively insignificant example of how throughout his life he has shot "awrie" at almost every mark, he ought rather to be pitied than blamed. The first sixteen lines include: an exordium to gain the good will of the judge, Lord Grey; a narration or brief account of the circumstances; and a proposition or brief, generalizing statement of the heart of the matter that is to be treated.

> MY woorthy Lord, I pray you wonder not,
> To see your woodman shoote so ofte awrie,
> Nor that he stands amased like a sot,
> And lets the harmlesse deare (unhurt) go by.
> Or if he strike a Doe which is but carren,
> Laugh not good Lord, but favoure such a fault,
> Take will in worth, he would faine hit the barren,
> But though his harte be good, his happe is naught:
> And therefore now I crave your Lordships leave,
> To tell you plaine what is the cause of this:
> First if it please your honour to perceyve,
> What makes your woodman shoote so ofte amisse,
> Beleeve me L. the case is nothing strange,
> He shootes awrie almost at every marke,
> His eyes have bene so used for to raunge,
> That now God knowes they be both dimme and darke.

[57] "*De Partitione Oratoria*," trans., H. Rackham in *Cicero*, The Loeb Classical Library (London: William Heinemann, Ltd., 1948), II, 333-57.

The next passage, consisting of about 85 lines, is devoted to confirming the truth of the proposition. He first "Shotte sometimes to hit Philosophie," next "to be a man of lawe," and then "to write the lawe by arte," but he lacked the necessary fortitude:

> . . . he most mislikte the thing,
> Which most might helpe to guide his arrow streight:
> He winked wrong, and so let slippe the string,
> Which cast him wide, for all his queint conceit.

Having despaired of serious occupations, he next "shotte to catch a courtly grace." But seeking dignity and preferment, he mistakes the means for achieving them and thus once again misses the mark. Gascoigne's self-criticism, as well as his implicit criticism of the Court, is the best writing of its kind since Wyatt's satires addressed to Poins and Brian.

> The blasing baits which drawe the gazing eye,
> Unfethered there his first affection,
> No wonder then although he shot awrie,
> Wanting the feathers of discretion.
> Yet more than them, the marks of dignitie,
> He much mistooke and shot the wronger way,
> Thinking the purse of prodigalitie,
> Had bene best meane to purchase such a pray.
> He thought the flattring face which fleareth still,
> Had bene full fraught with all fidelitie,
> And that such wordes as courtiers use at will,
> Could not have varied from the veritie.
> But when his bonet buttened with gold,
> His comelie cape begarded all with gay,
> His bumbast hose, with linings manifold,
> His knit silke stocks and all his queint aray,
> Had pickt his purse of all the Peter pence,
> Which might have paide for his promotion,
> Then (all to late) he found that light expence,
> Had quite quencht out the courts devotion.

Finally, having been led astray through a series of faulty choices and a weakness of the will, he "shootes to be a souldier in his age,"

> Mistrusting all the vertues of the minde,
> He trusts the power of his personage.
> As though long limmes led by a lusty hart,
> Might yet suffice to make him rich againe,
> But Flushyng fraies have taught him such a parte,
> That now he thinks the warres yeeld no such gaine.

But as a soldier he has also failed, though, in this instance, he has missed the mark not because of moral lassitude, but rather because of precisely the opposite:

> He cannot climbe as other catchers can.
> To leade a charge before himselfe be led,
> He cannot spoile the simple sakeles man,
> Which is content to feede him with his bread.
> He cannot pinch the painefull souldiers pay,
> And sheare him out his share in ragged sheetes,
> He cannot stoupe to take a greedy pray
> Upon his fellowes groveling in the streetes.
> He cannot pull the spoyle from such as pill,
> And seeme full angrie at such foule offence,
> Although the gayne content his greedie will,
> Under the cloake of contrarie pretence:
> And now adayes, the man that shootes not so,
> May shoote amisse, even as your Woodman dothe.

The next section of the poem maintains the semblance of a refutation by a strict qualification of all that has gone before. Gascoigne asserts that there are others who perhaps have shot "not so well." From Aristotle he learned at least temperance; Cicero taught him "somewhat to discerne/ Betweene sweete speeche and barbarous rudeness"; the books of law have acquainted him with lawlessness; and "The craftie Courtiers" have "put some experience in my mawe." But these acquisitions have not been sufficient for him to have mastered any art:

Yet can not these with many maystries mo,
Make me shoote streyght at any gaynfull pricke,
Where some that never handled such a bow,
Can hit the white, or touch it neare the quicke,
Who can nor speake, nor write in pleasant wise,
Nor leade their life by *Aristotles* rule,
Nor argue well on questions that arise,
Nor pleade a case more than my Lord Mairs mule,
Yet can they hit the marks that I do misse,
And winne the meane which may the man mainteyne.

And it is because he has been so preoccupied with this plight,
Gascoigne argues, that he has let the "hearde" go by. The next
and final section of the poem concludes the case by developing
a hypothetical example expanding the one point mentioned in
the narration that remains to be discussed. In what terms
might he excuse himself should he slay a doe that is carrying
a fawn? Some would interpret such an action as demonstrating
a lack of skill or as an accident of fortune; but Gascoigne holds
that such an event would be controlled by Providence and
would therefore constitute an act from which to learn a moral
lesson.

I say *Jehova* did this Doe advaunce,
And made hir bolde to stande before mee so,
Till I had thrust mine arrowe to hir harte,
That by the sodaine of hir overthrowe,
I myght endevour to amende my parte,
And turne myne eyes that they no more beholde,
Such guylefull markes as seeme more than they be:
And though they glister outwardely like golde,
Are inwardly but brasse, as men may see:
And when I see the milke hang in hir teate,
Me thinkes it sayth, olde babe now learne to sucke,
Who in thy youth couldst never learne the feate
To hitte the whytes whiche live with all good lucke.

Gascoigne has tightened the structure of the poem by developing the moral implications of the hunting trope within an
oratorical framework. The ethical doctrine and the deliberative

scheme have another important function. The notion of missing the mark provides Gascoigne with a methodology which focuses upon certain areas of his past experience as relevant, which excludes others, and which qualitatively determines the nature of his insights. The scheme of *dispositio*, too, though to a lesser extent, functions as a method, helping to order his perceptions and, inasmuch as he has committed himself to it, establishing from the outset a way of construing his theme.

The language of "Wodmanship" and the way in which the poem itself directly confronts the ethical dimensions of the role that the courtier must play if he is to win recognition suggest the old plain style and its didactic preoccupations. The particular mode of irony, so impressive in the middle and final sections of the poem, also suggests the plain style, specifically, the style and manner of Wyatt's satires of the Court. But influences of the eloquent tradition, already noticed with respect to the deliberative structure of the exposition, are also apparent in refinements of syntax and rhythm. Compare the opening lines of "Wodmanship" quoted above with the opening lines of "De profundis," a poem in which Gascoigne repeats the faults often present in the plain style as it appears in the early Elizabethan miscellanies:

> From depth of doole wherein my soule doth dwell,
> From heavy heart which harbours in my brest,
> From troubled sprite which sildome taketh rest.
> From hope of heaven, from dreade of darkesome hell,
> O gracious God, to thee I crye and yell.
> My God, my Lorde, to my lovely Lord aloane,
> To thee I call, to thee I make my moane.

In "Wodmanship" word order approximates that of expository prose, with syntax rather than the pentameter line and rhyme scheme functioning as the predominant principle of order. There are no inversions for the sake of rhyme or accent, and qualifying elements in the syntax observe parallelism and subordination. Parallelism in the passage from "De profundis" is also observed, but to a fault. The dominating structural principle is the rhymed couplet, and the syntactical units of clause and period are rigidly subordinated to its demands. The stiff regularity resulting is further accented by heavy alliteration and the unvaried occurrence in each line of a heavy cesura between the second and third feet.

One final example of the plain style in Gascoigne will suffice to conclude consideration of the early Elizabethans. I have in mind "The Lullabie of a Lover" which, in contrast to "Wodmanship" uses a medieval structure, but which discloses at the same time the same refinements in verse and syntax that I have noticed in that poem.

> Sing lullaby, as women doe,
> Wherewith they bring their babes to rest,
> And lullaby can I sing to,
> As womanly as can the best.
> With lullaby they still the childe,
> And if I be not much beguild,
> Full many wanton babes have I,
> Which must be stild with lullabie.

> First lullaby my youthfull yeares,
> It is nowe time to go to bed,
> For croocked age and hoary heares,
> Have wone the haven [within] my head:
> With Lullaby then youth be still,
> With Lullaby content thy will,
> Since courage quayles, and commes behind,
> Go sleepe, and so beguile thy minde.

> Next Lullaby my gazing eyes,
> Which wonted were to glaunce apace.
> For every Glasse maye nowe suffise,
> To shewe the furrowes in my face:
> With Lullabye then winke awhile,
> With Lullabye your lookes beguile:
> Lette no fayre face, nor beautie brighte,
> Entice you efte with vayne delighte.

> And Lullaby my wanton will,
> Lette reasons rule, nowe reigne thy thought,

Since all to late I finde by skyll,
Howe deare I have thy fansies bought:
With Lullaby nowe tak thyne ease,
With Lullaby thy doubtes appease:
For trust to this, if thou be styll,
My body shall obey thy will.

Eke Lullaby my loving boye,
My little Robyn take thy rest,
Since age is colde, and nothing coye,
Keepe close thy coyne, for so is best:
With Lulla[b]y be thou content,
With Lullaby thy lustes relente,
Lette others pay which hath mo pence,
Thou art to pore for such expence.

Thus Lullabye my youth, myne eyes,
My will, my ware, and all that was,
I can no mo delayes devise,
But welcome payne, let pleasure passe:
With Lullaby now take your leave,
With Lullaby your dreames deceive,
And when you rise with waking eye,
Remember then this Lullabye.

Both the theme and the lullaby as a convention are common
in collections of secular and religious medieval lyric, but the
invention is Gascoigne's. By treating his declining faculties as
small children whom he must lull to sleep, the aging lover
establishes a distance between himself and his subject and an
urbane attitude toward a past life spent in vigorous amorous
activities. The enumerative, repetitive structure is also medieval,
although it is complicated by the Renaissance psychology of
the passions in the third, fourth, and fifth stanzas: the passions,
stirred by sight, with the aid of fancy secure control of the
will, defeat reason, and then demand satisfaction (Robyn's
identity in the Renaissance as the phallus is a matter of common knowledge).

The poem, then, is medieval in style, structure, and convention. What distinguishes it as an example of the refined plain style is the extraordinary control of the refrain technique and the sophisticated way in which invention serves the purpose of tone and attitude. For example, there is the way in which Gascoigne in the opening stanza takes advantage of the fact that lullabies are ordinarily sung by women: "And lullaby can I sing to,/ As womanly as can the best." His admission here that with the loss of those powers which have made him a vigorous lover he approaches effeminacy is nicely ironic. Another example of the poet's sophistication occurs in the closing lines of the second stanza, in the pun on "content" in "Lullaby content thy will." The Lover's will is ordinarily "contented" in the sense of being satisfied by what he here realizes must be given up. It is also "contented" to the degree that it is able to accept what is not possibly avoided, that is, the weakening of the faculties that comes with old age. There is another ironic pun in the final line of this stanza. The word "beguile" here means to "divert attention in some pleasant way from anything painful or irksome" (N.E.D.). The final two lines mean then: since the heart (or vigor or lustiness) weakens, contemplate the generalization of which the lullaby sings and thus avoid the pain of the fact that it now applies specifically to you.

Literary historians have usually dismissed Googe, Turbervile, and Gascoigne as clumsy imitators of the verse in Tottel's *Miscellany*. They have not recognized the kind of experimentation with structure, especially in the elegy and the long reflective narrative, undertaken by these poets; and they have not acknowledged the perseverance of the vigorous plain style from Wyatt through Googe, Turbervile, and Gascoigne on into the Petrarchan period of Ralegh, Shakespeare, and Greville. Nor have they taken into account the presence of the eloquent tradition in mid-century verse and theory.

The reintroduction of Petrarchism with the appearance of Watson's *Passionate Century of Love* and Sidney's *Astrophil and Stella* is the beginning, certainly, of new directions and emphases in the English lyric. But those directions and emphases are not revolutionary in the sense that they are deliberately against prevailing notions of composition. They are in fact only to be understood rightly within the context of the theories of style and the experimentation with scheme, trope, and structure which since Tottel had characterized the English lyric. The plain and the eloquent styles retain their identities, even though both are substantially modified by new interests and refinements of technique, and by the recovery of classical literary theory which provided each style with authoritative support and prestige.

CHAPTER V

The Late Elizabethans: 1580-1600

THE PERIOD OF EARLY Elizabethan lyrical poetry ends abruptly in the 1580's with the appearance of the *Astrophil and Stella* manuscripts. The new poetry is distinguished by general refinements of language and verse techniques. Excessive aureation has been curbed and a good deal of the rigidity of syntax, often a characteristic of the earlier verse, has been eliminated. New and more sophisticated adaptations of classical conventions are commencing to emerge. The pentameter line, having absorbed many of the practices developed by the song writers, has acquired a new flexibility. And of course the impact of the Italian and French Petrarchans is everywhere apparent.[1]

The learned variety of the eloquent style, with its reliance upon neologisms, various long verse lines, balanced adjectives, alliteration, heavy mid-line caesuras and line end-stops, had reached a dead end in the *Gorgeous Gallery*. The courtly variety of the eloquent lyric still shows the influence of Tottel's *Miscellany* from time to time, as in the works of Dyer and Gorges, but the impact of Petrarch and the *Pléiade* is obvious in the pervasive concern for ingenuity of wit, and in the spread of neo-Platonism. The plain style, too, discloses extensive modifications. The medieval aphoristic style in conjunction with primitive structural techniques still appears, though much less frequently. At its most austere it is used by Ralegh in "The Lie" and in a number of his epigrammatical poems; by Nashe in "In Time of Pestilence"; and occasionally by anonymous contributors to the Songbooks. But generally it also discloses

[1] Sidney Lee's discussion of the extensive French influence on the English Petrarchans is still a useful summary. See *Elizabethan Sonnets*, I, Introduction, ix-cx.

Petrarchan influences in its increased structural and syntactical complexity and in its use of the sonnet form, and is further distinguished by its being put to use in the analysis of a broader range of subjects than ever before.

The eloquent lyric is still dominated, even in the poems closely imitating Petrarch or his French followers, by medieval theory. It remains an art of *elocutio*, and fine writing in verse, as well as in prose, is still cultivated as a courtly grace. Giles Fletcher in "The Epistle Dedicatory" to *Licea* grants that amorous verse may indeed be "a trifling labour" for a scholar to indulge in, but that it is, nonetheless, "an accomplishment of a Gentleman," for love is a matter "where every man takes upon himself to court exactly."[2] Even the scholarly Chapman agrees to complete *Hero and Leander* as a token of his gratitude to Lady Walsingham: ". . . were it not that wee must subject our accounts of these common receiued conceits to seruile custome; it goes much against my hand to signe that for a trifling subject, on which more worthines of soule hath been shewed, and weight of diuine wit, than can vouchsafe residence in the leaden grauitie of any Mony-Monger. . . . But he that shuns trifles must shun the world; out of whose reuerend heapes of substance and austeritie, I can, and will, ere long, single, or tumble out as brainles and passionate fooleries, as euer panted in the bosome of the most ridiculous Louer. Accept it therfore (good Madam) though as a trifle, yet as a serious argument of my affection."[3] Drayton discloses that the writing of love poems for others is still a common practice, and also that the old methods of verse composition are still in use:

> A witlesse gallant, a young wench that woo'd,
> (Yet his dull spirit her not one jot could move)
> Intreated me, as e'r I wish'd his good,
> To write him but one sonnet to his love:
> When I, as fast as e'r my penne could trot,

[2] Sidney Lee, *Elizabethan Sonnets*, II, pp. 30, 31.

[3] "To . . . The lady Walsingham," *The Poems of George Chapman*, ed., Phyllis Brooks Bartlett (New York: Modern Language Association, 1941), p. 132.

Powr'd out what first from quicke invention came;
Nor never stood one word thereof to blot,
Much like his wit, that was to use the same:
But with my verses he his mistres wonne,
Who doted on the dolt beyond all measure.
But see, for you to heav'n for phraze I runne,
And ransacke all Apollo's golden treasure;
    Yet by my froth, this foole his love obtaines,
    And I lose you, for all my wit and paines.

(Idea, 12)

Spenser's Amoretti and Epithalamion are praised for their display of learning, invention, and skillful decoration—characteristics of style which had been singled out for praise ever since Tottel's Miscellany:

. . . whether singing in some lofty vaine,
heroick deedes, of past, or present daies.
Or whether in thy louely mistris praise,
thou list to exercise thy learned quill,
thy muse hath got such grace, and power to please,
with rare inuention bewtified by skill.
As who therein can euer ioy their fill![4]

Whatever is new, therefore, in the eloquent lyric of the last decades of the century, beyond the general refinements concomitant with the coming of age of the vernacular, emerges within the limits circumscribed by the still vigorous tradition of medieval rhetoric. It emerges in response to a new emphasis upon originality and to a growing critical attitude toward courtly love verse. The earlier poets at the Court had been preoccupied with enriching the native tradition through rhetorical experimentation and the imitation of foreign models. They were not greatly concerned with putting what they had borrowed to original use, and though they frequently defended love as a valid subject for poetry, they made no real effort in

---

[4] The second dedicatory sonnet "To the Author of *Amoretti* and *Epithalamion*. In *Spenser's Minor Poems*, ed., Ernest de Sélencourt (Oxford: Clarendon Press, 1910).

their verse to avoid the accusation that they indulged in licentiousness. During the last decades of the century, however, the better poets stress above all else the importance of finding original conceits and try by various means to dignify love so as to avoid censure.

Implicit in the term *inventio* was the notion that the means selected for the development of a given subject must be new and ingenious. The notion lay behind the general Tudor and early Elizabethan movement to enrich the English verse tradition through foreign borrowing and imitation, but it assumes a new importance with the advent of Sidney. Controversies over methods of emulating the Classics still continue, such as the quarrels over inkhorn terms, native archaisms, rhyme, and prosody. The new concern, however, is the need to avoid slavish imitation and the importance of original, energetic invention. Gascoigne had urged originality of invention in *Certain Notes of Instruction*, but he showed little inclination to follow his own advice. The early poets were faced with the more immediate problems of an impoverished tradition—problems of diction, prosody, and modes of organization. But by 1580 the vernacular had come to be accepted as wholly adequate to all literary purposes, and the serious writers turned to what they accepted as their chauvinistic duty, the creation of a national body of poetry, continental in conception and English in spirit.[5]

Indications of this new concern in connection with the lyric are everywhere apparent. Thomas Watson's *Hecomtapathia: A Passionate Century of Love* reads as an illustrated text on the art of ingenious conceits. The majority of the poems are introduced with an open acknowledgment of their sources and brief descriptions of the techniques employed by the original authors in the development of their conceits. Thomas Nashe complains vigorously of the lack of inventiveness among English poets: "Such is this golden age wherein we live, and so replenished with golden asses of all sorts: that if learning had lost itself in a grove of genealogies; we need do no more but set an old goose over half a dozen pottle pots (which are, as

---

[5] See R. F. Jones, *The Triumph of the English Language*, p. 168.

it were, the eggs of invention) and we shall have such a breed
of books, within a while after, as will fill all the world with
the wild fowl of wits."[6] He also states: "Hence come our
babling Ballets, and our new found Songs and Sonets, which
euery rednose Fidler hath at his fingers end, and euery ignorant
Ale Knight will breath foorth ouer the potte, as soone as his
braine waxeth hote."[7] Sidney repeatedly expresses his contempt
for versifiers whose borrowings and antiquated mannerisms
"do bewray a want of inward touch" (15):

> YOU that do search for everie purling spring,
>   Which from the ribs of old *Parnassus* flowes,
>   And everie floure, not sweet perhaps, which growes
> Neare therabout, into your Poesie wring;
> You that do Dictionarie's methode bring
>   Into your rimes, running in ratling rowes:
>   You that poore *Petrarch's* long deceased woes,
> With new-borne sighes and denisend wit do sing;
>   You take wrong waies, those far-fet helpes be such,
>   As do bewray a want of inward tuch:
> And sure at length stolne goods do come to light.
>
> (ll. 1-11)[8]

Drayton in his introductory sonnet to *Idea* also condemns
uninspired imitation on the grounds that a lack of originality
belies a lack of genuine feeling.

> No far-fetched Sigh shall ever wound my breast!
> Love from mine eye, a Tear shall never wring!
> No "Ah me!"'s my whining sonnets drest!
> A Libertine! fantasticly I sing!
>
> (ll. 5-8)

[6] "Somewhat to read, for them that List," Preface to the first (sur-
reptitious) edition of *Astrophil and Stella* (1591). In Sidney Lee's
Elizabethan Sonnets, I, 9.

[7] "To the Gentleman Students of Both Vniversities," Preface to
Greene's *Menaphon*. In G. Gregory Smith's *Elizabethan Critical Essays*,
2 vols. (Oxford: Clarendon Press, 1904), I, 326-27.

[8] For similar criticism see Sonnets 6, 28, 55, 79, and 90; see also
the discussion of eloquence and amorous poetry in *The Defense of Poesy*.

His verse is his own and hence independently English:

> My Verse is the true image of my Mind,
> Ever in motion, still desiring change:
> And as thus, to variety inclined;
> So in all humours sportively I range!
>> My Muse is rightly of the English strain,
>> That cannot long one fashion entertain.
>>> (ll. 9-14)

Sir John Davies, too, aligns himself on the side of originality by expressing his contempt for the unimaginative and cliché-ridden labors of the gentleman victims of unrequited love:

> I cannot whine in puling Elegies
> Intombing Cupid with sad obsequies.
> I am not fashioned for these amorous times,
> To court thy beawtie with lascivious rimes:
> I cannot dally, caper, daunce, and sing,
> Oyling my saint with supple sonneting,
> I cannot busse thy fist, play with thy haire,
> Swearing by loue thou art most debonaire.
>> (*Ignoto*, 2, ll. 5-12)[9]

And in the nine "gulling sonnets" he attacks the lack of vigorous invention by parodying the most overworked conceits. Shakespeare, too, in both the sonnets and the plays frequently refers contemptuously to the excesses of the amorous vogues.

The effeminate vacuity of the current love poetry was also a favorite target of the early satirists. Eduard Guilpin's first satire is a fair example of the kind of attack leveled against amorous verse by writers in that genre:

> Fie on these *Lydian* tunes which blunt our sprights
> And turne our gallants to *Hemaphrodites*:
> Giue me a Doricke touch, whose *Semphony*,
> And daucing aire may with affinity
> Moue our light vaulting spirits and capering.

---

[9] *The Poems*, ed., Clare Howard (New York: Columbia University Press, 1941), p. 60.

Woo Alexander from lewd banquetting
To armes . . .
   Hence with these fidlers, whose oyle-buttred lines,
And Panders vnto lvsts, and food to sinnes,
Their whimpring Sonnets, puling Elegies
Slaunder the Muses; make the world despise,
Admired poesie, marre *Resolutions* ruffe
And melt true valour with lewd ballad stuffe.
   Heere one's Elegiack pen patheticall,
His parting from his Mistris doth bewaile:
Which when young gallant *Mutio* hath perus'd,
His valours crestfalne, his resolues abus'd,
For whatsoe're his courage erst did moue,
He'le goe no voyage new to leaue his Loue.[10]

Similar examples of violent antipathy directed toward love poetry are frequent in Hall, Marston, and Jonson. They are indicative of the more general dissatisfaction, evidenced by the emergence of literary satire, with the general decadence (or what was presumed to be decadence) of a court society.

The second force affecting the courtly lyric, the growing critical attitude toward the subject of love as immoral or of trivial significance—one sees signs of it in the Guilpin passage cited—is even stronger than the concern for originality. Such opposition is not new. Wyatt had been sharply critical of the Court and courtly love doctrine. Gascoigne had felt it necessary to defend his amorous "posies" on the grounds that such verse was expected of a gentleman seeking preferment and that it was for the good of the barren vernacular. Turbervile had published a recantation. But after 1580 accusations ranging from charges of licentiousness to foppery are critical commonplaces. Sidney acknowledges the moral opposition at least twice in *Astrophil and Stella*. Sonnet 14 is framed as an answer to a friend (perhaps Fulke Greville) who has criticized his amours as morally debilitating:

[10] *Skialetheia* (1598), ed., G. B. Harrison. Shakespeare Association Facsimiles No. 2 (London: Oxford University Press, 1931).

Alas have I not paine enough my friend,
  Upon whose breast a fiercer Gripe doth tire
  Then did on him who first stale downe the fire,
While *Love* on me doth all his quiver spend,
But with your Rubarb words yow must contend
  To grieve me worse, in saying that Desire
  Doth plunge my wel-form'd soule even in the mire
Of sinfull thoughts, which do in ruine end?

(ll. 1-8)

Sonnet 21 acknowledges similar criticisms: to surrender to love is to turn away from the "great expectations" which are the obligations of his noble birth:

YOUR words my friend (right healthfull caustiks) blame
  My young mind marde, whom *Love* doth windlas so,
  That mine owne writings like bad servants show
My wits, quicke in vaine thoughts, in vertue lame:
That *Plato* I read for nought, but if he tame
  Such coltish gyres, that to my birth I owe
  Nobler desires, least else that friendly foe,
Great expectation, weare a traine of shame.

(ll. 1-8)

Both Lodge and Nashe allow the validity of the charges of licentiousness and stupidity that Gosson had leveled against love poetry. Lodge would favor censorship: "I abhore those poets that sauor of ribaldry: I will with the zealous admit the expullcion of such enormities. . . . Beleeue mee the magistrats may take aduise . . . to roote out those odde rymes which runnes in euery rascales mouth, sauoring of rybaldry."[11] Nashe deplores the "fabulous follie" of verse in which "lust is the tractate of so many leaues, and loue passions the lauish dispence of so much paper." It is unfortunate, he continues, that Ovid's exile does not serve as a warning to those would-be "authors of Eloquence": it might "admonish such Idlebies to betake them to a new trade, the Presse should be farre better employed . . .

[11] *Defense of Poesy*, in G. Gregory Smith, I, 76.

English shoulde not be halfe so much Italianated as they are
. . . loue woulde obtaine the name of lust, and vice no longer
maske vnder the visard of virtue."[12]

Giles Fletcher refers specifically to Puritan opposition in "The
Epistle Dedicatory" to *Licea*. After granting that love has been
justly attacked as an idle and frivolous subject, he argues that
it need not necessarily be a source of corruption: "And howsoever LOVE, in this Age, hath behaved himself in that loose
manner as it is counted a disgrace to give him but a kind look:
yet I take the passion in itself to be of that honour and credit
as it is the perfect resemblance of the greatest happiness; and
rightly valued at his just price, in a mind that is sincerely and
truly amorous, an affection of the greatest virtue, and able of
himself to eternize the meanest vassal."[13] Continuing, he argues that "not only others in other countries, as Italy and
France, Men of Learning and great parts . . . have written
Poems and Sonnets of Love; but even amongst us, men of best
nobility and chiefest families to be the greatest Scholars and most
renowned in this kind."[14] That love is now an object of derision
is the fault of two things: "The one, that so many base com-
panions are the greatest Writers. The other, that our English
Genevian Purity hath quite debarred us of honest recreation:
yet the great Pillar, as they make him [i.e., Jean Calvin], of
that Cause hath shewed us as much wit and learning in this kind
as any other before or since."[15]

The kind of criticism reflected in Fletcher's defense, together
with the concern for originality and intellectual respectability,
had extremely important consequences. They are the major
causes for the reappearance in the eighties and nineties of the
religious lyric as a prominent genre and for developments within
the secular lyric which are the result of various attempts to make
love, morally and intellectually, a suitable subject for poetry.

Sidney, surveying in his *Defense of Poesy* the accomplishments of English writers, grants his opponents that the lyric has

---

[12] "To the Gentleman Students," *ibid.*, 322.
[13] *Elizabethan Sonnets*, II, 26.
[14] *Ibid.*, p. 27.
[15] *Ibid.* Jean Calvin is Lee's conjecture.

been confined to themes of secular love, and urges his contemporaries to celebrate divine love and to praise God: "Other sorts of Poetry almost haue we none, but that Lyricall kind of Songs and Sonnets: which, Lord, if he gaue us so good mindes, how well it might be imployed, and with howe heauenly fruite, both priuate and publique, in singing the prayses of the immortall beauty, the immortall goodnes of that God who gyueth vs hands to write and wits to conceiue: of which we might well want words, but neuer matter; of which we could turne our eies to nothing, but we should euer haue new budding occasions."[16] Clearly, Sidney sees the praise of a higher love as an antidote to the currently fashionable love poetry; and there are indications—"Leave me O Love, which reachest but to dust"; "Thou blind man's marke, thou foole's selfe chosen snare"; and the Psalm translations undertaken with his sister—that had he lived longer he might have written a substantial body of religious verse.

Sidney's views are shared by the Jesuit Robert Southwell and by Nicolas Breton. Southwell, in a prefatory letter to *Saint Peter's Complaint*, regrets that Christ's head "no garland weres" while poets waste their energies in paying homage to Venus:

> Stil finest wits are 'stilling Venus rose,
> In Paynim toyes the sweetest vaines are spent
> To Christian workes few have their talents lent.[17]
> (ll. 16-18)

Not only has the reputation of poetry suffered as a result; the poets who have used their talents to create "Paynim toyes" have abused an art which God chose as a medium of revelation: "Poets, by abusing their talent, and makeing the follies and faynings of loue the customarie subject of their base endeuours, haue so discreditied this facultie, that a poet, a louer, and a lyer, are by many reckoned but three words of one signification. But the vanitie of men cannot counterpoyse the authoritie of God,

---

[16] G. Gregory Smith, I, 201.
[17] "The Avthour to the Reader," in *The Complete Poems*, ed., Alexander Grosart (London: Robson and Sons, 1872), p. 9.

who deliuering many parts of Scripture in verse, and, by His Apostle willing vs to exercise our deuotion in hymnes and spiritual sonnets, warranteth the art to be good, and the vse allowable."[18] What is even worse, they have distorted their subject by ignoring the fact that proper love is truly a manifestation of *caritas*: "For as passion, and especially this of love, is in these daies the chiefe commaunder of moste mens actions, & the Idol to which both tongues and pennes doe sacrifice their ill bestowed labours: so is there nothing nowe more needefull to bee intreated, then, how to direct these humors into their due courses and to draw this floud of affections into the righte chanel. Passions I allow, and loues I approue, onely I would wishe that men would alter their object and better their intent. For passions being sequels of our nature, and allotted vnto vs as the handmaides of reason: there can be no doubt, but as their author is good, and their end godly; so ther vse tempered in the meane, implieth no offence. Loue is but the infancy of true charity, yet sucking natures teate, and swathed in her handes, which then groweth to perfection, when faith besides naturall motiues proposeth higher and nobler groundes of amitye."[19] Nicolas Breton in *A Solemne Passion of the Soules Loue* (1595)[20] allies himself with those who would encourage English poets to turn away from the praises of mistresses and to choose God as a subject. God is far superior as a source of inspiration:

> Come Poets yee that fill the world with fansies,
> Whose fauning Muses shew but madding fits,
> Which all too soone doo fall into those franzies,
> That are begotten by mistaking wits:
> Lay downe your lives, compare your love with mine
> And say whose vertue is the true divine.
>
> For further tryall let me give you leave,

[18] "The Author to his loving cosin?," *ibid.*, p. 4.
[19] "The Epistle Dedicatorie," to *Marie Magdalens Fvneral Teares* (London: printed by I. W. for G. C., 1591), A3 verso-A4 recto [HEH No. 69502].
[20] London: Iohn Danler, 1595 [HEH 80840], p. 48 of the photo copy.

To add a truth unto your ydle storyes,
Wherewith so oft you doo the wourld deceave,
And gayne your selves but ill conceyted gloryes:
Yet when you see where sweetest sights are showne,
Looke on my love, and blush to see your owne.

With sunny beautyes let your loves be blest,
The sunne doth fetch his light but from my loue,
You have your wonders from the Phoenix nest,
Mine honour lives but in the heavens aboue:
Your Muses doo your Ladyes prayses sing,
The Aungels sing in glory of my King.

It is clear that the religious lyric which emerges toward the end of the sixteenth century, developed quite specifically out of the awareness that the conventional attitudes toward love in the verse of the English Petrarchans made English poetry vulnerable to charges of vacuity and licentiousness. The religious poets themselves, however, were deeply indebted to the Petrarchans. The new religious lyric would not have appeared in the forms that it did if the Petrarchan vogue had not invaded English verse.

The indebtedness of the writers of religious lyric to the Petrarchans is not confined to the sonnet form or to the refinements of verse, syntax, and rhythm which the Petrarchan movement produced. It includes ways of examining states of mind and of handling those paradoxical feelings and attitudes which are a part of the devout Anglican's religious experience. The courtly conventions of praising a mistress, of asking that she offer or allow the petitioner some cause to hope that his love may be satisfied, or of describing the paradoxical feelings of unrequited love (despair, hope, sorrow and happiness, fear and assurance) which in the beginning had been introduced into the religion of love by the deliberate parody of religious experience are now, some three-and-a-half centuries later, reintroduced as ways of ordering thought and feeling within the very areas of experience from which they originally derived. The modes for praising a mistress and for asking for her love become the modes for praising God and asking for his grace; the modes for describing the malady of unrequited love become the modes for describing Christian despair; and the means by which the paradoxical feelings of unrequited love are examined become the means of examining the paradoxical feelings of love and fear that are inspired by meditation upon a God who is at once absolutely just and infinitely merciful, whose vexing "contraries meete in one."

What begins as a simple reaction against profane love poetry—in Constable and Southwell it is mainly a shift from the praise of a mistress to praises of Mary, Christ, and the Trinity, though occasionally, as in Southwell's "What Joy to Live" and "Dyer's Phancy Turned to a Sinner's Complaint," it is deliberate parody—culminates in Fulke Greville, John Donne, Ben Jonson, and George Herbert as the profound introspective analysis of the Christian in his attempt to make himself worthy of divine love. "What Joy To Live" is a parody of Petrarch's "I find no peace, and all my war is done" and "Dyer's Phancy," a parody of a lover's complaint by Edward Dyer. The parody of Petrarch begins with the following two stanzas:

> I wage no warr, yet peace I none enjoy;
> I hope, I feare, I fry in freesing colde;
> I mount in mirth, still prostrate in annoye;
> I all the worlde imbrace yet nothing holde.
> All welth is want where chefest wishes fayle,
> Yea life is loath'd where love may not prevayle.

> For that I love I long, but that I lacke;
> That others love I loath, and that I have;
> All worldly fraightes to me are deadly wracke,
> Men present happ, I future hopes do crave:
> They, loving where they live, long life require,
> To live where best I love, death I desire.

Following are several stanzas from Dyer's poem and Southwell's parody:

O fraile vnconstant kynd,   O frayle inconstant
                                                       Fleshe!

And safe in trust to noe
    man!
Noe woemen angells are
    yet loe!
My mistris is a woeman!

       (St. 24)

Alone I lye, whose like
By loue was never yet

Nor rich, nor poore, nor
    younge, nor old,
Nor fond, nor full of witt.

Hers still remaine must I,

By wronge, by death, by
    shame;
I cannot blot out of my
    mind
That loue wrought in her
    name.

I cannot set at naught
That I have held soe
    deare,
I cannot make it seem so
    farre
That is indeede soe neare.
      (Sts. 26-28)

Soone trapt in every
    gynn!
Soone wrought thvs to
    betray thy soule,
And plunge thy self in
    synne!
       (St. 24)

To moane a synner's case,
Then which was never
    worse,
In prince or poore, in
    young or old,
In blissd or full of curse.

Yet God's must I re-
    mayne,
By death, by wronge, by
    shame;
I cannot blott out of my
    harte
That grace wrote in His
    name.

I cannot sett at noughte
Whome I have held so
    deare;
I cannot make Him
    seeme afarre
That is in dede so neere.
    (Sts. 26-28)[21]

The secular love poetry, too, is deeply influenced by the criticism to which it is being increasingly subjected. It discloses that influence in a series of developments which taken together might be identified as leading to the "intellectualization" of the secular love poem, a series of developments which are the

[21] Robert Southwell, *The Complete Poems*, ed., Alexander Grosart (London: Robson and Sons, 1872).

result of various attempts to make love poetry morally and intellectually respectable.

One attempt to assure love poetry such respectability is the practice of imitating classical rather than continental models, especially the pastoral. Within the lyric that practice is represented by the verse in *England's Helicon* (1600). Another attempt among the writers of the "sugared" or courtly style is apparent in the new emphasis upon clever argument and the figures of amplification and embellishment that are carefully catalogued and illustrated in practically every treatise of rhetoric published in the century. And there is also evident in the verse of Sidney and his imitators a new concern with those grammatical tropes, or figures of thought, which proved useful in depicting the paradoxical emotions of unrequited love and in dramatizing the opposition, traditional in Christian ethical psychology, between reason and passion. According to Hallet Smith it was these "opposites and paradoxes" which Thomas Watson had found in Petrarch and which most interested the Elizabethan poet. They interested him, according to Smith, because "he was constantly trying to give to love poetry an intellectual and moral respectability; he was aware that to his audience this kind of verse might seem a 'toy' because of its subject matter. The way to avoid this was to complicate the technique. Ingenuity and wit might persuade the reader that the states of mind offered in the poem were not so frivolous or immature. The problem was to make love seem an almost heroic subject, and to do it by the insistence upon the consuming nature of the experience."[22] The evidence supporting Smith's explanation of the interest in ingenuity and wit is the poetry itself, particularly *Astrophil and Stella*, but also the sequences of Daniel, Drayton, and (though Smith does not mention them) Fulke Greville's amorous sonnets in *Caelica*. Of particular interest, as I shall

[22] *Elizabethan Poetry: A Study in Conventions, Meaning, and Expression* (Cambridge, Mass.: Harvard University Press, 1952), p. 138. Ralph Lever shares Smith's view: "The plethora of decorative conceits which marked the late Elizabethan sonnet reflected the intellectual curiosity of the age . . ." *The Elizabethan Love Sonnet* (London: Methuen, 1956), p. 161.

endeavor to show later on, is the method used by Sidney and Greville to dramatize, within a framework of scholastic psychology, the conflict of reason and will which both writers identify as the central one in the experience of love.

Finally, there are two other developments within the secular love poem which are inspired by the criticism of love poetry and which contribute to its intellectualization. One is the use of a modified version of the old plain style to develop inventions taken from the learned disciplines of philosophy, geography, law, and cosmology;[23] the other is the assertion and elaboration of a distinction between a "higher" and a "lower" love that is similar to the one assumed by Sidney and Southwell between divine and profane love. The sources of these developments within the secular love poem, as well as its rationale, are apparent in a second preface written by Fletcher in an effort to anticipate the arguments of the "Genevian" critics which the publication of *Licea* would most likely incur.

He opens his case with an attack upon excessive borrowings and a defense of the English language:

> This Age is learnedly wise, and faultless in this kind of making their wits known [*i.e.*, in the writing of love poetry]: Thinking so basely of our bare English, wherein thousands have travailed with such ill luck, that they deem themselves barbarous and the island barren, unless they have borrowed from Italy, Spain, and France their best and choicest con-

---

[23] Francis Meres observes that "that Poetrie dooth most delight which/ is mixt with Philosophy." (Poetry, St. 2, ll. 4-6)

John Hoskins urges writers to use intellectual metaphor, since it offers the most delight: ". . . to delight, generally, take those terms from ingenious arts to please the learned, and from several arts to please the learned of all sorts; as from the meteors, planets, and beasts in natural philosophy, from the stars, spheres, and their motions in astronomy from the better part of husbandry, from the politic government of cities, from navigation, from military profession, from physic; but not out of the depth of these mysteries . . . . But ever (unless your purpose be to disgrace) let the word be taken from a thing of equal or greater dignity." *Directions for Speech and Style*, ed. with Introduction and Notes by Hoyt H. Hudson (Princeton: Princeton University Press, 1935), p. 9.

ceits. For my own part, I am of this mind that our nation is so exquisite (neither would I overweeningly seem to flatter our home-spun stuff, or diminish the credit of our brave travellers) that neither Italy, Spain, nor France can go beyond us for exact invention. For if anything be odious amongst us, it is the exile of our old manners, and some base-born phrases stuft up with such new terms, as a man may sooner feel us to flatter by our incrouching eloquence than suspect it from the ear.[24]

The art of love is a gentleman's art, and only gentlemen are "fitted to write of Love." Others whose "debased minds" make them "unfit to know what Love means" are "deluded fondly with their own conceit" and take love to be "the contentment of themselves, the shame of others, the wrong of virtue; and the refiner of the tongue."[25] Continuing, he makes love a chaste goddess:

> . . . Love is a goddess (pardon me though I speak like a Poet) not respecting the contentment of him that loves but the virtues of the beloved, satisfied with wondering, fed with admiration, respecting nothing but his Lady's worthiness, made as happy by love as by all favours, chaste by honour, far from violence. . . . This is Love, and far more than this; which I know a vulgar head, a base mind, an ordinary conceit, a common person will not, and cannot, have.

The vulgar only confuse sensual lust with love. They are groveling followers of Cupid: "But the love wherewith Venus' son hath injuriously made spoil of thousands, is a cruel Tyrant: occasion of sighs, oracle of lies, enemy of pity, way of error, shape of inconstancy, temple of treason, faith without assurance, monarch of tears, murderer of ease, prison of hearts, monster of Nature, poisoned honey, impudent courtezan, furious bastard: and in one word, not Love." His Licea is no mistress in the

[24] "To the Reader," *Elizabethan Sonnets*, II, 30-3.
[25] Notice that Fletcher will not allow the argument that amorous poetry is to be condoned because it furthers the refinement of the vernacular.

ordinary sense. She is no courtesan to be worshiped in a false and sinful way: "If thou muse, What my LICIA is? Take her to be some DIANA, at the least chaste; or some MINERVA: no VENUS, fairer far. It may be she is Learning's Image, or some heavenly wonder: which the Precisest may not mislike. Perhaps under that name I have shadowed '[The Holy] Discipline.' It may be, I mean that kind courtesy which I found at the Patroness of these Poems, it may be some College. It may be my conceit, and pretend nothing." The sonnets written to Licia, however, contain no indication whatsoever of their author's professed intentions. It is impossible to distinguish Licea from the mistress of any other sonnet sequence produced by a Sidney imitator.

Nevertheless Fletcher's distinction between profane and spiritual love, and his insistence upon leaving open the possibility that Licia is not only a woman but perhaps represents Holy Discipline, is pretty clearly indicative of one of the causes for the widespread cultivation throughout the eighties and nineties of neo-Platonic love. Following the advice of Castiglione's *The Courtier* and the example of the Pléiade and of Petrarch, many of the Elizabethans found it to be both a means of purifying and elevating love and a source of learned and ingenious conceit.

George Chapman's *A Coronet for his Mistresse Philosophie*[26] carefully distinguishes between the divine and profane kinds of love by assuming the Platonic view of the separation of body and soul. The introductory sonnet makes the distinction between profane and spiritual love and condemns the poets who celebrate the profane:

> Muses that sing loues sensuall Emperie,
> And Louers kindling your enraged fires
> At *Cupids* bonfires burning in the eye,
> Blowne with the emptie breath of vaine desires,
> You that prefer the painted Cabinet
> Before the welthy Iewels it doth store yee,

[26] I have used a Photo Copy of the 1595 edition in the Huntington Library, copy number 49638.

And staine the liuing substance of your glory,
Abiure those ioyes, abhor their memory,
And let my loue the honord subiect be
Of loue, and honors compleate historie;
Your eyes were neuer yet, let in to see
The maiestie and riches of the minde,
But dwell in darknes; for your God is blinde.

The rest of the sequence elaborates the distinction in terms of the familiar neo-Platonic rationale and the current humor psychology. The worshipers of Cupid are blinded by the humor which falls from his eyes and tormented by the choler which flows up from the liver (2). Spiritual love, on the other hand, is

. . . the cordiall of soules
Teaching by passion what perfection is,
In whose fixt beauties shine the sacred scroules,
And long-lost records of your humane blisse
Spirit to flesh, and soule to spirit giuing.

(ll. 9-13)

Such love is the worship of pure and constant virtue, and of beauty which, because it is eternal, is not diminished by age, care, or torment (3). Divine virtue and beauty cannot be courted by the fashionable courtly means:

. . . not the weake disioint
Of female humors; nor the Protean rages
Of pied fac'd fashion, that doth shrink and swell,
Working poore men like waxen images
And makes them apish strangers where they dwell
Can alter her; titles of primacy,
Courtship of antick iestures, braineles iests,
Bloud without soule of false nobilitie,
Nor any folly that the world infests
Can alter her who with her constant guises
To liuing vertues turns the deadly vices.

(6. 4-14)

Love turns sin to virtue (7) and is a source of divine inspiration to poets who have discovered her (8), though no poet can ever hope to praise her adequately (9). The purpose of Chapman's argument is clear. The learned Chapman is, like Fletcher, agreeing with the accusations voiced by the critics of profane love and advocating a way to make love a suitable subject of poetry, a subject intellectually and morally respectable.

It is difficult to determine just how seriously the English took neo-Platonic theory. For some it was only a literary fashion to be followed by those who, according to Donne in "Love's Growth," "have no Mistresse but their muse." For others it made a distinction between levels of amorous experience which was borne out in some degree by personal experience. It was obvious to some poets who thought seriously about love that desire, easily satisfied in a moment of pleasure—a "love which reachest but to dust"—was something quite different from the feelings accompanying the unselfish admiration of a woman whose accomplishments and grace made her physical attractiveness relatively insignificant. Such admiration and respect were clearly in some way independent of the flesh, more like the friendship described by Cicero's *De Amicitia* than anything else. Also, neo-Platonic doctrine provided a vocabulary and rudimentary psychology which could be used to examine and describe the various states of mind and feeling that are a part of a lover's experience.

The emergence of the religious lyric and the intellectualization of secular love poetry during the last twenty-odd years of the sixteenth century make it difficult to understand Julius Lever's conclusions about the Elizabethan love poem. He finds that the other "imaginative creations of the age" were "profoundly influenced" by the "ferment of ideas and emotional responses" which "in the last decade of the sixteenth century would seem to have reached its climax in England," but not the love sonnet: "Despite Tudor modifications of the European tradition, despite Sidney's brilliant individual achievement, the conventional theme of courtly love remained in essence unchanged, and of its very nature impervious to the new spirit."[27]

[27] *The Elizabethan Love Sonnet*, p. 161.

Courtly love poetry in the Petrarchan vein of course does continue to be written well into the first half of the seventeenth century, but it is a decadent tradition by the mid-nineties. What is vigorous in the secular love poetry at the turn of the century is so because it has been deeply affected by the "ferment of ideas and emotional responses" to which Lever refers.

The neo-Platonism of Chapman's *A Coronet for his Mistresse Philosophie* represents only a beginning stage of an inquiry into the nature of love which engages some of the best minds of the period and which is reflected in drama and prose as well as in the new poetry. The neo-Platonism deriving from Ficino and the lesser Italian Platonists, to which the English were introduced by Spenser and the translators of Castiglione and Romei, stimulated that inquiry by raising a number of metaphysical and psychological difficulties of its own which men of the intelligence of Donne and Greville were quick to perceive. Advocating the contemplation of the beautiful, it runs counter to the active ideal which permeates English Renaissance thought as late as Marvell and Milton. Donne insists that "Love would sometimes contemplate and sometimes do,"[28] and works hard to demonstrate metaphysically and theologically that his position is the correct one. Shakespeare in the Comedies explores the conditions that must be fulfilled if a lover is to prove himself worthy of marriage, which in the Comedies represents the active life.[29] In fact, it is mainly in the "literary" poetry and in the books of courtesy, such as *The Courtier*, that one finds the contemplation of the Idea of Beauty presented seriously.

Among other difficulties raised by neo-Platonism was the sharp distinction between mind and body which Donne, an Aristotelian realist, could only construe as destroying the essential unity of man. If, as the Aquinian Pierre Charron insists, "The *Soule* is in the bodie, as the forme in the matter, extended and spred thorowout the body . . . and both of them together

---

[28] See "Love's Growth."

[29] A study of Shakespeare's comedies reveals that the moral purpose of comedy specified in the Donatan tradition, that life is to be embraced, is accepted by Shakespeare as a controlling comic idea and that marriage in the Romantic Comedies is presented as the embracing of life.

make but one *Hypostasis*, one intire subject, which is the creature, and there is no meane or middle that doth vnite and knit
them together,"[30] then love must involve the body as well as the
soul and the notion of a purely spiritual and contemplative act
is merely a fiction. Sidney, Donne, and Greville all recognized
this. Another difficulty raised by neo-Platonism, and it especially
interested Donne, was the way in which it reenforced a dichotomy between profane and sacred love. Donne, and Shakespeare, too, saw in that dichotomy a contradiction of *caritas*.
Donne throughout the *Songs and Sonets* and Shakespeare repeatedly in the Comedies identify the proper love between man
and woman as grounded in Christian charity and deny that the
body and its desires are necessarily evil. The result in both
writers is a resolution of the antithesis of the sacred and the
profane.

These, then, are some of the ideas which I expect to examine
in the verse of Sidney and Spenser, and later in Shakespeare,
Greville, and Donne. I expect also to consider the impact of
the various developments which are responsible for what I have
called the intellectualization of the lyric on poetic structures and
styles. The emphasis of my investigation shifts, however, from
considerations of structure and style to content, and necessarily,
in order to focus on what from 1580 on is the main interest of
the better poets. So long as their concern was to refine the
vernacular and prove it capable of eloquence, manner took
precedence over matter. But that initial stage in the evolution of
the lyric is over. Now in the final decades of the century it is
matter which gains attention. The consensus is that the language is now ready for any demands that might be made of it.
Spenser attempts an epic and, with an awareness that he is
endeavoring to accomplish in English what Virgil had in Latin,
he writes *The Shepheardes Calender*. Daniel and Shakespeare
promise to immortalize the people they praise by writing sonnets
in a vernacular which scarcely sixty years earlier had been
judged barren, rude, and even barbarous.

[30] *Of Wisdome*: Three Books, tr., Samson Lennard (London: printed
for Edward Blount and Witt Aspley, 1612) [HEH 5052, p. 31].

My approach to the lyric at end-century will undoubtedly be criticized for ignoring continental influences. How deeply the poets of Spenser's and Sidney's generation were actually influenced by the theory and arguments of the Italian and French defenders of their respective vernaculars is not easily determined. They were undoubtedly familiar with Sperone Speroni's *Dialogue on Languages,* either directly, or through Du Bellay's *Defense and Illustration of the French Language.* Certainly the various demonstrations by scholars of the extensive borrowings by the Elizabethans from the French Petrarchans is proof of the admiration which the English had for French courtly poetry and the literary ideals of *La Pléiade.* But literary influences are a complicated business. To imitate or to borrow is not necessarily to be "influenced" by. A poet *chooses* the models he imitates; and his choices reflect his tastes and critical preconceptions. Anterior to every borrowing or imitation there exists a body of assumptions about what is good and bad verse which therefore determines what is worth borrowing or imitating. If a poet approves of an ornate style, he will select ornate models. If he is impatient with Petrarchan cliché, he may very likely borrow inventions or adapt lines from French sonnets which are anti-Petrarchan.

The history of the Renaissance lyric in England cannot, therefore, be reliably presented in terms of literary influences or borrowings (the Italian sonnet form, is an excellent case in point), although both certainly have their place in any such account. Ultimately, that history must consider those ideas and attitudes which are at the center of Elizabethan culture and which are anterior to foreign borrowings and imitations.

Sir Philip Sidney and Edmund Spenser

The new concerns are immediately evident in *Astrophil and Stella.* Sidney repeatedly expresses his impatience with uninspired imitation and the ornate techniques of his contemporaries and pledges himself to sincerity of expression.

Some Lovers speake when they their Muses entertaine,
Of hopes begot by feare, of wot not what desires:

Of force of heav'nly beames, infusing hellish paine:
Of living deaths, deare wounds, faire stormes and freesing
    fires:
  Some one his song in *Jove*, and *Jove's* strange tales attires,
Broadred with buls and swans, powdred with golden raine:
Another humbler wit to shepheard's pipe retires,
Yet hiding royall bloud full oft in rurall vaine.
  To some a sweetest plaint, a sweetest stile affords,
  While teares powre out his inke, and sighs breathe out
    his words:
His paper, pale dispaire, and paine his pen doth move.
  I can speake what I feele, and feele as much as they,
  But thinke that all the Map of my state I display,
When trembling voice brings forth that I do *Stella* love.[31]

                              (No. 6)

But artlessness and plain statement are no part of the poetic
represented by the sequence. Sidney's craftsmanship is obvious
on every page, and it is a craftsmanship which is as much rhetorical as it is metrical. It is in matters of technique—his mastery
of the Petrarchan conventions and of tightly argued invention
within the structure of the sonnet—and in skillfully worked out
variations of themes that are sometimes as old as the code of
love itself that Sidney justifies his own claims of originality.

    Contrary to the textbook clichés, there is no evidence any-
where in the sequence of a revolution in literary theory.
Throughout, Sidney composes within the framework of the
eloquent poetic, "Ennobling new-found tropes with problems
old," occasionally, even working for eloquence in the old ornate manner by "enam'ling" "thoughts of gold" with the "pied
flowers" of *elocutio*. Nor are there signs of anything like a real
dissatisfaction with the code of love. Even in those poems in
which he appears to be most critical of the servant-mistress
relationship, Astrophil "courts exactly," writing within the
prescribed genres of praise, complaint, pledge, and plea and
always observing the rules of the courtly game.

[31] All quotations from Sidney's verse are from William A. Ringler's
The Poems of Sir Philip Sidney (Oxford: Clarendon Press, 1962).

Among the more "eloquent" praises and complaints that are scattered throughout the sequence (although most of them occur, curiously, among the last thirty or so sonnets),[32] Sonnet 9 is among the most interesting.

Queene *Vertue's* court, which some call *Stella's* face,
    Prepar'd by Nature's chiefest furniture,
    Hath his front built of Alablaster pure;
Gold is the covering of that stately place.
The doore by which sometimes comes forth her Grace,
    Red Porphir is, which locke of pearle makes sure:
    Whose porches rich (which name of cheekes endure)
Marble mixt red and white do enterlace.
The windowes now through which this heav'nly guest
Looks over the world, and can find nothing such,
Which dare claime from those lights the name of best,
Of touch they are that without touch doth touch,
    Which *Cupid's* selfe from Beautie's myne did draw:
    Of touch they are, and poore I am their straw.

[32] Richard B. Young notes that "the most 'mannered' sonnets are by and large confined to the beginning and end" of the sequence. He accounts for their conventionality in terms of what he sees as the dramatic structure of the sequence: "The Petrarchan convention throughout the sequence has delimited the world of Astrophel as lover, as contemporary affairs of state delimit the world of citizen and courtier. It functions as the universal to which, as lover and as poet, he must relate himself. . . . At first he imposes himself on the convention in an effort to overcome and eliminate it; it is public and impersonal and consequently the antagonist of the individual lover, who asserts the primacy of his unique personality over its generalizations, its assumptions, and its manners. His technique is that of the orator and advocate, attacking the conventional 'vice' in its various forms, praising virtue, and identifying himself as his 'proof.' By asserting himself through this technique he eliminates the superficial and therefore falsifying aspects of the convention, discovers and finally reaches Stella. By the end of the sequence, through his relation to Stella, Astrophel has been made aware of the nature of Love as the Petrarchan universal: he has discovered himself as part of the convention, which, by virtue of his participation in it has acquired permanent validity." "English Petrarke: A Study of Sidney's *Astrophel and Stella*," *Three Studies in the Renaissance* (New Haven: Yale University Press, 1958), pp. 40, 88.

The compliment appears, at least initially, to be Platonic—a chaste appreciation of Stella's spiritual beauty, in which originality is mainly a matter of the clever (and to modern tastes grotesque) fusion of the old catalogue technique and the equally old commonplace of the body's beauty being a reflection of an inner beauty. But, looking more closely at the poem, this does not turn out to be true. Cupid's entrance in the final couplet is the give-away. He has no business appearing in a poem which is supposed to be devoted to a lady's spiritual qualities; and Sidney knows it. Stella's eyes, the windows through which the "heav'nly guest looks over the world," affect Astrophil in a way which is decidedly un-Platonic. They may be the windows of Stella's soul, but they are composed of a mineral that has been mined by the god of erotic love and which like loadstone "without touching doth touch." Ringler is of the opinion that "Sidney here is thinking of the magnetic rather than the inflammatory property of Stella's eyes,"[33] and he is right in part. The property is magnetic and not inflammatory as tinder is; but it is capable of igniting tinder. The property is identified with Cupid, and hence with physical desire. It is this physical property in Stella's eyes, not the light of virtue shining in them, which arouses, or "inflames," Astrophil; and it is clear, finally, that the poem is not at all what it had first seemed, but an admission, instead, of Astrophil's failure as Platonic lover. He has been *touched* physically, and according to Ficino the sense of touch is active only in the "lower" love.

Sonnet 29 uses the same methods, although with less wit. Astrophil's purpose here is to proclaim his allegiance to Stella and to complain of his unrequited love. The invention is a likening of Stella's defenses to a military policy of strategic retreat and concession which is forced upon a ruler whose military powers are slight when compared to those of the threatening invader:

> Like some weake Lords, neighbord by mighty kings,
>> To keepe themselves and their chiefe cities free,
>> Do easly yeeld, that all their coasts may be

[33] *The Poems of Sir Philip Sidney*, Commentary, p. 464.

Ready to store their campes of needful things:
So *Stella's* heart, finding what power *Love* brings,
　To keepe it selfe in life and liberty,
　Doth willing graunt, that in the frontiers he
Use all to helpe his other conquerings:

She thus is able to save her heart from occupation by allowing
Love to use her "outer territories" and supplies to capture the
hapless Astrophil:

And thus her heart escapes, but thus her eyes
　Serve him with shot, her lips his heralds arre:
　Her breasts his tents, legs his triumphall carre:
　Her flesh his food, her skin his armour brave,
　And I, but for because my prospect lies
　Upon that coast, am giv'n up for a slave.

The grotesque extremes to which the invention is carried
(breasts as tents, legs as "triumphall carre"), is indicative of the
value placed upon invention by Sidney and his contemporaries.
The visual level of metaphor is among most of these poets a
matter of indifference; what is important is the ingenuity of the
conception expanded by metaphor, and the unlikely but witty
appropriateness of the metaphor selected.

Other examples of praise in the old eloquent mode include
Sonnet 22 in which the idea of Stella as the paragon of feminine
beauty is developed by a simple form of narration, and Sonnet
32 in which a listing of her spiritual virtues expands the old
conceit of the mistress as the most beautiful of all Nature's
creations. There is even one example of Rainolde's exercise of
"poetical narracoun": Sonnet 13 in which Astrophil relates how
Cupid emerged the victor in a contest with Jove and Mars as to
whose "armes the fairest were." It is Stella's picture on his
shield and a lock of her hair on his helmet which earns Cupid
the accolade.[34]

---

[34] Young has discovered in the description of the shield an allegorical
identification of Penelope Riche, but that does not alter the fact that the
poem is written according to the old notion of eloquence. See Young's
"English Petrarke," pp. 20-22.

The sequence also contains occasional examples of complaints written in the old manner. Sonnet 89 develops an analogy long popular in the courtly tradition: ". . . living thus in blackest winter night,/ I feele the flames of hottest sommer day." The same is true of Sonnet 108: ". . . in my woes for thee thou art my joy,/ And in my joyes for thee my only annoy."

In these poems Astrophil appears as the conventional lover with all the right symptoms, but as a poet who, in his dedication to the new concerns for originality and intellectual wit, displays a range of technical execution on every level of composition which the vernacular tradition had never before seen. In the feelings and attitudes they express, however, they assume un-critically the servant-mistress relationship and they confine their analysis of the various stages of that relationship to the more or less crude generalities of the courtly love psychology.

But there is another kind of poem in the sequence which considers the entire code of courtly love from a new perspective. In these poems Sidney follows the advice which in the *Arcadia* Musidorus offers to Pyrochles: "Separate yourself a little (if it be possible) and let your owne mind look to your owne pro-ceedings."[35] Sidney "separates" himself from his role as Astro-phil, the courtly lover, and examines the role itself. The new perspective has the advantage of greater objectivity and enables the poet to approach amorous experience analytically. He is able, for instance, to test the validity of courtly doctrine, in its original form, or as modified by neo-Platonic notions, against the empirical evidence of his own emotional experience.

The method is proclaimed in the opening two sonnets of the sequence as a source of originality and sincerity. Astrophil has begun by following the usual practice of laboring for the ap-propriate invention and seeking suggestions and inspiration in the works of other poets:

Loving in truth, and faine in verse my love to show,
That the deare She might take some pleasure of my paine:
Pleasure might cause her reade, reading might make her know,

[35] *The Complete Works of Sir Philip Sidney*, ed., A. Feuillerat, 4 vols. (Cambridge: University Press, 1912-26), I, p. 77.

Knowledge might pitie winne, and pitie grace obtaine,
I sought fit words to paint the blackest face of woe,
Studying inventions fine, her wits to entertaine:
Oft turning others' leaves, to see if thence would flow
Some fresh and fruitfull showers upon my sunne-burn'd
braine.

But the procedures are unsuccessful, and while still "great with child to speake, and helplesse in my throwes," his muse comes to his rescue: " 'Foole,' said my Muse to me, 'looke in thy heart and write.' " The Muse's advice is more than a conventional assertion of sincerity; it announces Sidney's intention to look directly at his own feelings rather than at the ways in which others have painted "the blackest face of woe." Analysis will take the place of description. The results are apparent in the second sonnet:

Not at first sight, nor with a dribbed shot
    Love gave the wound, which while I breathe will bleed:
    But knowne worth did in mine of time proceed,
Till by degrees it had full conquest got.
I saw and liked, I liked but loved not,
    I loved, but straight did not what *Love* decreed:
    At length to *Love's* decrees, I forc'd, agreed,
Yet with repining at so partiall lot.
    Now even that footstep of lost libertie
Is gone, and now like slave-borne *Muscovite*,
I call it praise to suffer Tyrannie;
    And now employ the remnant of my wit,
    To make my selfe beleeve, that all is well,
    While with a feeling skill I paint my hell.

The opening line indicates that the complaint is not to be another case history of a poet afflicted by the courtly malady. Courtly love is always love at first sight and often a matter of chance; but Astrophil's is founded, as Wyatt had recommended, on "knowne worth" and is a matter of choice.[36] In the beginning

---

[36] See Wyatt's "It was my choyse, yt was no chaunce," No. 121 in the Muir edition.

it had been rational and therefore moral.[37] The surrender to Cupid occurs in stages and over a period of time: first, the reluctant surrender to "Love's decrees," or passions; next, the loss of conscience, "that footstep of lost libertie"; and, finally, the use of "the remnant of my wit" to rationalize the rightness of servitude. Astrophil has not come out directly to condemn the love he is describing. He avoids making any explicit moral judgment; it is there only by implication.

The poem, then, dismisses the usual methods of finding suitable verbal equivalents for the emotions of unrequited love. Astrophil has looked into his passions and ignored the usual rhetorical approach.

Other sonnets follow the precedent set in Sonnet 2 by examining fully each of the stages enumerated in the sonnet by which passion gains sway over reason, or by dramatizing the conflict between reason and passion. Sonnet 4 examines the process of reasoning which has led Astrophil to identify Stella

---

[37] The question of whether love is based upon the "known worth" of its object, or whether the object becomes good because it is desired is debated in Shakespeare's *Troilus and Cressida* by Hector and Troilus in II, ii, ll. 51-93. Hector argues that Helen "is not worth what she doth cost/ The holding." But Troilus, seeing an analogy between his love for Cressida and Paris for Helen, disagrees and the debate proceeds:

> "*Tro.*: What is aught, but as 'tis valu'd?
>
> *Hector*: But value dwells not in particular will;
> It holds his estimate and dignity
> As well wherein 'tis precious of itself
> As in the prizer. 'Tis mad idolatry
> To make the service greater than the god;
> And the will dotes that is inclineable
> To what infectiously itself affects,
> Without some image of th' affected merit.
>
> *Tro.*: I take to-day a wife, and my election
> Is led on in the conduct of my will,
> My will enkindled by mine eyes and ears,
> Two traded pilots 'twixt the dangerous shores
> Of will and judgement: how may I avoid
> Although my will distaste what it elected,
> The wife I chose?

with virtue. The way in which the conflict caused by Virtue between "will" (passion) and "wit" (reason) is finally resolved is an example of how Astrophil has used "the remnant of my wit,/ To make my selfe beleeve, that all is well." After dismissing Virtue, "If vaine love have my simple soule opprest,/ Leave what thou likest not, deale not thou with it./ Thy scepter use in some old *Catoe's* brest," he proceeds to announce to Virtue that if he insists on meddling he will show him that his beloved is beyond reproach:

> But if that needs thou wilt usurping be,
> The litle reason that is left in me,
> And still th' effect of thy perswasions prove:
> I sweare, my heart such one shall shew to thee,
> That shrines in flesh so true a Deitie,
> That *Vertue*, thou thy selfe shalt be in love.

In other words, Astrophil would purge his passion by concentrating on the idea that the woman he loves is virtuous and that it is her virtue that he loves. But Sonnet 5 indicates that the enterprise has been a failure:

> It is most true, that eyes are form'd to serve
> The inward light: and that the heavenly part
> Ought to be king, from whose rules who do swerve,
> Rebels to Nature, strive for their owne smart.
> It is most true, what we call *Cupid's* dart,
> An image is, which for our selves we carve;
> And, fooles, adore in temple of our hart,
> Till that good God make church and Churchman starve.
> True, that true Beautie Vertue is indeed,
> Whereof this Beautie can be but a shade,
> Which elements with mortall mixture breed:
> True, that on earth we are but pilgrims made,
> And should in soule up to our countrey move:
> True, and yet true that I must *Stella* love.

Try as he will, Astrophil's interests cannot be transformed. He is not able to be Ficino's "contemplative" or even his

"human" lover; he remains, in the neo-Platonic view, a mere
"animal" lover. According to Ficino, all love has its beginnings,
just as Astrophil's has, with sight; but there resemblances
cease: "But the love of the contemplative man ascends from
sight into the mind; that of the voluptuous man descends from
sight into touch, and that of the practical man remains in the
form of sight. Love of the first is attracted to the highest
daemon rather than to the lowest, that of the second is drawn
to the lowest rather than to the highest, and that of the last
remains an equal distance from both. These three loves have
three names: love of the contemplative man is called divine;
that of the practical man, human; and that of the voluptuous
man, animal."[38] Astrophil has tried to become the contemplative lover. He sees properly a self-justifying rationalization
in the deterministic notion that to be struck by Cupid's dart is
to be "fated" to love, and he recognizes in the worship of Cupid
an heretical idolatry; but he is not able to alter his feelings.
Like Angelo in *Measure for Measure*, whose lust, ironically,
is stirred by Isabella's exceptional virtues, he is victimized by
Stella's moral beauty:

> The wisest scholler of the wight most wise
> By *Phoebus'* doome, with sugred sentence sayes,
> That Vertue, if it once met with our eyes,
> Strange flames of *Love* it in our soules would raise;
> But for that man with paine this truth descries,
> While he each thing in sense's ballance wayes,
> And so nor will, nor can, behold those skies
> Which inward sunne to *Heroicke* minde displaies,
> Vertue of late, with vertuous care to ster
> Love of her selfe, takes *Stella's* shape, that she
> To mortall eyes might sweetly shine in her.
> It is most true, for since I her did see,
> Vertue's great beautie in that face I prove,
> And find th'effect, for I do burne in love.

(No. 25)

[38] Marsilio Ficino, *Commentary on Plato's Symposium*, trans., Sears

There is nothing Platonic about the burning he suffers.

These poems suggest that Sidney did not seriously embrace neo-Platonism. He grants "that true Beautie Vertue is indeed," but rejects the notion that any woman can be its surrogate. He prefers to accept the irrascibility of the passions as a reality of man's condition. In other poems he openly attacks the Platonic notions that were so popular among his contemporaries:

> I beg no subject to use eloquence,
> Nor in hid wayes to guide Philosophy:
> Looke at my hands for no such quintessence;
> But know that I in pure simplicitie,
> Breathe out the flames which burne within my heart.
>
> (No. 28, ll. 9-13)

He is impatient with the absolute dualism of the Platonic view:

> A strife is growne betweene *Vertue* and *Love*,
>> While each pretends that *Stella* must be his:
>> Her eyes, her lips, her all, saith *Love* do this,
> Since they do weare his badge, most firmely prove.
> But *Vertue* thus that title doth disprove,
>> That *Stella* (ô deare name) that *Stella* is
>> That vertuous soule, sure heire of heav'nly blisse:
> Not this faire outside, which our hearts doth move.
>> And therefore, though her beautie and her grace
> Be *Love's* indeed, in *Stella's* selfe he may
> By no pretence claime any maner place.
> Well *Love*, since this demurre our sute doth stay,
>> Let *Vertue* have that *Stella's* selfe; yet thus,
>> That *Vertue* but that body graunt to us.
>
> (No. 52)

The cynical tone of the argument is unmistakable: If Stella's body isn't really Stella, then let Virtue give Astrophil her body; no one will be the worse, since Virtue will still have the real Stella, the real Stella will still be "sure heire of heav'nly bliss,"

R. Jayne, University of Missouri Studies, XIX, No. 1 (Columbia, Missouri: University of Missouri Press, 1944), p. 193.

and Astrophil and Love will have gotten what they wanted. The source of that cynicism is dissatisfaction with an idea which distorts the reality of experience. One may, according to Sidney, grant the supremacy of virtue, but when that supremacy is affirmed at the expense of the "whole" man, the truth is distorted. Virtue may inspire love, but it is impossible to deny the body: "So while thy beautie drawes the heart to love,/ As fast thy Vertue bends that love to good:/ 'But ah,' Desire still cries, 'give me some food.'" (No. 71, ll. 12-14)

It is impossible, finally, to be sure of what the motives behind such poems are. It may be that they only exploit the current psychology for the sake of a fiction which met the age's demand for a love poetry that was original and of substantial intellectual content. Or R. B. Young's interpretation may provide the answer.[39] But whatever the underlying intentions of the sequence may have been, these analytical sonnets reveal a lively intelligence psychologically and ethically engaged by the subject of human love and the difficulties of attempting to establish a means of distinguishing between eroticism and genuine human love—between a passion, virtually deified by courtly love doctrine, which "oft so clings to my pure Love, that I/ One from the other scarcely can descrie,/ While each doth blow the fier on my hart" (No. 72, ll. 2-4), and a virtuous love which, unlike the neo-Platonic, recognizes that men have bodies as well as souls.

There is no indication in *Astrophil and Stella* that Sidney ever reached a solution. He apparently settled instead for the commonly accepted distinction between profane and divine love, between a "love which reachest but to dust" and a love which aspires to God and the subsequent rejection of all temporality. At least that is what his remarks in the *Defense* suggest.

The difference between the two kinds of complaint in *Astrophil and Stella*—the one, confined entirely to the precepts of courtly love doctrine, the other, conceived psychologically— is significant to the intellectualization of the amatory lyric. So

[39] "English Petrarke."

long as Sidney and his contemporaries maintain their allegiance to courtly love, they are committed to the description of the generalized emotions that are defined by its doctrines. Courtly love is at best a civilizing code of manners. As a psychology it has the same limitations as any methodology which reduces human experience to arbitrary and overly simplified postulates. It is of little use to the poet whose interests are introspective. As a literary doctrine it remains, at this late date, a code of manners stressing intensity and conformity of feeling. In the long run any poem written within its limitations, tends to sound like any other poem written within the same limitations. The completed poem can only be at best a refinement of the premises it assumes. It cannot go beyond them. Sidney's "When sorrow (using mine owne fier's might)" which represents about as complete a mastery of Petrarchan metaphor as can be found among the Elizabethans writing in the "sugared" style, will illustrate my point:

> When sorrow (using mine owne fier's might)
>> Melts downe his lead into my boyling brest,
>> Through that darke fornace to my hart opprest,
> There shines a joy from thee my only light;
> But soone as thought of thee breeds my delight,
>> And my yong soule flutters to thee his nest,
>> Most rude dispaire my daily unbidden guest,
> Clips streight my wings, streight wraps me in his night,
>> And makes me then bow downe my head, and say,
> Ah what doth *Phoebus'* gold that wretch availe,
> Whom iron doores do keepe from use of day?
> So strangely (alas) thy works in me prevaile,
>> That in my woes for thee thou art my joy,
>> And in my joyes for thee my only annoy.
>
> (No. 108)

The old paradox stated in the closing couplet is cleverly expanded by the interplay of the images of darkness and light, the principle of order being furnished by the code of love. But the implications of the state of despair, the subject of the poem, are limited, necessarily, to those permitted by the courtly doctrine. The source of grief is taken for granted and left unexplored, while the metaphor is developed for its own sake. Because in this instance Sidney's only interest is in painting "the blackest face of woe," the sadness expressed by the poem is no different from that expressed by the numerous poems in Tottel's *Miscellany* which also describe by various kinds of analogy the same experience. All that the poem manages to say is summed up in the two-hundred-year-old platitude: "in my woes for thee thou art my joy,/ And in my joyes for thee my only annoy." The rest of the poem is ornament.

The Aristotelian psychology can also become, as a reading of any standard anthology of sixteenth-century English poetry will indicate, a facile means of reducing experience to overly simplified generalities; but it may also introduce a range of implication which the self-contained system of courtly love excludes as irrelevant. From a sixteenth-century point of view, at least, it views erotic love realistically, and it encourages an analytical in place of a purely descriptive approach to feeling. Whereas the code of love is primarily concerned with the description of feeling, taking more or less for granted its sources and motivations, the Aristotelian psychology that is the basis of Hooker's ethical system is mainly concerned with its sources and motivations. Its potentialities as such are demonstrable in:

Thou blind man's marke, thou foole's selfe chosen snare,
Fond fancie's scum, and dregs of scattred thought,
Band of all evils, cradle of causelesse care,
Thou web of will, whose end is never wrought;

Desire, desire I have too dearely bought,
With price of mangled mind thy worthlesse ware,
Too long, too long asleepe thou hast me brought,
Who should my mind to higher things prepare.

But yet in vaine thou hast my ruine sought,
In vaine thou madest me to vaine things aspire,
In vaine thou kindlest all thy smokie fire;

For vertue hath this better lesson taught,
Within my selfe to seeke my onelie hire:
Desiring nought but how to kill desire.

The poem is within the tradition of the penitential lyric. The doctrine of contrition furnishes the principle of organization just as it does in Wyatt's "Ffarewell Love and all thy Lawes for ever" and in Surrey's "Brittle beauty whom nature made so frail." It functions as a structural principle in the same way that the doctrine of courtly love functions in the conventional love complaint, "When sorrow (using mine owne fier's might)." The octave begins with a recognition of desire as the source of all sin and concludes with a hymnlike lamentation for having lived a life of sin. The first half of the sestet is an avowal of amendment stressing the baseness of the sin to be renounced; the second half of the sestet emphasizes that the poem is a declaration of "perfect contrition" rather than "attrition": an avowal of repentance inspired by a hatred of sin and a love of virtue and God rather than merely by a fear of punishment or by the recognition of the baseness of sin. The structure, in short, is theological.

The poem, however, is not simply a statement of contrition in the general terms of the bare theological doctrine. It is a closely reasoned analysis of the personal source of sin employing the psychology which Wyatt had frequently used in his love poems. In his only penitential sonnet, "Ffarewell Love and all thy Lawes for ever," Wyatt deals with moral turpitude in general terms, attributing it simply to "Love":

In blynde error when I did perseuer,
Thy sherpe repulse that pricketh ay so sore
Hath taught me to sett in tryfels no store
And scape fourth, syns libertie is lever.

But Sidney's treatment of the subject, insofar as it goes beyond Wyatt's, uses the same technique of analysis that Wyatt had used in poems such as "It was my choyse, yt was no chaunce." Sidney's poem concentrates on the psychological sources of sin in the manner of Wyatt's best verse: desire's object is self-chosen; with the aid of the imagination it overcomes reason and directs will to an unobtainable end; it lures reason to self-destruction, causing temporal goods to be placed before the true good. But paraphrase misses the stylistic qualifications which result from Sidney's use of Christian psychology as a refractive instrument to analyze what the more general doctrine of penance had brought into focus. By viewing his personal sin through a coherent system of ideas—which as a sixteenth-century Christian he took to be truly interpretive of human nature—he is able to examine his private experience with precision. Thought gains precision to the extent that the principles of the rationale by which it proceeds are adequate to human experience, and to the extent that the terminology of that rationale is sharply defined. In both respects Christian psychology is superior to the courtly code of manners.

Finally, Sidney's poem shows how the analytical method absorbed stylistic refinements from the eloquent tradition. From the opening series of rhetorical apostrophes to desire, with their calculated use of alliteration, to the paradoxical concluding line the poem makes use of many eloquent devices. But they are functional here rather than ornamental. Thus though the poem is in the courtly style, it is a contemplative poem, employing a method of self-analysis which Wyatt had used earlier and which Greville and Donne were to use to write some of the great contemplative poems in the tradition.

SPENSER: THE *Amoretti*

Few of Sidney's contemporaries approach him in ability. For the most part they are not interested in the analytical method, and their efforts on behalf of originality are largely confined to variations of old conceits or to a facile neo-Platonism. Even Spenser, who in so many ways is the innovator, seems mainly satisfied as a writer of sonnets to follow the conventions of his eloquent predecessors. Working within the several genres of amorous lyric, he often uses the old modes of *dispositio* which had been developed in conjunction with those genres. Sonnets 9, 15, and 26 use varieties of the catalogue for the purpose of eulogy. Others, such as Nos. 64 and 88, suggest Tottel as a source. And throughout the sequence, the burning and freezing so common in the lover's complaint are played upon and expanded according to the rules of the Code.

But if there is little in the way of technique in these sonnets that is dramatically new, refinements of syntax and facility in the handling of the sonnet structure are often as impressive as Sidney's. There is that same control of discursive exposition in certain sonnets in the sequence that is evident in *Astrophil and Stella*—that same ability to develop a closely reasoned argument in only fourteen lines. These poems are probably among the later poems to be written in the sequence, although there is no way of proving it. Certainly they suggest an advance in skill as well as in conception over such sonnets as No. 30 which echoes the poetry of an earlier period:

> My loue is lyke to yse, and I to fyre;
>> how comes it then that this her cold so great
>> is not dissolu'd through my so hot desyre,
>> but harder growes the more I her intreat?
> Or how comes it that my exceeding heat
>> is not delayd by her hart frosen cold:
>> but that I burne much more in boyling sweat,
>> and feele my flames augmented manifold?
> What more miraculous thing may be told
>> that fire which all thing melts, should harden yse:
>> and yse which is congeald with sencelesse cold,
>> should kindle fyre by wonderfull deuyse?
> Such is the powre of loue in gentle mind,
>> that it can alter all the course of kynd.[40]

The method of elaboration, as well as the diction, imagery, and the controlling paradox, suggests the old manner. It is illustrative—a matter of elaborating a commonplace rather than of reasoning from premises to a conclusion. The new

[40] All quotations from Spenser are from *Spenser's Minor Poems*, ed., Ernest De Sélincourt (Oxford: Clarendon Press, 1910).

method, along with certain other refinements, is apparent in Sonnet 41:

> Is it her nature or is it her will,
> to be so cruell to an humbled foe?
> if nature, then she may it mend with skill,
> if will, then she at will may will forgoe.
> But if her nature and her wil be so,
> that she will plague the man that loues her most:
> and take delight t'encrease a wretches woe,
> then all her natures goodly guifts are lost.
> And that same glorious beauties ydle boast,
> is but a bayt such wretches to beguile:
> as being long in her loues tempest tost,
> she meanes at last to make her piteous spoyle.
> O fayrest fayre let neuer it be named,
> that so fayre beauty was so fowly shamed.

The lover's analysis of the causes for the cruel way in which his mistress has treated him are indicative of the new concern for intellectuality in verse. It is obviously not advanced as a serious analysis, and, although it concludes with a persuasion based on a moral principle, it is not in any sense concerned with the moral implications of the servant-mistress relationship. Nevertheless, it is impressive for its ingenuity of logic and the skill with which it is expressed. There is also a kind of verbal play which anticipates the Shakespeare of the sonnets in such lines as: "If *will*, then she at *will*, may *will* forgoe," and "O *fayrest fayre* let neuer it be named,/ that so *fayre* beauty was so *fowly* shamed."

But it is primarily in his effort to synthesize Platonic and Christian notions of love that Spenser as a writer of sonnets distinguishes himself among his contemporaries. The differences elaborated in the *Fowre Hymnes* between sacred and profane love and heavenly and earthly beauty are assumed as the premises of the rationale advanced in the *Amoretti*. Sonnet 3 is one of several in which the poet identifies the mistress with the Divine Idea and the Divine Idea with the Godhead. The mistress, Beatrice-like, will raise the lover from baseness and cause him to contemplate in her "huge brightnesse" the heavenly source of all love and beauty:

> The souerayne beauty which I doo admyre,
>> witnesse the world how worthy to be prayzed:
>> the light wherof hath kindled heauenly fyre,
>> in my fraile spirit by her from basenesse raysed.
> That being now with her huge brightnesse dazed,
>> base thing I can no more endure to view:
>> but looking still on her I stand amazed,
>> at wondrous sight of so celestiall hew.
> So when my toung would speak her praises dew,
>> it stopped is with thoughts astonishment:
>> and when my pen would write her titles true,
>> it rauisht is with fancies wonderment:
> Yet in my hart I then both speake and write
>> the wonder that my wit cannot endite.

The seriousness with which such Platonic notions are advanced in the sequence will always be a matter of conjecture, especially difficult to settle because of the numerous poems throughout the sequence in which the old courtly views are assumed without the slightest signs of qualification by the Platonic. Nor is there any explanation to be discovered from the arrangement of the poems in the sequence. There are possibly identifiable groups within the sequence but no discernible over-all principle of progression, and one is left with two possible explanations: either such sonnets as No. 3 are experiments in neo-Platonism and are to be regarded as serious insofar as they use Platonism to express feelings of genuine admiration for a real lady, or they are among the poems in the sequence composed at a fairly late date which bear witness to a genuine conversion to neo-Platonic doctrine. One thing, however, of which we can be fairly certain is that they reflect Spenser's sensitivity to the general feeling in the period that love is an immoral subject and therefore not suitable as a subject for the English Muse. It was in response to such feeling that he wrote the *Hymnes*, "Of Heavenly Love" and "Of Heavenly Beavty."

Hauing in the greener times of my youth, composed these former two Hymnes in the praise of Loue and beautie, and finding that the same too much pleased those of like age and disposition, which being too vehemently caried with that kind of affection, do rather sucke out poyson to their strong passion, then hony to their honest delight, I was moued by the one of you two most excellent Ladies, to call in the same. But being vnable so to doe, by reason that many copies thereof were formerly scattered abroad, I resolued at least to amend, and by way of retraction to reforme them, making in stead of those two Hymnes of earthly or naturall love and beautie, two others of heauenly and celestiall.[41]

But to return to the *Amoretti* and the Christian-Platonic synthesis. The ennobling power of the higher love praised in Sonnet 3 requires the vigorous cooperation of the lover. He must discipline his contemplation, being careful to avoid any contaminating thoughts which might corrupt his devotions.

Let not one sparke of filthy lustfull fyre
    breake out, that may her sacred peace molest:
    ne one light glance of sensuall desyre
    Attempt to work her gentle mindes vnrest.
But pure affections bred in spotlesse brest,
    and modest thoughts breathd from wel tempred sprites
    goe visit her in her chast bowre of rest,
    accompanyde with angelick delightes.
There fill your selfe with those most ioyous sights,
    the which my selfe could neuer yet attayne:
    but speake no word to her of these sad plights,
    which her too constant stiffenesse doth constrayn.
Onely behold her rare perfection,
    and blesse your fortunes fayre election.

(Sonnet 84)

[41] "To the right honorable and most vertuous Ladies, the . . . Countesse of Cumberland, and the . . . Countesse of Warwicke."

The source of both the higher and lower loves (the celestial fire and the fire of passion) is the Godhead; both are therefore good. The lower love is essential to the reproduction of life:

> Thereby they all do liue, and moued are
> To multiply the likenesse of their kynd,
> Whilest they seeke onely, without further care,
> To quench the flame, which they in burning fynd.
> ("Of Love," ll. 99-102)

Only man loves for a reason beyond reproduction:

> But man, that breathes a more immortall mynd,
> Not for lusts sake, but for eternitie,
> Seekes to enlarge his lasting progenie.

> For hauing yet in his deducted spright,
> Some sparks remaining of that heauenly fyre,
> He is enlumind with that goodly light,
> Vnto like goodly semblant to aspyre:
> Therefore in choice of loue, he doth desyre
> That seemes on earth most heauenly, to embrace,
> That same is Beautie, borne of heauenly race.
> ("Of Love," ll. 103-12)

But man is frail, and through his frailty he is apt to allow Cupid the opportunity to exercise his tyranny; he may allow himself to be enslaved by the very beauty he ought to be transported by:

> For sure of all, that in this mortall frame
> Contained is, nought more diuine doth seeme,
> Or that resembleth more th'immortall flame
> Of heauenly light, then Beauties glorious beame.
> What wonder then, if with such rage extreme
> Fraile men, whose eyes seek heauenly things to see,
> At sight thereof so much enrauisht bee?

> Which well perceiuing, that imperious boy,
> Doth therwith tip his sharp empoisned darts;
> Which glancing through the eyes with countenance coy,
> Rest not, till they haue pierst the trembling harts,

And kindled flame in all their inner parts,
Which suckes the blood, and drinketh vp the lyfe
Of carefull wretches with consuming griefe.

("Of Love," ll. 113-26)

When the lover is successful in his contemplation, he sees in his lady's eyes only "the liuing fire/ Kindled aboue unto the maker neere." Cupid is forced into exile; the fire of the higher love is free to work its effects:

More than most faire, full of the liuing fire,
Kindled aboue vnto the make neere:
   no eies but ioyes, in which al powers conspire,
   that to the world naught else be counted deare.
Thrugh your bright beames doth not the blinded guest,
   shoot out his darts to base affections wound:
   but Angels come to lead fraile mindes to rest
   in chast desires on heauenly beauty bound.

(Sonnet 8, ll. 1-8)

When the lover fails, as he is bound occasionally to do, he must recognize that the agonies of unrequited love that accompany his failure are divine punishment to be endured as retribution:

When I behold that beauties wonderment,
   and rare perfection of each goodly part:
   of natures skill the onely complement,
   I honor and admire the makers art.
But when I feele the bitter balefull smart,
   which her fayre eyes vnwares doe worke in mee:
   that death out of theyr shiny beames doe dart,
   I thinke that I a new *Pandora* see;
Whom all the Gods in councell did agree,
   into this sinfull world from heauen to send:
   that she to wicked men a scourge should bee,
   for all their faults with which they did offend.
But since ye are my scourge I will intreat,
   that for my faults ye will me gently treat.

(Sonnet 24)

[207]

The myth alluded to here is a classical one, but the parodoxical powers of the lady's eyes derive from the fact that she is God's surrogate. She is both judge and redeemer, punishing the novitiate for his sins and rewarding him with something akin to the ecstasy of contemplating the countenance of God when his contemplation has been successfully purged of all baseness. She is also the one who has made him impatient with temporality itself by inspiring in him a longing for the eternal (Sonnet 83) and who has been the source of the inspiration he has needed to push on with the *Faerie Queene*: "the contemplation of whose heauenly hew,/ my spirit to an higher pitch will rayse." (Sonnet 80, ll. 11-12)

Platonism in the *Amoretti* is not, however, always the source of such elevated reflection. On at least two occasions Spenser expresses his disenchantment with his lady. In Sonnet 45, with a wit that is more commonly associated with Donne than with Spenser, the lover urges her to pity him so as to be able the better to satisfy her own self-love.

> Leaue lady in your glasse of christall clene,
>   Your goodly selfe for euermore to vew:
>   and in my selfe, my inward selfe I meane,
>   most liuely lyke behold your semblant trew.
> Within my hart, though hardly it can shew
>   thing so diuine to vew of earthly eye,
>   the fayre Idea of your celestiall hew,
>   and euery part remaines immortally:
> And were it not that through your cruelty,
>   with sorrow dimmed and deformd it were:
>   the goodly ymage of your visnomy,
>   clearer then christall would therein appere.
> But if your selfe in me ye playne will see,
>   remoue the cause by which your fayre beames
>   darkned be.

The wit here is present in the ingenious way in which the Platonic notion of spiritualized love is twisted to serve the purpose of the poem. Since nothing can be done about the lady's narcissism, the lover determines to turn it if he can to his advantage. If she will change mirrors, if she will stop admiring her "goodly selfe" in her own mirror and look into his heart, she will see there something more than her physical likeness; she will see "the fayre Idea" of her "celestiall hew." (The intended inference here, I think, is that in so doing she will see eventually how far she falls short of his idealized image of her.) But there is a difficulty: her reflection in the mirror of his heart will be clouded, "with sorrow dimmed and deformd," because she has been cruelly indifferent to him. She may therefore satisfy her own vanity the better if she will give him some satisfaction, since by doing so she will cleanse the mirror of his heart of the very things which now blur it.[42]

A similar disenchantment is expressed in Sonnet 79, this time with a wit that is more suggestive of Shakespeare than of Donne. The distinction between physical and spiritual beauty that is fundamental in Spenser's Christianized Platonism provides the standard in terms of which the disillusioned lover has judged his mistress and found her wanting. Men have rightly called her fair, for she is—at least in appearance. His disillusion is revealed indirectly in the way he gently rebukes her. The distinction between physical and spiritual beauty is of course a commonplace in the tradition, but Spenser develops it here with grace, restraint, and dignity.

> Men call you fayre, and you doe credit it,
> > For that your selfe ye dayly such doe see:
> > but the trew fayre, that is the gentle wit,
> > and vertuous mind, is much more praysd of me.
> For all the rest, how euer fayre it be,
> > shall turne to nought and loose that glorious hew:
> > but onely that is permanent and free
> > from frayle corruption, that doth argue you
> > to be diuine and borne of heauenly seed:

---

[42] I find that in my reading of this poem I have been partially anticipated by Murray Krieger. See *A Window to Criticism* (Princeton: Princeton University Press, 1964), pp. 83-85.

deriu'd from that fayre Spirit, from whom al true
and perfect beauty did at first proceed.
He onely fayre, and what he fayre hath made,
all other fayre lyke flowres vntymely fade.

Spenser is completely in control of his subject and technique.
The graceful variations in the relation of line and syntax, the
cadences, and the skilful repetition and play upon the word
"fair" anticipate the Shakespeare of the sonnets.[43]

Sidney and Spenser, as the poets receiving the fullest recognition of their contemporaries, established the norms of the
sugared style, and the majority of the minor sonneteers merely
perpetuate the genteel platitudes of the tradition or indulge in
extravagant excesses of conceit. Lodge adopts the pastoral
diction apparent in Sidney's songs and, along with Samuel
Daniel, carries on the neo-Platonic modes of polite compliment.
Giles Fletcher, in spite of his claims of originality and high
seriousness, writes mainly in the old sensual vein. Barnabe
Griffen's obsession with rhetorical schemes of repetition resulted
in poems which were easy targets for Sir John Davies. Griffen's
Sonnet 47 (in *Fidessa*) illustrates the extremes to which the
quest for originality was taken:

> I See, I hear, I feel, I know, I rue
> My fate, my fame, my pain, my loss, my fall;
> Mishap, reproach, disdain, a crown, her hue;
> Cruel, still flying, false, fair, funeral
> To cross, to shame, bewitch, deceive, and kill
> My first proceedings in their flowing bloom.
> My worthless pen fast chained to my will,
> My erring life through an uncertain doom,
> My thoughts that yet in lowliness do mount,
> My heart the subject of her tyranny:

[43] L. C. Knights in his excellent essay, "Shakespeare's Sonnets,"
Scrutiny, III (September 1934), 133-160, reprinted in *A Casebook on
Shakespeare's Sonnets*, eds., Gerald Willen and Victor B. Reed (New
York: Thomas Y. Crowell Co., 1964), pp. 173-97, observes that "the
Sonnets take their start from something that can . . . be called the
Spenserian mode . . ." (p. 178).

What now remains, but her severe account
Of murder's crying guilt (foul butchery!)
She was unhappy in her cradle breath;
That given was, to be another's death.[44]

From Sidney's *Astrophil and Stella* to Davison's miscellany, *A Poetical Rhapsody* (1604), the eloquent tradition is at a standstill. Given its controlling intention and the methods which from 1557 on had been in a process of development, it can proceed no further. It is as Thomas Carew describes it in "An Elegie upon the death of the Deane of Pauls, Dr. Iohn Donne": ". . . a garden with Pedantic weedes O'rspred," a poetry written in "soft melting Phrases" by poets who "each in others dust had rak'd for Ore."

Shakespeare's sugared sonnets are the obvious exception. In range of feeling and attitude and in grace of execution they are equalled only by the best efforts of Sidney, who was Shakespeare's only serious rival as a writer of sonnets. Despite signs of the carelessness and haste that were always characteristic of Shakespeare's work and some obviously inferior poems, his sonnets represent the best that the eloquent tradition was to achieve in the sixteenth century.

[44] Sidney Lee, *Elizabethan Sonnets*, II.

CHAPTER VI

Shakespeare's Sonnets

SHAKESPEARE, like Sidney before him, is impatient with the unimaginative repetition of Petrarchan themes and contemptuous of the excesses that the eloquent poetic has encouraged in the verse of his contemporaries. The evidence is abundant in the Dark Lady and Rival Poet groups.

Although the Dark Lady theory may have its basis in a real love affair, it is impossible to ignore her opposite, the Fair Mistress of the Petrarchan tradition, who always stands behind the Dark Lady in the Sonnets. The Fair Lady's prominence, together with the old habit of cataloguing her graces, is surely an indication of a satirical intent in "My mistress' eyes are nothing like the sun" (Sonnet 130).[1] Whatever we may conjecture about the Dark Lady's identity—whether she is a fiction conceived to mock Petrarchan conventions or a real mistress— the final couplet leaves no question as to how Shakespeare feels about extravagant praise: "And yet, by heaven, I think my love as rare/ As any she belied with false compare." Comparisons such as those he has enumerated and dismissed in the lines preceding are deceitful misrepresentations, a betrayal of the lady they are intended to honor.

A more complicated form of mockery occurs in the two sonnets following. In Sonnet 131 its targets are again the fair mistress, this time specifically her indifference which causes the lover to describe her beauty as proud and cruel, and the lover's customary habit of praising chastity while at the same time complaining of the great discomforts it is causing him.

> Thou are as tyrannous, so as thou art,
> As those whose beauties proudly make them cruel;
> For well thou know'st to my dear doting heart

---

[1] All quotations from the Sonnets are from Edward Hubler's *Shakespeare's Songs and Poems* (New York: McGraw-Hill, 1959).

Thou art the fairest and most precious jewel.
Yet in good faith some say that thee behold,
Thy face hath not the power to make love groan:
To say they err I dare not be so bold,
Although I swear it to myself alone.
And to be sure that is not false I swear,
A thousand groans, but thinking on thy face,
One on another's neck, do witness bear
Thy black is fairest in my judgment's place.
　　In nothing art thou black save in thy deeds,
　　And thence this slander, as I think, proceeds.

The method here is again essentially one of contradiction. The
poem opens with the claim that the Lady, even though she is
dark ("so as thou art"), can be just as proud and cruel and
just as tyrannical in her power over a lover's affections as any
fair mistress. However she may appear to others who maintain
that only a fair mistress has such powers, she has made a slave
of the speaker and fully exploited the advantage she has gained.
The sense of the seventh and eighth lines is ironic: "Who am
I to deny the venerable assumption that gentlemen prefer
blondes?" But if he will not openly deny what others have said,
"a thousand groans" bear witness to the fact that her swarthy
complexion has had the very effect upon him that only fair
mistresses are supposed to have on lovers. The final couplet, too,
upsets a convention by admitting that her behavior alone—her
black deeds—have given rise to the belief that she is not "fair."
Her lack of chastity may have caused others, but not the speaker,
to deny her beauty.

In Sonnet 132, again contrary to convention, the Dark Lady
has not been pitilessly indifferent. She has seen in his eyes the
pain her disdain has caused him:

　　　Thine eyes I love, and they as pitying me,
　　　Knowing thy heart torments me with disdain,
　　　Have put on black and loving mourners be,
　　　Looking with pretty ruth upon my pain.

The argument now takes an ingenious turn, and in a way which again contradicts the conventional plea. Seeing that the Lady pities him, the lover asks her, by way of a pun which violates drawing-room decorum, to spend the night with him:

> And truly not the morning sun of heaven
> Better becomes the grey cheeks of th' east,
> Nor that full star that ushers in the even
> Doth half that glory to the sober west,
> As those two mourning eyes become thy face:
> O, let it then as well beseem thy heart
> To mourn for me, since mourning doth thee grace,
> And suit thy pity like in every part.

The Lady's *mourning* eyes have become *morning* eyes. The couplet, too, gains in point when the convention it contradicts is recognized. Customarily, the lover pledges undying service to the lady, regardless of whether or not she graces him with her favor; furthermore, that service derives from his recognition that her physical beauty is a reflection of spiritual beauty. Now consider Shakespeare's couplet: "Then will I swear beauty herself is black,/ And all they foul that thy complexion lack." If she will spend the night with him and show "in every part" the pity her eyes have shown him, he will swear to a willful confusion of appearance and reality.

The Dark Lady may be more than a fiction created to mock the courtly conventions of praise, complaint, and plea, but there is little in the sonnets just discussed to indicate a more substantial identity. If she was indeed at one time Shakespeare's mistress, as other sonnets in the Dark Lady group suggest, the liberties he takes with Petrarchan materials in such sonnets as Nos. 130, 131, and 132 are, nonetheless, an indication of how indifferently he valued them.

In the Rival Poet group Shakespeare's targets are the insincerity and exaggeration that the eloquent poetic has produced in the verse of a rival. Sonnet 21, the first of the group, attacks the old habits of praise in a way that recalls Sidney. Extravagant comparisons are a weak substitute for the truth and are more suited to the peddler hawking his wares in the market place than to a lover sincerely praising a lady:

So is it not with me as with that Muse,
Stirr'd by a painted beauty to his verse,
Who heaven itself for ornament doth use,
And every fair with his fair doth rehearse,
Making a couplement of proud compare
With sun and moon, with earth and sea's rich gems,
With April's first-born flowers, and all things rare
That heaven's air in this huge rondure hems:
O let me, true in love, but truly write,
And then believe me, my love is as fair
As any mother's child, though not so bright
As those gold candles fix'd in heaven's air:
    Let them say more that like of hearsay well;
    I will not praise that purpose not to sell.

The Rival Poet's identity will doubtless always remain a matter for conjecture, but we can at least be certain of one thing. In Shakespeare's eyes he was guilty of rhetorical extravagance and vulnerable to the charge that he was more concerned with manner than with matter.

That charge is extended in Sonnets 32 and 82 to include the entire school of ornate verse. In the former the poet, referring to his own "poor rude lines" as "outstripped by every pen," asks the young man to read them for the true feelings they express and not for their style.

Reserve them for my love, not for their rhyme,
Exceeded by the heights of happier men.
O, then vouchsafe me but this loving thought:
"Had my friend's Muse grown with this growing age,
A dearer birth than this his love had brought
To march in ranks of better equipage;
    But since he died, and poets better prove,
    Theirs for their style I'll read, his for his love."

Again in Sonnet 82 the speaker allows that others may surpass him in eloquence, but

                   yet when thy have devis'd
    What strained touches rhetoric can lend,

Thou truly fair wert truly sympathiz'd
In true plain words by thy true telling friend.

The position that "true plain words" will suffice and that the
"colours" of rhetoric had best be saved for those who need them
is also taken in Sonnet 101: "Truth needs no colour, with his
colour fix'd;/ Beauty no pencil, beauty's truth to lay." Again
in Sonnet 103, Shakespeare says that a true rather than a
rhetorical description of the young man will be sufficient praise:

The argument, all bare, is of more worth
Than when it hath my added praise beside.
O blame me not, if I no more can write!
Look in your glass, and there appears a face
That over-goes my blunt invention quite,
Dulling my lines and doing me disgrace.
Were it not sinful then, striving to mend,
To mar the subject that before was well?
For to no other pass my verses tend
Than of your graces and your gifts to tell;
    And more, much more, than in my verse can sit,
    Your own glass shows you when you look in it.

Shakespeare, as any reader of the sonnets knows, can be just
as extravagantly rhetorical as any of his contemporaries; and
as with Sidney in his "anti-Petrarchan sonnets" these claims by
Shakespeare must be read as examples of skillful praise—as
poems in which invention is based upon the distinction assumed
in the current poetic between matter and manner. Nevertheless,
the criticism expressed of current literary practices tends to be
borne out by the sequence as a whole. Extravagant rhetoric in
the sonnets does occur, but not nearly so often as in the verse
of Shakespeare's minor contemporaries. And when it does it
usually takes the form of intellectual play, in ingenious puns
and arguments and in complex grammatical tropes.

The range of style in the sequence is wide—from the decorously ornate style of Sonnet 7, "Lo, in the orient when the
gracious light/ Lifts up his burning head," to the plain, direct

style of Sonnet 146, "Poor soul, the centre of my sinful earth,/ Fool'd by these rebel pow'rs that thee array" but the predominant style, at its purest in the early poems, is one of graceful, courtly compliment. It affects a simple, conversational intimacy; but it is not the old plain style which still appears occasionally at end-century, for instance in Ralegh. It avoids, in fact, those very colloquialisms that Ralegh, as Wyatt and Gascoigne had before him, deliberately cultivates as plain, forthright speech in opposition to what he regarded as the new-fangled sophistic of the court.[2] In the early sonnets the style assumes an intimacy between the speaker and the young man addressed which expresses itself in polite colloquialisms and often a tone that is gently chiding:

> Thou that art now the world's fresh ornament
> And only herald to the gaudy spring,
> Within thine own bud buriest thy content,
> And, tender churl, mak'st waste in niggarding.
> (No. 1)

> Then, beauteous niggard, why dost thou abuse
> The bounteous largess given thee to give?
> Profitless usurer, why dost thou use
> So great a sum of sums, yet canst not live?
> (No. 4)

> O, none but unthrifts! Dear my love, you know
> You had a father: let your son say so.
> (No. 13)

But such charges of churlish niggardness and prodigality are decorously polite in the highly complimentary contexts in which they appear. Forthrightness here is a convention assumed.

The differences between the old plain style and the Shakespearean version, at least in these early poems, derive ultimately from differences of attitude and intention. They are essentially

[2] As Hubler points out, "No one could mistake the new poetry [of which Shakespeare's sonnets are representative] for speech. It is characterized by its purged vocabulary, its word patterns and word play, its richness and melody." *Shakespeare's Songs and Poems,* xxi.

the same differences that distinguish Marlowe's "Come live with me and be my love" and Ralegh's "Reply." Marlowe's poem is a charming appeal to what man in every century has found attractive—escape into the Idyllic. Ralegh's answer insists upon confronting the world as it is, directly and without apology. Marlowe's concern is to express gracefully the pastoral impulse and that concern dictates style and tone; style and tone in Ralegh's poem are dictated by a concern to confront the realities of man's estate: *et in Arcadia ego*. Shakespeare's sonnets urging the young man to marry in order to preserve his beauty and to defy time, as well as the majority of those in which he promises the same young man immortality in verse, are not escapist in the sense that the Marlowe poem is; but they are like the Marlowe poem in that they do not seriously confront the serious issues they raise. Children are not the answer to the threat which time poses to one's identity.[3] Neither is the promise of immortality in verse. Nor is it likely that the poet who within a decade or so would write *Hamlet* and *Macbeth* seriously thought so. The intent of these poems is not to persuade but to praise. Style in these poems reflects that intention by carefully observing courtly decorum even while assuming intimacy.

It is, however, a style which is rich in possibilities. In Sonnet I the style produces an effect that is new to English verse. Transience is of course among the oldest of subjects. What is new in the poem is an awareness—perhaps it is an effect of the concern of humanism for temporal as well as eternal values—of the fact that the very awareness of the impermanence of beauty is a necessary condition of our appreciation of it. As a poet in our own century has written in lines which strongly suggest the Shakespearean sensibility:

> Death is the mother of beauty . . .
> She makes the willow shiver in the sun
> For maidens who were wont to sit and gaze
> Upon the grass, relinquished to their feet.

[3] But for a different view see Hubler, *The Sense of Shakespeare's Sonnets* (Princeton: Princeton University Press, 1952), pp. 64-77.

She causes boys to pile new plums and pears
On disregarded plate.
(Wallace Stevens, "Sunday Morning")

The opening quatrain of Sonnet 1 expresses that awareness beautifully:

From fairest creatures we desire increase,
That thereby beauty's rose might never die,
But as the riper should by time decease,
His tender heir might bear his memory.

The effectiveness of these lines is the result of elements that are extremely difficult to isolate. Roughly, they include a firmly structured but graceful syntax, a cadence established in the first two lines which is echoed in the second two, an absence in the rhyme scheme of consonantal stops, a pattern of muted assonance and alliteration, and a purity of diction that is new to the courtly tradition. Such effects are of course the product of a very great talent; but it should be remembered that it is a talent which has inherited a rhetorically conscious verse tradition and made the most of what it has to offer. They are evidence of the refinements of style accomplished by the repeated experimentations of the rhetorically conscious exponents of eloquent verse.

Sonnet 5 provides another fine example, especially of the effectiveness of diction which cannot be identified with any school. The opening three lines are not especially distinguished; they reflect the conventional diction and imagery of English Petrarchism and might have been written by any one of a number of Shakespeare's contemporaries:

Those hours that with gentle work did frame
The lovely gaze where every eye doth dwell
Will play the tyrants to the very same.

But with the fourth line the conventionality in the language disappears and the description becomes peculiarly Shakespeare's.

And that unfair which fairly doth excel;
For never-resting time leads summer on

To hideous winter and confounds him there,
Sap check'd with frost and lusty leaves quite gone,
Beauty o'ersnow'd and bareness everywhere.

The line, "And that unfair which fairly doth excel," with its curious but successful use of "unfair," introduces the conflict manifest in the cyclical process which the following four lines elaborate. These four lines are typical of the frequent passages devoted to process that one encounters throughout the sequence. They are crowded with connotation. "Never-resting" (with its sense of incompleted action), "leads on," and "confounds" sharpen the personification of time as a remorseless and tyrannical deceiver and reinforce the opposition between the forces of growth and corruption which the lines describe. The ambiguities of "leads on" and "confounds" are also skillfully managed. "Leads on" in the sense of "moves on" functions with the now archaic usage of "confounds" meaning "to destroy"; and in the same way "leads on" in the sense of "to delude" or "to mislead" works together with "confounds" in the sense of "to frustrate" or "to bewilder."

Rhythm also contributes to the connotative effect. Process is movement and the movement of the lines suggests the movement described. Lines 5 and 6 move lightly and regularly, but their cadence is violently interrupted by the heavy initial foot of line 7, the strong cesura after "frost," and the strong pause at the end of the line. The interruption suggests the violence and suddenness with which life's movement is "confounded."

These effects could not be accomplished in either the old plain or the eloquent style. They depend on a diction that is free from the conventional associations of Petrarchism and on variations in the relation of syntactical and verse units which the plain style tended to discourage. The particular importance of fresh diction to such effects may be seen by comparing the following two sonnets.

Lo, in the orient when the gracious light
Lifts up his burning head, each under eye
Doth homage to his new-appearing sight

Serving with looks his sacred majesty;
And having climb'd the steep-up heavenly hill,
Resembling strong youth in his middle age,
Yet mortal looks adore his beauty still,
Attending on his golden pilgrimage;
But when from highmost pitch, with weary car,
Like feeble age, he reeleth from the day,
The eyes, 'fore duteous, now converted are
From his low tract and look another way:
　　So thou, thyself out-going in thy noon,
　　Unlook'd on diest, unless thou get a son.

(No. 7)

How like a winter hath my absence been
From thee, the pleasure of the fleeting year!
What freezings have I felt, what dark days seen,
What old December's bareness every where!
And yet this time remov'd was summer's time;
The teeming autumn, big with rich increase,
Bearing the wanton burthen of the prime,
Like widowed wombs after their lord's decease:
Yet this abundant issue seem'd to me
But hope of orphans and unfather'd fruit;
For summer and his pleasures wait on thee,
And, thou away, the very birds are mute;
　　Or, if they sing, 'tis with so dull a cheer
　　That leaves look pale, dreading the winter's near.

(No. 97)

The differences between the two poems are easily recognized. The gracefully extended comparison of the young man's life to the sun's daily journey in Sonnet 9 fulfills a courtly intention, even to the point of assuming the position of subservience required in Petrarchan verse. All look up to the young man in his ascendency to do him "homage." The diction, too, reflects the courtly convention. "Orient," "gracious light," "burning head," "sacred majesty," "heavenly hill," "mortal looks," "feeble age"—each has an aura of familiarity. The over-all effect is one of polite praise couched in a language of embellishment rather than of perception.

Metaphor and diction in Sonnet 97, on the other hand, disclose a quite different concern. Metaphor here is a means of objectifying a state of feeling—the barren loneliness endured by the speaker while separated from his friend—and this difference of intent calls for a different kind of language, language showing no trace of studied eloquence or Petrarchism. The development of metaphor here is essentially associational; logical consistency in the development of the several figures is ignored, although strict adherence to the quatrain and couplet units of the English sonnet gives the progression the appearance of logical rigor. Both metaphor and language are devoted to the securing of connotative effects. Feelings inspired in the speaker by winter's destruction of summer's plenitude are defined and then equated with the experience of separation. The result is a wandering series of impressive details which is emotionally powerful but logically impenetrable.

The logical development of the initial comparison is clear enough through line 6: The time of absence has been like the cold, barren days of December, even though it actually occurred at the height of the summer harvest. The difficulty develops in lines 6 and 7. The connotative import of autumn the fertile mother is comprehensible, but its only logical function seems to be to prepare for the contrast between the rich fruition of the harvest season and the speaker's own feelings of despair and sterility.

The more closely one looks at the poem the more it resists logical analysis, and yet, as Hubler remarks, "it makes its impact and is, in part at least, unforgettable.[4] Its success is due, I believe, to the connotative power of a pure language employed in the drawing of comparisons from nature, and from elements of style that are characteristically Shakespearean in their "music" —cadences reinforced by patterns of assonance and alliteration. Such effects of style are not innovations. They occur in *Astrophil and Stella* and the *Amoretti*, although rarely with the suc-

[4] *Shakespeare's Songs and Poems*, p. 104.

cess which seems so effortlessly achieved by Shakespeare. They are the accomplishment of a generation of poets dedicated to achieving eloquence in the mother tongue. Shakespeare's triumph is his realization of the potentialities for subjective reflection that are available in the tradition he has inherited. His most striking contribution to the tradition is a language that is suitable to the expression of a wide range of nuance but which is also, because of its simplicity and precision, equal to the most demanding kind of close psychological analysis.

A similar use of language and metaphor is apparent in Sonnet 73, a poem much discussed since John Crow Ransom's now famous essay, "Shakespeare at Sonnets."[5]

> That time of year thou mayst in me behold
> When yellow leaves, or none, or few, do hang
> Upon those boughs which shake against the cold,
> Bare ruin'd choirs, where late the sweet birds sang:
> In me thou see'st the twilight of such day
> As after sunset fadeth in the west;
> Which by and by black night doth take away,
> Death's second self, that seals up all in rest:
> In me thou see'st the glowing of such fire,
> That on the ashes of his youth doth lie,
> As the death-bed whereon it must expire,
> Consum'd with that which it was nourish'd by.
>> This thou perceiv'st, which makes thy love more
>> strong,
>> To love that well which thou must leave ere long.

Ransom's objection to line 4, that it "compounds" the preceding figure, is technically sound. "It is one thing," he writes, "to have the boughs shaking against the cold," but "it is another thing to represent them as ruined choirs where the birds no longer sing . . . the two images cannot in logical rigour co-

[5] *Southern Review*, III (January 1938), 531-53. Reprinted in *The World's Body* (New York: Scribners, 1938); also in *A Casebook on Shakespeare's Sonnets*, eds., Gerald Willen and Victor B. Reed (New York: Thomas Y. Crowell Co., 1964), pp. 198-218.

exist."⁶ Close analysis of the sort undertaken by Ransom discloses another difficulty which he does not mention. The sharply realized details of line 4 lead the analytical reader to suppose that each has an equally precise figurative meaning; hence, the description of the boughs as "choirs" directs him to read "sweet birds" metaphorically as referring to those monks who formerly sang in those choirs—a reading which is humorously absurd. But again as in Sonnet 97, in spite of the difficulties arising out of close analysis, the connotative power of the quatrain successfully conveys the speaker's emotional response to the approaching winter of life. In fact, the very line which violates the logic of the trope is especially powerful in its conveying of the sense of time's encroachment.

The second and third quatrains show no signs of the kind of inconsistency apparent in the first. In the second quatrain's identification of night as "death's second self," each detail has a corresponding figurative significance; but the metaphor is less effective than either of the figures that are developed in the first and third quatrains. This is probably because it is developed by general rather than sharply realized detail. The figure in the final quatrain, on the other hand, is easily the most impressive in the poem. The basis for the comparison of the dying fire and dying man involves what in the current Aristotelian metaphysics were considered "essential" as distinguished from "accidental" properties of being. Similarities of color, weight, size, and shape are, according to that metaphysics, "accidental"; similarities deriving from the very conditions of existence are "essential." The fire exists only so long as the process of wood becoming ash is incomplete. Man's existence is analogous: to live is, in this sense, to be in motion and to be in motion is to be moving toward death. Both fire and man consume themselves in the act of existing.

There is nothing arbitrary about the comparison; nor is there any margin of the imprecision that is evident when "accidental" qualities (for example, the lack of consciousness in sleep and death in the preceding figure) are compared. It is

⁶ *A Casebook on Shakespeare's Sonnets*, p. 215.

possible in the brilliant summary line, "Consum'd with that which it was nourish'd by," to point to the carefully balanced contraries, *consum'd* and *nourish'd*, as constituting a trope. But the trope here is only the exact means of expressing the paradox which Shakespeare sees as underlying all temporal existence.

There is a similar precision of figure and language in Sonnet 64.

> When I have seen by Time's fell hand defaced
> The rich proud cost of outworn buried age,
> When sometime lofty towers I see down rased,
> And brass eternal slave to mortal rage;
> When I have seen the hungry ocean gain
> Advantage on the kingdom of the shore,
> And the firm soil win of the wat'ry main,
> Increasing store with loss and loss with store;
> When I have seen such interchange of state,
> Or state itself confounded to decay,
> Ruin hath taught me thus to ruminate
> That Time will come and take my love away.
>> This thought is as a death, which cannot choose
>> But weep to have that which it fears to lose.

The heightened rhetoric of the opening lines, due partly to the sustained periodic structure of the syntax and partly to the personification of time, is firmly supported by the seriousness of the theme. Especially impressive is the shift from the changes wrought by time to great monuments of civilization over the centuries to the almost imperceptible but continuous change that is present in the endless erosion of the land by the sea. Each—the towers rased, the brass corroded, and the land worn away—is an instance of the same law; each is part of the kingdom ruled by the tyrant Time. Again, as in the second quatrain of Sonnet 73, a brilliant summary line contributes to the success of the octave: "Increasing store with loss and loss with store." The concluding couplet, however, is another matter. The experience it discloses is surely a valid one. There is no reason why reflection upon mutability should not lead to the painful realization that it will destroy the most intimate of personal relationships, but as here stated it seems anticlimactic and formulary. Line 12 is flat, and the couplet suggests that Shakespeare was more interested in concluding the poem with a paradox than he was in the summarizing content of the lines. How can a death "choose" or "fear"? The identification of "this thought" as a kind of death and then the personification of death, moreover, appear to be mainly a preparation for the easy paradox of the final line, "But *weep to have* that which it *fears to lose*." Still, the brilliant lines of the first two quatrains, especially those in the second in which the metaphysical concept of change is represented by an absolutely precise metaphor, make the sonnet one of the most memorable in the entire sequence.

This extraordinary delineation of metaphors drawn from nature rather than books to represent the imperceptible movements of change provides some of the finest passages in the sonnets:

> Like as the waves make towards the pibbled shore,
> So do our minutes hasten to their end,
> Each changing place with that which goes before,
> In sequent toil all forwards do contend.
> (No. 60, ll. 1-4)

> Ah, yet doth beauty, like a dial hand
> Steal from his figure, and no pace perceiv'd
> (No. 104, ll. 9-10)

> Thou by thy dial's shady stelth mayst know
> Time's thievish progress to eternity.
> (No. 77, ll. 7-8)

> When I perceive that men as plants increase,
> Cheer'd and check'd even by the selfsame sky,
> Vaunt in their youthful sap, at height decrease,
> And wear their brave state out of memory.
> (No. 15, ll. 5-8)

In passages such as these the abstraction "lives" in the concrete particulars of the metaphor.

I intend now to consider another kind of trope which appears in a number of variations throughout the sequence, the grammatical trope of antithesis. Paradox and oxymoron are of course common in English love poetry from the beginning to the end of the century. The Lover's Malady is defined by contraries—fever and chills, hope and despair—and variations upon them are innumerable in love poetry from Tottel on. What I am interested in, however, are those particular schemes which are listed and illustrated in the current handbooks of rhetoric and which in the sonnets are peculiarly characteristic of Shakespeare.

Any doubts as to Shakespeare's familiarity with the handbooks of rhetoric are dispelled by the elaborate structures of word and sound repetition and balanced parallelism in such sonnets as No. 129. There is, in fact, strong evidence suggesting that Thomas Wilson's *Arte of Rhetorique* is the source of Sonnet 129.[7] The subject of the poem is a Renaissance commonplace which Shakespeare could have found anywhere, but the manner of the poem is extraordinary:

Th' expense of spirit in a waste of shame
Is lust in action; and till action, lust
Is perjur'd, murd'rous, bloody, full of blame,
Savage, extreme, rude, cruel, not to trust;
Enjoy'd no sooner, but despised straight;
Past reason hunted; and no sooner had,
Past reason hated as a swallowed bait
On purpose laid to make the taker mad:
Mad in pursuit, and in possession so;
Had, having, and in quest to have, extreme;
A bliss in proof, and prov'd, a very woe;
Before, a joy propos'd; behind, a dream.
 All this the world well knows; yet none knows well
 To shun the heaven that leads men to this hell.

The likely source occurs in a short section in which Wilson

[7] The discussion following is a slightly revised version of an earlier article, "A Probable Source for Shakespeare's Sonnet CXXIX," *Shakespeare Quarterly*, v (Autumn 1954), 381-84.

outlines and illustrates the schemes of sentences "like among themselves," "gradation," and "regression."[8]

Wilson's discussion of sentences "like among themselves" discloses thematic as well as structural parallels: "Sentences are called like when contraries are set together, and the first taketh asmuch as the other following: and the other following taketh as much awai, as that did which went before. As thus. Lust hath overcome shamefastness, impudence hath overcome feare, and madnesse hath overcome reason." The opening line and a half of the sonnet closely parallels "Lust hath overcome shamefastness," and lines 6 through 10 are an amplification of "madness hath overcome reason." Since reason overcome by lust is commonplace, the thematic parallel, and even the verbal echoes, by themselves would have little significance; but the structural parallel puts them in an entirely different light. Shakespeare has cast the opening line in the antithetical form (which, incidentally, is manifest throughout the sonnet) exactly as it is defined and illustrated by Wilson. "Waste of shame" is the "contrary" of "expense of spirit"; it "taketh as much awai, as that did which went before." Likewise, the second type of sentences defined and illustrated by Wilson as "like among themselves" provides a structural parallel, perhaps even the model, for the third and fourth lines of the sonnet. Here is Wilson's definition and first example: "Or els sentences are said to be like among themselves, when every part of one sentence is egall, and of like waight one with an other. As thus. Is it knowne, tried, proved, evident, open, and assured that I did such a deed?" Here again are the lines in the sonnet: "Is perjur'd, murd'rous, bloody, full of blame,/ Savage, extreme, rude, cruel, not to trust." The scheme, more commonly known as a species of *synonymia*, occurs nowhere else in the sonnets, a fact which when considered along with the other parallels, strengthens the probability that the poem derives from Wilson.

In the sections immediately following Wilson again affords parallels that are both thematic and stylistic:

[8] Edited by G. H. Mair (Oxford: Clarendon Press, 1909), pp. 202-05.

Gradation, is when we rehearse the word that goeth next before and bring an other word thereupon that encreaseth the matter, as though one should goe up a pair of stayres and not leave till he come at the top. Or thus. Gradation is when a sentence is dissevered by degrees, so that the word which endeth the sentence going before doeth begin the next. . . . Of sloth cometh pleasure, of pleasure cometh spending, of spending cometh whoring, of whoring cometh lack, of lack cometh theft, of theft cometh hanging, and there an end for this world.

The sonnet does not closely follow either variation of "gradation," but its structure does consist essentially of a series of balanced antitheses which, by contrasting the several stages of lust, progresses by steps to its conclusion. Wilson, in fact, defines "progression" as that which "standeth upon contraries, which aunswere one another" (p. 202). There is, then, a general resemblance between the treatment of related themes in the sonnet and in the example devised by Wilson.[9]

Wilson next treats "regression": "That is called regression, when we repeat a word eftsone that hath bin spoken and rehersed before, whether the same be in the beginning, in the middest, or in the latter end of a sentence. . . . In the latter ende, thus. Man must not live to eate, but eate to live. Man is not made for the sabboth, but the sabboth is made for man." Shakespeare uses the trope in lines 2 and 14: "Is *lust in action*; and *till action, lust*"; "*All* this the world *well knows*; yet *none knows well*." But what is of particular interest is that one of Wilson's examples of regression is apparently inspired by an epigram by Petronius which has been cited as a parallel and possible source for the sonnet.[10] Here is Petronius' epigram:

[9] Notice also that Shakespeare in line 11 uses the word "prov'd" in the same sense as it is used in the example from Wilson cited above. Shakespeare also uses the noun "expense" in line 1 in the same sense that Wilson uses the gerundive "spending" (see quotation immediately following), that is, as a variant of the verb "spend" in the sense of waste or loss through extreme indulgence.

[10] See ed., H. E. Rollins, *Variorum Edition of Shakespeare's Sonnets* (Philadelphia: J. B. Lippincott Co., 1944), I, 330.

"Foeda est in coitu et brevis voluptas,/ Et taedet veneris statim peractae." Wilson's example: "If man do any filthy thing, and take pleasure therein:/ the pleasure goeth away, but the shame tarieth still." If either is a source for the poem, the passage from *The Arte of Rhetorique* is the more likely one.

Two more purely stylistic parallels deserve notice. In all but the third, fourth, and tenth lines of the sonnet there is a regular placing of cesuras to set off clauses or phrases of equal or nearly equal length. It is likely that Shakespeare's rigorous adherence to this manner of reinforcing the effect of balanced antithesis was inspired by Wilson's definition of "egall members": "Egall members are such when one half of the sentence answers the other, with just proportion of number, not that the Sillables of necessitie should bee of just number, but that the eare might judge them to be so egall, that there may appear small difference." The regular placing of the cesura, however, is only one of several auditory devices that Shakespeare uses to strengthen the antithetical effect. Lines 5, 6, and 7 disclose the use of *homoioteleuton*, the use of like endings of words in corresponding positions within successive clauses:

> Enjoy'd no sooner, but despised straight
>
> Past reason hunted; and no sooner had,
>
> Past reason hated.

Lines 10 and 11 employ *traductio*, the repetition of words with the same root but with different case endings: "*Had, having*, and in quest *to have*, extreme; A bliss in *proof*, and *prov'd*, a very woe." Wilson in his discussion of "contraries" does not mention these schemes by name, but he does speak of the delightful effects "when contrary things are repeated together: when that once again is altered which before was spoken: when sentences are turned and letters are altered."

Whether or not the *Arte of Rhetorique* is the source for the sonnet is, finally, not important. What is important is the undeniable evidence of Shakespeare's familiarity with and use of the kinds of schemes that Wilson discusses. In spite of the slight distortion of thought in the final couplet to satisfy the requirements of the antithetical pattern, "All this the world well knows, yet none knows well/ To shun the heaven that leads men to this hell," the sonnet is a brilliant example of the way in which Shakespeare has adapted devices of *elocutio* which were cultivated initially as ornaments of style to the precise expression of thought and feeling. The antithetical structure of the syntax functions exactly as other verse structures—the pentameter line, the quatrain and final couplet units in the English sonnet, or the conventions of complaint, pledge, plea, and praise—as ways of selecting, approaching, and ordering experience. The undistinguished poet, in laboring to meet the exigencies of the formal principles he has imposed on himself in his initial decision as to the kind of poem he will write is more often than not defeated by them, compromising meaning for the sake of rhyme, selecting a word to keep accent—in short, settling for satisfying the demands of the formal limitations he has chosen to work within, rather than accomplishing something by means of them. Shakespeare in Sonnet 129 has brought a commonplace to life by means of the antithetical structure he has set up for himself. What in the verse of his lesser contemporaries remains a cliché has become the occasion for an extremely moving statement of the corrupting power of lust. The only trace of compromise— of satisfying formal requirements at the expense of matter—is in the final couplet, but it hardly detracts from what has been so brilliantly sustained in the preceding twelve lines.

From the beginning of the sequence on, varieties of antithesis are among the most frequently recurring schemes, although they are not always used so effectively as in Sonnet 129. In the early sonnets, especially, their use often reflects the courtly taste for euphuistic variation. This is true, for instance, of the following examples from Sonnets 1 and 2:

Making a famine where abundance lies.

(No. 1, l. 7)

This were to be new made when thou art old,
And see thy blood warm when thou feel'st it cold.

(No. 2, ll. 13-14)

Each passage functions figuratively in a context of graceful and witty compliment, and its value in context is the extent to which it contributes to the graceful, witty tone. Neither is serious in the sense that Sonnet 129 is serious. The first passage is an hyperbole sustaining the figure of a beauty which devours itself; and the second, although there is a sense in which the satisfactions it affirms are true—a father's heart may be warmed when discovering resemblances to himself in a son—is a charming extravagance.

On other occasions, as in Sonnet 8, "contraries" and "egall members" are used to develop an invention which in its very conception is antithetical. The argument for marriage in Sonnet 8 is based upon the notion (a commonplace in Shakespeare's plays) that the man who dislikes music is himself "out of tune" with the Natural Order. The young man addressed in the poem hears music "sadly" because he remains "unnaturally" single. If he will marry he will live in harmony with the Natural Order and hence will discover the pleasures of music. Stylistically, all elements are devoted to the contraries which define the discrepancy between what is and what ought to be:

Music to hear, why hear'st thou music sadly?
Sweets with sweets war not, joy delights in joy:
Why lov'st thou that which thou receiv'st not gladly,
Or else receiv'st with pleasure thine annoy?
If the true concord of well-tuned sounds,
By union married, do offend thine ear,
They do but sweetly chide thee, who confounds
In singleness the parts that thou shouldst bear:
Mark how one string, sweet husband to another,
Strikes each in each by mutual ordering;
Resembling sire and child and happy mother,
Who all in one, one pleasing note do sing:
   Whose speechless song, being many, seeming one,
   Sings this to thee: "Thou single wilt prove none."

The use of sound and word recurrence throughout the poem to underscore antithesis and paradox recalls Wilson's discussion of sentences "like among themselves." This is true especially of the opening and concluding sections of the poem where there are excellent examples of the delightful effects remarked by Wilson "when contrary things are repeated together: when that once again is uttered which before was spoken: when sentences are turned and letters are altered."

A similar play with syntax and sound is evident in the opening lines of Sonnets 142 and 152:

> Love is my sin, and thy dear virtue hate,
> Hate of my sin, grounded on sinful loving.
>
> (No. 142, ll. 1-2)

> In loving thee thou know'st I am forsworn,
> But thou art twice forsworn, to me in love swearing.
>
> (No. 152, ll. 1-2)

Content in neither instance justifies the syntactical complexity. The governing concern is with wit. Other examples of the same concern are easily found:

> Th' imprison'd absence of your liberty.
>
> (No. 58, l. 6)

> When most I wink, then do mine eyes best see,
> For all the day they view things unrespected;
> But when I sleep, in dreams they look on thee,
> And darkly bright, are bright in dark directed.
> Then thou, whose shadow shadows doth make bright,
> How would thy shadow's form form happy show
> To the clear day of thy much clearer light,
> When to unseeing eyes thy shade shines so!
> . . . .
> All days are nights to see till I see thee,
> And nights bright days when dreams do show thee me.
>
> (No. 43, ll. 1-8, 13-14)

The preoccupation with such patterns is indicative of a period in the development of the vernacular when men of learning, enthusiastic over the degree of refinement to which it had been brought, admired the virtuoso performance.

There is a good deal of such performing in the sonnets, but it is not always so easy as in the passages cited above to draw the line between verbal elaborations which are play and those which are inseparable from the meaning Shakespeare intends. The very nature, for instance, of the experience reflected on in the widely praised Sonnet 30 seems logically to call for antithesis as a means of elaboration:

> When to the sessions of sweet silent thought
> I summon up remembrance of things past,
> I sigh the lack of many a thing I sought
> And with old woes new wail my dear time's waste;
> Then can I drown an eye unus'd to flow,
> For precious friends hid in death's dateless night,
> And weep afresh love's long since cancell'd woe,
> And moan th' expense of many a vanish'd sight;
> Then can I grieve at grievances foregone,
> And heavily from woe to woe tell o'er
> The sad account of fore-bemoaned moan,
> Which I new pay as if not paid before:
>> But if the while I think on thee, dear friend,
>> All losses are restor'd and sorrows end.

Antithesis seems the natural way to express the contrasts between old aspirations and present achievements and between the poet's former world with its "precious friends" and that world as it now is. But what of the verbal embellishment? Does the alliteration in "old woés néw wáil my dear time's waste," which to the modern ear is excessive, contribute to the affective content of the line? The two spondees juxtaposed perhaps provide the contraries—old causes of grief newly lamented—with a justifiable rhetorical stress; but "wail" is troublesome. One cannot avoid the suspicion that it was chosen to satisfy the rhetorical scheme nor ignore the connotations that have accrued to it as a result of its repeated use in the current love poetry to describe unrequited love. The line following is also contaminated by Petrarchan connotations, and its detail functions primarily to sustain the antithetical structure of the preceding two lines: *lack—many, old—new, drown—unus'd to flow*. On the other hand, the structure of line 7 is functional and the repetition in lines 9 through 12 sustains the tone of grief by suggesting through the recurrence of similar sounds the experience of recurring grief. But the preparation for the final couplet in "Which I *new pay* as if *not paid* before" is easy and obvious. The closing couplet, itself, shows the characteristic weakness which other critics have noticed in the sonnets. It dismisses through a resolution that is only verbal the seriousness of all that precedes it. It is not that the truth of what it affirms is a cause for doubt; it is flat, formulary, and unpersuasive because it stands in context as an undeveloped assertion.

The frequency with which varieties of paradox and antithesis occur in the sonnets, besides indicating Shakespeare's interest in the potentialities of schematic structures and the general fascination of the Elizabethans for verbal wit, is perhaps also indicative of something deeper. Initially, paradox and antithesis appear in Tudor verse as a more or less primitive means of indicating psychological and emotional conflict. That at least appears to be its function in the early love poetry. But by the time of Sidney they are well established as the natural means for elaborating contraries that in the Elizabethan view are definitive of the universe and man's place in it. In a religious and philosophical dualism in which existence, the nature of man, and even the nature of God are defined by contraries, antithesis is a natural means of expressing fundamental oppositions (body and soul, reason and passion, growth and decay, time and eternity, absolute justice and infinite mercy).

In an earlier section of this chapter I cited passages from the sonnets dealing with mutability in which metaphor functions as a figure of thought and in which I also noticed, in passing, that antithesis occurs naturally, defining the paradoxical nature of time and the enigma of change. Shakespeare uses the same schemes to dramatize the oppositions within man—between passion and reason and body and mind—to depict

[235]

the stages by which a lust masquerading as love causes the lover to forsake reality for appearance.

In the poems devoted to this process there are occasionally traces of verbal play, as in Sonnets 142, 149, and 152; but they mainly reflect a seriousness of intent which is not apparent in Sidney's earlier treatments of the same experience. The tone of disillusionment and self-disgust, and even of frustration at the failure to accept emotionally what reason has made clear, contrasts sharply with the conversational but decorously polite tone of Sidney's efforts. Antithesis is frequent, but as in Sonnet 129 it is functional, elaborating a conflict in man which has its source in antithesis. Occasionally, as in No. 137, antithesis also has a rhetorical purpose—that of suggesting the lover's frustration at being unable to extricate himself:

Thou blind fool, Love, what dost thou to mine eyes,
That they behold and see not what they see?
They know what beauty is, see where it lies,
Yet what the best is take the worst to be.
If eyes, corrupt by over-partial looks,
Be anchor'd in the bay where all men ride,
Why of eyes' falsehood hast thou forged hooks,
Whereto the judgment of my heart is tied?
Why should my heart think that a several plot
Which my heart knows the wide world's common place?
Or mine eyes seeing this, say this is not,
To put fair truth upon so foul a face?
In things right true my heart and eyes have erred,
And to this false plague are they now transferred.

The lover knows that the mistress, the Dark Lady, is faithless; and he is able to express that knowledge with a violent disgust. But the disgust is with himself for knowing that "Fair is foul and foul is fair" and being unable to bring his heart to accept it. This peculiar kind of servitude, paradoxical because self-imposed and morally enervating because the antithesis between soul and body (or will and reason) has been resolved through the subversion of soul and reason, is also the subject of Nos.

138, 141, 142, and 147-152. In each of these poems antithesis provides the structure of analysis and elaboration.

Antithesis also provides a structural principle for Nos. 35, 66, and 146. The latter, the familiar "Poor soul, the centre of my sinful earth," is the one renunciation sonnet in the entire sequence. It assumes the conventional oppositions between body and soul and worldly and heavenly goods, and construes the attainment of Christian resignation as a paradox satisfactorily resolved. The purpose of the poem is "rhetorical," not in the sense that it is informed by the eloquent poetic (in fact, in tone, attitude, and diction its main affinities are with the old plain style) or that it endeavors to persuade its readers of anything, but in the sense that certain of Fulke Greville's religious sonnets and the majority of Donne's *Holy Sonnets* are. Its concern is one of self-persuasion; its aim, action—that of rejecting one set of values for another. Action, as rhetoricians from Aristotle to Thomas Wilson never ceased to point out, requires more than intellectual assent. It requires the moving energies of emotion, and those energies are most effectively aroused by visual images which appeal directly to the imagination. That is the purpose here of the concretely developed antitheses. They are the means of bringing a familiar commonplace to life so that a newly discovered awareness of its personal implications will lead to a rejection of the temporal in favor of the eternal.

No. 66 has certain stylistic affinities with No. 146, especially in matters of diction and tone, but the antithetical structure serves a quite different purpose. The poem also reminds one, until the final line, of Wyatt's "Mine own John Poins since ye delight to know," Gascoigne's "Wodmanship," and Ralegh's "The Lie." It shares with them a common focus, attitude, and diction.

> Tir'd with all these, for restful death I cry:
> As to behold desert a beggar born,
> And needy nothing trimm'd in jollity,
> And purest faith unhappily forsworn,
> And gilded honour shamefully misplac'd,
> And maiden virtue rudely strumpeted,

And right perfection wrongfully disgrac'd,
And strength by limping sway disabled,
And art made tongue-tied by authority,
And folly, doctor-like, controlling skill,
And simple truth miscall'd simplicity,
And captive good attending captain ill:
    Tir'd with all these, from these would I be gone,
    Save that to die, I leave my love alone.

The moral tone of the summary statement is here sharpened by the antithetical pattern imposed; and although, unlike the majority of Shakespeare's sonnets and the better verse of his contemporaries, the poem shows no discursive progression, the cumulative effect, as in Ralegh's "The Lie," of the particulars elaborating the social ills which have distressed the poet is powerful.

Sonnet 35, more similar in both method and style to Sonnets 147-150 than the two sonnets just discussed, uses antithesis to sustain a closely reasoned analysis of the personal consequences of excusing another's indulgences. No poem of Donne's or Marvell's is more closely reasoned or more concise in its wit.

No more be griev'd at that which thou hast done:
Roses have thorns, and silver fountains mud;
Clouds and eclipses stain both moon and sun,
And loathsome canker lives in sweetest bud.
All men make faults, and even I in this,
Authorizing thy trespass with compare,
Myself corrupting, salving thy amiss,
Excusing thy sins more than thy sins are;
For to thy sensual fault I bring in sense—
Thy adverse party is thy advocate—
And 'gainst myself a lawful plea commence:
Such civil war is in my love and hate
    That I an accessory needs must be
    To that sweet thief which sourly robs from me.

Antithesis here, besides being logically suggested by the dualistic terms assumed by the analysis, functions both rhetorically and conceptually, contributing decisively to the tone and making possible the extraordinary compression of the argument. The recommendation of the opening line is based on a faulty deduction in which the major premise—in itself supported by antithetical enthymemes which are intentional clichés (ll. 2-4)—is applied to something that does not fall within the class it specifies: "Since imperfection is the condition of all things, you need not feel sorry for what you have done." The fifth line appears initially to be a confirming summary statement of the fallacious conclusion, "All men make faults"; but the second half of the line, by a clever maneuver which forces the reader to reconsider the first half of the line, admits the fallacy. The conclusion that "All men make faults," on which the speaker has urged the person he is addressing not to feel guilty, now becomes a statement about man's fallen nature which he sees as confirmed by his own sin: "By excusing your sin 'with compare' I corrupt myself." The fallacy in the exonerating comparisons is implied rather than stated; they ignore the currently held distinction between natural and moral imperfection. A muddy fountain or a worm-infested rose is one thing; a deceitful man is quite another. Lines 8 and 9 advance the analysis by explaining how the speaker corrupts himself in the act of forgiving and, in fact, commits a worse transgression than the one he is so anxious to excuse. His sin involves his reason and not merely the senses and their passions. This is made evident by the line, "For to thy *sensual fault* I bring in *sense*,"[11] in which *sense* as reason stands in opposition to *sensual fault* as sensuality. The speaker has allowed his love to enlist reason in its service to excuse what is not excusable. That is the nature of the corruption. "Adverse party" in the following line is a pun elaborating the statement of line 9. It designates the speaker who should rightfully be the accuser but who has become the "advocate" and also his rational faculty which ought to oppose sensuality but which now defends it. The final

---

[11] The line is further complicated by the pun noticed by Hubler on "in sense" (*Songs and Poems*, Notes, p. 40), but the pun reinforces rather than contradicts my reading of the line.

lines, continuing the legal metaphor introduced in line 10, are mainly summary, with the couplet, in which the speaker alludes to the third party as a "sweet thief" who "sourly robs" concluding the poem with a familiar verbal antithesis.

Although rhetorical schemes of antithesis are common throughout the poetry of the period, in the sonnets they are a definitive characteristic of style, functioning conceptually and connotatively and sometimes even structurally as a means of dramatizing inner conflict. Among the other poets writing in the courtly tradition they are used mainly to produce a verbal wit of the kind that is only occasionally evident in the sonnets.[12] They also occur in Donne and George Herbert; antithesis and paradox are virtually synonymous with what is commonly called "metaphysical wit." But among the Metaphysicals they do not ordinarily appear in the forms of trope that are listed by the rhetoricians under *Elocutio*. Donne, Herbert, and Marvell, like Shakespeare, are in various ways preoccupied with problems arising out of a philosophical dualism and use antithesis to dramatize and explore familiar oppositions between soul and body, reason and desire, sacred and secular love, action and contemplation, and constancy in change; but they are strongly opposed, especially Donne and Herbert, to studied eloquence as well as to courtly love poetry and avoid those schemes which in the sonnets contribute to the mellifluousness of the sugared style. The remarkable thing is that Shakespeare could use such highly artificial devices so naturally that their artifice often goes unnoticed.

In attempting to fix the position of the sonnets in relation to the plain and eloquent traditions, it is essential to realize that although by 1590 the two styles have undergone a series of refinements which make them no longer so easily distinguishable, each continues to reflect its social origins. The eloquent

---

[12] For example, Daniel's:

> Fair is my love, and cruel as she's fair:
> Her brow shades frowns, although her eyes are sunny,
> Her smiles are lightning, though her pride despair,
> And her disdains are gall, her favors honey.
>
> (*Sonnets to Delia*, No. 6)

style remains the courtly style, reflecting the literary and social norms of an aristocratic institution. The plain style, no longer the "rude" or "vulgar" didactic medium, nevertheless retains plain-speaking in the "honest," "homespun" vernacular as a convention and continues to be identified by noncourtly and deliberately anticourtly attitudes.

Shakespeare, as we have seen, occasionally attacks courtly literary practices and sometimes turns to the plain style, but the sonnets are predominantly representative of the Court. The old plain style appears in the several sonnets devoted to the psychological analysis of a diseased love; in "Tir'd with all these, for restful death I cry," although the final couplet returns to the courtly norm to affirm the restorative power of love when a weariness with the world has momentarily made death seem attractive; and in the renunciation sonnet, "Poor soul, the centre of my sinful earth." In these poems Shakespeare assumes the manner or convention of plain-speaking as a means of indicating either a noncourtly or an openly anticourtly attitude. Numerous other sonnets throughout the sequence have qualities that one does not ordinarily encounter in courtly verse— sonnets in which one finds a diction and imagery that is mainly free of courtly associations, a functional rather than decorative use of trope and scheme, and allusions made to common rather than courtly areas of life. In the many sonnets which for one reason or another consider time and change, even the effects are often very close to those achieved by the plain stylists in contemplative poems devoted to the theme of transiency:

> Since brass, nor stone, nor earth, nor boundless sea,
> But sad mortality o'er-sways their power,
> How with this rage shall beauty hold a plea,
> Whose action is no stronger than a flower?
>
> (No. 65, ll. 1-4)

> No longer mourn for me when I am dead
> Than you shall hear the surly sullen bell
> Give warning to the world that I am fled
> From this vile world, with vildest worms to dwell.
>
> (No. 71, ll. 1-4)

In other poems, language and allusion result in a simplicity and directness that is quite distinct from the plain, but studied, simplicity that is occasionally assumed by Spenser and Sidney and by Shakespeare, himself. It is a simplicity that shows no traces of the genteel manner.

> If there be nothing new, but that which is
> Hath been before, how are our brains beguil'd,
> Which, labouring for invention, bear amiss
> The second burthen of a former child!
>
> (No. 59, ll. 1-4)

> Then hate me when thou wilt; if ever, now;
> Now, while the world is bent my deeds to cross,
> Join with the spite of fortune, make me bow,
> And do not drop in for an after loss.
>
> (No. 90, ll. 1-4)

> Alas, 'tis true I have gone here and there,
> And made myself a motley to the view,
> Gor'd mine own thoughts, sold cheap what is most dear,
> Made old offences of affections new;
> Most true it is that I have look'd on truth
> Askance and strangely. . . .
>
> (No. 110, ll. 1-6)

There is also the fact (noted earlier) that Shakespeare, as Sidney before him, uses on a number of occasions the plain stylists' argument that although his verse lacks the eloquence ordinarily expected of the poet who would observe "The perfect ceremony of love's rite" (No. 23), its very plainness is proof of its integrity. But to assume the conventions of a style is also to assume a set of values and attitudes, and the majority of the sonnets assume the conventions of the courtly rather than of the plain style: the servant-mistress (modified to that of servant-master) relationship; the generic modes of praise, complaint, plea, and pledge; a diction which however plain it may often be usually observes courtly decorum; and the various rhetorical means of writing with elegance and wit.

[242]

I have concerned myself mainly with those conventions which are specifically stylistic or structural. To have dealt fully with the values of love and friendship which the sonnets celebrate in terms of the servant-master relationship, and which confirm their identification with the courtly tradition, would have required an investigation of those values as they are revealed in the Comedies, and thus have taken me considerably beyond the limits of the present study. I shall therefore conclude by offering only some general observations which might suggest a starting point for further investigation and confine those observations to the sonnets in which the Friend is virtually a surrogate of divine love, who redeems time and all its contingencies for the lover.[13]

It is easy enough in those poems to point to the ways in which they echo the idealism of Petrarch, affirming as they do the lover's constancy, his utter dependence upon the beloved, his sorrows of unreturned devotion, and the ennobling and inspiring effects which his love has had upon him. But such a generalization applies about equally well to *Astrophil and Stella*, *Amoretti*, and *Delia*. The problem is to locate, if possible, the sources of the characteristics which distinguish the conception of ennobling love that is expressed in the sonnets. The problem is made the more difficult by the fact that the sonnets relevant to it are poems of assertion, proclaiming the effects of love, rather than developing any kind of a rationale from which it might be possible to deduce an articulate theory. One must rely on hints and parallels which might prove illuminating when followed up. The tempest-tossed bark in Sonnet 116 ("Let me not to the marriage of true minds"), for instance, offers that possibility.

[13] Leishman remarks that many of these "more hyperbolical sonnets must seem in the strict sense idolatrous, for in them the supreme object of the poet's contemplation is a human life, regarded, not as the symbol or incarnation of something that transcends it, but as in itself transcendent: all-supplying, all-restoring, all-sufficing. Shakespeare might almost be saying, blasphemously parodying St. Paul: 'I live; yet not I, but my friend liveth in me.' " *Themes and Variations in Shakespeare's Sonnets* (London: Hutchinson & Co., 1961), p. 217.

The notion that a love which is a "marriage of true minds" is unaffected by temporality or adversity because it is a relationship between spiritual substances is familiar enough in the poetry at end-century; but the particular way in which the tempest-tossed bark is used introduces some interesting variations. Such love "is an ever fixed mark,/ That looks on tempests and is never shaken;/ It is the star to every wandering bark,/ Whose worth's unknown, although his height be taken." (ll. 5-8) The figure of the storm-tossed ship has a long and interesting literary tradition behind it. It is repeatedly used throughout the sixteenth century to represent the troubled state of unrequited love and most often in that capacity to represent the lover's despair. That is its function in Wyatt's "My galy charged with forgetfulness":

> A rayn of teris, a clowde of derk disdain,
>> Hath done the wered cordes great hinderaunce;
>> Wrethed with errour and eke with ignoraunce.
> The starres be hid that led me to this pain;
>> Drowned is reason that should me consort,
>> And I remain dispering of the port.

The same connotations of desperation are evident in the nautical imagery which Capulet uses to describe what he takes to be Juliet's response to the news of Tybalt's death:

> In one little body
> Thou counterfeits a bark, a sea, a wind:
> For still thy eyes, which I may call the sea,
> Do ebb and flow with tears; the bark thy body is,
> Sailing in this salt flood; the winds, thy sighs,
> Who, raging with thy tears, and they with them,
> Without a sudden calm, will overset
> Thy tempest-tossed body.

(III. 5. 131-39)[14]

[14] Quotations from Shakespeare's plays are cited from *The Complete Plays and Poems of William Shakespeare*, eds., William A. Neilson and Charles J. Hill (Cambridge, Mass.: Houghton Mifflin Co., 1942).

And they are also obviously present in Romeo's final words·

> Come, bitter conduct, come unsavoury guide!
> Thou desparate pilot, now at once run on
> The dashing rocks thy sea-sick weary bark.
>
> (V. 3. 116-18)

In each of these passages the lover's "ship" is threatened by love's "tempests," so severely in Romeo's case that he destroys himself. But in Sonnet 116 it is love which provides the bearing by which the lover charts his course, rides out the tempest, and brings his ship finally to a safe harbor. It may be that in the sonnet Shakespeare through this contradiction is simply stressing the difference between a love which is something less than a "marriage of true minds," and therefore liable to catastrophe and despair, and a rational love which is a constant source of hope and indifferent to tempests. But another common Renaissance usage of the storm-tossed ship suggests a more complicated concern behind its appearance in the sonnet.

The ship successfully riding out the storm is a common Christian emblem of patience (or constancy) in adversity. The patient man, whose faith in the ways of Providence to man remains strong in the midst of affliction, does not give up the helm of his ship and even welcomes a "sea of troubles" as a divine gift which allows him the opportunity to prove and exercise his faith. Thus, according to Du Vair, "the Sailor groweth to be a Pilote amongst tempests and stormes: and man becomes not a man indeed, that is, constant and courageous, but in adversitie. It is affliction makes him know his strength."[15] The Friar in Brooke's *Romeus and Juliet* draws the same analogy and to the same purpose when advising a distraught Romeus:

> A wise man in the midst of troubles and distres,
> Still standes not wayling present harme, but seeks his harmes
>   redres
> As when the winter flawes, with dredfull noyse arise,

[15] Guillaume Du Vair, *A Buckler Against Aduersitie* (London, 1622), p. 94. Huntington Library Copy No. 60013.

And heave the fomy swelling waves up to the starry skies,
So that the broosed barke in cruell seas betost,
Dispayreth of the happy haven in daunger to be lost.
The pylate bold a helme, cryes, mates strike now your sayle
And turnes her stemme into the waves, that strongly her
    assayle,
Then, driven hard upon the bare and wrackfull shore,
In greater daunger to be wract, then he had been before
He seeth his ship full right against the rocke to ronne,
But yet he dooth what lyeth in him the perilous rocke to shunne.
Sometimes the beaten boate, by cunning government,
The ancors lost, the cables broke, and all the tackle spent,
The roder smitten of, and over boord the mast,
Doth win the long desyred porte, the stormy daunger past.
But if the master dread, and overprest with woe,
Begin to wring his handes, and lets the gyding rodder goe
The ship rents on the rocke, or sinketh in the deepe,
And eke the coward drenched is. So, if thou still beweepe
And seke not how to helpe the chaunges that do chaunce,
Thy cause of sorow shall increase, thou cause of thy
    mischaunce.

(ll. 1358-1380)[16]

In the sonnet, love is the "ever fixed mark that looks on tempests and is never shaken" and the "star to every wandering bark," just as in the passages cited divine love is the source of an enduring hope which enables man to endure the severest of life's storms. In both, love is the source of constancy and necessarily contains an element of faith.

These similarities suggest the possibility that Shakespeare may construe human love as an analogue of divine love, and there is evidence elsewhere in the sonnets and the comedies which would appear to confirm that possibility. In "Tir'd with all these, for restful death I cry," as I have remarked earlier, it is love which rescues the lover from a weariness with life:

[16] *The Tragical Historie of Romeus and Juliet,* in *Narrative and Dramatic Sources of Shakespeare* ed., Geoffrey Bullough (London: Routledge and Kegan Paul, 1957), I.

"Tir'd with all these, from these I would be gone,/ Save that to die, I leave my love alone"; from a bitter hatred of self and impatience in "When in disgrace with fortune and men's eyes" (No. 29); from an overwhelming sense of failure and isolation in "When to the sessions of sweet, silent thought" (No. 30). Other sonnets suggest that love, in addition to being a source of redeeming hope, is also a source of purification (in the theological sense) and even of being born anew. In "Alas, 'tis true I have gone here and there" (No. 110) the lover, after confessing his past transgressions and renouncing them, pledges himself to a new life. The echoes of Christian resignation are strong:

> Now all is done, have what shall have no end:
> Mine appetite I never more will grind
> On newer proof, to try an older friend,
> A god in love, to whom I am confin'd.
> > Then give me welcome, next my heaven the best,
> > Even to thy pure and most most loving breast.
>
> (ll. 9-14)

Theological overtones are even more distinct in the sonnet immediately following, in which the lover addresses the Friend as a penitent might in prayer approach Christ.

> O, for my sake do you with Fortune chide,
> The guilty goddess of my harmful deeds,
> That did not better for my life provide
> Than public means which public manners breeds.
> Thence comes it that my name receives a brand,
> And almost thence my nature is subdu'd
> To what it works in, like the dyer's hand:
> Pity me then and wish I were renew'd;
> Whilst, like a willing patient, I will drink
> Potions of eisel 'gainst my strong infection;
> No bitterness that I will bitter think,
> Nor double penance, to correct correction.
> > Pity me then, dear friend, and I assure ye
> > Even that your pity is enough to cure me.

The opening passage of seven lines consists of the penitent's confession. In choosing the public world he has made himself vulnerable to Fortune, the goddess who presides over that world, and despite the efforts of his Friend, who has tried to intervene on his behalf, he has been victimized by the "guilty goddess." But the choice of the public world was his, and, as he implicitly acknowledges, he has only himself to blame for what he has become. Thus he has acknowledged his "sin" and expressed a due hatred toward it. Now the penitent asks his Friend again to intervene and to extend to him the pity which like theological grace will make possible the renewal which he so ardently longs for. This time he will cooperate. Having rejected the world, he will now welcome whatever penance he must do, as purgative, stressing even his readiness to do "double penance, to correct correction," if he should err again by failing to perform his penitential obligations.

The theological parallels in this and other sonnets discussed are too exact to be accidental. How they are to be taken, however, is difficult to say. If they occurred only in an occasional sonnet, they might be dismissed as examples of a kind of parody that is not uncommon in the amorous poetry of the century, but their occurrence in the sonnets is more than occasional. Furthermore, they occur in the Comedies, and in contexts which make it difficult to dismiss them as frivolous or fanciful.

The proving of love by adversity, for instance, is recurrent in both the late and early Comedies. Prospero tests Ferdinand's devotion to Miranda by making him pile logs, a task considerably beneath his princely rank, and his readiness to "feel what wretches feel" is as much a proof of his love as Lear's readiness is proof of his recently discovered charity. On the other hand, Cressida's love for Troilus fails the test of time and adversity. It cannot "admit impediments" and it "bends with the remover [Diomedes] to remove." In *Love's Labour's Lost* "every Jack hath not his Jill" because love has not been tested. The King's request that love be granted at "the latest minute of the hour" is rejected by the French Princess on the grounds that the "latest minute" is "a time . . . too short/ To make a world-without-end bargain in" (5.2.797-799). Navarre must retire from the world for a year and live as a hermit. If his love withstands the tests of prolonged self-examination and of time, the Princess promises to grant it.

> If this austere unsociable life
> Change not your offer made in heat of blood;
> If frosts and fasts, hard lodging and thin weeds
> Nip not the gaudy blossoms of your love;
> Then, at the expiration of the year,
> Come challenge me, challenge me by these deserts
> And . . .
> I will be thine.
>
> (V.2. 809-17)

Biron, too, is directed to purge himself and prove his love by assuming a penitential burden. It is a burden which will prove that he has discovered humility and charity and thus prove that he is qualified for romantic love and marriage.

> You shall this twelvemonth term from day to day
> Visit the speechless sick and still converse
> With groaning wretches; and your task shall be,
> With all the fierce endeavor of your wit
> To enforce the pained impotent to smile.
>
> (V.2. 860-64)

Shakespeare's position seems to be that unless a lover is able to feel a humility and a compassion that are informed by an awareness of the conditions that all men share, that unless he has attained the virtue of charity and is willing to reject temporality and the world, he is not able to embrace temporality and the world in the form of romantic love. Love and friendship for Shakespeare would in fact seem to be expressions of the theological virtue. The actions of Adam and Celia in the opening action of *As You Like It* provide further evidence of such a view. Each readily gives up temporal security and comfort, each risks the future for the sake of a friend. Adam's readiness is especially suggestive. Orlando's position seems hopeless: he faces either living as a thief or beggar or death at the hands of a malicious brother. But Adam intervenes on his behalf, offering him the 500 crowns he has managed to save for his retirement. He places his future entirely in the hands of Providence:

> Take that, and He that doth the ravens feed,
> Yea, providently caters for the sparrow
> Be comfort to my age. Here is the gold.
>
> (II.3. 43-45)

Orlando might appropriately have replied: "O, for my sake do you with Fortune chide."

Orlando's actions, especially late in the play, also suggest the Christian ethic. The trial of his love that is set for him by the disguised Rosalind is specifically one involving time. He must learn punctuality, and he fails the first test by being late for a meeting with Rosalind. He is also late a second time, but on this occasion because he has risked his own life to save his enemy's. That act is not merely extenuating; it is proof that he is able to love the man whose malice and envy have cruelly denied him his birthright. Consequently, he has proved himself worthy of Hymen's blessing of a marriage which will not "admit impediments," a marriage which "no cross shall part" (V.4. 137). He has ignored time (his appointment with Rosalind) in order to honor a nontemporal obligation—Love thine enemy!—and thus earned a love which will be unaffected by time. Touchstone and Audrey, on the other hand, have agreed finally to marriage as a means of getting what they want—she, a position in the world; he, a bed-partner. They can look forward, as Jaques predicts, "to wrangling, for thy loving voyage/ Is but for two months victuall'd." (V.4. 197-98) One needs more than physical provisions when commencing upon the voyage of love.

Whatever a more extensive examination of the notions of love and friendship in the Comedies and the sonnets might discover, the secular and religious parallels I have briefly noted suggest at the very least that those notions are the expression of something considerably beyond the rationale of courtly love and English Petrarchism. Certainly they deserve further study.

As the values informing the style of the mature sonnets, these notions of love and friendship still identify Shakespeare with the courtly tradition; but to the extent that they go beyond the Petrarchan assumptions of his courtly contemporaries, by implying the resemblances between human and divine love that I have been discussing, they distinguish that style from what can be generally identified as the stylistic norm in Spenser, Sidney, Daniel, and Shakespeare's own marriage sonnets. The distinction is more than a matter of diction, imagery, and cadence, although these are pertinent; it is also a matter of attitude. On the other hand, while these sonnets may go considerably beyond the sentiments of English Petrarchism, and may, in fact, reveal general characteristics of style that suggest the plain tradition, they do not reject the tradition in which they find their sources; instead, they sustain it, refining it on all levels to achieve an excellence which it does not achieve again.

The relation to the courtly tradition of the next sonnet sequence discussed, Fulke Greville's *Caelica*, is a different matter. Greville begins the sequence as a courtly poet, although one who is uneasy in his role and unwilling (or unable) to assume the graceful, mellifluous manner; but he soon begins to reveal his dissatisfaction with the values and assumptions represented in the current love poetry and eventually, a little more than halfway through the sequence, rejects his mistresses, Myra and Caelica, for God. Shakespeare refines and extends the tradition with which he began; Greville revolts, dismissing the courtly for the devotional after exploring the rationale of the former in a style that has its origins in the plain tradition.

CHAPTER VII

Fulke Greville's *Caelica*

THE MAJOR DEVELOPMENTS within the lyric tradition during the final decades of the sixteenth century are evident in the changes of attitude that characterize the progression of the sonnets in Fulke Greville's *Caelica*.[1] The sequence begins with a more or less conventional group of praises, complaints, and petitions depicting the familiar role of suffering or admiring lover, but in the course of the sequence the poems become increasingly critical of that role, until the neo-Platonic religion, along with the worship of Cupid as God of erotic desire, are renounced in favor of the divine love made available to undeserving man through Christ. The secular poems, even the earliest ones, reflect the processes of intellectualization which have been noticed in *Astrophil and Stella*, either in the exploitation of philosophical and theological doctrine for purposes of ingenious invention and extravagant compliment or in the extensive analysis of the limitations of the currently fashionable views of love. *Caelica*, then, is a poetry of ideas, philosophical reflection, and scrupulous self-examination.

The style of *Caelica* is, substantially, the native plain style, although considerably refined by syntactical techniques developed within the eloquent tradition by experimentation with the "schemes" of grammar. Even the earliest sonnets in the sequence show no trace of the "sugared" style and bear out Greville's disavowal in *A Treatie of Humane Learning* of "the craft of words" currently in use:

> *Rhetorike* . . .
> Is growne a *Siren* in the formes of pleading,

[1] It is generally agreed that "evidence of style and thought . . . suggests (broadly) a chronological arrangement." Geoffrey Bullough, *Poems and Dramas of Fulke Greville* (New York: Oxford University Press, 1945), I, Introduction, 36. Subsequent quotations from Greville's verse will be from Bullough's edition.

[252]

Captiuing reason, with the painted skinne
Of many words; with empty sounds misleading
  Vs to false ends, by these false forms abuse,
  Brings neuer forth that Truth, whose name they vse.

Besides, this Art, where scarcity of words
Forc'd her, at first, to *Metaphorike* wings,
Because no Language in the earth affords
Sufficient Characters to expresse all things;
  Yet since, she playes the wanton with this need,
  And staines the Matrone with the Harlots weed.

Whereas those words in euery tongue are best,
Which doe most properly expresse the thought;
For as of pictures, which should manifest
The life, we say not that is fineliest wrought,
  Which fairest simply showes, but faire and like:
  So *words must sparkes be of those fires they strike.*

For the true Art of *Eloquence* indeed
Is not this craft of words, but formes of speech,
Such as from liuing wisdomes doe proceed;
Whose ends are not to flatter, or beseech,
  Insinuate, or perswade, but to declare
  What things in Nature good, or euill are.

(St. 107-10)

"The true Art of *Eloquence*" is devoted to the declaration of truth and the elimination of deceptive appearances. It seeks the means which "most properly express the thought" itself and not the means of clothing it in attractive language. It employs metaphor only when clarity of thought requires it. It is the art of direct statement, simple and unadorned.

The first six sonnets in *Caelica* introduce the higher and lower loves of the Italian neo-Platonists and as a group indicate what for Greville were, finally, the inadequacies of any attempt to define love as a religion of chaste devotion. Sonnets 1 and 2 introduce the two loves without any explicit indication of the ways in which they are contradictory. Sonnets 3 and 4 are

devoted to the higher love and Sonnet 5 to the lower, still
without any acknowledgment of the opposition. But in Sonnet
6 that opposition is made the subject of the poem.

Sonnet 1 is a eulogy based on the familiar neo-Platonic commonplace: the mistress as the incarnation of infinite virtue and
beauty:

Loue, the delight of all well-thinking minds;
Delight, the fruit of vertue dearely lov'd;
Vertue, the highest good, that reason finds;
Reason, the fire wherein mens thoughts bee prov'd;
    Are from the world by Natures power bereft,
    And in one creature, for her glory, left.

Beautie, her couer is, the eyes true pleasure;
In honours fame she liues, the eares sweet musicke;
Excesse of wonder growes from her true measure;
Her worth is passions wound, and passions physicke;
    From her true heart, cleare springs of wisdome flow,
    Which imag'd in her words and deeds, men know.

Time faine would stay, that she might never leave her,
Place doth reioyce, that she must needs containe her,
Death craues of Heauen, that she may not bereaue her,
The Heauens know their owne, and doe maintaine her;
    Delight, Loue, Reason, Vertue let it be,
    To set all women light, but only she.

The mistress of Sonnet 2 is a "Faire Dog" in the employ of
Cupid, who throughout the sequence will represent eroticism
and variability:

Faire Dog, which so my heart dost teare asunder,
That my liues-blood, my bowels ouerfloweth,
Alas, what wicked rage conceal'st thou vnder
These sweet enticing ioyes, thy forehead showeth?
Me, whom the light-wing'd God of long hath chased,
Thou hast attain'd, thou gau'st that fatall wound,
Which my soules peacefull innocence hath rased,
And reason to her seruant humour bound.

[254]

Kill therefore in the end, and end my anguish,
Give me my death, me thinks euen time vpbraideth
A fulnesse of the woes, wherein I languish:
Or if thou wilt I liue, then pittie pleadeth
 Helpe out of thee, since Nature hath reuealed,
 That with thy tongue thy bytings may be healed.

The contrast between the two loves in these two poems is too extensive to be unintentional. The lady of the first sonnet is "passions physicke," her heart is constant and a source of wisdom, and her temperance inspires "excess of wonder." Her beauty and her honor appeal to the senses of sight and hearing which, according to Ficino, are associated with Venus Urania, the higher love: they are, respectively, "the eyes *true* pleasure" and the "eares sweete musicke."[2] The "Faire Dog" of the second sonnet is a mistress whose "sweet enticing ioyes" stir up desire and bind "reason" to the "humours" over which she formerly had command, and whereas the beauty of the lady in the first sonnet is only a reflection of her inner beauty— "Beautie, her couer is"—the "sweet enticing ioyes" of the lady of the second sonnet conceal some form of "wicked rage." The Platonic mistress is both "passions wound, and passions physicke," but the mistress of Sonnet 2 has inflicted a "fatall wound" for which only death (surely, the sexual pun is intended here) or the lady's tongue offer any potential relief. Her identification with desire is completed by these references to the senses of touch and taste which distinguish the lower love from the higher.[3] She is the mistress of change, the object of animal passion.

The next two sonnets return to the Platonic mistress. In Son-

[2] "Since, therefore, the mind, the sight, and the hearing are the only means by which we are able to enjoy beauty, and since Love is the desire for enjoying beauty, Love is always limited to the pleasures of the mind, the eyes, and the ears. What need is there of the senses of smell, taste, and touch?" Ficino's *Commentary*, p. 130.

[3] "Odors, flavors, heat, cold, softness, hardness, and like qualities are the objects of these senses [i.e. smell, taste, and touch]. None of these is human beauty . . . beauty pertains only to the mind, sight and hearing." *Ibid.*

net 3 the initiate pledges to worship her and asks that she
return his devotion: "If in my heart all Saints else be defaced,/
Honour the Shrine, where you alone are placed." (ll. 5-6) The
lover continues his deliberate religious parody in Sonnet 4 with
a remarkable ingenuity:

> You little starres that liue in skyes,
> And glory in *Apollo's* glorie,
> In whose aspects conioined lyes
> The Heauens will, and Natures storie,
> Ioy to be likened to those eyes,
> Which eyes make all eyes glad, or sorie,
>   For when you force thoughts from aboue,
>   These ouer-rule your force by loue.
>
> And thou O *Loue*, which in these eyes
> Hast married *Reason* with *Affection*,
> And made them Saints of beauties skyes,
> Where ioyes are shadowes of perfection,
> Lend me thy wings that I may rise
> Vp not by worth but thy election;
>   For I haue vow'd in strangest fashion,
>   To loue, and neuer seeke compassion.

The opening stanza proclaims the power of Love to intervene
and overrule the astrological influence of the stars as they carry
out the laws of nature and effect the will of God. Love's
power is analogous to the power by which God can offer salvation to the individual or momentarily suspend natural law.
This Christian side of the analogy is extended in the second
stanza, and in a particularly interesting way. The poet prays to
Love that he may be raised up on the wings of grace, but not
because he has made himself worthy of such a gift. The god of
Love, like the God of Calvinism and of Anglicanism, does not
recognize the efficacy of good works; his bestowal of saving
grace is a gift and not a reward; and the poet-lover has vowed
"in strangest fashion" to serve his deity exactly as the devout
Anglican or Calvinist must serve his. The rest of the stanza
carries out the religious analogue. The lady's eyes are identified

as "Saints of beauties skyes," and her face (that is, "beauties skyes") as the finite incarnation of perfect beauty and virtue whose "joyes are shadows" of the beatitude which the Elect will enjoy after death.[4]

Sonnet 5, a complaint, returns again to the sorrows encountered by those who have trusted Cupid, the god of desire and change. The "shadows of perfection" in "beauties skyes" have been replaced by darkness: the lover has been "eclipsed from my Sunne" (l. 5) and lives now in "shadowes of an Earth, quite ouer-runne" (l. 6). The contrast between the divine and profane loves that has been developed in the four preceding poems is now complete. The divine has been presented by images of "heauenly fire," "beauties skyes", "Shadowes of perfection," Saints, and divine influence; the profane, by the blind Cupid, animal savagery, the sun in eclipse, and earthly shade (images, incidentally, which recur throughout the rest of the sequence whenever Greville returns to the contrasting of the celestial with the sublunary). The next sonnet then proceeds to present the two loves for the first time in a single poem in order to explain the poet-lover's failure to sustain his chaste worship of the lady:

> Eyes, why did you bring vnto me those graces,
> Grac'd to yeeld wonder out of her true measure,
> Measure of all ioyes, stay to phansie-traces,
>   Module of pleasure?
>
> Reason is now growne a disease in reason,
> Thoughts knit vpon thoughts free alone to wonder,
> Sense is a spie, made to doe phansie treason,
>   Loue goe I vnder.
>
> Since then eyes pleasure to my thoughts betray me,
> And my thoughts reasons-leuell haue defaced,
> So that all my powers to be hers, obey me,
>   Loue be thou graced.

---

[4] Sonnet 7 also develops an heretical religious analogy. Myra, the lady, is given God's position. She is absolute perfection, beyond the processes of change and, in fact, first and final cause ("the doome") "of all Change."

Grac'd by me Loue? no, by her that owes me.
She that an Angells spirit hath retained
In *Cupids* faire skie, which her beauty showes me,
    Thus haue I gained.

The lover here confesses his failure as a follower of the Platonic religion. He has been undone by his own passions, "Reason is now growne a disease"; and the ladies "graces," which he had praised in Sonnet 1 as sources of "excesse of wonder," now inspire only lust. Her physical beauty, which in Sonnet 1 he had recognized as "a cover" for her virtue and had praised as "the eyes *true* pleasure," is now for him merely a sensual stimulus, "eyes pleasure." She still "graces" Love, but he is the captive of desire; she retains "an Angells spirit," but her face, "beauties skyes" in Sonnet 4, appears to him now as "Cupid's faire skie." His vision has been impaired by his failure to sustain his role as Platonic admirer.

From this point on in the sequence Greville's view of Platonic love is that it is noble but hopelessly idealistic. No daughter of Eve could possibly embody the ideals of virtue and beauty that the neo-Platonists insist upon, nor could any son of Adam worship such ideals in a woman without finding his own fallen nature an unsurmountable obstacle. Greville, as he acknowledges in his *Life of Sidney*, preferred to view the problems of man in terms of this world:

> For my owne part, I found my creeping Genius more fixed upon the Images of Life, than the Images of Wit, and therefore chose not to write to them on whose foot the blacke Oxe had not already trod, as the Proverbe is, but to those only, that are weather-beaten in the Sea of this World, such as having lost the sight of their Gardens, and groves, study to saile on a right course among Rocks, and quick-sands.[5]

Greville expresses his objections toward Platonic love in the companion pieces, Sonnets 9 and 10. In the former, Love, the "mortall sphere of powers diuine," is a tyrant, who thinks to

[5] *Sir Fulke Greville's Life of Sir Philip Sidney*, ed., Nowell Smith (London: Clarendon Press, 1907), p. 224.

[258]

guard his kingdom by fear and sorrow, and the usurper of reason (ll. 14-15). Sonnet 10 concludes that ideal love can exist only as a heavenly idea. Having tried and failed to worship the divine in the person of a woman, Greville ponders the reasons for his failure:

> What Angells pride, or what selfe-disagreeing,
> What dazling brightnesse hath your beames benighted,
> > That fall'n thus from those ioyes which you aspired,
> > Downe to my darkened minde you are retired?
>
> > > > (ll. 5-8)

The celestial ideal has escaped him, leaving him deeply disillusioned and his faculties violently disordered:

> Within which minde since you from thence ascended,
> Truth clouds it selfe, Wit serues but to resemble,
> Enuie is King, at others good offended,
> Memorie doth worlds of wretchednesse assemble,
> Passion to ruin passion is intended,
> My reason is but power to dissemble;
> > Then tell me *Loue*, what glory you diuine
> > Your selfe can find within this soule of mine?
>
> > > > (ll. 9-16)

He concludes, therefore, that the "divine idea" cannot endure in a world of change among men and women who are imperfect, and he rejects as hopelessly unrealistic the attractive conceit which equates Caelica with the "divine idea":

> Rather goe backe vnto that heauenly quire
> Of Natures riches, in her beauties placed,
> And there in contemplation feed desire,
> Which till it wonder, is not rightly graced;
> For those sweet glories, which you doe aspire,
> Must, as *Ideas* only be embraced
> > Since excellence in other forme enioyed,
> > Is by descending to her Saints destroyed.
>
> > > > (ll. 17-24)

Only the attributes of the Ideal are properly the subject of admiration and worship. Only such love can be kept pure. Platonic worship of a woman would only be possible in another Golden Age—as a later sonnet claims, in another Eden,

> . . . when the world was yong,
> Nature so rich, as Earth did need no sowing,
> Malice not knowne, the Serpents had not stung,
> Wit was but sweet Affections ouerflowing.
>
> (44, 1-4)

For then

> Desire was free, and Beauties first-begotten;
> Beauty then neither net, nor made by art,
> Words out of thoughts brought forth, and not forgotten,
> The Lawes were inward that did rule the heart.
>
> (44, 5-8)

The present, however, is a "Brasen Age," when the

> . . . Earth is worne,
> Beauty growne sicke, Nature corrupt and nought,
> Pleasure vntimely dead as soone as borne,
> Both words and kindnesse strangers to our thought.
>
> (44, 9-12)

One might have expected to find wisdom, constancy, and the honoring of vows in that "Golden Age," when "Saturne rul'd alone." But now, when each of the planets exerts its influence upon the world below, desire and variability are the rule.

If Greville is emphatic in his insistence that ideal love cannot endure the vicissitudes and imperfections of the sublunary world, he nevertheless insists upon the reality of such a love. He develops this position most fully in Sonnet 16, in which the Ptolemaic cosmology furnishes the rationale for distinguishing love from desire and for affirming the eternality of the former:

> Fye foolish Earth, thinke you the heauen wants glory,
> Because your shadowes doe your selfe be-night?
> *All's darke vnto the blind*, let them be sory,
> The heauens in themselves are euer bright.

[260]

Fye fond desire, thinke you that Loue wants glory,
Because your shadowes doe your selfe benight?
The hopes and feares of lust, may make men sorie,
But *loue still in her selfe finds her delight.*

Then Earth stand fast, the skye that you benight
Will turne againe, and so restore your glory;
Desire be steady, hope is your delight,
An orbe wherein no creature can be sorie;
   Loue being plac'd aboue these *middle* regions,
   Where euery passion warres it selfe with legions.

The poem, in its affirmation of the transcendent existence of a love which is indeed constant and eternal, anticipates those religious sonnets later in the sequence (for instance, Sonnet 85, "*Loue* is the Peace, whereto all thoughts doe striue") in which Greville identifies love as the one source of hope in these "middle regions." If man stands fast in the knowledge that such a love is a reality, he will be constant in his desire, for he will have the assurance that Love will again shine on him and thus restore his lost glory. In the religious poems it is of course God who is the source of such love, and it is through Christ's atonement that it is made available to man.[6]

If ideal love and the imperfections of the sublunary world are incompatible, it is impossible for any woman to be Love's surrogate. The heavenly Caelica is consequently divested of her heavenly raiments with a witty whimsicality that reminds one of John Donne:

Caelica, when I did see you euery day,
I saw so many worths so well vnited,
As in this vnion while but one did play,
All others eyes both wondred and delighted:

---

[6] Sonnets 17, "*Cynthia*, whose glories are at Full for euer," and 55, "*Cynthia*, because your Hornes looke diuerse ways," employ a variation of the cosmological conceit present in Sonnet 16 for what may be the purpose of complimenting Elizabeth: The moon's variability is only apparent; in reality she is "euer round, and neuer varies" (55). Her apparent variability is due to "*Shadowes and distance*" which "*doe abuse the eye*" (55).

Whence I conceau'd you of some heauenly mould,
Since Loue, and Vertue, noble Fame and Pleasure,
Containe in one no earthly metall could,
Such enemies are flesh, and blood to measure.

And since my fall, though I now onely see
Your backe, while all the world beholds your face,
This shadow still shewes miracles to me,
And still I thinke your heart a heauenly place:
    For what before was fill'd by me alone,
    I now discerne hath roome for euery one.
                        (Sonnet 64)

The fact that Caelica has betrayed him has restored the poet-lover to his senses. He realizes that the divinity she seemed to possess was merely his own invention and, by implication, that the Platonic notion of love is a lot of nonsense.[7] His response to her betrayal is urbane: he is not disillusioned, only amused by the naïveté of his preconceptions.

Following his dismissal of Platonic love, Greville turns to treat love as an erotic game whose rules have been conceived by Cupid. It is a game which is innocent enough so long as its participants do not mistake Cupid for a god or the game for a religion. The prize for winning the game is physical satisfaction, nothing more. When Caelica, now no longer viewed in celestial raiments, complains of his inconstancy and of his failure to worship her properly—

I offer wrong to my beloued Saint,
I scorne, I change, I falsify my loue,
Absence and time haue made my homage faint,
With *Cupid* I doe euery where remoue.

. . . .

I grudge, she saith, that many should adore her,
Where loue doth suffer, and thinke all things meet,
She saith, All selfe-nesse must fall downe before her—

he rejects her complaints: "I say, Where is the sauce should

---

[7] The second quatrain almost certainly refers to Sonnet 1, and line 4 of the sestet, to Sonnet 3.

make that sweet?" (18) Love as the poet-lover now conceives it depends upon variety and change. Constancy is its
enemy and those who expect a mistress to be faithful are false
to Cupid:

> Alas poore soule, thinke you to master *Loue*,
> With constant faith; doe you hope true deuotion
> Can stay that God-head, which liues but to moue,
> And turne mens hearts, like Vanes, with outward motion.
>
> .   .   .   .
>
> No hereticke, thou *Cupid* dost betray
> And with religion wouldst bring Princes vnder;
>
> By merit banish Chance from Beauties sky,
> Set other lawes in Womens hearts, than will;
> Cut Changes wings, that she no more may flye,
> Hoping to make that constant, which is ill;
>   Therefore the doome is, wherein thou must rest,
>   *Myra* that scornes thee, shall loue many best.
>   (Sonnet 41, ll. 1-4, 15-22)[8]

Honor, too, is Cupid's enemy (Sonnets 27, 35), but absence is
necessary to his health. It is essential as a stimulus to jaded
appetites:

> *Absence*, the noble truce
> Of *Cupids* warre:
> Where though desires want vse,
> They honoured are.
> Thou art the iust protection,
> Of prodigall affection,
> Haue thou the praise;

---

[8] Compare with John Donne's *The Indifferent* in which Venus levels
the same punishment for the same heresy:

> She [Venus] went, examin'd, and return'd ere long,
> And said, alas, Some two or three
> Poore Heretiques in love there bee,
> Which thinke to stablish dangerous constancie.
> But I have told them, since you will be true,
> You shall be true to them, who'are false to you.
>   (ll. 23-28)

When bankrupt *Cupid* braueth,
Thy mines his credit saueth,
With sweet delayes.

. . . .

Absence, like dainty Clouds,
On glorious-bright,
Natures weake senses shrowds,
From harming light.
Absence maintaines the treasure
Of pleasure vnto pleasure,
Sparing with praise;
Absence doth nurse the fire,
Which starues and feeds desire
With sweet delayes.
(Sonnet 45, 1-10, 21-30)

The only danger risked by those in the service of Cupid is a loss of perspective. If the lover confuses desire with love and assumes that vows made at Cupid's altar are sacred, he is bound to be unhappily disillusioned (Sonnet 68). The lover must therefore always remember that "Who worships *Cupid*, doth adore a boy," that boys "for a new, soone leave their dearest toy" (Sonnet 62, 1, 3), and that whenever man worships an idol he creates for himself his own punishment:

Mercurie, Cupid, Mars, they be no Gods,
But humane Idols, built vp by desire,
Fruit of our boughs, whence heauen maketh rods,
And babyes too for child-thoughts that aspire:
Who sees their glories, on the earth must prye;
Who seeks true glory must looke to the skye.
(ll. 19-24)

Caelica establishes Greville's position in the tradition of the secular lyric about midway between Sidney and Donne. Stylistically, the sequence shows that Greville is consistent with his own notion of eloquence, even in those early poems devoted to the most extravagant kind of praise. He does not use rhetoric to decorate the surface of a poem, although he frequently uses verbal and grammatical figures as aids to the expression and organization of thought. *Caelica* is, in short, written in the native plain style enriched by rhetorical practices. Sidney, too, had disavowed rhetorical eloquence and in *Astrophil and Stella* claimed to be speaking plainly; but the styles of Sidney and Greville do not have much in common. Most of the sonnets in Sidney's sequence are written in a conversational style, colloquial but polite, often to the point of affectation. It is genteel in a courtly sense even when it incorporates the technical terminology of scholasticism. Greville, too, often assumes a conversational manner, but it is never the genteel manner of Sidney. Greville relies far more extensively upon a philosophical vocabulary and abstraction, and his style is the most highly compressed version of the plain style yet to appear in the English lyric. Occasionally it suggests in its whimsical wit and sudden turns of irony Donne's *Songs and Sonets*, but its cadences are more formal than is customary in Donne's secular verse.

In content and attitude *Caelica* reflects the processes of intellectualization that are evident in *Astrophil and Stella* and which reach significant fulfillment in Donne's *Songs and Sonets*. They show a predilection for philosophical invention that is present in Sidney but to a degree that exceeds anything in *Astrophil and Stella*, or, for that matter, anything in the lyrical verse of his contemporaries, excepting Donne's. Greville uses the scholastic psychology to examine the emotions of courtly love in ways reintroduced by Sidney and subsequently used by Donne. Both Sidney and Greville are avowed anti-Petrarchans; but whereas the majority of the sonnets in *Astrophil and Stella* assume the norms of feeling and attitude that are represented by English Petrarchism, *Caelica* mocks them with a wit and urbanity that again suggests Donne. Greville's mockery of constancy, his denial of the feminine ideal, his perverse praise of absence as an erotic stimulant, and his candid explorations of erotic experience all suggest the so-called cynical verse in the *Songs and Sonets*. The point that needs stressing here, however—and it has also led to the consistent misinterpretation of Donne—is that the method of mockery and ridicule shared by Greville and Donne is not directed at woman or constancy but at the fashionable attitudes toward women and constancy that are assumed in the conventions of English Petrarchism. Both men are mocking fatuous ways of viewing amorous experience.

Both Sidney and Greville raise the problem of arriving at a definition of love which adequately distinguishes between a selfless esteem for the beloved and a selfish desire to possess the beloved as an object of appetite. Both consider the neo-Platonic doctrines as a possible solution to the problem but finally dismiss it as totally unrealistic. But whereas Sidney continues to insist that although love is not what the neo-Platonists claim it to be, it is nevertheless something more than desire, Greville, after rejecting the Platonic view, dismisses all love between man and woman as an erotic game, pleasant and harmless enough so long as it is not mistaken for something more than it really is. Both men raise a question that is of the greatest interest to the intellectuals of the period, only to dismiss it unanswered and then concentrate on sacred subjects; in doing so they preserve the dichotomy between divine and profane love which is the common assumption present in virtually every discussion or portrayal of love in the sixteenth century, unless, of course, the context is Petrarchan. It remained for Donne to attempt a metaphysical definition of human love which did not dismiss either mind or body and which eliminated the dichotomy between the human and the divine by insisting that human love is a true analogue of the divine.

Consideration of Greville's place in the tradition of the religious lyric, generally, and of the penitential lyric in particular, follows.[9]

The history of the development of the penitential lyric from its inception in the Middle Ages to its full realization at about the close of the sixteenth century can be described generally as a movement away from the formulary and didactic toward the

[9] Lily B. Campbell's *Divine Poetry and Drama in Sixteenth-Century* is a valuable history of religious verse, original and in translation, from its beginnings early in the century. Especially relevant to my consideration of Greville's penitential verse is Miss Campbell's discussion of the translations of the Psalms during the reigns of Edward VI and Elizabeth, Chapters 5 and 6.

highly personal and introspective. Its medieval representatives are usually either versified paraphrases of the steps that are necessary for repentance, or formulary prayers that include confessions of sin, avowals of contrition or of the willingness to make atonement, and pleas for grace addressed to the Virgin or one of the persons of the Trinity. This formulary and didactic strain can be traced into the early years of Elizabeth's reign where it is represented by the numerous poems in the miscellanies and works of minor poets that are devoted to the Christian's preparations for death, and occasionally by impressive contemplative poems such as Gascoigne's "Lullabie."

A new variation of the penitential lyric, which is less specifically doctrinal than the old medieval types and which often adopts the sonnet form, appears in Tottel's *Miscellany*. Its earliest examples are Wyatt's "Farewell, love, and all thy joys forever" and Surrey's "Brittle beauty, that nature made so frail." It is distinguished from the medieval and predominantly didactic variety by the nature of its content and its style. It is confined to the renunciation of amorous desire and the code of courtly love and proceeds to justify the renunciation, not on the grounds that renunciation is necessary for salvation, but on the grounds that desire is self-inflicted privation. The theme and method of this new variety of repentance lyric have become established conventions by the time *Astrophil and Stella* first appears in print in 1591.[10] Examples of the type after 1591 include Ralegh's "Farewell false love, the oracle of lies," Campion's "Vaine men, whose follies make a god of love," Sidney's "Thou blind man's marke, thou foole's selfe chosen snare" and "Leave me o Love, which reachest but to dust," and Shakespeare's "Th' expense of spirit in a waste of shame" and "Poor soul, the center of my sinful earth." What is apparent in the "renunciation" convention is a confluence of traditions, as the psychological methods of analysis developed within the courtly

[10] The fact that the renunciation sonnet frequently contains a statement of literary intent as well as a religious vow is further evidence of the widespread resistance among the Elizabethans to a native verse tradition which has confined itself to themes of secular love.

tradition are introduced into the penitential lyric. Sidney's two sonnets probably represent the most sophisticated of the type yet to appear: the fusion of the "sugared" style of English Petrarchism and religious subject is complete, even to the point of their use of the song cadences of the secular tradition.

The earliest published examples in English of sonnets dealing exclusively with the experiences of the devout Christian appear in Henry Loc's *Svndry Christian Passions Contained in two hundred Sonnets Diuided into two equall parts: The first consisting chiefly of Meditations, Humiliations, and Prayers. The second of Comfort, Ioy, and Thanksgiuing* (1593).[11] Loc's subjects are the "passions" of penitential experience—fear of Divine Justice, sorrow for sins committed, despair, love of Christ, and hope—but there is nothing to indicate in either of the two parts of the collection that Loc thought of the sequence in terms of the theological doctrines of confession, contrition, and satisfaction. His purpose is more general. It is his hope that by recounting the history of his own religious experiences he will provide his readers with a testimonial

> In which (as in a glasse) may be seene, the state of a regenerate soule, sicke with sinne, sometimes (Ague-like) shivering with cold dispaire, straight waies inflamed with feruencie of faith and hope. One while yeelding under the burthen of sinne to eternall death, and presently incouraged to runne cheerfully forward the appointed course of this pilgrimage, and like a practized traueller, vsed to the change of companie, diet, heate, cold, paine, pleasure, plentie, and wante, not to amaze himselfe long with anie chaunge; but by a consideration of pleasures passed or rest expected, patientlie to passe ouer this world full of incomberances. (p. 4)

He has seen no reason to organize his sequence beyond that of the simple two-part classification identified in the collection's title: ". . . as for the cause of my so preposterous placing of them and deuision onely into two sorts, I confesse indeed I am per-

---

[11] I have used a photostat copy of the Huntington Library copy, No. 12919.

swaded their disorder doth best fit the nature of mankind, who commonly is delighted with contraries, and exercised with extremes, and also as they were by God ministred to my minde . . ." (p. 5) Greville's religious sonnets, on the other hand, disclose a concern for sequential order. Greville's sonnets are further distinguished from Loc's by the fact that they suggest a different source of literary inspiration. Behind Loc's collection one discerns the sonnet sequences of the Petrarchans,[12] whereas behind Greville's, one is aware of the century-long tradition of Psalm translation. The language and the paradoxes of the secular love poetry are frequently suggested by Loc's sonnets, even though he announces at the outset his commitment to the plain style.[13] But the range of experience and the emotional content of Greville's poems strongly suggest an attempt to write a series of poems similar in subject and spirit to the Psalms.

The initial group of divine sonnets in *Caelica* discloses an order of progression that has not been noticed. The Warwick Manuscript indicates that Greville had intended to use Sonnet 82 as a general introduction to the penitential group which follows:

> You that seeke what Life is in Death,
> Now find it aire that once was breath.
> New names vnknowne, old names gone:
> Till time end bodies, but soules none.
> > *Reader*! then make time, while you be,
> > But steppes to your Eternitie.

[12] Miss Campbell attributes Loc's sequence to the enormous popularity of the secular love sequences of the period, and I think rightly so: ". . . this list of sonnet sequences is enough to make clear why it seemed necessary that divine sonnets should be written if Biblical story was to compete with the chronicles of love's agonies and ecstasies" (p. 130).

[13] "I do not greatly seeke the praise of a curious Architector . . . herein haue [I] rather folowed the force of mine owne inward feeling, then outward ornaments of Poeticall fictions or amplifications, as best beseeming the naked cloathing of simple truth, & true Analogie of the nature of the Histories whereto they alude, and harmonie of scriptures whence they are borrowed" (pp. 5-6).

Under this poem in the Warwick Manuscript there is a note in
Greville's hand, " 'This to (come?) after wth the rest.' "[14] The
page following is blank. Following the blank page is the long
secular love poem, "Who Grace, for Zenith had, from which
no shadowes grow" (Sonnet 83), which according to the
Warwick Manuscript is misplaced.[15] Bullough's conjecture is
that the blank page is for " 'the rest' " of a poem, of which
these lines may have been intended as a conclusion.[16] But if the
misplaced Sonnet 83 is removed, it is clear that the notation,
"This to come after wth the rest," instructs a copyist or printer
to place "This poem" [Sonnet 82], with "the rest" of the
poems following the misplaced sonnet, and that it serves to locate
the subject matter of the rest of the following group in the
central Christian experience of preparing oneself for death.

The first "steppes" in preparing for "Eternitie" are the renouncing of worldly desires and the embracing of God as the
first and final cause of man's existence. These are the steps
represented by Sonnets 84 and 85:

Sonnet 84

Farewell sweet Boy, complaine not of my truth;
Thy Mother lou'd thee not with more deuotion;
For to thy Boyes play I gaue all my youth,
Yong Master, I did hope for your promotion.

While some sought Honours, Princes thoughts obseruing,
Many woo'd *Fame, the child of paine and anguish,*
Others iudg'd inward good a chiefe deseruing,
I in thy wanton Visions ioy'd to languish.

I bow'd not to thy image for succession,
Nor bound thy bow to shoot reformed kindnesse,
Thy playes of hope and feare were my confession,
The spectacles to my life was thy blindnesse;

[14] *Fulke Greville*, I, Notes, p. 275.
[15] *Ibid.*, Notes to 76, 268-69 and Notes to 88, 275.
[16] *Ibid.*, 82, 275.

But *Cupid* now farewell, I will goe play me,
With thoughts that please me lesse, & lesse betray me.

Sonnet 85

Loue is the Peace, whereto all thoughts doe striue,
Done and begun with all our powers in one:
The first and last in vs that is aliue,
End of the good, and therewith pleas'd alone.

Perfections spirit, Goddesse of the minde,
Passed through hope, desire, griefe and feare,
A simple Goodnesse in the flesh refin'd,
Which of the ioyes to come doth witnesse beare.

Constant, because it sees no cause to varie,
A Quintessence of Passions ouerthrowne,
Rais'd aboue all that change of obiects carry,
A Nature by no other nature knowne:
  For Glorie's of eternitie a frame,
  That by all bodies else obscures her name.

The poems correspond generally to Sidney's "Thou blind man's
marke, thou foole's selfe chosen snare" and "Leave me o Love,
which reachest but to dust." They assume a significance by
virtue of their position in the *Caelica* sequence and their position
in the penitential group, however, which the Sidney poems do
not have. They serve as summary commentaries on the poems
preceding them and as prefatory statements initiating the
spiritual labors necessary to the attainment of the divine love
identified in the latter of the two sonnets as man's first and final
cause. This latter poem defines metaphysically a Deity of Love
who must become for the penitent an emotional reality, if he is
going to experience the presence of divine love as saving grace.
Later poems in the sequence are devoted to the discovery of that
emotional experience; but here the concern is identification of
the abstract concept, and Greville proceeds to define Christian
love as first and final cause of man's existence and everlasting
happiness, as personal perfection, and as absolute and unchang-
ing. Created by an act of love, man is able to find enduring

happiness only in loving God. By striving toward God as his
proper end, he approaches personal perfection through the
realization of his human potentialities. But final fulfillment
requires divine aid, aid which is forthcoming only if man has
fulfilled the rigorous demands of the doctrine of contrition.
How those demands are to be fulfilled becomes the subject of the
next poems in the sequence.

"The Earth with thunder torne, with fire blasted" (86)
treats of the need to endure "the body of this death"—of the
need to look to heaven to acquire the strength of Christian
patience. "When as Mans life, the light of humane lust" (87)
is a warning to the man who is not "absolute for death." The
next poem, "Man, dreame no more of curious mysteries,"
introduces what for Greville is the first preparatory step in the
exercises leading ultimately to contrition. By reflecting upon
God's law one commences the purification which is preparatory
for redemption through love:

> *First, let the Law plough vp thy wicked heart,*
> *That* Christ *may come, and all these types depart.*

> When thou hast swept the house that all is cleare,
> When thou the dust hast shaken from thy feete,
> When Gods All-might doth in thy flesh appeare,
> Then Seas with streames aboue thy skye doe meet;
> For *Goodnesse onely doth God comprehend,*
> *Knowes what was first, and what shall be the end.*

> (ll. 11-18)

The poem advises man to dismiss all questions of a theological
nature—Adam's life, what Eden was like, the geographical
positions of heaven and hell—which are irrelevant to salvation
and to consider only "mans renewed birth" and how it may
be gained. One begins by letting *"the Law plough vp thy
wicked heart,/ That* Christ *may come, and all these types
depart."* Bullough in his notes for this poem cites passages from
Calvin which would seem to indicate that Greville had Calvinist
leanings.[17] But the Calvinist doctrine involved had already be-

[17] *Fulke Greville,* II, 279-80.

come a part of Anglican orthodoxy. It is the doctrine which insists that repentance inspired by fear of punishment alone is insufficient and which advises the penitent to contemplate his sins in the light of the Law as a preparatory step toward "saving sorrow." By such contemplation he will realize that Absolute Justice demands death as a punishment for his transgressions; he will consequently come to hate sin and realize the truth of the fact that his only hope is to turn to Christ who is infinitely merciful. In this way he may "plough vp his wicked heart" and allow Christ to save him from "these types" of retribution (the antecedents are in lines 7-9) promised in the Old Testament.

The next sonnet, "The *Manicheans* did no Idols make" (89), continues the discussion of the Law and the purgation that it demands. The poem warns against the assumption that the saving presence of Christ can be experienced without the purgation demanded by the Law. The poem develops a comparison between two erroneous notions of Divine Presence in order to stress that a mere knowledge of Christ's atoning sacrifice is insufficient. Such knowledge is no less idolatrous than a form of idolatry practiced by the Manicheans. They did not worship wooden idols,

> Yet Idolls did in their *Ideas* take,
> And figur'd *Christ* as on the crosse he stood.
> Thus did they when they earnestly did pray,
> Till clearer Faith this Idoll tooke away.

Current members of the faith ". . . seeme more inwardly to know the Sonne,/ And see our owne saluation in his blood;" but they err no less than the Manicheans if

> When this is said, we thinke the worke is done,
> And with the Father hold our portion good:
> As if true life within these words were laid,
> For him that in life, neuer words obey'd.

The Father demands more than lip service; He demands that Justice be satisfied by the purgation of evil. If mere lip service to the doctrine of the atonement "be safe, it is a pleasant way,/

The Crosse of Christ is very easily borne:/ But *sixe dayes labour
makes the sabbath day*." But verbal acknowledgment is a false
way. The preparations for Christ's saving presence are stringent:

> *The flesh is dead before grace can be borne.*
> *The heart must first beare witnesse with the booke,*
> *The earth must burne, ere we for Christ can looke.*

The following poem, "The Turkish gouernment allowes no
Law," digresses from the subject of the preceding poems. It is
a more general treatment of the Law which distinguishes
Christian society from the Turkish by citing the willing subjection of Christian society to civil laws based upon the natural law.
Subjection to the law is essential to the notion of Christian
freedom. The final six lines of the poems are difficult and can
only be understood after the allusion in the final line back to
the preceding poem is recognized:

> Our *Christian* freedome is, we haue a law,
> Which euen the Heathen thinke no Power should wrest;
> Yet proues it crooked as power lists to draw,
> The rage or grace that lurkes in Princes brests.
> *Opinion bodies may to shadowes giue,*
> *But no burnt* Zone *it is, where People liue.*

The sense of the passage seems to be that "Christian freedome"
may be abused by Princes who bend the law to their own purposes. The laws thus bent are no longer truly laws; they have
only the appearance of law, as shadows may assume the appearance of substance. The concluding line in all probability
refers back to the final line of the preceding poem: "*The earth
must burne, ere we for Christ can looke.*" It apparently means
that "People liue" in an imperfect world and thus can only
expect that laws be abused. Only after the world as we now
know it has ended, only after it has been purged by fire and
Christ has descended to rule, can man expect the laws to be
administered with perfect justice.

The relation of this poem to the one preceding it inheres only
in the implied but real relationship between God's law before

which every descendant of Adam is guilty and the civil law which in the Renaissance view is a reflection of Divine Law but which is administered by men who are free to abuse it—by men who are free to bend it "as power lists to draw." At the same time, the relationship of Sonnet 90 to the next two poems is quite specific. They examine the temptations which cause rulers to abuse the authority they have assumed by virtue of the law and thus to abuse the law itself. Sonnet 91 identifies "Nobilitie and Fame" as the "Rewards of earth" which most commonly entice rulers. They are the "Calues of brasse" by which subjects as well as kings are deceived. Sonnets 92 and 93 then proceed to consider nobility and fame, respectively, and to dismiss each as hollow "Rewards of Earth." The next two poems conclude the discussion of the enticements which lead governors to abuse the power of their offices and bend the law to their own purposes. "Men, that delight to multiply desire" (94) and "Malice and Loue in their waies opposite" (95) condemn covetousness and hate.

The next poem, "In those yeeres, when our Sense, Desire and Wit" (96), returns to the theme of personal redemption. It summarizes, in preparation for the highly personal penitential poems which immediately follow, the "Rewards of Earth" (elaborated upon in the poems immediately preceding) that must be thrown over by the penitent and it traces the course of the Christian's pilgrimage. As a prisoner of his passions, he is brought to the edge of despair. He has found no happiness in pleasure, only confusion:

> In which confused sphere Man being plac'd
> With equall prospect ouer good or ill;
> The one unknowne, the other in distaste,
> Flesh, with her many moulds of Change and Will,
> So his affections carries on, and casts
> In declination to the errour still;
>   As by the truth he gets no other light,
>   But to see *Vice, a restlesse infinite.*
>
> By which true mappe of his Mortality,
> Mans many Idols are at once defaced,

And all hypocrisies of fraile humanity,
Either exiled, waued, or disgraced;
Falne nature by the streames of vanity,
Forc'd vp to call for grace aboue her placed:
    Whence from the depth of fatall desolation,
    Springs vp the height of his Regeneration.

(ll. 25-40)

Recognizing the sinfulness of his past life, he fears punishment. Fear leads to remorse and finally to full repentance and salvation:

Which light of life doth all those shadowes warre
Of woe and lust, that dazell and inthrall,
Whereby mans ioyes with goodnesse bounded are,
And to remorse his feares transformed all;
His sixe dayes labour past, and that cleere starre,
Figure of Sabboths rest, rais'd by this fall;
    For God comes not till man be ouerthrowne;
    Peace is the seed of grace, in dead flesh sowne.

Flesh but the *Top*, which onely *Whips* make goe,
The *Steele* whose rust is by afflictions worne,
The *Dust* which good men from their feet must throw,
A *liuing-dead thing*, till it be new borne,
A *Phenix-life*, that from a selfe-ruine growes,
Or *Viper* rather through her parents torne,
    A *boat*, to which the world it selfe is Sea,
    Wherein the minde sayles on her fatall way.

(ll. 41-56)

The next four poems deal with Greville's own struggle to meet the requirements of repentance. The group then concludes with nine poems which, though outside the strict penitential scheme, deal with the general sins of humanity: in the body politic (101, 106, 108), in the church (104, 109), and in the general history of Adam's descendants (102, 103, 105, 106). These poems round off the penitential group and represent the final stage of Greville's development as a lyric poet. They are all

distinguished by their seriousness and skill and establish Greville
as a religious-contemplative poet of the first order.

To examine in detail each of the poems in this group would
be to go beyond the purpose of this study. It will suffice here to
select for analysis the three poems (97, 98, 99) that deal in the
most personal terms with the poet's own struggle to experience
contrition. They will afford an excellent opportunity for summarizing tendencies in contemplative and penitential verse that
had been developing for at least a century and that were being
fully realized in the late Renaissance by Greville and his better-
known contemporary, John Donne. They will also afford some
indication of the intense scrutiny of conscience demanded of the
Protestant ascetic and of the method of self-analysis that is
responsible for what critics generally agree is the largest collection of great devotional verse in the history of English poetry.
Here, then, are the three poems:

Sonnet 97

Eternall Truth, almighty, infinite,
Onely exiled from mans fleshly heart,
Where ignorance and disobedience fight,
In hell and sinne, which shall haue greatest part:
   When thy sweet mercy opens forth the light,
Of Grace which giueth eyes vnto the blind,
And with the Law euen plowest vp our sprite
To faith, wherein flesh may saluation finde;
   Thou bidst vs pray, and wee doe pray to thee,
But as to power and God without vs plac'd,
Thinking a wish may weare out vanity,
Or habits be by miracles defac'd.
   One thought to God wee giue, the rest to sinne,
Quickely vnbent is all desire of good,
True words passe out, but haue no being within,
Wee pray to *Christ*, yet helpe to shed his blood;
   For while wee say *Believe*, and feele it not,
Promise amends, and yet despaire in it,
Heare *Sodom* iudg'd and goe not out with *Lot*,

Make Law and Gospell riddles of the wit:
  We with the *Iewes* euen *Christ* still crucifie,
  As not yet come to our impiety.

Sonnet 98

Wrapt vp, O Lord, in mans degeneration;
The glories of thy truth, thy ioyes eternall,
Reflect vpon my soule darke desolation,
And vgly prospects o're the sprites infernall.
  Lord, I haue sinn'd, and mine iniquity,
  Deserues this hell; yet Lord deliuer me.

Thy power and mercy neuer comprehended,
Rest lively imag'd in my Conscience wounded;
Mercy to grace, and power to feare extended,
Both infinite, and I in both confounded;
  Lord, I haue sinn'd, and mine iniquity,
  Deserues this hell, yet Lord deliver me.

If from this depth of sinne, this hellish graue,
And fatall absence from my Sauiours glory,
I could implore his mercy, who can saue,
And for my sinnes, not paines of sinne, be sorry:
  Lord, from this horror of iniquity,
  And hellish graue, thou wouldst deliuer me.

Sonnet 99

Downe in the depth of mine iniquity,
That vgly center of infernall spirits;
Where each sinne feeles her owne deformity,
In these peculiar torments she inherits,
  Depriu'd of humane graces, and diuine,
  Euen there appeares this *sauing God* of mine.

And in this fatall mirrour of transgression,
Shewes man as fruit of his degeneration,
The errours ugly infinite impression,
Which beares the faithlesse downe to desperation;

Depriu'd of humane graces and diuine,
Euen there appeares this *sauing God* of mine.

In power and truth, Almighty and eternall,
Which on the sinne reflects strange desolation,
With glory scourging all the Sprites infernall,
And vncreated hell with vnpriuation;
    Depriu'd of humane graces, not diuine,
    Euen there appeares this *sauing God* of mine.

For on this sp'rituall Crosse condemned lying,
To paines infernall by eternall doome,
I see my Sauiour for the same sinnes dying,
And from that hell I fear'd, to free me, come;
    Depriu'd of humane graces, not diuine,
    Thus hath his death rais'd up this soule of mine.

To assure a correct reading of these poems and to clarify further the approach to the writing of poetry that they embody, certain qualifications of Greville's theological position must first be established. First, as a Protestant, Greville's responsibilities are directly to God. His repentance goes by way of no church intermediary: sin and salvation are matters he must take up directly with God. Second, and in this, too, he is in general agreement with Protestantism, his definition of contrition differs essentially with the official Catholic definition. The Council of Trent had defined the act of contrition as "in essence" the "dissent of the will from evil" and the accompanying feeling of sorrow as the consequence of the essential act.[18] It further distinguished between perfect and imperfect contrition (attrition) in terms of what has motivated the dissent of the will. Dissent motivated by a fear of Divine punishment was defined as attrition; dissent motivated by a hatred of sin itself and a love of God was defined as contrition. Although the latter is the more desirable, either, according to the Catholic church, is sufficient for salvation.[19] Greville, on the other hand, accepts

[18] *The Catholic Encyclopedia*, "Contrition."
[19] *Ibid.*

the feelings of sorrow as the essence of contrition and denies that anything short of perfect contrition is sufficient for salvation.[20] Since Greville's object as a would-be penitent is a state of feeling, the problem that immediately confronts him is a twofold one: he must scrupulously examine his conscience to discover the obstacles preventing him from experiencing the desired state of sorrow, and he must discover and contemplate the proper objects that will prepare him to receive divine aid without which he will never experience that state. The resolution of this twofold problem is Greville's object in the three poems in question.

There can be little doubt that Greville intended these poems to appear in the order they have been published. The insights into sin provoked by its analysis in the first poem become the means of penetrating more deeply into the consequences of sin in the second, and the insights provoked in the second lead to a still deeper penetration of the causes and nature of sin in the third. Each poem, in short, defines a specific kind of Christian sorrow that is exactly in accord with the conception of sin that has determined it, and it is possible to illustrate how in each poem the emotion changes as the conception of sin changes.

"Eternal Truth, almighty, infinite" considers sin simply as willful disobedience and ignorance—the causes which together have prevented him from experiencing the "preparatory sorrow" that precedes contrition. But "disobedience" and "ignorance" are Christian commonplaces, and Greville is content merely to state them as such. He then turns to explore their consequences; for commonplaces, as such, are valueless. They are empty generalizations, "true words" that "haue no being

---

[20] Greville's position would appear to be similar to Thomas Hooker's. Attrition is preparatory or "saving" sorrow; contrition is "sanctifying sorrow" and is a sign of God's presence: ". . . you must know there is a double sorrow. First, there is a sorrow in preparation. Secondly, there is a sorrow in sanctification." The former is preliminary to the state of grace. It is the sorrow felt by the man who "is truly sensible of his sin and the vilenes of it, and abhors himselfe for it" but who has "not yet settled on Christ." The latter "comes after justification, and after the soule hath received faith and grace." (*The Soules Preparation for Christ. Or A Treatise of Contrition* . . . ," London, 1632, pp. 167-68.)

within," until their consequences are fully realized by the individual's intelligence and embraced by his emotions. Greville's purpose, then, is so to realize these commonplaces that they may become motives for sorrow. His method is to treat the commonplaces of disobedience and ignorance as a self-inflicted paradox that he must either resolve or be damned by: although he is desirous of salvation, aware of the extent of his ignorance and sin, and even outwardly sorry for having broken God's law, he continues, nevertheless, willfully to exclude God, who is infinite, from his fleshly and finite heart. The strategy employed to explore the consequences of the paradox in an effort to resolve it, and thus to experience "preparatory sorrow," is one which is logically suggested by it—rhetorical antithesis (ll. 13-22). Greville has, in short, taken over a rhetorical device endlessly employed by the Petrarchans in the interest of paradox for its own sake and used it to explore a paradox that is a fundamental obstacle in the Christian's quest for salvation. None of the consequences of sin and ignorance considered by Greville are in any sense original; the ideas stated in the concluding series of antitheses, in fact, were commonplaces in medieval religious poetry. But they have a cumulative effect that justifies the emotional climax of the concluding couplet. Each member of the series is a consequence of ignorance and guilt, and the series is the means by which the powerful irony of the concluding generalization is earned. They are the means by which the poet has come to recognize the weight of his transgressions and, in accordance with that recognition, to experience "preparatory sorrow."

The realization of the extent of his guilt leads Greville in the next poem, "Wrapt vp O lord, in mans degeneration," to consider the ultimate consequences of his disobedience, that is, to consider the punishment of sin that is demanded by Eternal Law. His "degeneration" has isolated him from God; his future promises only "vgly prospects o're the sprites infernal," a "hellish graue," and "fatall absence from my Sauiours glory." These consequences would seem inevitable. Absolute Justice must and will be satisfied; disobedience to Eternal Law is justly deserving of infinite and eternal punishment. Greville has attained the state of "preparatory sorrow": he recognizes the extent of his deprivation, is willing to endure his punishment as wholly justified, and in all humility is able to pray for deliverance: "Lord, I haue sinn'd, and mine iniquity/ Deserues his hell; yet Lord deliuer me." His recognition of God's infinite mercy justifies the hope implicit in the refrain; but contrition is not complete. He remains confounded by the paradox that had confounded Luther and Calvin—a God who is at once infinitely just and infinitely merciful:

> Thy power and mercy neuer comprehended,
> Rest lively imag'd in my Conscience wounded;
> Mercy to grace, and power to feare extended,
> Both infinite, and I in both confounded.

But even though he is able to hope, his contrition is not yet perfect. His sorrow is motivated by the fear of punishment (even though he recognizes his punishment as just) rather than by a hatred of sin in itself and by the love of God. "Sanctifying sorrow" requires a fuller understanding of both sin and God: sin and its punishment must be recognized as self-inflicted, and God must be recognized as all-merciful as well as perfectly just:

> If from this depth of sinne, this hellish graue,
> And fatall absence from my Sauiours glory,
> I could implore his mercy, who can saue,
> And for my sinnes, not paines of sinne, by sorry:
>> Lord, from this horror of iniquity,
>> And hellish graue, thou wouldst deliuer me.

The concluding poem of the group, "Down in the depth of mine iniquity," discloses that Greville has finally overcome the last obstacle to contrition. The resolution of the paradox of a God who is at once all-merciful and perfectly just, achieved through the contemplation of the Crucifixion, has brought him from the edge of despair to the state of saving grace and enabled him to be sorry for sin in itself:

> For on this sp'rituall Crosse condemned lying,

To paines infernall by eternall doome,
I see my Sauiour for the same sinnes dying,
And from that Hell I fear'd, to free me, come.

He is therefore able finally to see sin in its proper perspective, to hate it as the willful privation of being and a self-inflicted punishment, and to love God for His infinite mercy.

These poems are not merely versified dogma or formulary prayers. Nor are they "poetic imitations" of Christian meditations. They are explorations of conscience which seek to discover those states of feeling which are essential to the central Protestant experience. They are genuine modes of discovery, and they are great poems—as good as the best of Donne's religious verse.

Considered historically, Greville's religious verse is an achievement of the native plain style and of the contemplative verse traditionally written in the plain style. As such, it discloses a close logical structure that was made available to the writer of English lyric by the earlier verse exercises in *refutatio* and *dispositio* and by the elaborate rhetorical argumentation within the verse of Sidney and the other English Petrarchans; the mastery of the method and terminology of the scholastic psychology for purposes of introspection and analysis of feeling; and a precise and firm syntax that had emerged from nearly a half-century of extensive experimentation with the numerous and varied grammatical schemes of repetition and antithesis—a syntax that is wholly adequate to the intensive demands for logical exposition that Greville's philosophical speculations and analyses of conscience made upon it.

The religious verse in *Caelica* also shows that Greville is working in the same devotional tradition and employing virtually the same methods of approaching religious experience that are used by Donne, George Herbert, Vaughan, and Crashaw. Greville does not use the meditative exercises that Martz has identified in the works of those poets;[21] and he does not employ metaphysical conceits. His penitential concerns, with the result-

[21] *The Poetry of Meditation* (New Haven: Yale University Press, 1954).

ing emphasis upon the examination of feelings in terms of their motives, and his use of the methods of logical exposition, however, have a good deal in common with the concerns and methods of those poets, especially with the concerns and methods of Donne.

CHAPTER VIII

John Donne

DONNE'S POSITION in relation to the plain and courtly traditions is essentially one of opposition to the courtly. He is indebted as a love poet to the courtly tradition for various themes and conventions, and by engaging issues inherent in the absolute dualism of Italian neo-Platonism, he continues the line of philosophical concern which I have previously noticed in *Astrophil and Stella*, *Amoretti*, *A Coronet for His Mistress Philosophy*, and *Caelica*. But with respect to manner and attitude his major antecedents are to be found in the tradition of the plain style.[1] In his religious verse he devotes his energies to themes of Christian resignation which since the fourteenth century had been assumed to be proper to the noncourtly tradition; and although his devotional verse often shows in manner and structure the newer influences of the meditative exercises,[2] it retains essential characteristics of the old plain style. The *Holy Sonnets* and such occasional poems as "A Hymn to God the Father" can in fact be said to represent the culmination of a continuously developing kind of contemplative poem with its beginnings in the medieval didactic lyric and traceable in the sixteenth century through Dunbar, Skelton, Wyatt, Vaux, Gascoigne, Southwell, Loc, Sidney, and Greville. The *Songs and Sonets*, too, along with the Satires and the Elegies, represent a continuous line of development: the assumption of the conventions of the plain

---

[1] Rosemond Tuve (*Elizabethan and Metaphysical Imagery*, pp. 196-214 *passim*) is doubtless right in claiming that Donne's observance of stylistic decorum is evidence of orthodoxy, but I do not find that his traditionalism in this sense is particularly relevant. " 'Abbasing a matter' " may require, according to the principle of stylistic decorum, a lowering of style; nevertheless, the questions remain: What are the objects of Donne's attack, and what are the precedents, if any, for the low style he assumes as most suitable to his attack?

[2] See Helen Gardner, *John Donne: The Divine Poems* (Oxford: Clarendon Press, 1952), Introduction; and Louis Martz, *The Poetry of Meditation*.

style to express opposition to the Court as legislator of social and literary norms.

In the *Songs and Sonets* Donne avoids the "sugared" style of his courtly contemporaries, striving instead for what he himself refers to as a style of "masculine persuasive force" ("Elegie 16," l. 4) and Carew, as "a line/ Of masculine expression" ("Elegy on Donne," ll. 38-39).[3] One finds no evidence of the "sudden arbours and groves" of Renaissance pastoral. Shepherds and their flocks have been banished along with Cupid and all the rest of that "goodly exil'd traine/ Of gods and goddesses" which Carew (ll. 63-64) feared would return to English poetry after Donne's death. Nor is there any evidence of the stylized and sometimes lovely sensory detail of which the elegant surfaces of the "sugared" style are mainly comprised, or of those schemes of *elocutio* which contribute so much to its harmonies. In contrast to a style of "soft melting Phrases" (Carew, l. 53) and "language whose tun'd chime/ More charmes the outward sense" (Carew, ll. 46-47), Donne's, as has been frequently remarked, is often colloquial and conversational in its idiom, suggesting in its rhythms an intentional harshness which Arnold Stein attributes to a deliberate attempt to avoid the "modulations" of Elizabethan song.[4] It is a style with a wide range of variation, wider than is sometimes recognized; but nevertheless consistent in its noncourtly attitude—from the indignation of the spoken retort of the opening of "The Canonization" to the restraint and measured grace of the song, "Sweetest love, I do not goe"; from the heretical contrariness of Donne's particular mode of mockery in "The Indifferent," or the parody in "Communitie" of Castiglione's pseudo-scholastic debate of woman's virtues,[5] to the totally committed seriousness and metaphorical complexity of "A Valediction: of my name, in the window." It is a style which when devoted to the satirical treatment of courtly commonplaces or conventions

[3] Reference to a "masculine" style implies a contrast. Courtly effeminacy by the end of the century has become a literary commonplace.

[4] *John Donne's Lyrics* (Minneapolis: University of Minnesota Press, 1962), p. 20.

[5] *The Courtier*, Everyman edition (London: Dent, 1928), pp. 177-84.

[286]

is informed by precisely the intentions which Stein is convinced are behind its harsh rhythms:

> Whether we like the effects or not, his verse character-istically sounds different from the verse of most of his con-temporaries. The difference would seem to oppose the Renaissance idea of necessary pleasantness—the dish with the delicate sauce. For Donne is a conscious master of harsh-ness. . . . One becomes aware that, beyond the context, and sometimes even beyond Donne's own dominant taste for metrical sound, there is an attitude that requires harshness. . . . This attitude may comment on conventional love situations. It may comment on popular verse styles, or on popular social manners. It may cultivate harshness as a comment on those who cultivate grace. (pp. 24-25)

In contrast to Greville, whose *Caelica* is the history of his shifting from a courtly to a noncourtly position, Donne never reveals any sympathy with the Court as a cultural institution. He is an outsider who speaks of the world of courtly and political preferment with all of the vehemence of one whose expectations in that world, and we know that they were once very promising, have been disappointed.[6] He writes an occa-sional poem of compliment to a patroness or a friend, extrava-gant in its sentiments and heavy with hyperbole; but even in such poems the texture is that of closely woven argument.

From the beginning Donne was a representative of the new intellectual and cultural center in London, the Inns of Court, which during the nineties successfully challenged the Court's venerable position in those areas. It is his sharing of anticourtly

---

[6] J. B. Leishman, in discussing "The Canonization" and similar poems in which Donne expresses contempt for the world of aspiration and political preferment while praising the private world of his love, refuses to discount the unfortunate practical consequences of Donne's marriage: ". . . I find it impossible not to feel that Donne, whose pros-pects of worldly advancement seemed at the time, and long continued to seem, irreparably blighted by the consequences of his clandestine marriage, is trying to persuade himself, or at least defiantly proclaim-ing, that, in return for the private world which he and his wife have been able to create, the public world has been 'well lost.' " *Themes and Variations in Shakespeare's Sonnets*, p. 218.

views with the members of the Inns-of-Court group which accounts for his affinities in matters of attitude and style with those poets who, like Jonson, Hall, and Davies, were identified in one way or another with the intellectual life at the Inns: the avoidance of *eloquence* in the old sense, the stress upon logical and philosophical complexity, the impatience with courtly affectation, the plain and vigorous and sometimes violent diction, the favoring of the theory and practice of the anti-Virgilian poets of the first century A.D. and of the classical genres of Satire, Epistle, Ode, and Epigram.[7]

There are, needless to say, some stylistic differences between Donne and the members of the so-called Jonsonian school, but they are neither so numerous nor so radical as has been commonly supposed. Jonson is rarely so harsh, rhythmically, as Donne and more frequently adopts the conventions and cadences of Elizabethan song. Donne in the *Songs and Sonets* rarely uses the tetrameter couplet, one of Jonson's favorite forms. On the other hand, one does not find in Jonson anything resembling the metaphysical conceit. But these differences should not cause us to overlook important affinities of attitude and language and a common emphasis upon closely argued content.

The metaphysical conceit, a characteristic of Donne's style which most dramatically distinguishes it from Jonson's (although I would maintain it is a distinction that has commonly been made too much of), may naturally raise some questions about the accuracy of identifying Donne with the tradition of the plain style, until it is remembered that the plain style was never identified by a lack of trope but rather by its avoidance of decorative trope. Wyatt's "Blame not my lute for he must sownde," Gascoigne's "Lullabie," and Shakespeare's "Poor soul, the centre of my sinful earth" develop metaphorically; and George Herbert, whose style is at least as "conceited" as Donne's, describes his own verse as plain in its avoidance of decorative "fictions."[8] The fact that the Donnean conceit

[7] Wesley Trimpi, *Ben Jonson's Poems, A Study of the Plain Style* (Stanford: Stanford University Press, 1962).
[8] See "Jordon" I and II.

[288]

usually has, as Leonard Unger has shown,[9] a function within an argumentative, or "conceptual," structure aligns Donne with the plain stylists, who freely use metaphor as a figure of thought, even though the tradition of the plain style contains nothing in the way of specific stylistic precedent for it.

But the question remains: If both Donne and Jonson represent the tradition of the plain style, what lies behind Donne's distinctive use of metaphor? It is possible to argue that his particular interests led him to models which were of little interest to Jonson. There is in continental verse a "metaphysical" poetry which has characteristics in common with Donne's;[10] but even if we allow the inference that a continental tradition has directly influenced Donne, we are still faced with the need to explain why that particular tradition and not another was attractive to him. In short, we are still confronted by the question of why Donne selects the figures he does and by the need to discover the purpose behind the directions in which he develops them.[11] In any event, I believe the solution is nearer at hand—in the native traditions and in Donne's particular response to the kinds of issues which seem especially to have interested him.

As Donne's commentators have frequently observed,[12] the *Songs and Sonets* disclose an obsessive interest in the soul-body relationship, specifically in the ways in which the soul and the body are involved in romantic love. Thus he continues the line of controversy which I have already discussed in the sonnet collections of Spenser, Sidney, and Greville; and it is that controversy, carried on as it is within the framework of a radical dualism, which furnishes an illuminating context for at least

[9] "Donne's Poetry and Modern Criticism," in *The Man in the Name* (Minneapolis: University of Minnesota Press, 1956), pp. 30-104. See especially pp. 83-85.

[10] Frank Warnke, *European Metaphysical Poetry* (New Haven and London: Yale University Press, 1961).

[11] I do not have in mind here those figures which, as in "The flea" or "Communitie," are immediately recognizable as conceived to shock the expectations of readers schooled in courtly decorum.

[12] See, for instance, A. J. Smith's "The Metaphysic of Love," *Review of English Studies*, n. s. IX (1958), 362-75.

one kind of conceit in the *Songs and Sonets*. In Greville and Sidney (the evidence in Spenser is not conclusive) the effort to approach the neo-Platonic ideal, a love removed from the claims of the body is judged, finally, to be bound to fail. For Greville, and perhaps for Sidney, as well, the alternative is the absolute rejection of temporality and of any love which "reachest but to dust" for the sake of divine love—not the Platonic version, although Platonic assumptions are present, but the Christian. The dichotomies that are assumed in neo-Platonism between the profane and the divine, reason and appetite, matter and spirit, and body and soul are thus implicitly accepted in Christian rejections of the earthly for the divine. But in Donne, allowing for the occasional exception in such poems as "The Undertaking"—those dichotomies are denied in an effort to vindicate, as Grierson observed, "the interconnexion and mutual dependence of body and soul."[13] It is this effort, I believe, which accounts in the *Songs and Sonets* for a kind of extended comparison that reaffirms and elaborates correspondences between modes of being and action which in the neo-Platonic view are construed as irreconcilably antithetical.

The simile which begins "A Valediction: forbidding mourning" is one example of the kind of figure I have in mind. The point of comparison that Donne finds significant is not simply that the lovers ought to part quietly, since parting like death is inevitable and demands resignation, but the correspondence between the virtuous man's relationship to God, which his faith assures him will not be destroyed in death, and the lovers' relationship to each other, which ought to provide them with a comparable assurance. No two things, particularly in the neo-Platonic view, would appear to be more unlike than the virtuous man's release from temporality to enjoy beatitude and the lovers' sublunary parting. But the "occult resemblance" which Donne discovers is between the spiritual relationships of the virtuous man's soul to God and the lovers' souls to each

[13] *The Poems of John Donne*, ed., H. J. C. Grierson (Oxford: Clarendon Press, 1912), Vol. 2, p. 41. All quotations from Donne's secular poetry will be from Grierson's edition.

other. Both, incidentally, are represented by Donne by the circle, the symbol of perfect motion and purity—the latter, of course, in the closing stanzas of the poem under discussion, the former in the elegy on the death of Lord Harrington:

> O Soule, O circle, why so quickly bee
> Thy ends, thy birth and death, clos'd up in thee?
> Since one Foot of thy compasse still was plac'd
> In heav'n, the other might securely have pac'd
> In the most large extent, through every path,
> Which the whole world, or man the abridgement hath.
>
> (ll. 105-10)

Just as God makes the good man's life circular by affording him a fixed point, it is the beloved who makes Donne's "circle just,/ And makes me end, where I begunne."

Another example of this technique of reconciling neo-Platonic opposites occurs in "The Sunne Rising," "The Anniversary," and "The Canonization"—in the figure of the lovers' world which is in time and yet unaffected by it, frankly sensual and active in its fulfillment and yet contemplative and otherworldly in its serenity, a world which combines the two worlds ordinarily regarded as irreconcilable by poets, secular as well as devotional, who assume a radical dualism. The figure as it appears in "The Sunne Rising" is suitable to my present purpose; Marlowe's "The passionate Sheepheard to his love" and Ralegh's "The passionate mans Pilgrimage" (his second reply to Marlowe's Shepherd), representing as they do the diametrically opposed views which Donne's poem reconciles, will serve as a suitable context in which to consider Donne's method.

Marlowe's Shepherd invites his mistress to share a world of love in which time and the trivia of the quotidian are of no significance.[14] The life he promises is one of devotion and complete serenity in which all pleasures may be "proved" without the threat of satiety. The pastoral convention used is the one used so frequently in its various adaptations from Wyatt's "Myne owne

---

[14] The poem appears in *The Poems of Sir Walter Ralegh*, Agnes Latham, ed. (Cambridge: Harvard University Press, 1951), pp. 15-16.

John Poynz, sins ye delight to know" to Milton's "Lycidas" and Marvell's "The Garden" to set in dialectical opposition the values of the Court (or town) and country, of the active and contemplative ideals, and of the secular and heavenly worlds. It is also evident in both the Ralegh and Donne poems, although in the latter it is stripped of the pastoral fiction and retains only the traditional juxtaposition of mutually exclusive opposites. In Ralegh's poem[15] the opposites juxtaposed are the real world, the world of fallen man, and Christian Paradise, or true Arcadia. In place of the "shallow Riuers" and "Vallies, groues, hills and fieldes" which the Passionate Shepherd promises his lady, the Passionate Man accepts "the bowle of blisse" promised by the Shepherd Christ, whose passion has made the lost pastoral of Eden once again available. Christian Arcadia is a land of "Nectar fountaines" and "milken Hills" where a "staffe of Faith" is more suitable than a shepherd's crook and a "Gowne of Glory" more attractive than the one of "finest wooll" which the Passionate Shepherd promises. The world rejected is the one which Ralegh reminds the Passionate Shepherd of in "The Reply," and to which in another poem he gave the lie. It is the world of reality which the plain tradition had always insisted upon confronting directly and honestly.

The worlds celebrated by Marlowe and Ralegh are as directly opposed to each other as they are opposed to the single world from which they promise eventual escape. The world of Donne's lovers not only shares qualities with both the Passionate Shepherd's and the Passionate Man's worlds; it is *already* possessed. Furthermore, it retains its reality, as time and place indicate, in the world which the Marlowe and Ralegh visions reject. The poem is, simultaneously, a denial of *carpe diem* and a jubilant celebration of sensuality. The lovers, together in bed, greet the morning sun to discover that, having died sexually, they have been born anew in a world which has important qualities in common with Christian Arcadia. It is a world knowing no season and in which all of the riches of the East and all kingdoms have been contracted. The happiness of a love

[15] *Ibid.*, 49-51.

that is "all alike" makes wealth, honor, and fame—those sources
of pleasure in the ordinary world—seem pallid and inconsequential. It is a sensual happiness, but as its purity, serenity, and
constancy imply, it is also contemplative. Donne's lovers enjoy
the best of both Marlowe's and Ralegh's worlds.

It seems to me, therefore, that at least one kind of conceit in
Donne's love poetry has its origins in that body of verse in which
the dualism of neo-Platonic thought gives rise to the question
of how mind and matter participate in the experience of love.
Through the figure of the lovers' world neo-Platonic antitheses
of time and eternity, matter and spirit, and the profane and the
heavenly have been reconciled. Presented in their new unity,
they are definitive characteristics of what Donne elsewhere
refers to as "substantial love."

The question of how seriously Donne intends his concept of
"substantial love" is a difficult one. It is possible that the im-
patience with Petrarchism and courtly fashion which lies behind
such poems as "The Indifferent," "Communitie," and
"Womans constancy" is also behind "The Sunne Rising" and
"The good-morrow," or that the values governing all of the
Songs and Sonets are generally those of wit and originality.
Leishman, in a stimulating discussion of what he calls the theme
of "compensation" in Shakespeare's Sonnets and in Donne's
"The good-morrow," "The Canonization," and "The Sunne
Rising," describes the problem well:

> To "vent wit" was always one of Donne's keenest pleasures
> and most besetting temptations, and even in the poems I have
> mentioned I am not sure whether this rather than, as with
> Shakespeare, a profound conviction, was not the main source
> of his inspiration. In their defiance and their sweepingness
> there is something Shakespearean, but, on the other hand,
> splendid as they are, do they not convey some impression of
> bravado, theatricality, and even attitudinising, such as we
> never find in Shakespeare's sonnets—something of the bra-
> vado and contemptuous defiance of one who has, or who is
> pleased for the moment to regard himself as having, in
> modern phraseology, "contracted out"? Did this paradoxical

antithesis between the lovers' world and the great world arise in Donne as the spontaneous expression of a profound and permanent way of thinking and feeling, or did it suddenly present itself to him as a wonderful subject for the venting of wit. . . ?[16]

On the other hand, there is much to support the view that Donne is seriously concerned to articulate a metaphysic of love which honors the integrity, or unity, of man and at the same time justifies romantic love as an analogue of divine love.

Just such a correspondence between romantic and divine love is clearly implied, for instance, in the devotional sonnet on the death of Anne Donne:

> Since she whome I lovd, hath payd her last debt
> To Nature, and to hers, and my good is dead,
> And her soule early into heaven ravished,
> Wholy in heavenly things my mind is sett.
> Here the admyring her my mind did whett
> To seeke thee God; so streames do shew the head.
>
> (ll. 1-6)

There is no question here of opposition between the earthly and the divine; in an absolutely serious context romantic love is referred to as having its source in divinity itself.

Another kind of evidence, inconclusive, perhaps, but nevertheless pertinent to the question of the seriousness with which Donne intends his figure of the lovers' world and the view of love it represents are the circumstances of his own marriage.[17] The fact is that Donne did in effect reject the world for love. Before his secret marriage he had apparently every reason to look forward to a bright future in the world of the Court. In Sir Thomas Egerton, the Lord Keeper, he had a powerful patron who would see that he gained the preferment that his intelligence and talents warranted. His marriage, of course, destroyed those expectations and for fifteen years Donne lived in poverty. Whether he was aware of what the consequences of his

---

[16] *Themes and Variations in Shakespeare's Sonnets*, pp. 222-23.
[17] *Ibid.*, 218.

marriage would be will never be known, although the fact that he felt it necessary to marry secretly is an indication that he must at least have had some unsettling anticipations. In any event, it is difficult to believe that a man of his reflective nature did not ponder over those feelings which led to the marriage and ended a most promising career, or that he was totally insensitive to the reactions of his friends, as well as to those of his father-in-law, to what could only have seemed to them an extremely rash venture.

Something of what those reactions may have been is suggested by "The Canonization." As its opening lines indicate, the poem is a reply to someone who has chided the speaker for falling in love and thus depriving himself of wealth and royal preferment. The impatient defiance of the speaker's opening statement is equally pronounced in the stanza in which he meets the charge that sexual passion has deprived him of judgment by admitting the passion, "Call us what you will, wee are made such by love;/ Call her one, mee another flye,/ We are Tapers too, and at our owne cost die," and then denying the shame and satiety which are symptomatic of mere passion: "Wee dye and rise the same." By the end of the poem the tone has changed to one of exultant self-vindication.

The New Criticism has made us wary of using biographical material to recover poetic intention; but it is foolish to discount the circumstances and consequences of Donne's marriage as irrelevant to the view of love he expresses in the *Songs and Sonets*. The charges he meets in "The Canonization" are the charges that such a marriage might very well have occasioned. That he should have endeavored to vindicate to himself a marriage which ended his promising expectations is not in the least unlikely.

But the case for the seriousness of Donne's intentions—and hence for my conclusion that the *Songs and Sonets* belong in the tradition of the plain style—does not depend on the support of biographical conjecture. That he is not engaging in a virtuoso display of wit in such poems as "The Sunne Rising" is borne out by a reading of the collection in the context of anticourtly sentiment provided by the tradition of the plain style.

It discloses a consistently held view of love, sustained by the so-called cynical as well as by the serious poems, that is based upon a fully articulated metaphysic which, as A. J. Smith has shown,[18] Donne almost certainly discovered in the Italian neo-Aristotelians.

The Songs and Sonets

Donne's anti-Platonism is commonly recognized. Besides the explicit criticism of the Platonic position in "Loves growth," "The Primrose," "Negative Love," "Loves Alchymie," "The Extasie," and "Elegie XVIII," it is obvious that the mistress addressed in such poems as "Womans constancy," "The Flea," and "Witchcraft by a picture" is the antithesis of the neo-Platonic prototype and that the various poems in praise of indifference, variety, and inconstancy mock the notion of chaste service due a mistress whose physical beauty is a reflection of the ideal virtues. What seems not so commonly recognized is the fact that these poems are not merely "witty and paradoxical elaborations of general Petrarchan theses," expressions of a youthful cynicism. They are poems which attack fashionable clichés through mockery and contradiction.[19] They are identical in purpose and method to the *Paradoxes and Problems,* which "carry with them a confession of there lightnes . . . but indeed they are made rather to deceaue tyme then her daughter truth: although they haue beene written in an age when any thing is strong enough to overthrow her: if they make you to find better reasons against them they do there office: for they are but swaggerers: quiet enough if you resist them. If perchaunce they be prettyly guilt, it is there best for they are not hatcht: they are rather alarums to truth to arme her then enemies."[20] They

---

[18] "The Metaphysic of Love." This essay is one of the major contributions to Donne scholarship in recent years.

[19] For an interesting discussion of seventeenth-century wit which tends to corroborate my view that Donne employs wit to mock absurdity and thus to defend truth, see Arnold Stein's *John Donne's Lyrics,* pp. 92-99.

[20] "Letter to a friend" (probably Henry Wotton) in Evelyn M. Simpson's *A Study of the Prose Works of John Donne* (Oxford: Clarendon Press, 1948), pp. 316-17.

are poems which as "alarums to truth" attack neo-Platonic truisms by affirming their dialectical contraries.

The method of mockery through contradiction is present in "Goe and catch a falling star," "Womans constancy," and "Communitie." In the first two poems Donne attacks neo-Platonic conventions of eulogy and the assumptions about human nature that they presuppose. "Goe and catch a falling star" attacks the practice of deifying a mistress by describing her attributes as if they were absolutes, a practice exemplified by Greville's "The world, that all containes, is euer mouing" (*Caelica*, 7). Myra in that poem is the only constant agent in a universe in constant motion: "Onely like fate sweet Myra neuer varies,/ Yet in her eyes the doome of all change carries." Donne attacks hyperbole with hyperbole by asserting the equally preposterous contrary: "No where/ Lives a woman true, and faire." The grounds for Donne's rejection of the notion of the mistress who is fair and true, insofar as they appear in this poem, are implied in the relationship between the speaker and the audience. The speaker has looked for a woman who is both fair and true, and he has failed. He speaks therefore with the authority of experience. The lesson he has learned and would pass on to his listeners is that such a woman would be a miracle less likely to occur than the impossibilities listed in the first two stanzas. The notion of the ideal mistress is meaningless. It is contradicted by experience; and to search for such a woman is inevitably to be disappointed and an easy prey to cynicism.[21]

If the ideal mistress is only an illusion, the constancy and chaste admiration that are required of the Platonic lover are obviously meaningless. This is the conclusion reached in "Womans constancy," in which the method of contradiction

[21] The grounds for Donne's objection to the neo-Platonists' Ideal Mistress, at least insofar as they are suggested in "Goe and catch a falling star," are the same as those expressed by Jonson in his criticism of Donne's own "Anniversary": "That Donne's Anniversary was profane and full of blasphemies; that he told Mr Donne, if it had been written of the Virgin Mary it had been something; to which he answered that he described the Idea of a Woman and not as she was." "Conversations with Drummond," *Ben Jonson*, eds., Herford and Simpson, I, 133.

results in the destruction of another neo-Platonic formula. The mistress has been allowed those "gifts of the mind" which the Platonic lover never tires of enumerating, but they are gifts which she will almost certainly abuse. The wit of the poem resides in the perversion of those platitudes of eulogy and in the sophistry of the arguments justifying inconstancy, but its effectiveness as a criticism of a courtly cliché is in the implications suggested by the attitude assumed by the speaker at the end of the poem: If women are false by nature (and the title of the poem indicates that the poem is intended to apply to women in general), and thus can only be true to their own nature by being false, then lovers owe them no undying service and ought not be disillusioned by behavior that falls short of the ideal.

These implications are more fully developed in the deliberately sophistical "Communitie":

> Good wee must love, and must hate ill,
> For ill is ill, and good good still,
> But there are things indifferent,
> Which wee may neither hate, nor love,
> But one, and then another prove,
> As wee shall finde our fancy bent.
>
> If then at first wise Nature had
> Made women either good or bad,
> Then some wee might hate, and some chuse,
> But since shee did them so create,
> That we may neither love, nor hate,
> Onely this rests, All, all may use.
>
> If they were good it would be seene,
> Good is as visible as greene,
> And to all eyes it selfe betrayes:
> If they were bad, they could not last,
> Bad doth it selfe, and others wast,
> So, they deserve nor blame, nor praise.
>
> But they are ours as fruits are ours,
> He that but tasts, he that devours,
> And he that leaves all, doth as well:

Chang'd loves are but chang'd sorts of meat,
And when hee hath the kernell eate,
    Who doth not fling away the shell?

Donne's audience at the Inns would have recognized this poem as an "alarm to truth," and found immediately "reasons against" its argument. The conclusion of the argument rests upon three fallacies, each involving an intentional blurring of a single metaphysical distinction. The first occurs in the minor premise of the central syllogism: Since men may use indifferently whatever is neither good nor evil, and since women are neither good nor evil, men may use women indifferently. The argument ignores a scholastic distinction between moral and ontological good. According to Aquinas, it is true that *morally* nature has created woman neither good nor evil. Virtue and sin are of mankind's doing, not nature's. But *ontologically* any being is good insofar as it exists. The second and third fallacies occur in the development of the minor premise, itself. Each fallacy is an instance of the same kind of equivocation. There is first the assertion that the good is easily discovered, is, in fact, self-evident:

If they were good it would be seene,
Good is as visible as greene,
    And to all eyes it selfe betrayes.

The ontological good is self-evident since it pertains to the very existence of things. The man with normal sight has no trouble "seeing" grass or a woman; but from Augustine to Hooker, Christian moralists agree that faulty moral choice results from the failure to distinguish between appearance and reality, that errors in judgment testify to the fact that the *moral* good does not betray itself to all eyes—is not "as visible as greene." Donne is again equivocating on the term *good*. *Good* in the first reference, "If they were good it would be seen," is to the *moral* good; in the second reference, "Good is as visible as greene," *good* is the ontological referent.

The same deliberate equivocation occurs in the argument showing that women are not evil: "If they were bad, they could

not last,/ Bad doth it selfe, and others wast. . . ." Ontological
evil is the privation of being; a deformed arm or blindness is
evil in the ontological sense. Moral evil, on the other hand, is
the result of faulty moral choice. Moral evil results in the
privation of being, but no one, except the man bent on suicide,
seeks his own destruction, although he may of course inadvert-
ently bring it about by a series of faulty choices, as Macbeth
does. It is true, therefore, that moral evil destroys itself and
others—"Bad doth it selfe, and others wast"—but moral privation is a matter of individual responsibility. Any number of
women may thus eventually destroy themselves, but the sur-
vival of Woman (the poem speciously assumes that she is a
distinct *genus*) has nothing to do with moral privation or good.
Woman's ontological existence lies outside moral consideration.

There are other poems among the *Songs and Sonets* which
attack the postures of the Platonic lover through contradiction.
The eighteenth "Elegie" celebrates sensuality to mock the
lover who would pretend that his affections are uncorrupted by
desire. To claim to love a woman only for her virtue, her
beauty, or her wealth is to feign love. This is the import of
Donne's assertion that to love a woman for any of the con-
ventionally announced reasons is to love only her possessions:

> Can men more injure women then to say
> They love them for that, by which they're not they?
> Makes virtue woman? must I cool my bloud
> Till I both be, and find one wise and good?
> May barren Angels love so. But if we
> Make love to woman; virtue is not she:
> As beauty'is not nor wealth: He that strayes thus
> From her to hers, is more adulterous
> Then if he took her maid.
>
> (ll. 19-27)

Love must have as its object the beloved herself, and not her
attributes. Virtue, like wealth, is acquired. Beauty, on the other
hand, is an accidental and physical quality and therefore not
part of a woman's essential nature. Only barren angels, that is,
pure substances, may love virtue in one another, for virtue is

part of their essence. In "Confined Love," after scornfully attributing constancy to "Some man unworthy to be possessor/ Of old or new love, himself being false or weake," the free indulgence of women is argued with a sophistry as flagrant as that present in "Communitie." And other examples of the antithetical method include "The Indifferent," "A Jeat Ring sent," "The Prohibition," "Negative Love," and the second, third, and eighth "Elegies."

Once the method of contradiction used in the mocking poems is understood, it is possible to resolve the apparently contradictory attitudes, say, between the "Valediction" poems and "Communitie" without recourse to biographical conjectures suggesting that the cynical and obscene poems were written before and the serious poems after Donne's marriage to Anne More. The antitheses set up in the mocking poems between fashionable attitudes and their opposites are logical contraries that negate each other. The cynicism and disillusionment present in these poems are therefore not indicative of Donne's attitude toward women or love but rather of his attitude toward currently fashionable views of women and love. His own attitudes toward women and love are founded, as we shall eventually see, upon a psychology which provides for a resolution of the attitudes set in opposition in the mocking poems.

The grounds for Donne's rejection of Platonism are revealed only by implication in the mocking poems, but they are revealed openly in "The Primrose," "The Blossome," and "Loves growth." They bear out what the mocking poems suggest—that his fundamental objections are like Greville's and Sidney's: Neo-Platonism has no basis in reality; it ignores the imperfections of human nature and dismisses, or excludes as improper, a range of feeling that is essential to the experience of human love. The kind of perfection sought by the Platonic suitor is an impossibility, human nature being what it is. This is the argument presented in "The Primrose":

> I walke to finde a true Love; and I see
> That 'tis not a mere woman, that is shee,
> But must, or more, or lesse then woman bee.

Yet know I not, which flower
I wish; a sixe, or foure;
For should my true-Love less then woman bee,
She were scarce any thing; and then, should she
Be more then woman, shee would get above
All thought of sexe, and thinke to move
My heart to study her, and not to love;
Both these were monsters; Since there must reside
Falshood in woman, I could more abide,
She were by art, then Nature falsify'd.   (ll. 8-20)

Again Donne insists that theory conform to reality. The ideal
mistress would be more than a woman; she would be unnatural,
no less a monstrosity than if she were less than a woman, and
no more desirable. It is preferable to have women as they are,
for although there is falsehood in them it is better that they
reveal it in affectation than that nature should have created
them as something other than they are. Love is more than
chaste admiration; it involves body as well as mind. Therefore,
if women were "above all thought of sex," love would simply
not be possible. The same conclusion is intimated in "The
Blossome," in which a departing lover speaks to a flower
(symbolizing his heart or affections) that he plans to leave with
a woman whose interest in him has been only Platonic:

Meet me at London, then,
Twenty dayes hence, and thou shalt see
Mee fresher, and more fat, by being with men,
Then if I had staid still with her and thee.
For Gods sake, if you can, be you so too:
I would give you
There, to another friend, whom wee shall find
As glad to have my body, as my minde.
(ll. 33-40)

"The Primrose" and "The Blossome" show Donne's insistence
on a definition of love which acknowledges that the whole man
is involved in whatever amorous relationship he may enter.
There is nothing perverse in this insistence. He is not indulging

in sophisticated argument to persuade a mistress to go to bed
with him. He is levelling a criticism against Platonic love from
a position which insists that man is not a soul in a body but a
composite of both. If, then, man is such a composite, whatever
experiences he may have will involve, for better or for worse,
the body and its appetites as well as the mind.

"Loves growth," one of the most impressively developed
poems in the entire Donne canon, discloses Donne's objections
to the neo-Platonic theory more clearly and fully than any
other poem in the collections.

> I scarce beleeve my love to be so pure
>   As I had thought it was,
>   Because it doth endure
> Vicissitude, and season, as the grasse;
> Me thinkes I lyed all winter, when I swore,
> My love was infinite, if spring make'it more.
>
> But if this medicine, love, which cures all sorrow
> With more, not onely bee no quintessence,
> But mixt of all stuffes, paining soule, or sense,
> And of the Sunne his working vigour borrow,
> Love's not so pure, and abstract, as they use
> To say, which have no Mistresse but their Muse,
> But as all else, being elemented too,
> Love sometimes would contemplate, sometimes do.
>
> And yet no greater, but more eminent,
>   Love by the spring is growne;
>   As, in the firmament,
> Starres by the Sunne are not inlarg'd, but showne.
> Gentle love deeds, as blossomes on a bough,
> From loves awakened root do bud out now.
> If, as in water stir'd more circles bee
> Produc'd by one, love such additions take,
> Those like so many spheares, but one heaven make,
> For, they are all concentrique unto thee;
> And though each spring doe adde to love new heate,
> As princes doe in times of action get

New taxes, and remit them not in peace,
No winter shall abate the springs encrease.

The opening stanza announces the poet's discovery of a discrepancy between his preconceived idea of love and the evidence
of his own experience. He has discovered that his love has been
affected by the vicissitudes of the seasonal cycle, enduring winter
only as the grass (the connotations of the Biblical "All flesh is
grass" are surely intended here) has endured. His original
assumption, therefore, about the purity and infinitude of his
love must have been erroneous, since quintessential purity is
outside of change and the infinite admits of no degree.

The discrepancy requires a decision in favor either of the
theory or of experience, and the poet decides in favor of experience by dismissing the notion of love as "pure" and "infinite" as a notion cultivated only by those who "have no
Mistresse but their Muse." His experience has shown him that
love is "mixt of all stuffes" because the whole man is involved,
and not just his mind; love must be more than contemplative;
it must be fulfilled in action. Love may inflict pain of both
"soule" and "sense" (mind and body) since both the rational
and animal natures of man are involved in the experience of
love. Even the vegetative level of man, the level of insensitive
growth and reproduction is involved, since love "borrows," just
as grass may be said to borrow, "working vigour" from the sun.

But the acceptance of the fact that the whole man participates
in love raises the serious problem of demonstrating philosophi-
cally that constancy in human love is possible. The evidence of
the speaker's experience has indicated that his love has "grown";
and what is subject to growth is equally subject to decay. The
evidence indicates, in short, that the existence of his love is no
different than the existence of anything else in the sublunary
world where all things are subject to the laws of change. His
love, like all other things which exist in time, appears to be
transient and therefore inconstant. But Donne rescues his love
from variability in the final two stanzas by deciding that it has
not really grown. He grants that love is in some way affected
by change but that whatever change it manifests is "accidental"

rather than "substantial." His love is "substantially" no greater in the spring. Its "essence" or "substantial nature" is spiritual and therefore outside of change. It is only more "eminent" in the spring because of the quickened forces of nature which invigorate physical activity. Just as vegetation is revitalized in the spring—as the grass grows and as blossoms appear in the spring—so man's "vegetable soul" is enlivened. The essence of his love therefore remains constant, while its apparent growth is really only its realization in action and increased feeling. Its "additions" do not destroy its unity; parts are not added to parts.

The poem, then, is not simply an excursion into wit. It is a serious statement about the relationship of love and of the constancy that is possible between two beings whose existence is contingent upon change.

If the idea of spiritual love, represented by Venus Urania, is unacceptable to Donne because it assumes an absolute separation between mind and body and proceeds to dismiss the validity of the body's participation in love, he finds the worship of Eros no more satisfactory. The point consistently made throughout the *Songs and Sonets* is that the religion of courtly love is implicitly voluntaristic. In assuming the unrequited lover's helplessness and his absolute servility to his feelings, the followers of Eros deny the notion of human freedom and responsibility. Donne would have agreed with Iago's reply to Roderigo's complaint that he cannot stop loving Desdemona because he lacks the "virtue" (in the sense of power):

> Virtue! a fig! 'tis in ourselves that we are thus or thus. Our bodies are our gardens, to the which our wills are gardeners; so that if we will plant nettles or sow lettuce, set hyssop and weed up thyme, supply it with one gender of herbs or distract it with many, either to have it sterile with idleness or manured with industry, why, the power and corrigible authority of this lies in our wills. If the balance of our lives had not one scale of reason to poise another of sensuality, the blood and baseness of our natures would conduct us to most preposterous conclusions; but we have reason to cool our raging motions, our carnal stings, our unbitted lusts. . . . (I, iii, 322-37)

On the other hand Donne avoids the view that passion is necessarily "a lust of the blood and a permission of the will" (I, iii, 329) depriving man of his freedom. His own position seems to be that although the appetite for sex may assume the proportions of lust and thus deprive man of his freedom in the manner that Sidney, Greville, and Shakespeare have described in various sonnets, it need not necessarily do so. For the man who is able to maintain his sense of proportion, and thus maintain his freedom, it may remain a source of pleasure.

It is on the grounds summarized above that Donne attacks the courtly Roderigos and the moral extremists in "Loves diet." Whereas the lovers of the "I burn, I freeze" school complain of unfulfilled desires and lament their involuntary servitude and the moralists desire "nought but how to kill desire," the speaker in "Loves diet" celebrates a whimsical indifference. He has kept his appetite from growing to a "burdenous corpulence" by tempering fancy. He has refused to imagine courtly love as anything more than a game of deceit:

> Above one sigh a day I'allow'd him not,
> Of which my fortune, and my faults had part;
> And if sometimes by stealth he got
> A she sigh from my mistresse heart,
> And thought to feast on that, I let him see
> 'Twas neither very sound, nor meant to mee.
>
> (ll. 7-12)

Thus he has remained free of entanglements and indifferent as to how his desires are satisfied:

> Thus I reclaim'd my buzard[22] love, to flye
> At what, and when, and how, and where I chuse;
> Now negligent of sport I lye,
> And now as other Fawkners use,

[22] Cf. *Macbeth*, IV, iii, 73-76:
> We have willing dames enough; there cannot be
> *That vulture in you to devour so many*
> As will to greatness dedicate themselves,
> Finding it so inclin'd. [Italics mine]

I spring a mistresse, sweare, write, sigh and weepe:
And the game kill'd, or lost, goe talke, and sleepe.

(ll. 25-30)

He is now able to play at love with equanimity, to observe the rules of courtship; but whether he is successful or not is of little consequence. The game is easily come by. Win or lose, he is free to try again since there is freedom in variety and indifference.

Variety, indifference, and freedom are defended on the same grounds in the seventeenth *Elegie*, a poem of particular interest since it reveals the actual process of resolving the extreme positions set in opposition (variety and constancy, Platonic admiration and erotic sensuality, freedom and servitude) in the mocking poems. It makes clear in the resolutions of those extremes that Donne's celebration of sexual license is a way of ridiculing what he held to be false views of love. The poem begins as a typical mocking poem with a specious argument for variety in which precedent is extravagantly abused:

The heavens rejoyce in motion, why should I
Abjure my so much lov'd variety,
And not with many youth and love divide?
Pleasure is none, if not diversifi'd:
The sun that sitting in the chaire of light
Sheds flame into what else so ever doth seem bright,
Is not contented at one Signe to Inne,
But ends his year and with a new beginnes.
All things doe willingly in change delight,
The fruitfull mother of our appetite:
Rivers the clearer and more pleasing are,
Where their fair spreading streames run wide and farr;
And a dead lake that no strange bark doth greet,
Corrupts it self and doth live in it.

(ll. 1-14)

Hence variety in mistresses is wholly justified: "Let no man tell me such a one is faire,/ And worthy all alone my love to share." (ll. 15-16) One ought to share a good mistress; nor should one consider her faithlessness a motive for jealousy:

[307]

Nature in her hath done the liberall part
Of a kind Mistresse, and imploy'd her art
To make her loveable, and I aver
Him not humane that would turn back from her.
(ll. 17-20)

The next section of sixteen lines turns the courtly code of
chivalric service back upon itself by exploiting familiar puns on
die, serve, and *service* and by contradicting its basic tenets and
ideals:

I love her well, and would, if need were, dye
To doe her service. But followes it that I
Must serve her only, when I may have choice
Of other beauties, and in change rejoice?
The law is hard, and shall not have my voice.
(ll. 21-25)

The "law" demands that the lady be fair, virtuous, and of
noble birth and that the lover serve her only. But the speaker
has found many women pleasurable, each offering felicities
that the others do not. A fair mistress "holds me in the Sun-
beames of her hair;/ Her nymph-like features such agreements
have/ That I could venture with her to the grave." (ll. 27-29)
But there are others who are not fair:

Another's brown, I like her not the worse,
Her tongue is soft and takes me with discourse.
Others, for that they well descended are,
Do in my love obtain as large a share;
And though they be not fair, 'tis much with mee
To win their love onely for their degree.
(ll. 30-35)

At this point the poem shifts from the playful defense of
sexual indulgence to a serious defense of several kinds of valid
admiration. One woman may be honored for her beauty, another for her social graces, and another for her "degree" and
possible patronage.

The second half of the poem begins like the first and also

gradually shifts from mockery to seriousness. The opening
passage attacks "law" or custom. Variety in love was recognized in primitive times: "Women were then no sooner asked
then won/ And what they did was honest and well done."
(ll. 44-45) But custom has since destroyed the pleasures and
freedom of variety:

> But since this title honour hath been us'd,
> Our weake credulity hath been abus'd;
> The golden laws of nature are repeald,
> Which our first Fathers in such reverence held;
> Our liberty's revers'd our Charter's gone,
> And we're made servants to opinion,
> A monster in no certain shape attir'd
> And whose originall is much desir'd,
> Formlesse at first, but goeing on it fashions,
> And doth prescribe manners and laws to nations.[23]
>
> (ll. 46-55)

Sensual license is a deliberate perversion of nature's "golden
laws." It functions as an "alarum to truth." But the commentary on fashion is intended literally. The following remarks
on the ill effects suffered by love when subjected to custom are
also intended literally:

> Here love receiv'd immedicable harmes,
> And was dispoiled of his daring armes.
> A greater want then is his daring eyes,
> He lost those awfull wings with which he flies;
> His sinewy bow, and those immortall darts
> Wherewith he'is wont to bruise resisting hearts.
>
> (ll. 56-61)

The customs of society have imposed such severe restrictions
upon physical passion that it no longer has the power to
"bruise resisting hearts"; the means of "courting exactly" have
preempted Cupid's power. Now that custom has been substituted for passion, only the few outsiders, those who have

[23] The argument at this point in the poem suggests Greville's Sonnet
44, "The Golden-Age was when the world was yong."

resisted custom, honoring nature rather than submitting to that "monster in no certain shape attir'd," maintain their freedom:

> Onely some few strong in themselves and free
> Retain the seeds of antient liberty,
> Following that part of Love although deprest,
> And make a throne for him within their brest,
> In spight of modern censures him avowing
> Their Soveraigne, all service him allowing.
>
> (ll. 62-67)

Freedom from the restrictions of custom turns out to be a different kind of subjection: the complete and willing subjection to whatever Cupid dictates and the readiness to satisfy desire with any and all mistresses who make themselves available. As one of those independent few, the speaker celebrates his allegiance to Eros:

> I glory in subjection of his hand,
> Nor ever did decline his least command:
> For in whatever forme the message came
> My heart did open and receive the same.
>
> (ll. 70-73)

The immediate targets of the poem's wit are the customs which deny the natural force of Eros in the experience of love and hold captive those who embrace them. And yet Eros is kept in his place. While he may be the awe-inspiring god of passion, he is not, finally, the god of love. There will eventually come a time when the speaker will be obliged to leave off his service to Eros and commit himself to an allegiance which is more binding and yet, paradoxically, allowing him genuine freedom:

> But time will in his course a point discry
> When I this loved service must deny,
> For our allegiance temporary is,
> With firmer age returnes our liberties.
> What time in years and judgement we repos'd,
> Shall not so easily be to change dispos'd,

Nor to the art of severall eyes obeying,
But beauty with true worth securely weighing,
Which being found assembled in some one,
We'll love her ever, and love her alone.

(ll. 74-83)

The preoccupation with wit in the poem is unquestionable, but beyond the obvious intent to shock the expectations of readers long accustomed to courtly sentiments, there is also evident an attitude toward the subject of eroticism which is indicative of Donne's basic disagreement with the views of desire and the body that are commonly expressed in most of the verse of his contemporaries. Besides his insistence that without Eros there can be no romantic love, he also indicates that the kind of love to which he will finally give himself will have nothing to do with custom. If sensuality is a kind of servitude, it is not so extreme as the moralists are inclined to judge it. To understand it is to avoid being consumed by it. But to define it as love and then proclaim, along with the Roderigos of the world of Court, that its powers are as deterministic as Fate is to surrender to custom. On the other hand, to treat desire as intrinsically evil is to assume that the body and the soul are irreconcilable enemies and that the soul can be victorious only by denying the body.

The difference between Donne's view of desire and this latter view of the Christian Platonists can be demonstrated by comparing his "Farewell to Love" with Shakespeare's Sonnet 129. The similarities of the views expressed in these two poems seem, initially, to be very close. For Shakespeare desire is an "expense of spirit":

Enjoy'd no sooner, but despised straight;
Past reason hunted; and no sooner had,
Past reason hated as a swallowed bait
On purpose laid to make the taker mad;
Had, having, and in quest to have, extreme;
A bliss in proof, and prov'd, a very woe;
Before, a joy propos'd; behind, a dream.

For Donne it is

> the thing which lovers so
> Blindly admire, and with such worship wooe;
> Being had, enjoying it decayes:
> And thence,
> What before pleas'd them all, takes but one sense
> And that so lamely, as it leaves behind
> A kinde of sorrowing dulnesse to the minde.

But the difference in their views emerges clearly in the concluding passages. It is a difference in attitude resulting from a difference in the ways the two poets assess the consequences of desire. Shakespeare's conclusion is a moral generalization lamenting the fact that man lacks the will to avoid what he knows beforehand will be morally debilitating: "All this the world well knows, yet none knows well/ To shun the heaven, that leads men to this hell." Donne's conclusion is a whimsical statement of a personal resolution:

> Since so, my minde
> Shall not desire what no man else can finde,
> I'll no more dote and runne
> To pursue things which had indammag'd me.
> And when I come where moving beauties be,
> As men doe when the summers Sunne
> Growes great,
> Though I admire their greatnesse, shun their heat;
> Each place can afford shadowes. If all faile,
> 'Tis but applying worme-seed to the Taile.

Donne's whimsicality—"If I succumb to beautiful women in the future, the worst that I shall have experienced is no more than that of an aphrodisiac"—is unquestionably a reaction against the attitudes that are typically expressed in the renunciation sonnets of his contemporaries. He is dismissing the judgment that passion is necessarily a madness which leaves its victim morally scarred.

Donne's own view of the roles of soul and body and of the faculties of each is basically Aristotelian and almost certainly derived from the Aristotelian school at Padua.[24] The crucial doctrine for Donne and the Italian neo-Aristotelians is Aristotle's conception of the soul-body relationship as an instance of "form" realizing itself in "matter." Man is indivisible. Although his soul may be immaterial, it is incapable of an independent existence, at least in this world, and is powerless except for the body's faculties. Man, then, is no more a purely intellectual substance that thinks than he is only a sensibility that perceives and feels. It follows from this doctrine that although it is possible to make distinctions between thought and passion or idea and sensation for the purpose of analysis, they are not real distinctions; and that while in any given instance of man's consciousness, thought or feeling may dominate, neither can exist without the other.

Given this essential "oneness" of man, love, as Donne concludes in "Loves growth," must be "mixt of all stuffes, paining soule, or sense"—including even the lowest level of life in man, the nutritive, which borrows "working vigour" from the sun. It will necessarily involve the sense faculties, since it is dependent on them, in its origins as well as in its consummation; and it will necessarily be active, rather than exclusively contemplative, inasmuch as man's existence for the Aristotelian is an act of form realizing itself in matter.

If the Aristotelian conception of the soul-body relationship denies the Platonic division, and with it the antitheses deriving from it, it nevertheless preserves analytical distinctions between matter and spirit, passion and reason, desire and will and thus furnishes Donne with a basis for distinguishing between a love which "takes but one sense" and what he refers to in "A Valediction: of my name, in the window" as "firme substantiall love." The former is dominated by sexual desire and seeks only a selfish physical satisfaction without regard for the integrity of the other person involved. The latter, as the Aristotelian term "substantial" suggests, is a relationship in which the rational (or substantial) soul comprehends "true worth" in the beloved and thus dominates the physical nature of the relationship. In contrast to the momentary satisfaction of a love "whose soule is

[24] See A. J. Smith, "The Metaphysic of Love."

sense" it provides something analogous to what Donne identifies as "essentiall joy" in "The second Anniversary":

> This is essentiall joy, where neither hee [God]
> Can suffer diminution, nor wee;
> 'Tis such a full, and such a filling good;
> Had th'Angels once look'd on him, they had stood.
>
> (ll. 443-46)

It is something like "essential" joy that the lovers in "The good-morrow" experience following their resurrection:[25]

> And now good morrow to our waking soules,
> Which watch not one another out of feare;
> For love, all love of other sights controules,
> And makes one little roome, an every where.
> Let sea-discovers to new worlds have gone,
> Let maps to other, worlds on worlds have showne,
> Let us possesse one world, each hath one, and is one.
>
> (ll. 8-14)

Substantial love will necessarily be parodoxical—in time but resistant to change, erotic but spiritual, worldly and otherworldly, contemplative and active—because it is a relationship between beings whose very substance is, paradoxically, both matter and spirit. It links the spiritual and the material worlds precisely because it is a relationship between beings whose position in the chain of being is midway between those two worlds. So long as the lover permits reason to order his experience, his love will remain substantial, a natural expression of the rationality which defines his position in the chain. He will not confuse desires "which reachest but to dust" with those "higher things" which are the proper object of human aspiration.

[25] Clay Hunt observes that "the poem derives from two related genres in Renaissance love poetry: the *aubade*, a morning serenade of a lover to his mistress, and a similar popular literary form, the *aube*, a love poem which presents a conversation between two lovers as they awaken at dawn after a night of love." *Donne's Poetry: Essays in Literary Analysis* (New Haven: Yale University Press, 1954), p. 54.

It is also probable that the Aristotelian theory of cognition furnishes the rationale for that perfect union of lovers in which, according to Donne, each participant assumes the other's identity, or "becomes" the other:

My face in thine eye, thine in mine appeares,
And true plaine hearts doe in the faces rest,
Where can we find two better hemispheares
Without sharpe North, without declining West?
("The good-morrow," ll. 16-19)

The exchanging of identities by lovers is a popular notion among the neo-Platonists, and Donne may have discovered it in their commentaries, perhaps Ficino's,[26] but it can also have come from a source that is more consistent with the predominantly Aristotelian position represented in such poems as "The good-morrow." As I have proposed, for Donne the condition of substantial love is understanding, and understanding for Aristotle is in itself a mode of possessing and becoming. One is said to possess and in a sense to become an object, according to the Aristotelian view, insofar as he understands it. The intellect is both "passive" and "active": actively, it abstracts the intelligible from sensation: passively, it is *informed* by what it has actively made intelligible.[27] In these terms, then, Donne's lovers possess each other insofar as the active intellect of each understands the other perfectly; and each becomes the other insofar as his passive intellect has "become" the other. It is possession on the level of understanding that has made sexual consummation in "The

[26] Ed. and trans. Sears Jayne, *Commentary on Plato's Symposium*, pp. 144-45.
[27] Citing Aristotle as his authority, Aquinas describes the twofold function of the intellect as follows: "He plainly wishes to show that the possible [i.e. passive] intellect is understood, as are other intelligible objects, from the fact that *the possible intellect, so far as it is actually understanding, is identical with that which is understood.* Moreover, Aristotle had remarked a little before that the possible intellect 'is in a sense potentially whatever is intelligible, though actually it is nothing until it has exercised its power of understanding'; and here he explicitly gives us to understand that *by actually knowing*, the possible intellect becomes its objects" [Italics mine]. *Summa Contra Gentiles*, trans. James F. Anderson, II, Chap. 78, p. 252.

Sunne Rising" and "The good-morrow" a "dying" into happiness rather than a brief pleasure followed by "a sorrowing
dulnesse of the minde."

Lovers, however, exist in time. Constancy is precarious—
threatened by all the vicissitudes that define existence in a
sublunary world—and the "essential joy" of substantial love is
finally for Donne a pale substitute for the supreme moment of
Beatitude:

> . . . what essentiall joy can'st thou expect
> Here upon earth? what permanent effect
> Of transitory causes? Dost thou love
> Beauty? (And beauty worthy'st is to move)
> Poore cousened cousenor, *that* she, and *that* thou,
> Which did begin to love, are neither now;
> You are both fluid, chang'd since yesterday;
> Next day repaires, (but ill) last dayes decay.
> Nor are, (although the river keepe the name)
> Yesterdaies waters, and to daies the same.
> So flowes her face, and thine eyes, neither now
> That Saint, nor Pilgrime, which your living vow
> Concern'd, remaines; but whil'st you thinke you bee
> Constant, you'are hourely in inconstancie.
> *(Anniv. II,* 387-400)

At best, his own beloved has been a source of happiness that is
as permanent as can be found this side of the grave. She is not
Deity, nor is the world of love he shares with her heaven. Like
Elizabeth Drury she may have

> kept by diligent devotion,
> Gods Image in such reparation,
> Within her heart, that what decay was growne,
> Was her first Parents fault, and not her owne,
> *(Anniv. II,* 455-58)

and thus have

> made this world in some proportion
> A heaven, and here became unto us all,
> Joy, (as our joyes admit) essential.
> (ll. 468-70)

But the shadows of change are always imminent, threatening the lovers' world and perhaps for that very reason making it the more valuable as the one relatively constant relationship which offers resistance to the flow of change.

In any event, it is Donne's intense awareness of the precariousness of love in a world of time and change which accounts for some of his most moving poems—poems in which he treats complaisance, separation, and death as threats to the lovers' world which can be successfully withstood through the mutual efforts of its inhabitants.

Only love "all alike no season knowes," and such love can not remain static and still endure. Paradoxically, although its essence is spiritual and unaffected by the natural processes of change, the condition of its duration is constant growth. It is "a growing, or full constant light; / And his first minute, after noone, is night." ("A Lecture upon the Shadow") It is only by fulfilling this condition that the lovers can preserve the completeness and timelessness of their love. They must continue to understand each other so perfectly that nothing external may intrude upon their relationship. This is the import of the lecture in "loves philosophy" that Donne presents in "A Lecture upon the Shadow."

> Stand still, and I will read to thee
> A Lecture, Love, in loves philosophy.
> These three houres that we have spent,
> Walking here, Two shadowes went
> Along with us, which we our selves produc'd;
> But, now the Sunne is just above our head,
> We doe those shadowes tread;
> And to brave clearnesse all things are reduc'd.
> So whilst our infant loves did grow,
> Disguises did, and shadowes, flow,
> From us, and our cares; but, now 'tis not so.
>
> That love hath not attain'd the high'st degree,
> Which is still diligent lest others see.
>
> Except our loves at this noone stay,
> We shall new shadowes make the other way.

As the first were made to blinde
Others; these which come behinde
Will worke upon our selves, and blind our eyes.
If our loves faint, and westwardly decline;
    To me thou, falsly, thine,
And I to thee mine actions shall disguise.
The morning shadowes weare away,
But these grow longer all the day,
But oh, loves day is short, if love decay.

Love is a growing, or full constant light;
And his first minute, after noone, is night.

Although in the early stages of their relationship the lovers, perhaps out of necessity, were concerned to disguise their feelings and were beset by cares, they are now completely indifferent to the reactions of outsiders. But if deception and worries are allowable in "infant" love or love's "morning," once love's "noon" is reached they are indications of love's decline. Love must remain at "noone." Once marred by deception, even if it is of the most innocent sort, love is not on its way to destruction, it has been destroyed. The permanent or constant admits of no degree.

If concerns for the ordinary world, either for its values or the reactions of others, are signs of love's decay, indifference is, conversely, proof of its vigor. Thus the lover in "The Canonization" impatiently dismisses the friend who has urged him to attend a little more to the affairs of the world, and then defiantly announces his indifference as to how his behavior may be interpreted by others. Fame, fortune, wealth, political and social preferment, even health and approaching age, are matters of indifference to the lover. Nor is he affected by those who disapprove of his attachment. If they see only sexuality in his behavior, it is of no matter; he rests confident in the knowledge that his love is substantial. However it may appear to others, he knows that his love is not confined to, although it includes, sex, since "Wee dye and rise the same." He knows that he enjoys a virtuous love, and he advises his critics to emulate it. It is a reflection of *caritas*; he and his beloved are, figuratively, saints who may intercede between God and man on man's behalf.

It is a love which fulfills a pattern "begged from above"; it is proper to man's nature and therefore in accord with God's law.

If love is precarious, requiring constant diligence and admitting no intrusions of any sort, it must also prove itself able to endure parting and separation. If love is substantial, that is, essentially spiritual, it can endure separation for the reasons expressed in a "Valediction: forbidding Mourning":

> Dull sublunary lovers love
> (Whose soule is sense) cannot admit
> Absence, because it doth remove
> Those things which elemented it.
>
> But we by a love, so much refin'd,
> That our selves know not what it is,
> Inter-assured of the mind,
> Care lesse, eyes, lips, and hands to misse.

Separation, however, is separation; and though lovers who are "inter-assured of the mind" may "care *lesse*" than sublunary lovers during periods of absence about not being able to enjoy their love, they do care. Their sorrow may be both profound and enduring, since, as the song "Sweetest love, I do not goe" indicates, each lover experiences in parting the other's grief as well as his own:

> When thou sigh'st, thou sigh'st not winde,
> But sigh'st my soule away,
> When thou weep'st, unkindly kinde,
> My lifes blood doth decay.

The lover has no alternative but to accept his grief and be consoled by the assurance that his love is able to endure separation. Like "virtuous men" who "passe mildly away," secure in their faith that their love of God is sufficient to assure them beatitude in being united with Him, the lovers must be confident that their love is such that they will be reunited finally and that their happiness will be resumed.

Donne's approach to the theme of separation is another indication of his lack of sympathy with neo-Platonic theory.

Separation for the Platonic lover, according to Bembo in the fourth book of *The Courtier*, is a trivial matter:

[The lover] shal not take thought at departure or in absence, because he shall evermore carrie his precious treasure about with him shutte fast within his hart.

And beside, through the vertue of imagination, hee shall fashion with himselfe that beautie much more faire than it is in deede. But among these commodities, the lover shall find another yet farre greater, in case hee will take this love for a stayre (as it were) to climbe up to another farre higher than it. The which he shall bring to passe, if he will goe and consider with himselfe, what a straight bond it is to bee alwaies in the trouble to behold the beautie of one bodie alone. And therefore to come out of this so narrowe a roome, hee shall gather in his thought by litle and litle so many ornaments, that meddling all beautie together, he shal make an universall conceite, and bring the multitude of them to the unitie on one alone, that is generally spred over all the nature of man. And thus shall he beholde no more the particular beautie of one woman, but an universall, that decketh out all bodies.[28]

Bembo's resolution of the problem of separation dismisses what for Donne is the real issue—the preservation in the face of necessary separation of the absolutely unique and most intimate of human relationships. He is not interested in the sublimation of his feelings or the kind of transcendence Bembo advises. Bembo's position presupposes that ideas are more real than things, for things only imperfectly reflect ideas. It follows, therefore, that to remember a particular woman, that is, to retain her image in the mind, is a more substantial mode of possession than to possess her actually; that to imagine her as being more beautiful than she really is, is more desirable than to remember her merely as she actually is; and, finally, that to contemplate universal feminine beauty is more desirable than to contemplate the idealized image of any specific woman. In these terms the lover approaches truth and the good as he moves from the particular and the concrete to the universal and the abstract. The reverse

[28] *The Courtier*, Everyman Edition, pp. 317-18.

is true for Donne; he is only interested in the specific and absolutely unique experience of the two lovers.

For Donne there is, finally, no way to eliminate the sorrows of separation. They can only be endured with the assurance that since substantial love is beyond the physical, it is able to survive such physical obstacles as separation. Whatever the metaphysical arguments and means available to demonstrate that parting lovers have no cause to fear inconstancy, it is finally only the inexplicable "magique" of love that can provide any such guarantee. This is the import of the brilliantly executed "A Valediction: of my name, in the window," a poem curiously ignored even by Donne's most enthusiastic admirers. The opening three stanzas introduce the notion that the lovers may preserve their relationship during separation only if they remember each other in detail:

> My name engrav'd herein,
> Doth contribute my firmnesse to this glasse,
> > Which, ever since that charme, hath beene
> > As hard, as that which grav'd it, was;
> Thine eye will give it price enough, to mock
> > The diamonds of either rock.

> 'Tis much that Glasse should bee
> As all confessing, and through-shine as I,
> > 'Tis more, that it shewes thee to thee,
> > And cleare reflects thee to thine eye.
> But all such rules, loves magique can undoe,
> > Here you see mee, and I am you.

> As no one point, nor dash,
> Which are but accessaries to this name,
> > The showers and tempests can outwash,
> > So shall all times finde mee the same;
> You this interenesse better may fulfill,
> > Who have the patterne with you still.

The lover's name engraved upon the window as a binding commitment of his "firmnesse" will only be more valuable than either the African or Indian diamond, if the beloved regards it properly as an object of contemplation. If she follows the instructions offered in the second and third stanzas, his signature will bear witness to the substantiality of the speaker's love. The conceit here is an extraordinary one: The window glass and the lover share the property of transparency, for the lover is fully known by the beloved. The function of the glass is to reveal the world beyond; but it also reflects. The beloved need only focus her eyes properly upon its surface to take advantage of its mirror-like quality. But both the natural powers of the glass—to reveal what is beyond and to reflect the image of the observer— may be transcended by "loves magique." If the beloved will contemplate the lover's name, and thus ignore the world beyond the window, she will see, simultaneously, the transparent name and her own image: "Here you see mee, and I am you." This is one of the few instances in the *Songs and Sonets* in which detail on both the figurative and literal level of metaphor are perfectly applicable. The signature and the reflected image on the glass are one, just as the lovers, who have "become" each other are one. The requirement to be met if the name is to be properly an object of contemplation is that the name and the reflected image—not what lies beyond them—must be the sole object of perception and thought.

The initial conceit is further complicated by the introduction in the third stanza of the metaphysical concept of "identity." The first four lines, which establish a fairly obvious analogy between the resistance of the signature to the wind and rain and the "firmness" of the lover's vow, conclude the initial phase of the poem, the lover's pledge. The closing couplet, however, complicates the preceding analogy by introducing a concept which suddenly throws the "points" and "dashes," the "accessaries to this name," into a new perspective. Separately, the points and dashes are no more the name than are the separate parts of the human body the man behind the name. They are "accidental" attributes given unity and the relationship of parts to a whole by the informing principle that organizes them and thus makes the signature a meaningful symbol of identity, rather than a mere collection of points and dashes. Just as the letters on the glass become meaningful, so, too, the separate parts of the body become meaningful and intelligible as parts of man when informed by the soul. The analogy is carried even further: the dots and lines are the "matter" of which the signature is composed, and as "matter" they constitute the principle, in the Aquinian system, of "individuation." They make it this particular signature and no other in the same way that matter, the body, makes the man behind the name "this man" and no other. The full meaning of the closing lines is now available: "You this interenesse better may fulfill,/ Who have the patterne with you still." The "accessaries to this name" do indeed "fulfill" the name, but the name is only a symbol of identity. The lover's identity may only be fulfilled by the beloved. She brings him to life when by contemplating his name and her own reflected image she "becomes" him.

The fourth stanza dismisses the original conceit and with it the complex metaphysical learning on which it is based. The "learning" in the first three stanzas may have been "too hard and deepe" to serve the purpose for which it was conceived, and so the lover now invites his beloved to consider his name, a symbol of identity in the first three stanzas, as having only a physical significance. She may meditate upon the bony signature en*graved* on the window as a death's-head, a reminder of "lovers mortalitie," or as a skeleton of the lover whom she may resurrect through meditation:

> Or, if too hard and deepe
> This learning be, for a scratch'd name to teach,
>   It, as a given deaths head keepe,
>   Lovers mortalitie to preach,
> Or thinke this ragged bony name to bee
>   My ruinous Anatomie.
>
> Then, as all my soules bee,
> Emparadis'd in you, (in whom alone
>   I understand, and grow, and see,)
>   The rafters of my body, bone
> Being still with you, the Muscle, Sinew, and Veine,
>   Which tile this house, will come againe:

Till my returne, repaire
And recompact my scattered body so.
  As all the vertuous powers which are
  Fix'd in the starres, are said to flow
Into such characters, as graved bee
    When these starres have supremacie:

  So since this name was cut
When love and griefe their exaltation had,
  No doore 'gainst this names influence shut;
  As much more loving, as more sad,
'Twill make thee; and thou shouldst, till I returne,
  Since I die daily, daily mourne.

Both alternatives stress the body and the physical consequences of separation. The first, the signature as a death's-head,
may be of use in two ways. It may remind the beloved of death
and separation at the grave's edge and thus make the present
parting easier to accept, or it may lead to acceptance of temporary separation and thus prepare for the parting that must
inevitably come with death. Resignation to temporary separation can be, in short, an exercise in preparation for death, as
Donne remarks in "Sweetest love, I do not goe":

    . . . since that I
  Must dye at last, 'tis best,
  To use my selfe in jest
    Thus by fain'd deaths to dye.

The second alternative, the signature as the lover's skeleton
which may be resurrected through meditation, is the more fully
developed. The concern behind it is precisely the opposite of
what the reader of Donne's other valedictory poems has come
to expect. The lover is here anxious to encourage mourning.
He would have his beloved experience repeatedly the extreme
love and grief that he had experienced at the moment of their
parting.

    What Donne is recommending to his beloved in this second
lesson of meditation is essentially the same method recommended in the Ignatian *Spiritual Exercises* for stimulating love

and sorrow.[29] The Christian penitent, seeking to experience the sorrow and love that constitutes the experience of full contrition, is advised by Loyola to meditate upon the wounds of Christ, for instance, and to stimulate grief and love by imagining as concretely as possible the ugliness of the wounds. Donne asks his beloved to visualize him at the time of their parting as concretely as possible in order to stimulate and thus to re-experience the love and grief he had felt at the moment of their parting.

The astrological analogy employed in the sixth and seventh stanzas to develop this final consequence of meditation is self-explanatory; but the final line of the seventh stanza, "Since I die daily, daily mourne," is difficult. It appears to have two distinct though not contradictory meanings. First, the lover "dies daily" inasmuch as the passing of time, the passing of each day, brings him closer to death. It may also be, however, that we are to understand that the name on the window "dies" nightly when it fades from the window and is no longer visible.

The next three stanzas (eight through ten) anticipate possible distractions that might intrude upon the beloved's meditation and suggest how they might lead back to the name on the window. They reassert the importance of the full recollection of the absent lover in all his particularity. They are simpler than the preceding stanzas, but beautifully managed; especially the eighth stanza, in which the speaker anticipates the possibility of a new suitor who might draw the beloved's attentions to the world lying beyond the window:

> When thy inconsiderate hand
> Flings ope this casement, with my trembling name,
> To looke on one, whose wit or land,
> New battry to thy heart may frame,
> Then thinke this name alive, and that thou thus
> In it offendst my Genius.

The flung-open window trembles and the name comes alive with a movement expressing exactly the feeling caused by the

[29] Martz does not notice Donne's indebtedness to the meditative tradition in this particular poem.

inconsiderate offense done to the lover. The final stanza is
equally successful although more difficult:

> But glass, and lines must bee,
> No meanes our firme substantiall love to keepe;
> Neere death inflicts this lethargie,
> And this I murmure in my sleepe;
> Impute this idle talke, to that I goe,
> For dying men talke often so.

The complexity results from the puns on "death" and "dying."
First of all, "death" designates parting; the lovers are represented on the edge of "death." The sexual meaning may also
be present, the implication being that the act has just been
completed. Hence the lover can now look forward only to
separation; since in spite of the ways outlined in preceding
stanzas for preserving substantial love, only his real presence
and physical reaffirmation will guarantee its security.

The one remaining threat to substantial love that Donne
considers is death. It is the subject of "A nocturnal upon S.
Lucies day" and "The Anniversary." The resolution of the
problem in each of these poems is consistent with the view of
love that is affirmed in "The good-morrow" and "The
Extasie."

If the attainment of perfect love is to gain a world outside of
time and to experience "joy (as our joyes admit) essential," it
follows that to lose the beloved is to suffer spiritual death and a
sorrow analogous to that suffered throughout eternity by the
damned who are denied the Beatific Vision.[30] The speaker in
"A nocturnal" has apparently suffered such a loss. The death of
his beloved has resulted, metaphorically, in his spiritual death.[31]

[30] I agree with Martz's conjecture that "Donne wrote the 'Nocturnall'
after his wife's death in 1617; though it might have been composed
on some occasion of severe illness . . ." *Poetry of Meditation*, p. 215.

[31] Martz offers a somewhat different reading: The poem is "a
'Vigill,' commemorating the death of his beloved—his saint. He recalls
the passionate fluctuations of their worldly career, in terms that suggest
a long period of frustrated spiritual devotion. . . . But with her death
his physical life has died, and he is 're-begot Of absence, darkenesse,
death': in him love has 'wrought new Alchimie' by expressing 'A

Whereas all other beings endure the temporary subsidence in winter of the life forces because of their dependence upon God, the speaker has been deprived of the final cause on which his existence depends:

> All others, from all things, draw all that's good,
> Life, soule, forme, spirit, whence they beeing have;
> I, by loves limbecke, am the grave
> Of all, that's nothing. Oft a flood
> Have wee two wept, and so
> Drownd the whole world, us two; oft did we grow
> To be two Chaosses, when we did show
> Care to ought else; and often absences
> Withdrew our soules, and made us carcasses.
>
> But I am by her death, (which word wrongs her)
> Of the first nothing, the Elixir grown;
> Were I a man, that I were one,
> I needs must know; I should preferre,
> If I were any beast,
> Some ends, some means; Yea plants, yea stones detest,
> And love; All, all some properties invest;
> If I an ordinary nothing were,
> As shadow, a light, and body must be here.
>
> But I am None; nor will my Sunne renew.
>
> (ll. 19-37)

In contrast to other sorrows he has experienced as the result of lesser privations, this sorrow is absolute. The lovers' world of which he has been a part, that unity achieved by a mutual understanding so complete that each has become the other, has been submerged by tides of grief, the griefs of one becoming the griefs of the other. He has endured the chaos of that world when concerns of the outside world have proved to be distractions. And he has experienced the "death" of parting, when "absences withdrew our soules and made us carcasses." But now

---

quintessence even from nothingnesse. His only life now lies in the spiritual realm where she now lives . . ." *Ibid.*, 214.

the beloved's actual death has caused his spiritual death. He is now "the grave of all, that's nothing."

The effects of the beloved's death on the speaker are analogous to what the consequences would be if somehow God should cease to be. Just as the world's continued existence depends upon God as efficient and final cause, so the lover's world depends upon his beloved as efficient and final cause. When describing himself as "of the first nothing, the Elixir grown," the lover asks the reader to imagine a state of "nothingness" more extreme than the nothingness that existed before the Creation. Before the Creation there was chaos and God, non-being and Being. If the reader can imagine that not even God existed before the Creation, he can comprehend the "quintessence of non-being" which the speaker conceives his present state to be: deprived of his beloved upon whom he and his world have been absolutely dependent, he now endures a Godless void. He has been deprived of being on all levels—the rational, the sensible, the nutritive, and the inanimate. He is deprived even of apparent but unreal being, as the extraordinary hyperbole in the following lines indicate: "If I an ordinary nothing were,/ As shadow, a light, and body must be here." All created being inclines toward God by fulfilling its being according to its substantial form; the lover, at least in the world of love, has been deprived of the efficient and final cause on which his own existence and the existence of the world in which he has formerly lived depends.

The lesson to be learned from the lover's tragedy is now clear. To those who may have discovered the kind of love the speaker has formerly enjoyed, he offers a warning: "Study me then, you who shall lovers bee/ At the next world, that is, at the next Spring." (ll. 10-11) They should bear in mind the contingency of their happiness and must remember that if love is potentially the source of the greatest temporal happiness, it is also the potential source of the deepest sorrow. They must expect to follow the speaker's example and "prepare" themselves through a similar "Vigill" for eventual reunion "At the next world." As for those who enjoy only their lust, they had best take advantage of what a brief "summer" allows:

> You lovers, for whose sake, the lesser Sunne
> At this time to the Goat is runne
> To fetch new lust, and give it you,
> Enjoy your summer all.
>
> (ll. 38-41)

It will be all the love that they will have. As for the speaker in the poem, his world is ended; his only recourse is to prepare for the next world where his beloved enjoys "her long night's festivall" and where they may perhaps again be reunited.

The question of whether or not lovers will be reunited in the next world is raised again in "The Anniversary." The opening stanza presents summarily what Donne has worked out in detail in such poems as "Loves growth," "The good-morrow," and "A Valediction: forbidding mourning": substantial love is constant because it is essentially a relationship of minds. What is new in the poem is the affirmation that after death and resurrection the lovers will continue to enjoy their love.[32] Although the lovers' "world," in which each lover is, simultaneously, subject and ruler, would appear, finally, to be no different than the sublunary world where all things "to their destruction draw," the lovers may be sure that since their love is proper it will be blessed. After resurrection it will be at least as great as it is now, and perhaps even greater (presumably, because of the purification of the body and its senses that is supposed to occur in resurrection). Neither lover, therefore, has cause for fears of any sort. Fear of separation is a false fear and should be dismissed; and the lovers may also dismiss "true feares," for the only fear (true fear) which need concern man is that of failing to repent and thus failing to merit blessing on the day of resurrection.

By insisting in this poem that his love is "blessed," Donne again implicitly rejects the dichotomy between profane and divine love that is generally accepted among his contemporaries. Substantial love will be blessed because it is founded on values rationally apprehended and characterized by emotions properly ordered. It is specifically *human* love involving the whole man,

---

[32] Henry King assumes a similar position in "The Exequy."

his body as well as his mind; and we shall see in the concluding section of this chapter that when Donne turns from human love to religious devotion and those states of feeling which are requisite to salvation, it is still the whole man who must be involved. Emotions which are partially or imperfectly understood in terms of the revealed truths which motivate them, emotions which are deficient or excessive, are dangerous in the critical matter of redemption. Fear inspired by the contemplation of Absolute Justice may lead to despair; sorrow wrongly or inadequately motivated may lead to false assurance. On the other hand, intellectual acknowledgement of Justice and Mercy is not enough. The paradoxical nature of the Christian Deity must be comprehended by the whole man, and the proof of such comprehension consists of the emotional states experienced when the paradoxical nature of Justice and Mercy is made the subject of meditation.

The Holy Sonnets

Although nearly a century of innovation and refinement separates Skelton's "Upon A Dead Man's Head" and Donne's "Oh my blacke Soule! now thou art summoned," the poems disclose affinities of style, structure, and intention that are evidence of an uninterrupted tradition of renunciation and penitential lyric. The genre remains for Donne what it had been for Skelton—a mode of intense meditation aimed at discovering the immediate personal relevance of commonplaces that are at the center of Christian experience. The feelings awakened in such verse are the measure of its success; if they are of sufficient strength they will move the novitiate to take the necessary steps leading to redemption and salvation. For Donne as for Skelton the penitential lyric is a poetry of self-persuasion; hence, their similar reliance upon strategies which most effectively dramatize the penitent's position. He must see and feel death's imminence and the ineluctability of the categories of transience and original sin; he must experience the unrelenting logic of Absolute Justice and discover in the Passion the emotion of redeeming love.

To accomplish these ends the writers of penitential lyric

customarily relied upon the resources of the plain style—its convention of direct statement and its unadorned vernacular, rich in proverbial wisdom, simple metaphor, and realistic concrete detail. Although as the century progresses and the genre develops greater complexity by utilizing the sonnet form and conventions of Elizabethan song and by appropriating to its purposes structures from the art of meditation, it continues to concentrate upon the moment and consequences of death in a language of direct statement. In early examples, in Skelton and Vaux for instance, texture is dominated by physical detail, medieval in its folk quality, that stresses the ugliness of the enemy death, or the inevitability of advancing age, and dramatizes the urgency of renunciation and repentance. Vestiges of the medieval version of the plain style are especially strong in Skelton:[33]

> I have well espied
> No man may him hide
> From Death hollow-eyed,
>   With sinews wyderëd
> With bonës shyderëd,
> With his worm-eaten maw,
> And his ghastly jaw
> Gasping aside,
> Naked of hide,
> Neither flesh nor fell.
>
> .   .   .   .
>
> Our days be dated
> To be checkmated
> With draughtës of death
> Stopping our breath:
> Our eyen sinking,
> Our bodies stinking,
> Our soules brinning.
>
> ("Upon A Dead Man's Head," ll. 9-18, 29-35)

In Vaux[34] a more accomplished rhythm and the assumption of the persona of courtly lover are evidence of the kind of refine-

[33] *The Complete Poems of John Skelton*, ed., Phillip Henderson.
[34] *The Poems of Lord Vaux*, ed., Larry P. Vonalt (Denver: Swallow Press, 1960).

ment which the genre will continue to undergo throughout the century; nevertheless, the medieval manner persists, especially in the quality of detail and direct statement:

> The wrinkles in my brow,
> The furrows in my face,
> Say, limping age will hedge him now
> Where youth must give him place.
> The harbinger of death,
> To me I see him ride;
> The cough, the cold, the gasping breath
> Doth bid me to provide
> A pickaxe and a spade,
> And eke a shrouding sheet,
> A house of clay for to be made
> For such a guest most meet.
> Methinks I hear the clerk
> That knolls the careful knell,
> And bide me leave my woeful work,
> Ere nature me compel.
> ("The Aged Lover Renounceth Love," ll. 19-34)

Vaux's enumeration of stark detail is succeeded in Gascoigne by reflective general statement reinforced by the concrete details of an appropriate metaphor:

> The dreadfull night with darkesomnesse,
> Had over spread the light,
> And sluggish sleepe with drowsyness,
> Had over prest our might:
> A glasse wherin you may beholde,
> Eche storme that stopes our breath,
> Our bed the grave, our clothes lyke molde,
> And sleepe like dreadfull death.
> (Gascoigne's "Good-Morrow," ll. 17-24)

In Ralegh the medieval has given way to a new idiom, one reflecting extensive courtly refinement on all levels, but the manner remains direct and the old motive behind the use of concrete detail is still dominant:

[332]

The Light, the Belly, lipps and breath,
He [Time] dimms, discolours, and destroyes,
With those he feedes, but fills not death,
Which sometimes were the foode of Joyes;
Yea Time doth dull each liuely witt,
And dryes all wantonnes with it.
("Nature that washt her hands in milke," ll. 25-30)

Seeing my flesh must die so soone,
And want a head to dine next noone,
Iust at the stroke when my vaines start and spred
Set on my soule an euerlasting head.
("The passionate mans Pilgrimage," ll. 54-57)

Donne continues the technique of visualizing the moment of death, but with a shift of focus from the physical to the spiritual realities of the moment. The result is a more deeply introspective and dramatic verse than is ordinarily to be found in earlier examples of the genre.

Oh my blacke Soule! now thou art summoned
By sicknesse, deaths herald, and champion;
Thou art like a pilgrim, which abroad hath done
Treason, and durst not turne to whence hee is fled,
Or like a thiefe, which till deaths doome be read,
Wisheth himselfe delivered from prison;
But damn'd and hal'd to execution,
Wisheth that still he might be imprisoned.
(No. 4, ll. 1-8)[35]

This is my playes last scene, here heavens appoint
My pilgrimages last mile; and my race
Idly, yet quickly runne, hath this last pace,
My spans last inch, my minutes last point,
And gluttonous death, will instantly unjoynt
My body, and soule, and I shall sleepe a space,
But my'ever-waking part shall see that face,
Whose feare already shakes my every joynt.
(No. 6, ll. 1-8)

[35] Quotations from Donne's religious verse are from Helen Gardner's *John Donne: The Devotional Poems* (Oxford: Clarendon Press, 1952).

The shift is due to the influence of the Art of Meditation, especially to that of the Ignatian exercises in meditation upon the Last Things; but rather than altering the course of the tradition of renunciation and penitential verse, the Art contributes to its refinement by making available a highly developed method of self-analysis and self-persuasion. The Art also provides powerful support for the tradition of the plain style by insisting upon simplicity, directness, and homely humility. Edward Dawson, whose *Practical Methode of Meditation*[36] is described by Louis Martz as providing "the essence of the advice for meditation that was being offered by spiritual counselors throughout Europe, as well as by the underground priests in England,"[37] recommends the familiar and the ordinary as the most suitable source of similitudes—". . . we may help ourselves much to the framing of spirituall conceites, if we apply unto our matter familiar similitudes drawne from our ordinary actions. . ." (p. 14)—and advises that in prayer the novitiate "talke with God as a servant with his Maister, as a sonne with his Father, as one friend with another, as a spouse with her beloved bridgrome, or as a guilty prisoner with his Judge. . ." (p. 17). Donne's verse is stylistically more complex, especially in its syntax and rhythms, than Skelton's, Vaux's, or Gascoigne's. This is due in part to the refinements and innovations which English verse has undergone during the years intervening and partly to the shift from earlier habits of reflecting upon the physical details of death to Donne's own habit of concentrating upon death's spiritual ramifications. Nevertheless, the *Holy Sonnets* by observing the stylistic norms recommended in the treatises on meditation, preserve the old straightforward and unadorned manner of the tradition of the plain style.

The persistence of the tradition of penitential verse in the *Holy Sonnets* is also evident in the sequential order they reveal in Helen Gardner's fine edition.[38] As a group they constitute the

[36] In Louis Martz's *The Meditative Poem: An Anthology of Seventeenth-Century Verse* (New York: Doubleday and Co., 1963), pp. 3-23.
[37] *Ibid.*, Introduction, xviii.
[38] The following discussion of the *Holy Sonnets* is a slightly revised

most complete account yet to appear in the lyric of the devout Anglican's quest for "saving sorrow," showing in their structure and progression how Anglican disciplines developed to lead the penitent to redemption appropriated Catholic habits of meditation to a specifically Protestant end. The fear and love which Gardner has identified as the respective themes of the two groups of six that comprise the 1633 sequence are identified by Donne as essential preliminaries to contrition:

> Place the affection . . . upon the right object, God, and I have, in some measure, done that which this Text directed, (*Taught you the fear of the Lord*) if I send you away in either disposition, *Timorous*, or *amorous*; possessed with either, the fear, or the love of God; for, this fear is inchoative love, and this love is consummative fear; the love of God begins in fear, and the fear of God ends in love; and that love can never end, for God is love.[39]

The stimulation of fear in the first half of the sequence of 1633 prepares for the stimulation of love in the second half, which in turn prepares for the "contrite" sorrow that is the theme of the four sonnets of 1635 and the three Westmoreland sonnets.

Both Catholic and Anglican doctrines agree that contrition is essentially a state of feeling, a "sorrow of heart and detestation for sin committed, with the resolve to sin no more." Anglican doctrine, however, insists absolutely that sorrow must be motivated by a hatred for sin in itself and that it must be precipitated by love for God.[40] Donne is simply quoting orthodox doctrine when he insists that sorrow must issue from love and that fear is only a preliminary to love. Fear is merely attrition and, in itself, not sufficient for salvation.

> Our new *Romane Chymists* . . . can change any foulness into cleanness easily. They require no more after sin, but . . .

version of "John Donne's *Holy Sonnets* and the Anglican Doctrine of Contrition," *Studies in Philology*, LVI, 3 (July 1959), 504-18.

[39] *The Sermons of John Donne*, eds., Evelyn M. Simpson and George R. Potter (Berkeley: University of California Press, 1953), VI, 113.

[40] See above, p. 340.

A little slight inward sorrow, and that's enough. For, they have provided an easier way then *Contrition*; for, that which they have induc'd, and call *Attrition*, is not an affection . . . That hath proposed God, for the mark, that it is directed to . . . but it is such an affection as may be had without any concurrence or assistance of grace, and is onely . . . a natural sorrow, proceeding onely out of a servile fear of torment. And yet, a Confession made with this Attrition and no more, is enough for salvation, say they; and he that hath made a confession with such a disposition as this . . . shall never need to repent any farther for his sins. . . . This is Attrition, to be displeased with our sins, but not more with our sins, then with any thing else. . . To have a purpose to leave a sin, but not the sin rather then any thing else, this is their *Attrition*, and this is their enough for salvation. A sigh of the *penitent*, a word of the *Priest*, makes all clean, and induces an absolute pureness.[41]

As Donne implies in this passage, the Anglican's penitence must be made directly to God; he cannot rely on any church intermediary; he receives no assurance from his priest that he has satisfied the requirements of contrition. Assurance is entirely a matter of conscience.

The consequences of such doctrine for a man whose belief is as rigorous as Donne's are an intensive and sometimes tortuous examination of conscience, and equally intensive meditation upon the consequences of sin and those Christian commonplaces that ought, God willing, to stimulate proper love and sorrow. But the effect toward saving sorrow is difficult. Such sorrow can be only an effect of grace; and since it is a state of emotional conviction, not merely a rational acknowledgment of sin and of the debt of love that man owes God, the question of assurance is exceedingly difficult. To be too easily convinced of saving sorrow is to risk the sin of complacence; to be overly scrupulous is to risk despair. The avoidance of either extreme is doubly difficult, since contrition is a suprarational experience— a state of feeling that cannot be confirmed by rational means.

[41] *The Sermons of John Donne*, I, 203-04.

The penitent's only recourse, therefore, is to follow disciplines advocated by the church and designed to help him cooperate with God in the hope that with their aid his efforts will be rewarded with saving grace.[42]

Those disciplines are the disciplines employed in the Ignatian art of meditation for the stimulation of religious fervor, and it is in the interest of experiencing contrition that Donne employs the Exercises in the sonnets of 1633. He has not composed "two contrasting sets of six [sonnets]" to "create an image of himself at prayer"; nor is he committed "to showing himself as he would be rather than as he is,"[43] except in the obvious sense that any man of Donne's religious convictions prefers salvation to damnation. The *Holy Sonnets* represent a series of efforts to experience those states of feeling that either precede or are concomitant with contrition. Once this is recognized, the stages of progression in the sequence of 1633 are clearly evident.

The introductory poem, "As due by many titles I resigne," poses the problem that the sequence attempts to resolve. The penitent, having satisfied the preliminary requirements of re-pentance by a declaration of faith and an acknowledgment of sin (ll. 1-10), must now seek the grace that is essential to contrite sorrow:

Except thou rise and for thine owne worke fight,
Oh I shall soone despaire, when I doe see
That thou lov'st mankind well, yet wilt'not chuse me,
And Satan hates mee, yet is loth to lose mee.

But grace is not immediately forthcoming. The penitent must first dissuade his will from sin; and it is to this end that fear of punishment is stimulated in the next three sonnets. Donne's procedure here is confirmed by Richard Hooker, who stresses the function of fear as prerequisite to repentance: Although "fear is impotent and unable to advise itself; yet this good it hath, that men are thereby made desirous to prevent, if possibly they may, whatsoever evil they dread . . . fear of divine revenge

[42] See Richard Hooker, *The Works of Richard Hooker* (Oxford: Clarendon Press, 1865), II, 239-40.
[43] Gardner, xvi.

and punishment, where it taketh place, doth make men desirous to be rid . . . from that inward guiltiness of sin, wherein they would else securely continue."[44] For the stimulation of fear Hooker advises meditating on the Ignatian "Last Things": "The resurrection of the dead, the judgment of the world to come, and the endless misery of sinners being apprehended, this worketh fear" (p. 241). Such meditation, however, must also include a consideration of both the means and possibility of avoiding "revenge and punishment":

> Howbeit, when faith hath wrought a fear of the event of sin, yet repentance hereupon ensueth not, unless our belief conceive both the possibility, inasmuch as God is merciful, and most willing to have sin cured; the means, because he hath plainly taught what is requisite and shall suffice unto that purpose. (p. 241)

Donne's employment of the Ignatian topics is thoroughly in accord with Hooker's instructions. "Oh my blacke Soule! now thou art summoned" meditates in the octet upon "the endless misery" that confronts the sinner at the point of death and in the sestet contemplates the possibility and means of averting punishment. The possibility is made manifest, of course, through Christ; the means is repentance or, more exactly, that proper sorrow, as well as the acceptance of the Atonement, which allows grace to be operative:

> Yet grace, if thou repent, thou canst not lacke;
> But who shall give thee that grace to beginne?
> Oh make thy selfe with holy mourning blacke,
> And red with blushing, as thou art with sinne;
> Or wash thee in Christs blood, which hath this might
> That being red, it dyes red soules to white.

It should be noticed here that "holy mourning blacke" and "red with blushing" imply sorrow for sin rather than sorrow occasioned by fear of punishment. The procedure in the next poem, "This is my playes last scene, here heavens appoint" is the same except for one interesting variation. This time the

44 *The Works of Richard Hooker*, II, 240.

"means" and "possibility" of avoiding the punishment demanded by absolute justice—Hooker's essential preliminaries to
repentance—are founded on an argument which is deliberately
fallacious, and one which dates back at least to the medieval
"Debate of the Body and Soul": Since it has been my body
that has sinned, and since at the moment of death my body
will be separated from my soul, I shall be thus purged of evil
and may therefore legitimately hope that "God will impute me
righteous." What is particularly interesting is that Donne rejects
this argument as fallacious in the following poem on "the resurrection of the dead" by pointing out that it is the whole man—
not the soul alone—that will be judged on Doomsday:

> At the round earths imagin'd corners, blow
> Your trumpets, Angells, and arise, arise
> From death, you numberlesse infinities
> Of soules, and to your scattred bodies goe. . . .

Furthermore, it is futile to hope for pardon on the Day of
Judgment. There is only one way of receiving pardon: full
repentance "here on this lowly ground":

> 'Tis late to aske abundance of thy grace,
> When wee are there; here on this lowly ground,
> Teach mee how to repent; for that's as good
> As if thou'hadst seal'd my pardon, with thy blood.

At this point in the sequence the first phase of the discipline
is concluded. The following two poems, "If poysonous mineralls, and if that tree" and "Death be not proud, though some
have called thee," are transitional sonnets in the sequence which
look forward to the next phase of contrition, the transcendence
of fear through love. "If poysonous mineralls, and if that tree"
questions the justice and mercy of God in order to dramatize the
futility of attempting to resolve by reason the mystery of God's
justice:

> If lecherous goats, if serpents envious
> Cannot be damn'd; Alas; why should I bee?
> Why should intent or reason, borne in mee,
> Make sinnes, else equall, in mee more heinous?

And mercy being easie, and glorious
To God, in his sterne wrath, why threatens hee?

To argue such questions—to dispute the paradoxical concept of
a deity who is at once absolutely just and infinitely merciful—is
pointless. The penitent is obliged to accept God and His decrees
on faith and to throw himself upon His mercy. Thus the stimulation of fear by meditating upon God as absolute justice brings
home to the penitent the need to make full repentance. The
poem ends with a plea for the grace that will transform sorrow
incited by fear to sorrow incited by love:

But who am I, that dare dispute with thee?
O God, Oh! of thine onely worthy blood,
And my teares, make a heavenly Lethean flood,
And drowne in it my sinnes blacke memorie.
That thou remember them, some claime as debt,
I thinke it mercy, if thou wilt forget.

"Death be not proud, though some have called thee" dismisses
death as a motive of fear. Fear of death is a "natural fear"
and, according to Donne, natural fears are transcended by
"Feare of the Lord": "when the feare of the Lord is entred
into my naturall feare, my feare is more conversant, more
exercised upon the contemplation of *Good*, then *Evill*, more
upon the glory of God . . . than upon the afflictions of this life,
how malignant, how manifold soever."[45]

The sequence now proceeds to the final prerequisite to contrition, the love for God.[46] The first three poems (Sonnets 7,
8, and 9) are devoted to the goodness and mercy of God,
subjects which, according to Hooker, are the best means of
stimulating the love that "moveth unto repentance":

Our love and desire of union with God ariseth from the
strong conceit which we have of his admirable goodness. The

[45] *The Sermons of John Donne*, VI, 106.
[46] Miss Gardner observes that "meditation, designed to deepen religious fear, needs to be followed by a meditation to awaken love"
(Introduction, xlii), but she does not develop the point in any way that
suggests she is aware of the disciplines of contrition that I have been
discussing.

goodness of God which particularly moveth unto repentance, is his mercy towards mankind, notwithstanding sin: for let it once sink deeply into the mind of man, that howsoever we have injured God, his very nature is averse from revenge, except unto sin we add obstinacy; otherwise always ready to accept our submission as a full discharge or recompense for all wrongs; and can we choose but begin to love him whom we have offended? or can we but begin to grieve that we have offended him whom we now love? (p. 242)

The first of these three poems, "Spit in my face yee Jewes, and pierce my side," expresses for the first time in the sequence a sorrow that is not motivated by fear. By considering sin as cruelty to Christ, Donne approaches the sorrow for which he had prayed in "If poysonous mineralls, and if that tree." The sestet then moves to what is also the subject of meditation in the next two poems, a consideration of divine mercy:

> Oh let mee then, his strange love still admire:
> Kings pardon, but he bore our punishment.
> And *Jacob* came cloth'd in vile harsh attire
> But to supplant, and with gainfull intent:
> God cloth'd himselfe in vile mans flesh, that so
> Hee might be weake enough to suffer woe.

The next poem, "Why are wee by all creatures waited on?" reconsiders the hierarchical creation, which had been the subject of "If poysonous mineralls, and if that tree." Whereas the earlier poem had considered reason only as the faculty whereby man was made responsible for his transgressions, it is now treated as the gift that enables man to rule the natural world and second only to the Atonement as an indication of God's love. The progression from reason as a source of culpability to reason as a source of nobility is the direct result of the different phase of repentance involved. The same thing occurs in the next poem, "What if this present were the worlds last night?", which, like "This is my playes last scene, here heavens appoint," imagines the imminence of Doomsday. In the earlier poem fear was stimulated by contemplating God as judge. Now, to dispel fear, the subject of meditation is the mercy and love of God that is evident in the Crucifixion. The face of God "whose feare already shakes my every joynt" is supplanted by the face of Christ, mercy suffusing wrath:

Marke in my heart, O Soule, where thou dost dwell,
The picture of Christ crucified, and tell
Whether that countenance can thee affright,
Teares in his eyes quench the amasing light,
Blood fills his frownes, which from his pierc'd head fell,
And can that tongue adjudge thee unto hell,
Which pray'd forgivenesse for his foes fierce spight?

With a final declaration of assurance, "This beauteous forme assures a pitious minde" (l. 14), another step toward contrition has been taken. The next step is, of course, to return God's love. This once accomplished, proper sorrow ought to follow. Thus it is the debt of love to God that provides the subject for the final three poems of the sequence.

"Batter my heart, three person'd God; for, you" is a prayer for the grace that is necessary for the consummation of contrition. The penitent has co-operated in so far as he is able:

I, like an usurpt towne, to'another due,
Labour to'admit you, but Oh, to no end,
Reason your viceroy in mee, mee should defend,
But is captiv'd, and proves weake or untrue. . . .

Sufficient love for God requires divine aid:

Divorce mee, 'untie, or breake that knot againe,
Take mee to you, imprison mee, for I
Except you'enthrall mee, never shall be free,
Nor ever chast, except you ravish mee.

The plea here is nearly identical to the plea made in the introductory poem, "As due by many titles I resigne." It differs only in the intensity of feeling. The penitent has experienced the full implications of what in the earlier poem was stated simply as a truism:

Oh I shall soone despaire, when I doe see
That thou lov'st mankind well, yet wilt'not chuse me,
And Satan hates mee, yet is loth to lose mee.

The spiritual effort undertaken in the intervening eight sonnets culminates in this more intense desire and more urgent need to satisfy the requirements of contrition. After the next sonnet, "Wilt thou love God, as he thee! then digest," which only reaffirms the tenet that grace will not be forthcoming until the penitent's love for God is sufficient, the sequence is concluded by "Father, part of his double interest"—a summarizing affirmation of the tenet that mercy transcends justice and that the command to love, by which God's law is abridged, offers the only means and possibility for hope to the penitent.

The sequence ends, therefore, with no indication that the efforts it represents have been successful: each of the preliminary stages which ought to lead to contrition are represented, but so far there has occurred no expression of contrite sorrow. There are indications of such success, however, in the "penitential" sonnets of 1635. These four poems, while not sequentially related to the sequence of 1633, consummate, nevertheless, the disciplines represented by it. Richard Hooker concludes his discussion of the methods of bringing about contrition by describing what are in effect the subjects and feelings of the sonnets of 1635:

> From these considerations, setting before our eyes our inexcusable both unthankfulness in disobeying so merciful, and foolishness in provoking so powerful a God, there ariseth necessarily a pensive and corrosive desire that we had done otherwise; a desire which suffereth us to foreslow no time, to feel no quietness within ourselves, to take neither sleep nor food with contentment, never to give over supplications, confessions, and other penitent duties, till the light of God's reconciled favour shine in our darkened soul (p. 243).

The first three sonnets of the 1635 group are clearly expressions of that "pensive and corrosive desire" described by Hooker. "Thou hast made me, And shall thy worke decay?" is both a

[343]

"supplication" and "confession." "I am a little world made cunningly" and "O might those sighes and teares returne again" are lamentations for sin, expressing "a desire that we had done otherwise" and prayers for "God's reconciled favour." The fourth and concluding poem, "If faithfull soules be alike glorifi'd," on the other hand, is not an expression of contrition, but a summarizing commentary of the success of the disciplines undertaken in the preceding fifteen sonnets. The admission here is one of assurance: "captive reason" (Sonnet 10) is now capable of "white truth"; sorrow is now "true griefe." The penitent is convinced that he enjoys a state of grace: "valiantly I hels wide mouth o'rstride."[47]

There is, then, a clearly realized principle of unity and of progression in the sixteen sonnets that have so far been discussed. The sequence of 1633 is devoted to those preliminary stages of feeling, of fear and of love, that ought to lead to contrite sorrow; the first three of the sonnets of 1635 are expressions of contrite sorrow, and the fourth is a statement of assurance. Furthermore, it is also evident that the next group, the Westmoreland sonnets, are about contrition and hence are neither "entirely unconnected with each other" nor "distinct in their inspiration from the sixteen which precede them in the manuscript."[48]

"Show me deare Christ, thy spouse, so bright and cleare" fulfills one of the obligations of the Anglican who would properly love God; to love God is also to love Christ's "bride," the spiritual church.[49] Donne mourns the state of the temporal

[47] Donne's conjecture as to whether or not the souls of the dead perceive intuitively is also relevant to the subject of contrition, specifically, to the question of assurance. Contrition is a matter of inner conviction, achieved only with the aid of grace, and, consequently, suprarational. It cannot, therefore, be perceived through the senses but only intuitively. It is a mode of knowing possessed only by God, angelic substances, and, perhaps, by the souls of the dead. The point that Donne makes implicitly is this: although his sorrow may appear outwardly to be proper, the only real evidence are the feelings of his own heart; thus only God, angels, and perhaps the souls of the dead can know whether his assurance is justified.

[48] Gardner, xli.

[49] To maintain that the sonnet is inspired by the desire to fulfill the

church abroad and in England and then prays that the true church, the "mild Dove," be revealed and accepted by "most men."

> Betray kind husband thy spouse to our sights,
> And let myne amorous soule court thy mild Dove,
> Who is most trew, and pleasing to thee, then
> When she'is embrac'd and open to most men.

Love and sorrow is expressed; again Donne's concern is with feelings proper to contrition. The penitent is obliged to feel the weight of the sins of all humanity, of which the abuses in the temporal church are a part. The obligation is accepted by Fulke Greville in "*Syon* lyes waste, and thy *Ierusalem*,"[50] and it is here accepted by Donne.

The other two Westmoreland sonnets, "Since she whome I lov'd, hath payd her last debt" and "Oh, to vex me, contraryes meete in one," round out the *Holy Sonnets* as a group of poems dedicated to the experience of contrition by considering difficulties that are apt to arise if the penitent is inclined to excessive scrupulosity.[51] "Since she whome I lov'd, hath payd her last debt" has customarily been read as a lament for the poet's deceased wife; but her death is only incidental to the real subject of the poem, only an event Donne introduces to explain his present feelings toward God:

> Since she whome I lov'd, hath payd her last debt
> To Nature, and to hers, and my good is dead,

---

obligations of contrition does not contradict Miss Gardner's excellent explication of the poem. See Appendix C in her edition, pp. 121-27.

[50] *Caelica*, No. 109.

[51] Hooker describes the effects of overscrupulosity: "Now there are . . . others, who doubting not of God's mercy toward all that perfectly repent, remain notwithstanding scrupulous and troubled with continual fear, lest defects in their own repentance be a bar against them. These cast themselves first into very great, and peradventure needless agonies, through misconstruction of things spoken about proportioning our griefs to our sins, for which they never think they have wept and mourned enough. . . . Yet do what they can, they are still fearful, lest herein also they do not that which they ought and might." *Works*, II, 323.

And her soule early into heaven ravished,
Wholy in heavenly things my mind is sett.

Through her the poet's longing for God has been sharpened,
but the real subject of the poem is a kind of spiritual sickness:

Here the admyring her my mind did whett
To seeke thee God; so streames do shew the head,
But though I have found thee, and thou my thirst hast fed,
A holy thirsty dropsy melts mee yett.

The sickness is an inordinate desire that God provide him with
further indications of His love, some assurance that he is in a
state of grace. The sickness is correctly diagnosed in the sestet:

But why should I begg more love, when as thou
Dost wooe my soule, for hers offring all thine:
And dost not only feare least I allow
My love to saints and Angels, things divine,
But in thy tender jealosy dost doubt
Least the World, fleshe, yea Devill putt thee out.

It is sufficient assurance that the penitent feel in his heart that
God desires his love and would see him remain free from sin.

It may be that the spiritual difficulty treated by Donne in
"Since she whome I lov'd, hath payd her last debt" arose as a
consequence of his wife's death. One would suppose that for
the Christian a loss such as Donne's would be more easily
interpreted as an indication of God's displeasure than as an
indication of His love. Nevertheless, Donne's main concern in
this sonnet is an inordinate desire for assurance, not his wife's
death.

The difficulty confessed in "Oh, to vex me, contraryes meete
in one" is even more serious. Inconstancy in devotion has become habitual; hence, contrition is imperfect:

As humorous is my contritione
As my prophane love, and as soone forgott:
As ridlingly distemperd, cold and hott,
As praying, as mute; infinite, as none.

The initial "contraryes" are defined clearly enough: "inconstancy" has become "a constant habit." But it is only after we are aware of the theological doctrines behind the poem—those formulations from which the precise definitions of the key terms, "love" and "fear" depend—that we recognize the source of inconstancy and thus are able to appreciate the full range of the sonnet's implications. The inconstancy of Donne's devotions are the result of his failure to resolve another set of contraries, contraries which he had defined in "If poysonous minerals, and if that tree." He is confounded by a deity who is at once absolutely just and infinitely merciful, and his feelings waver between "true fear" and an insincere love that can express itself only in "flattering speaches":

I durst not view heaven yesterday; and to day
In prayers, and flattering speaches I court God:
To morrow I quake with true feare of his rod.
So my devout fitts come and go away
Like a fantastique Ague: save that here
Those are my best dayes, when I shake with feare.

Until we realize that for the Anglican, fear alone is not sufficient for salvation, that in fact, unless fear is transcended by love, it is damning, we are unable to appreciate the terrible irony of the concluding line or to recognize that the sonnet is an admission of near-despair, reflecting a moment of spiritual dryness brought on, perhaps, by the overscrupulosity that appears to have been a characteristic of Donne's asceticism.[52]

Thus, in spite of their diversity of subject, the Westmoreland sonnets are not, strictly speaking, "entirely unconnected with each other" or "distinct in their inspiration from the sixteen which precede them in the manuscript." It is true that they are not related schematically to the sonnets of 1633; nor do they contain such explicit statements of contrite sorrow as are ap-

[52] The distinction between sorrow motivated by fear and sorrow motivated by love is familiar in Renaissance literature. Fulke Greville in *Caelica*, No. 97 confronts the same paradox that has confounded Donne. See above, pp. 342-43. See also my "A Note on *Measure for Measure*," *Notes and Queries* (April 1964), 135-37.

parent in the sonnets of 1635. Nevertheless, they have their place in a complete representation of the Anglican experience of contrition.

To show that the *Holy Sonnets* have a unity of purpose is not to argue that their value as poetry is thereby enhanced, but, ultimately, an informed criticism ought to take into account the ramifications in individual poems of the theological doctrine which informs the sonnets as a group. The reasons for this should be obvious. For one thing, the meaning of individual sonnets is qualified by their relationships with other sonnets in the group. For another, the terminology of individual sonnets is given finer definition by their theological context, in several instances providing a deeper and more accurate reading than is otherwise possible. As for their value as a sequence of poems devoted to the theme of penitential contrititon, the *Holy Sonnets* represent the culmination of a major genre within the tradition of the plain style. Although a number of poets have written memorably of renunciation and repentance—Dunbar, Wyatt, Vaux, Gascoigne, Shakespeare, Sidney, Ralegh, and Jonson— no poet contributing to the genre, save Greville in *Caelica* and perhaps Herbert in "The Sacrifice," has written at such length and with such sustained intensity and power as the author of the *Holy Sonnets*.

Conclusion

RECOGNITION OF THE *plain* and *eloquent* traditions makes possible a more comprehensive and I believe a more accurate account of the evolution of the short poem, or lyric, in the sixteenth century than any previously proposed. It makes clear, for instance, that the domestication of the sonnet and English Petrarchism, which the standard literary histories have always stressed as being of central importance, are only minor events within a larger context of developments, and that the grouping of Tudor poets by Lewis into a "Drab" and a "Golden" school is arbitrary and at the expense of major continuities. Furthermore, it locates precedents for Donne's anti-Petrarchan sentiments that qualify his position as an innovator and identify him with an anticourtly movement that is nearly a century old. Finally, it leads to an appreciation of the literary ramifications of "degree" in a hierarchically ordered society by revealing that the plain and eloquent styles represent, from their inception to the end of the sixteenth century, and regardless of whatever technical modifications they happen to disclose at any given moment in their evolution, the values of distinct cultural groups.

Initially, there is no indication of critical disagreement between advocates of the respective styles. Each style appears to be accepted as having its proper use, a use determined by the class distinction and intention out of which it emerged.

The plain style is the "popular" or "vulgar" style. Its characteristics—direct summary statement tending toward folk aphorism, a predominantly Anglo-Saxon diction, folk proverb and metaphor, a tone of moral severity—reflect its didactic concern. Devoted to the purpose of encouraging a parochial audience to embrace and act upon the ethical and theological truths of Christianity, it assumes the idiom of the common man. In its earliest phase it is not supported by anything that can be identified as a "poetic"; it has no body of precepts articulating a theory of verse composition. Nor is there any evidence of "literary" awareness among its proponents. Its characteristics

[349]

simply reflect its didactic purpose and the audience it endeavors to reach.

The eloquent style, on the other hand, is as radically distinguished from the plain as the courtier's clothes and manners are from those of the commoner, and on the same grounds of "degree." It is the literary manner deemed appropriate to occasions of state and the Court. Although its subjects initially show some variety, by the time of Chaucer the eloquent style is mainly devoted to the sentiments and service of *Amour Courtois*. The idea of *eloquence* itself derives from a late-classical tradition of rhetoric in which the art of persuasion has been reduced to *Elocutio*, the means of beautifying style through the embellishments of grammatical and verbal tropes. Hence, the *eloquent* style.

Whereas the plain style by the time of Wyatt has been adapted to purposes other than didactic and is no longer exclusively identified with the popular classes, the eloquent style retains its identity with the Court to the end of the century; and although it eventually discards much of its original ornateness, it continues, even as late as Shakespeare's Sonnets, to emphasize eloquence in the old sense. No better expression of the eloquent tradition's governing ideal and of the concept of decorum on which it is premised can be found than the following passage from Puttenham:

> And as we see in these great Madames of honour, be they for personage or otherwise neuer so comely and bewtifull, yet if they want their courtly habillements or at leastwise such other apparell as custome and ciuilitie haue ordained to couer their naked bodies, would be ashamed or greatly out of countenaunce to be seen in that sort, and perchance do then thinke themselues more amiable in euery mans eye, when they be in their richest attire, suppose of silkes or tyssewes & costly embroderies, then when they go in cloth or in any plain and simple apparell. Euen so cannot our vulgar Poesie shew it selfe either gallant or gorgious, if any lymme be left naked and bare and not clad in his kindly clothes and coulours, such as may convey them somwhat out of sight, that is from the

common course of ordinary speech and capacitie of the vulgar iudgement, and yet being artificially handled must needs yeld it much more bewtie and commendation. This ornament we speake of is giuen to it by figures and figurative speeches, which be the flowers as it were and coulours that a Poet setteth vpon his language by arte, as the embroderer doth his stone and perle, or passements of gold vpon the stuffe of a Princely garment, or as th'excellent painter bestoweth the rich Orient coulours vpon his table of pourtraite (pp. 137-38).

"Custome and ciuilitie" demand eloquence of the courtly poet. It is his obligation to avoid the "common course of ordinary speech" by using the "flowers" and "coulours" of *Elocutio* to adorn his noble thoughts and sentiments just as the "embroderer doth his stone and perle" to adorn a "Princely garment."

Although there are no indications of critical disagreement between the early representatives of the two styles, the sources of eventual disagreement are present from the beginning in the eloquent poetic's stressing of the importance of surface embellishment and in the narrow identification of the eloquent style with the Court; and it is precisely these two points which are raised by the early critics of the eloquent style. In the *Canterbury Tales*, for instance, the eloquent or "high" style is identified with courtly affectation and criticized further for devoting itself to niceties that are not essential to the conveying of the "matter." In fact, Oure Hooste's stated preference for a simple, plain style has the ring of authorial assent to an already well-established literary credo, a credo which maintains the superiority of the plain style on moral grounds.

The moral connotations of such objections to the eloquent style as are found in Chaucer are even more pronounced in the ironic apologies with which so many fifteenth-century and early sixteenth-century writers preface their works: "Although I am unskilled in the colours of rhetoric," the typical apology begins, "I can speak plainly and truthfully." By the time of Skelton what is inferential in these earlier apologies has become an open condemnation: Eloquence is committed to appearances at the expense of truth and reality. If it is indeed, as the Court insists, the mark of a courtier, according to its critics it is the mark of his affectation and hypocrisy—proof of the general affectation and hypocrisy that is bred at Court.

If Oure Hooste's remarks and the ironic apologies indicate the emergence of opposition to eloquence and Court, they also indicate that the old didactic manner has acquired a new identity. So long as the plain style was confined to instruction, its characteristics and subjects reflected its function and the supposed predilections of the audience it endeavored to reach. The didactic poet simply assumed the idiom of the commoner in order to remind him of the truths that he could not afford to ignore. But with the emergence of anticourtly sentiment the homespun, direct manner and the vulgar didactic idiom is adopted by writers who wish to attack the Court directly (Skelton's "Colin Clout," Wyatt's three satires) or whose concerns are noncourtly or contemplative (Dunbar's "Lament for the Makaris," Skelton's "Upon a Dead Man's Head"). It becomes a convention which preserves the folk idiom of didactic verse to exploit its reputation for honesty and devotion to the simple truth.

In its new capacity as an anticourtly and contemplative convention the plain style is identified by its advocates with the Christian Contemplative Ideal and advanced as the antithesis of the eloquent style which, in turn, has been identified with courtly worldliness. The Contemplative Ideal is premised on the assumption that temporal goods are illusory in their promise of happiness. It is their appearances that deceive; once they are comprehended as illusions, they can be rejected for the sake of the ultimate realities of God and Eternity. This ethic provides the plain stylists not only with a basis for condemning the worldly commitments represented by the courtly style—preferment, service to a lady as prescribed by the code of love, emulation of the continental model of the Ideal Courtier—but also with a poetic which makes a moral virtue of plain statement. In contrast to the eloquent, which in concentrating upon surface embellishment stresses appearances, the plain style is dedicated only to content—to truth and reality. Furthermore, it is the defender of the truth against those who "make the crow singing as the swane," or who "Vse vertu as it goeth now a dayese/ in word alone to make . . . langage swete."

By the time of Wyatt the otherworldly/worldly antithesis between the plain and eloquent styles is firmly established; and continuous lines of development from Wyatt to Greville and Donne are evidence of a tradition of the plain style whose continuity has its sources in anticourtly and otherworldly ends. For instance, there is the mode of irony initiated by Wyatt in his attacks on the Court in the satires addressed to Poins and Brian and traceable through Gascoigne's "Wodmanship" and "Memories 3"; Googe's "Of Money"; Turbervile's "Retraction"; Ralegh's "The Lie" and "The Passionate Man's Pilgrimage." There is also the "renunciation" poem in which the poet as disillusioned lover rejects worldly love and dedicates himself to contemplation: Wyatt's "Ffarewell Love and all thy Lawes for ever"; Surrey's "Brittle beautie, that nature made so frail"; Vaux's "I loathe that I did love"; Gascoigne's "Lullabie," "Good-Morrow," and "The Green Knight's Farewell to Fancy"; Ralegh's "Farewell Love, thou oracle of lies"; Greville's "Farewell sweet Boy, complaine not of my truth." And there is the lyric of contemplation devoted to the commonplace of death and the various stages of penitential experience.

It is the eloquent courtly tradition, however, which dominates the lyric throughout most of the century. During the reign of Henry VIII it is sanctioned by a monarch who endeavored successfully to establish a court society in the image of the continental model, and it enjoys the prestige of humanist support in the movement to refine the vernacular. For three-quarters of a century eloquence is both a courtly and a literary ideal: to write well is to write as the courtier writes—in the lyric to "court exactly," expressing in a language suitably polished for the occasion the sentiments of courtly service and love. It is no wonder that the eloquent style is the dominant mode throughout most of the century. In fulfilling his social obligation and approaching the image of the Ideal Courtier by writing ornately of courtly love, the court poets were also advancing the cause of the English language.

During the last decades of the century, however, and particularly in the nineties, there is evidence of widespread and deep dissatisfaction with the Court as cultural and social center and with the literature most representative of its values. Anti-courtly commentary becomes more strident. The voice of the disillusioned courtier is still heard—in Ralegh's poems and to a lesser extent in Fulke Greville—but the new voices are of those (Southwell, Nashe, Hall, Donne, Marston, Jonson) who have never entertained any sympathy for the Court. Instead of expressing disillusionment with an institution which they once accepted but which has betrayed them, they either urge rejection of the world as well as of the Court for the sake of Christian devotion, or they mock the vices and follies of a society dominated by the Court. Both critics, the defender of Christian devotion and the satirist of a court-ridden society, are united in their opposition to the love poetry of the Court. It is sophistical, it is an affectation, it is "Italianate," and it celebrates the passions of the body.

The results of such criticism upon the courtly tradition are efforts at reform and a reassertion of the ideal to which it is committed. The new emphasis is upon originality and integrity and an effort to meet the critics' charge of "Italianate" worldliness by insisting upon the ennobling power of service to a lady. Sidney in *Astrophil and Stella* proclaims the honest inspiration of his own poems, contrasting them with the uninspired and derivative efforts of Petrarch's imitators. They have looked for inventions, and even inspiration, in the works of others; he has looked into his own heart and written honestly and plainly of his feelings. Giles Fletcher feels he must defend his sonnet sequence by explaining that Licea is no ordinary mistress, no "impudent courtezan," but perhaps "Holy Discipline," "Learning's Image," or "some College." Drayton announces that his sonnets are "rightly of the English strain." Others, among them most notably Spenser, turn to neo-Platonism as an answer to the moral accusations levelled against secular love poetry—as a secular and temporal alternative to the Christian Contemplative Ideal in the form of a religion proclaiming that a woman as a surrogate of divinity may be contemplated and that such contemplation may purify and ennoble its advocate. Shakespeare affirms that a love which is a "marriage of true minds" (a love which looks very much as though it were conceived as an analogue of *caritas*) is the one constant value redeeming an otherwise valueless world of shifting illusions.

But even while the tradition of courtly lyric witnesses its most impressive achievements in Sidney and Shakespeare, the contemplative and anticourtly tradition is gaining a prominence it will not relinquish until after the Restoration. Donne in the *Songs and Sonets* adopts a rough manner and mocks the sugared style and conventions of the courtly tradition. Greville in *Caelica* systematically explores the religion of courtly love, eventually denying Cupid his divinity and dismissing neo-Platonic contemplation as having little value for Adam's sons. The epigram, the verse epistle, and the formal verse satire emerge as new anticourtly modes in which a new generation of poets, whose affiliations are with the Church and the Inns of Court, attack the follies and vices of a society dominated by the Court. The contemplative lyric, since Wyatt's translations of the Psalms mainly confined to the general themes of death and renunciation of the world, emerges—often in acknowledged opposition to the genres devoted to profane love—as a major genre dedicated to divine love and the disciplines of self-examination leading to contrition.

Stylistically, the contemplative or noncourtly tradition is no longer so easily identified. The old convention of plain speaking still occurs in Ralegh and occasionally in Greville, Shakespeare, Donne, and Jonson; but even in its most severe form, for instance in Ralegh's "The Passionate Man's Pilgrimage," it reflects the influences of the poets and songwriters of the court circle. The new and more common version of the plain style often uses the tropes, schemes, and rhythms of the eloquent tradition and frequently adopts the structures inherent in the courtly pledge, complaint, and plea. It is no longer so narrowly committed to summary statement or to the language of homely metaphor and folk adage; and it may use techniques of extended metaphor that were first introduced into English verse by the

[355]

Petrarchans. Nevertheless, in its opposition to rhetorical eloquence the new contemplative and anticourtly manner retains its
identity as the plain style and in fact acquires new prestige as the
idiom of integrity. The devotional poets discover in the tradition
of religious meditation new precedents for a style using image
and metaphor from the familiar world of everyday occurrences.
Prayer and supplication require a language of simplicity and
humility. At the same time, the classical tradition provides a
theory of the plain style (at least as old as Plato and adopted
in the first century A.D. by Roman poets who were opposed to
Virgilian eloquence) which when domesticated, powerfully reinforces the native theory. Like its native predecessor this classical theory insists upon using "language, such as men doe vse,"
rejecting ornament and rhetorical affectation as not pertaining
to the truth.

During the last decade of Elizabeth's reign the emergence
of the plain style as the dominant lyric tradition marks the end
of the Court's domination of the lyric. Even in Shakespeare's
sonnets, the last distinguished collection of lyrics to represent the
courtly tradition, courtly norms on the levels of both style and
attitude have been deeply modified by a sensibility that owes at
least as much to the popular as it does to the aristocratic culture.
Admittedly, traces of the courtly tradition can be found in
Jonson, especially in those poems in which he honors, nostal-
gically, the sentiments of neo-Platonism or assumes the graceful
modes of Elizabethan song to praise a lady. But even in *A
Celebration of Charis* and the elegy, "Though Beautie be the
Marke of praise," poems which owe a good deal to the courtly
tradition, Jonson's adherence to the classical plain style is unmistakable. Equally apparent is the fact that much of the
vigor of his satire in short verse forms derives from his contempt
for the hypocrisy and affectation bred at Court. The norm for
Jonson and the Tribe of Ben is a classical rather than a courtly
urbanity. In the other new lyricists of eminence, the devotional
poets, evidence of the waning influence of the Court is even
stronger. George Herbert, Vaughan, Crashaw, and Traherne
continue a tradition of anticourtly and otherworldly verse

originating in the simple didactic poetry of the Middle Ages and becoming in the seventeenth century the dominant and most vigorous mode of English lyric. The verse of Jonson and the Tribe of Ben and of the devotional poets is proof of a revolution which is social as well as literary.

Bibliography

Aquinas, Saint Thomas. *Basic Writings of Saint Thomas Aquinas,* ed., Anton C. Pegis. 2 vols. New York, 1945.

Aristotle. *The Rhetoric of Aristotle,* tr., Lane Cooper. New York, 1932.

Ascham, Roger. *The Scholemaster,* ed., Edward Arber. London, 1869. (Arber English Reprints.)

Atkins, J. W. H. *English Literary Criticism: The Medieval Phase.* Cambridge (Eng.), 1944.

———. *English Literary Criticism: The Renascence.* London, 1947.

Bacon, Francis. *The Advancement of Learning,* ed., William A. Wright. Oxford, 1900.

Baldi, Sergio. *La Poesia di Sir Thomas Wyatt.* Florence, 1953.

Baldwin, Charles S. *Medieval Rhetoric and Poetic (to 1400).* New York, 1928.

Bennett, Joan. *Five Metaphysical Poets.* Cambridge (Eng.), 1964.

———. "The Love Poetry of John Donne," in *Seventeenth Century Studies Presented to Sir Herbert Grierson.* Oxford, 1938.

Berdan, John M. *Early Tudor Poetry, 1485-1547.* New York, 1920.

Berners, Dame Juliana. *The Gentlemans Academie, or the Booke of S. Albans,* ed., Gervase Markham. London, 1595.

Breton, Nicholas. *Marie Magdalens Loue.* London, 1595.

———. *A Solemne Passion of the Soules Loue.* London, 1598.

Brook, G. L., ed. *The Harley Lyrics.* Manchester, 1948. (Old and Middle English Texts.)

Brooke, Arthur. "The Tragical Historie of Romeus and Juliet," in vol. 1 of *Narrative and Dramatic Sources of Shakespeare,* ed., Geoffrey Bullough. London, 1957.

Brown, Carleton, ed. *Religious Lyrics of the Fifteenth Century.* Oxford, 1939.

Brown, John Russell, and Bernard Harris, eds. *Elizabethan Poetry.* New York, 1960. (Stratford-upon-Avon Studies, No. 2.)

Bush, Douglas. *Mythology and the Renaissance Tradition in English Poetry.* Minneapolis, 1932.

Campbell, Lily B. *Divine Poetry and Drama in Sixteenth-Century England.* Berkeley and Los Angeles, 1959.

Campion, Thomas. *Campion's Works*, ed., Percival Vivian. Oxford, 1909.

Carew, Thomas. *The Poems of Thomas Carew*, ed., Rhodes Dunlap. Oxford, 1949.

Case, Arthur E. *A Bibliography of English Poetical Miscellanies, 1521-1750*. Oxford, 1935.

Castiglione, Baldassare. *The Book of the Courtier*, tr., Sir Thomas Hoby. New York, 1928. (Everyman's Library.)

Chambers, E. K. *English Literature at the Close of the Middle Ages*. Oxford, 1945. (*Oxford History of English Literature*, vol. 2, pt. 2.)

————. *Sir Thomas Wyatt and Some Collected Studies*. London, 1933.

————, and F. Sidgwick, eds. *Early English Lyrics: Amorous, Divine, Moral and Trivial*. London, 1921.

Chapman, George. *Ouids Banquet of Sence: A Coronet for His Mistresse Philosophie*. London, 1595.

————. *The Poems of George Chapman*, ed., Phyllis Brooks Bartlett. New York, 1941.

Charron, Pierre. *Of Wisdome, Three Bookes*, tr., Samson Lennard. London, 1612 (?).

Chaucer, Geoffrey. *The Complete Works of Geoffrey Chaucer*, ed., F. N. Robinson. Boston, 1933.

Cicero, Marcus Tullius. *The Booke of Freendeship*. London, 1562.

————. "De Partitione Oratoria," in vol. 2 of *De Oratore*, tr., H. Rackham. London, 1948. (Loeb Classical Library.)

Clark, Donald L. "Ancient Rhetoric and English Renaissance Literature," *SQ*, II (1951), 195-204.

————. *Rhetoric and Poetry in the Renaissance*. New York, 1922.

Clements, Robert J. "Condemnation of the Poetic Profession in Renaissance Emblem Literature," *SP*, XLIII (1946), 213-32.

Coffin, Charles Monroe. *John Donne and the New Philosophy*. New York, 1958.

Cox, Leonard. *The Arte or Crafte of Rhethoryke*, ed., Frederic Ives Carpenter. Chicago, 1899.

Craig, Hardin. *The Enchanted Glass*. New York, 1936.

Crane, William G. *Wit and Rhetoric in the Renaissance*. New York, 1937. (Columbia University Studies in English and Comparative Literature, No. 129.) Reprinted: Gloucester (Mass.), 1964.

Cunningham, J. V. "Logic and Lyric," *MP*, LI (1953), 33-41.

————. *Tradition and Poetic Structure*. Denver, 1960.

Daniel, Samuel. *Poems and A Defence of Ryme*, ed., A. C. Sprague. Cambridge, Mass., 1930.

Davies, Sir John. *The Poems of Sir John Davies*, ed., Clare Howard. New York, 1941.

Davison, Francis. *A Poetical Rhapsody*, ed., Hyder Rollins. 2 vols. Cambridge (Mass.), 1931-32.

Donne, John. *The Divine Poems*, ed., Helen Gardner. Oxford, 1952.

————. *The Poems of John Donne*, ed., H. J. C. Grierson. 2 vols. London, 1933.

————. *The Sermons of John Donne*, eds., George R. Potter and Evelyn Simpson. 10 vols. Berkeley, 1953-61.

Donner, Henry W. "The Significance of Minor Poets," in *English Studies Today*, eds., C. L. Wrenn and G. Bullough. London, 1951.

Doran, Madeleine. *Endeavors of Art: A Study of Form in Elizabethan Drama*. Madison, 1954.

Drayton, Michael. *The Poems of Michael Drayton*, ed., John Buxton. 2 vols. Cambridge (Mass.), 1953. (The Muses' Library.)

Du Bellay, Joachim. *The Defense and Illustration of the French Language*, tr., Gladys M. Turquet. London, 1939.

————. *La Deffence et Illustration de la Langue Francoyse*. Paris, 1948. (*Société des Textes Français Modernes*.)

Dunbar, William. *The Poems of William Dunbar*, ed., John Small. 3 vols. Edinburgh, 1884-1893. (The Scottish Text Society.)

Du Vair, Guillame. *A Buckler Against Adversitie*, tr., Andrew Court. London, 1622.

————. *The True Way to Vertue and Happinesse*. London, 1623. (Re-titled reissue of *A Buckler Against Adversitie*.)

Edwards, Richards, comp. *The Paradise of Dainty Devices (1576-1606)*, ed., Hyder Rollins. Cambridge (Mass.), 1927.

Ellrodt, Robert. *L'Inspiration Personnelle et l'Esprit du Temps chez les Poètes Métaphysiques Anglais*. Vol. 1. Paris, 1960.

Elyot, Thomas. *The Boke Named the Gouernour*, ed., Henry S. Croft. 2 vols. London, 1883.

England's Helicon, ed., Hyder Rollins. Cambridge (Mass.), 1935.

Engelhardt, George J. "Medieval Vestiges in the Rhetoric of Erasmus," *PMLA*, LXIII (1948), 739-44.

Evans, Maurice. *English Poetry in the Sixteenth Century*. London, 1955.

Farr, Edward, ed. *Select Poetry, Chiefly Devotional, of the Reign of Queen Elizabeth*. 2 vols. Cambridge (Eng.), 1845.

Fellowes, E. H. *English Madrigal Verse, 1588-1632*. Oxford, 1950.
Fenton, Geoffrey. *Golden Epistles*. London, 1575.
Ficino, Marsilio. *Commentary on Plato's Symposium*, tr., Sears R. Jayne. Columbia (Mo.), 1944. (University of Missouri Studies, XIX, No. 1.)
Fraunce, Abraham. *The Arcadian Rhetorike*, ed., Ethel Seaton. Oxford, 1950. (Luttrell Society Reprints.)
Fulwood, William. *The Enimie of Idlenesse*. London, 1568.
Gardner, Helen. *The Metaphysical Poets*. London, 1961.
Gascoigne, George. *The Complete Works of George Gascoigne*, ed., J. W. Cunliff. 2 vols. Cambridge (Eng.), 1907-10.
Googe, Barnaby. *Barnabe Googe. Eclogs, Epytaphes, & Sonettes. 1563*, ed., Edward Arber. London, 1910. (Arber English Reprints.)
Gorges, Sir Arthur. *The Poems of Sir Arthur Gorges*, ed., Helen E. Sandison. Oxford, 1953.
Greville, Fulke. *Poems and Dramas of Fulke Greville*. 2 vols. New York, 1945.
————. *Sir Fulke Greville's Life of Sir Philip Sidney*, ed., Nowell Smith. Oxford, 1907.
Grierson, H. J. C., ed. *Metaphysical Lyrics and Poems of the Seventeenth Century, Donne to Butler*. Oxford, 1921.
Guilpin, Edward. *Skialetheia, 1598*, ed., G. B. Harrison. London, 1931. (Shakespeare Association, Facsimiles, No. 2.)
Hall, Joseph. *Meditations and Vowes Divine and Morall, Devided into Two Bookes*. London, 1605.
Harding, D. W. "The Rhythmical Intention in Wyatt's Poetry," *Scrutiny*, XIV (1946), 90-102.
Hawes, Stephen. *The Pastime of Pleasure*, ed., W. E. Mead. London, 1928. (EETS, original series, No. 173.)
Hawkins, John Erskine. *The Life and Works of John Turbervile*. Lawrence (Kan.), 1940. (University of Kansas Publications, Humanistic Series, No. 25.)
Herbert, George. *The Works of George Herbert*, ed., F. E. Hutchinson. Oxford, 1941.
Herrnstein, Barbara, ed. *Discussions of Shakespeare's Sonnets*. Boston, 1964. (Discussions of Literature.)
Hietsch, Otto. *Die Petrarcaübersetzungen Sir Thomas Wyatts; eine sprachvergleichende Studie*. Vienna, 1960. (*Wiener Beiträge zur englischen Philologie*, N. 67.)
Hogarde, Miles. *A Mirrour of Loue*. London, 1555.

Hollander, John. *The Untuning of the Sky: Ideas of Music in English Poetry, 1500-1700.* Princeton, 1961.

Hooker, Richard. *The Works of Richard Hooker.* 2 vols. Oxford, 1865.

Hooker, Thomas. *The Soules Preparation for Christ.* London, 1632.

Hoskins, John. *Directions for Speech and Style,* ed., Hoyt H. Hudson. Princeton, 1935.

Howell, Wilbur Samuel. *Logic and Rhetoric in England, 1500-1700.* Princeton, 1956.

Hubler, Edward, ed. *The Riddle of Shakespeare's Sonnets.* New York, 1962.

————. *The Sense of Shakespeare's Sonnets.* Princeton, 1952. (Princeton Studies in English, No. 33.)

Hudson, Hoyt H. *The Epigram in the English Renaissance.* Princeton, 1947.

Hunt, Clay. *Donne's Poetry: Essays in Literary Analysis.* New Haven, 1954.

Ing, Catherine. *Elizabethan Lyrics; A Study in the Development of English Metres and Their Relation to Poetic Effect.* London, 1951.

John, Lisle Cecil. *The Elizabethan Sonnet Sequences: Studies in Conventional Conceits.* New York, 1964.

Jones, Richard Foster. "The Moral Sense of Simplicity," in *Studies in Honor of Frederick W. Shipley.* St. Louis, 1942. (Washington University Studies, n.s., Language and Literature, No. 14.)

————. *The Triumph of the English Language.* Stanford, 1953.

Jonson, Ben. "Conversations with Drummond," in vol. 1 (*The Man and His Work*) of *Ben Jonson,* ed., C. H. Herford, Percy and Evelyn Simpson. Oxford, 1925.

————. "Explorata: or, Discoveries," in vol. 8 (*The Poems, The Prose Works*) of *Ben Jonson,* eds., C. H. Herford, Percy and Evelyn Simpson. Oxford, 1947.

Knights, L. C. "Shakespeare's Sonnets," *Scrutiny,* III (1934), 133-60.

Krieger, Murray. *A Window to Criticism: Shakespeare's Sonnets and Modern Poetics.* Princeton, 1964.

Landry, Hilton. *Interpretations in Shakespeare's Sonnets.* Berkeley, 1963.

La Primaudaye, Pierre de. *The French Academie,* tr., T. Bowes. Third edition. London, 1594.

Leishman, James Blair. *The Metaphysical Poets: Donne, Herbert, Vaughan, Traherne.* New York, 1963.

———. *The Monarch of Wit; An Analytical and Comparative Study of the Poetry of John Donne.* London, 1951.

———. "Variations on a Theme in Shakespeare's Sonnets," in *Elizabethan and Jacobean Studies Presented to Frank Percy Wilson,* eds., Herbert Davis and Helen Gardner. Oxford, 1959.

———. *Themes and Variations in Shakespeare's Sonnets.* London, 1961.

Lever, Julius Walter. *The Elizabethan Love Sonnet.* London, 1956.

Lewis, Clive Staples. "Donne and Love Poetry in the Seventeenth Century," in *Seventeenth Century Studies Presented to Sir Herbert Grierson.* Oxford, 1938.

———. *English Literature in the Sixteenth Century, Excluding Drama.* Oxford, 1954.

Lok, Henry. *Sundry Christian Passions Contained in Two Hundred Sonnets.* London, 1593.

Louthan, Doniphan. *The Poetry of John Donne, A Study in Explication.* New York, 1951.

McKeon, Richard. "Rhetoric in the Middle Ages," *Speculum,* xvii (1942), 1-32.

Manning, Stephen. *Wisdom and Number. Toward a Critical Appraisal of the Middle English Religious Lyric.* Lincoln, 1962.

Martz, Louis L., ed. *The Meditative Poem: An Anthology of Seventeenth-Century Verse.* Garden City, 1963.

———. *The Poetry of Meditation.* New Haven, 1954.

Mason, Harold Andrew. *Humanism and Poetry in the Early Tudor Period.* London, 1959.

Mazzeo, Joseph Anthony. "A Critique of Some Modern Theories of Metaphysical Poetry," in *Seventeenth Century English Poetry; Modern Essays in Criticism,* ed., William R. Keast. New York, 1962.

Meres, Francis. *A Comparative Discourse of Our English Poets, Painters & Musicians,* ed., Edward Arber. London, 1903. (Arber English Reprints.)

Milton, John. *The Complete Poetical Works of John Milton,* ed., Douglas Bush. Boston, 1965.

Moore, Arthur K. *The Secular Lyric in Middle English.* Lexington (Ky.), 1951.

Muir, Kenneth. *Life and Letters of Sir Thomas Wyatt.* Liverpool, 1963.

Nash, Thomas. *The Vnfortunate Traveller.* Vol. 2 of *The Works of Thomas Nash,* ed., Ronald B. McKerrow. London, 1904-10.

Padelford, Frederick Morgan. *Early Sixteenth Century Lyrics.* Boston, 1907. (The Belles-Lettres Series.)

Parker, William R. "The Sonnet in 'Tottel's Miscellany,'" *PMLA*, LIV (1939), 669-77.

Patterson, Frank A. *The Middle English Penitential Lyric.* New York, 1911.

Peacham, Henry. *The Garden of Eloquence, 1593*, ed., W. G. Crane. Gainesville, 1954. (Scholars' Facsimiles & Reprints.)

Peterson, Douglas L. "John Donne's *Holy Sonnets* and the Anglican Doctrine of Contrition," *SP*, LVI (1959), 504-18.

———. "*Measure for Measure* and the Anglican Doctrine of Contrition," *N&Q*, XI (1964), 135-37.

———. "A Probable Source for Shakespeare's Sonnet CXXIX," *SQ*, V (1954), 381-84.

Proctor, Thomas, comp. *A Gorgeous Gallery of Gallant Inventions, 1578*, ed., Hyder Rollins. Cambridge (Mass.), 1926.

Prouty, Charles Tyler. *George Gascoigne, Elizabethan Courtier, Soldier, and Poet.* New York, 1942.

Puttenham, George. *The Arte of English Poesie*, eds. G. D. Willcock and A. Walker. Cambridge: Cambridge University Press, 1936.

Rainolde, Richard. *The Foundacion of Rhetorike*, ed., Francis R. Johnson. New York, 1945. (Scholars' Facsimiles & Reprints.)

Ralegh, Sir Walter. *The Poems of Sir Walter Ralegh*, ed., Agnes M. C. Lathan. Cambridge (Mass.), 1951.

Ransom, John Crowe. "Shakespeare at Sonnets," *Southern Review* (La.), III (1938), 531-53. Reprinted in *The World's Body* (New York, 1938) and in *A Casebook on Shakespeare's Sonnets* (New York, 1964).

Renwick, W. L. *Edmund Spenser: An Essay on Renaissance Poetry.* London, 1925.

Robbins, Rossell H., ed. *Secular Lyrics of the XIVth and XVth Centuries.* Oxford, 1952.

Rollins, Hyder, ed. *A Handful of Pleasant Delights.* Cambridge, Mass., 1924.

———. "Marginalia on Two Elizabethan Poetical Miscellanies," in *John Quincy Adams: Memorial Studies*, ed., J. G. McManaway, and others. Washington, D.C., 1948.

———. *The Paradise of Dainty Devices.* Cambridge, Mass., 1927.

———. "A Small Handful of Fragrant Flowers (1575)," *Huntington Library Bulletin*, IX (April 1936), 27-35.

Romei, Annibale. *The Courtiers Academie*, tr., J. Kepers. London, 1598.

Rubel, Veré L. *Poetic Diction in the English Renaissance from Skelton through Spenser.* New York, 1941.

Schelling, Felix E. *English Literature During the Lifetime of Shakespeare.* Rev. edn. New York, 1927.

——. *The Life and Writings of George Gascoigne.* Boston, 1893. (University of Pennsylvania Series in Art, Literature, and Archeology, Vol. 2, No. 4.)

Schlauch, Margaret. *The English Language in Modern Times, (Since 1400).* Warsaw, 1959.

Seccombe, Thomas, ed. *Elizabethan Sonnets Newly Arranged and Indexed,* with an introduction by Sidney Lee. 2 vols. Westminster, 1904.

Shakespeare, William. *The Complete Plays and Poems of William Shakespeare,* eds., William A. Neilson and Charles J. Hill. Cambridge (Mass.), 1942.

——. *Songs and Poems,* ed., Edward Hubler. New York, 1959.

——. *The Sonnets,* ed., Hyder Rollins. 2 vols. Philadelphia, 1944. (*A New Variorum Edition of Shakespeare.*)

Sherry, Richard. *A Treatise of Schemes & Tropes.* London, [1550].

——. *A Treatise of the Figures of Grammer and Rhetorike.* London, 1555.

Shirmer, Walter F. "The Importance of the Fifteenth Century for the Study of the Renaissance, with Special Reference to Lydgate," in *English Studies Today,* eds., C. L. Wrenn and G. Bullough. London, 1951.

Sidney, Sir Philip. *The Complete Works of Sir Philip Sidney,* ed., A. Feuillerat. 4 vols. Cambridge (Eng.), 1912-26.

——. *The Poems of Sir Philip Sidney,* ed., William A. Ringler. Oxford, 1962.

Simpson, Evelyn. *A Study of the Prose Works of John Donne.* Second edition. Oxford, 1948.

Skelton, John. *The Complete Plays of John Skelton, Laureate,* ed., Philip Henderson. Second rev. edn. London, 1948.

Smith, A. J. "Donne in His Time: A Reading of *The Extasie,*" *RLMC,* x (1957), 260-75.

——. "The Metaphysic of Love," *RES,* n.s., ix (1958), 362-75.

——. "New Bearings in Donne: 'Aire and Angels'," *English,* xiii (1960), 49-53.

——. "Sources of Difficulty and of Value in the Poetry of John Donne," *LM,* vii (1957), 182-90.

Smith, G. Gregory, ed. *Elizabethan Critical Essays*. 2 vols. Oxford, 1904.

Smith, Hallett. "The Art of Sir Thomas Wyatt," *HLQ*, IX (1946), 323-55.

———. *Elizabethan Poetry; A Study in Conventions, Meaning, and Expression*. Cambridge (Mass.), 1952.

———. "English Metrical Psalms in the Sixteenth Century and Their Literary Significance," *HLQ*, IX (1946), 249-71.

Southall, Raymond. *The Courtly Maker: An Essay on the Poetry of Wyatt and His Contemporaries*. New York, 1964.

Southwell, Robert. *The Complete Poems of Robert Southwell, S.J.*, ed., Alexander Grossart. London, 1872.

———. *Marie Magdalens Funeral Teares*. London, 1590.

———. *Moeoniae. Or, Certaine Excellent Poems & Spirituall Hymnes*. London, 1595.

Spearing, A. C. *Criticism and Medieval Poetry*. New York, 1964.

Speirs, John. *Medieval English Poetry: The Non-Chaucerian Tradition*. London, 1957.

Spencer, Theodore, ed. *A Garland for John Donne*. Cambridge (Mass.), 1931.

Spenser, Edmund. *Spenser's Minor Poems*, ed., Ernest de Sélincourt. Oxford, 1910.

Speroni, Sperone. "Dialogo delle Lingue," in *Tesoro della Prosa Italiana*, ed., E. Albéri. Second edition. Florence, 1848.

Stein, Arnold. *John Donne's Lyrics: The Eloquence of Action*. Minneapolis, 1962.

Stevens, John E. *Music and Poetry in the Early Tudor Court*. London, 1961.

Stirling, Brents. "A Shakespeare Sonnet Group," *PMLA*, LXXV (1960), 340-49.

Surrey, Henry Howard, Earl of. *The Poems of Henry Howard, Earl of Surrey*, ed., Frederick Morgan Padelford. Rev. edn. Seattle, 1928. (University of Washington Publications, Language and Literature, No. 5.)

Swallow, Alan. "The Pentameter Lines in Skelton and Wyatt," *MP*, XLVIII (1950), 1-11.

———. "Principles of Poetic Composition from Skelton to Sidney." (Unpub. Ph.D. Dissertation, Louisiana State University, 1941.)

Swart, J. *Thomas Sackville; A Study in Sixteenth-Century Poetry*. Groningen, 1949.

Sweeting, Elizabeth J. *Early Tudor Criticism, Linguistic and Literary*. New York, 1964.

Tate, Allen. *On the Limits of Poetry*. New York, 1948.

Thaler, Alwin. "Literary Criticism in *A Mirror for Magistrates*," *JEGP*, XLIX (1950), 1-13.

Thomson, Patricia. *Sir Thomas Wyatt and His Background*. London, 1964.

Tottel, Richard, comp. *Tottel's Miscellany (1557-1587)*, ed., Hyder Rollins. 2 vols. Cambridge (Mass.), 1928-29.

Trimpi, Wesley. *Ben Jonson's Poems, A Study of the Plain Style*. Stanford, 1962.

Turbervile, George. Epitaphes, Epigrams, Songes and Sonets, 1567. In *The Works of the English Poets*, ed., Alexander Chalmers (London: Johnson, 1910), II.

Tuve, Rosemund. "A Critical Survey of Scholarship in the Field of English Literature of the Renaissance," *SP*, XL (1943), 204-55.

——. *Elizabethan and Metaphysical Imagery*. Chicago, 1947.

Unger, Leonard. *The Man in the Name; Essays on the Experience of Poetry*. Minneapolis, 1956.

Vaux, Lord. *The Poems of Lord Vaux*, ed., Larry P. Vonalt. Denver, 1960.

Wallace, Karl R. "Rhetorical Exercises in Tudor Education," *QJS*, XXII (1936), 28-51.

Warnke, Frank. *European Metaphysical Poetry*. New Haven & London, 1961.

Watson, Foster. *The English Grammar Schools to 1660*. Cambridge (Eng.), 1908.

Watson, Thomas. *The Hekatompathia, or Passionate Centurie of Love*. London, 1575.

——. *An Ould Facioned Loue*. London, 1594.

——. *Poems*, ed., Edward Arber. London, 1870. (Arber English Reprints.)

——. *The Tears of Fancie, or, Loue Disdained*. London, 1593.

Webbe, William. *A Discourse of English Poetrie*. London, 1586.

Willen, Gerald, and Victor B. Reed, eds. *A Casebook on Shakespeare's Sonnets*. New York, 1964.

Williamson, George. "The Convention of *The Extasie*," in *Seventeenth Century English Poetry*, ed., William R. Keast. New York, 1962.

——. *The Donne Tradition*. New York, 1958.

Wilson, Thomas. *The Rule of Reason, Conteining The Arte of Logique*. London, 1552.

———. *Wilson's Arte of Rhetorique, 1560*, ed., G. H. Mair. Oxford, 1909.

Winters, A. Y. "The Sixteenth-Century Lyric in England," *Poetry*, LIII (1939), 258-72 and 320-35; and LIV (1939), 35-51.

Wyatt, Sir Thomas. *Collected Poems of Sir Thomas Wyatt*, ed., Kenneth Muir. Cambridge (Mass.), 1949.

———. *The Poems of Sir Thomas Wiat*, ed., A. K. Foxwell. 2 vols. New York, 1964.

———. *Some Poems of Sir Thomas Wyatt*, ed., Alan Swallow. New York, 1949.

Young, Richard B. "English Petrarke: A Study of Sidney's *Astrophel and Stella*," in *Three Studies in the Renaissance: Sidney, Johnson, Milton*. New Haven, 1958.

Index

Aphthonius, *Progymnasmata*: popular school text, 42; use in the Grammar School, 52; methods of praise and dispraise in *Tottel's Miscellany*, 53; as adapted by Rainolde, 53n, 144; medieval theory of eloquence, 76; methods of praise, 82; methods of confirmation and refutation, 126

Aquinas, Saint Thomas, *Summa Theologica*: psychological basis for theories of persuasion, 49n; on the will as influenced by the imagination, 107-109, 108n, 109n; moral and ontological goods distinguished, 299 —*Summa Contra Gentiles*: theory of cognition, 315n

Ariosto, mentioned by Puttenham, 46

Aristotle, his psychology as mode of analysis, 199; distinction between "primary" and "accidental" properties of being, 224; mentioned, 50, 157. *See also* John Donne —*Rhetoric*: purpose of plain style, to teach, 48n; psychological basis for theories of persuasion, 49n; praise and dispraise, function of deliberative oratory, 54n; degrees of probability, 114; emotional assent a condition of persuasion, 237

Ascham, Roger, *The Scholemaster*: doctrine of imitation, 39; on Surrey's blank verse, 39n, 40n; condemnation of love

poetry, 48; on eloquence as "plain and sensible utterance," 49-50; plain style, as best suited to treatment of matter, 120 —*Toxophilus*: on excessive admiration of Chaucer and Petrarch, 50

Bacon, Sir Francis, *Advancement of Learning*: view of aphoristic style, 151-52

Baldwin, C. S., *Medieval Rhetoric and Poetic*: on confusion of rhetoric and poetic in Middle Ages, 25n; on *Ars Dictaminis* as preserving classical divisions of oration, 30-31; *Ars Dictaminis*, pedagogical importance in Middle Ages, 130

Baldwin, William, *A Treatise of Moral Philosophy*: as commonplace book, 52n

Berdan, John M., *Early Tudor Poetry*: on Wyatt's literary influence on his successors, 91

Breton, Nicolas, *A Solemne Passion of the Soules Love*: opposition to love poetry, 173, 174-75

Brooke, Arthur, *Tragical Historie of Romeus and Juliet*: pilot-tempest emblem, 245-46

Brown, Carleton, *Religious Lyrics of the Fifteenth Century*: commonplace verse, No. 183, 9-10, No. 175, 10, No. 181, 11-13; enumerative structure, No. 176, 12-13; doctrinal structure, No. 163, 13, No.